Developmental Cognitive Neuropsychology

Christine M. Temple
University of Essex

Psychology Press

An imprint of Erlbaum (UK) Taylor & Francis

Copyright © 1997 by Psychology Press, an imprint of
Erlbaum (UK) Taylor & Francis Ltd.

Psychology Press, Publishers
27 Church Road
Hove
East Sussex, BN3 2FA
UK

British Library Cataloguing in Publication Data

A catalogue record for this book is available from the British Library

ISBN 0-86377-400-8 (Hbk)
ISBN 0-86377-401-6 (Pbk)

Printed and bound in the United Kingdom by T. J. International Ltd.

To Alexander

Contents

Brain Damage, Behaviour and Cognition
Developments in Clinical Neuropsychology

Series Editors
Chris Code, University of Sydney, Australia
Glyn Humphreys, University of Birmingham, UK
Dave Müller, University College Suffolk, UK

Published titles

Cognitive Rehabilitation Using Microcomputers
Veronica A. Bradley, John L. Welch and Clive E. Skilbeck

The Characteristics of Aphasia
Chris Code (Ed.)

Classic Cases in Neuropsychology
Chris Code, Claus-W. Wallesch, Yves Joanette, and André Roch Lecours (Eds)

The Neuropsychology of Schizophrenia
Anthony S. David and John C. Cutting (Eds)

Neuropsychology and the Dementias
Siobhan Hart and James M. Semple

Clinical Neuropsychology of Alcoholism
Robert G. Knight and Barry E. Longmore

Acquired Neurological Speech/Language Disorders in Childhood
Bruce E. Murdoch (Ed.)

Neuropsychology of the Amnesic Syndrome
Alan J. Parkin and Nicholas R.C. Leng

Clinical and Neuropsychological Aspects of Closed Head Injury
John T.E. Richardson

Unilateral Neglect: Clinical and Experimental Studies
Ian H. Robertson and J.C. Marshall (Eds.)

Apraxia: The Neuropsychology of Action
Leslie J. Gonzalez Rothi and Kenneth Heilman (Eds.)

Acquired Apraxia of Speech in Aphasic Adults
Paula A. Square (Ed.)

Developmental Cognitive Neuropsychology
Christine Temple

Cognitive Rehabilitation in Perspective
Rodger Wood and Ian Fussey (Eds.)

Series Preface

From being an area primarily on the periphery of mainstream behavioural and cognitive science, neuropsychology has developed in recent years into an area of central concern for a range of disciplines. We are witnessing not only a revolution in the way in which brain–behaviour–cognition relationships are viewed, but a widening of interest concerning developments in neuropsychology on the part of a range of workers in a variety of fields. Major advances in brain-imaging techniques and the cognitive modelling of the impairments following brain damage promise a wider understanding of the nature of the representation of cognition and behaviour in the damaged and undamaged brain.

Neuropsychology is now centrally important for those working with brain-damaged people, but the very rate of expansion in the area makes it difficult to keep up with findings from current research. The aim of the *Brain Damage, Behaviour and Cognition* series is to publish a wide range of books which present comprehensive and up-to-date overviews of current developments in specific areas of interest.

These books will be of particular interest to those working with the brain-damaged. It is the editors' intention that undergraduates, postgraduates, clinicians and researchers in psychology, speech pathology and medicine will find this series a useful source of information on important current developments. The authors and editors of the books in this series are experts in their respective fields, working at the forefront of contemporary research. They have produced texts which are accessible and scholarly. We thank them for their contribution and their hard work in fulfilling the aims of the series.

CC and GH
Sydney, Australia and Birmingham, UK
Series Editors

CHAPTER ONE

Introduction to Developmental Cognitive Neuropsychology

THEORETICAL QUESTIONS

The questions, which are addressed by developmental cognitive neuropsychology, include:

- How independent are different components of cognitive skills during development?
- Is the modularity seen in studies of adult neuropsychological disorders, mirrored by modularity in development?
- Are developmental neuropsychological disorders explicable against cognitive models?
- What restrictions are there to developmental plasticity? How many routes are there to competence?
- Is there a single developmental pathway?
- What do disorders of cognitive development tell us about normal developmental processes?

As will be reflected in the forthcoming chapters, in certain cognitive domains the field is well developed in conducting relevant studies and analyses to address the questions. In other areas, pertinent studies are just beginning, although interesting routes for future enquiry are evident.

Developmental cognitive neuropsychology has its most recent origins in adult neuropsychology, and an understanding of its history, assumptions and objectives is an important background to any discussion of the developmental field.

ADULT NEUROPSYCHOLOGY

There are currently two distinct approaches to adult neuropsychology; one is broadly more dominant in North America and the other is broadly more dominant in Europe. The approaches differ fundamentally in both their methods and objectives.

The first approach could be called *classical neuropsychology* and is concerned with the issue of localisation of brain function and the identification of symptoms, characteristic of particular brain disorders. The emphasis has been not upon how the brain conducts a cognitive process but upon where within the brain the process is conducted. This interest in which bits of the brain do what has been a consistent focus of study, since Broca's (1861) report that productive speech was associated with the third frontal convolution of the left hemisphere. Although some have questioned the utility and validity of the localisation exercise, it has remained a dominant theme throughout the 20th century. Further impetus was provided following the Second World War, when patients became available for study who had circumscribed brain lesions and who displayed a range of cognitive and intellectual deficits (Newcombe, 1969). This enabled the establishment of research programmes, investigating groups of patients typically selected on the basis of a common location of lesion. Standardised or novel tests were then administered to determine what was distinctive about the pattern of cognitive impairment. There was further impetus for such studies, in the days before the widespread availability of brain scanners in a clinical context, since having established knowledge of the patterns of distinctive cognitive impairments linked to specific lesions, in subsequent patients behavioural symptomatology could be used to predict the localisation of a patient's brain lesion. A similar approach has been adopted with children with acquired brain lesions and in the study of some developmental disorders.

The second approach within adult neuropsychology is more recent in its development. *Cognitive neuropsychology* is a quite different tradition, established largely in the UK but now the dominant approach to neuropsychology in Europe and certain centres in the US and Canada. The origins of cognitive neuropsychology are found in part within human experimental psychology, as cognitive psychologists and neuropsychologists working together realised that patients with brain lesions could provide data of considerable interest for both testing and developing theories and models of normal cognition. Further, having integrated patient data with theoretical models in cognition, it then became possible to provide theoretically coherent analyses of new patients in relation to the models, which provided a constructive backdrop for both planning remediation and monitoring recovery.

Thus, cognitive neuropsychology has two fundamental aims (Ellis & Young, 1988a). The first aim is "to explain the patterns of impaired and intact cognitive performance seen in brain-damaged patients in terms of damage to one or more components of a theory of normal cognitive functioning". The second aim is "to draw conclusions about normal, intact cognitive processes from the patterns of impaired and intact capabilities seen in brain-injured patients" (Ellis & Young, 1988a). Group data are far less relevant to this exercise than single cases that showed patterns of dissociation in cognitive function.

Cognitive neuropsychologists have little interest in mapping brain behaviour relationships or describing typical sequelae of brain injury, since this information says little about how the patients are processing information, in functional terms. They are interested in finding, studying and reporting cases which provide information about the architecture of the cognitive processes. They also argue that, without a clear model of how a system is working, it is not always evident which functions one should even be attempting to map. One function of a cognitive model is to represent an analysis of an area of intellectual processing, in which a "black box" is specified in more detail, both in relation to its constituent subcomponents and to the activities of which they are capable (Temple, 1990b). Within those cognitive domains which are now well modelled by cognitive neuropsychology, it has become of interest to determine whether metabolic regional scanners support anatomically discrete localisation of the component elements within the models, by using tasks designed to tap specific elements during activation, but this is a late development in the research objectives. Without a well-formulated view of how a system may operate, the most sophisticated scanners can provide only unfocused information, as the selection of tasks during the activational recording is likely to be inappropriate, generating less informative results.

The seminal study in the development of cognitive neuropsychology from which many others were spawned was reported in 1966, with the publication by Marshall and Newcombe of details of a brain-damaged war veteran, GR, who displayed a pattern of reading deficit, which they labelled deep dyslexia. GR had no phonological reading skills, being unable to read aloud even the simplest non-word. Yet, GR could read aloud correctly and understand many concrete words. Errors to single words presented in isolation with no context, were dominated by semantic paralexias (e.g. canary → parrot), for which it was evident that some element of the semantic features of the target had been accessed. The paper was of considerable significance for three reasons. First, it challenged the prevalent models of reading of the time by demonstrating that semantic information could be attained from written text, without the need for a phonologically based access code. It thus contributed, with evidence emerging from studies of normal subjects, to the modification of the previously held model of normal reading, within which phonological decoding of written words preceded any access to a word's meaning. In similar fashion, the case of KF (Shallice & Warrington, 1970) who had a severe impairment of short-term memory but normal long-term memory, challenged the prevalent view at that time, that short-term memory was a temporary store within which material had to be held *en route* and before any entry to long-term memory. The modification and enhancement of cognitive models of normal function remains a central objection of cognitive neuropsychology.

The second reason for the significance of the study of GR was that it documented the semantic errors of deep dyslexia which occurred when patients attempted to read aloud individual words presented in isolation (Table 1.1). These errors were intriguing and intrinsically entertaining, and thereby captured the interest of many subsequent researchers. Although such errors could be collated across subjects, analysis of the errors within the distribution of error types from an individual subject, and in relation to other components of reading performance from that subject, was necessary in order to indicate their prevalence and significance. The analysis therefore favoured case studies, another core aspect of many cognitive neuropsychological analyses. If Marshall and Newcombe (1966, 1973), had merely studied GR as one of a group of patients with reading disorders, and averaged performance measures across subjects, the interesting dissociations within the performance of their patient would have been missed. Cognitive neuropsychology emphasises the study of dissociations within subjects, employing them to "carve cognition at its seams" (McCarthy & Warrington, 1990). The performance patterns from individual case studies, are used throughout

TABLE 1.1
Examples of Semantic Errors Made in Deep Dyslexia

antique	→	"vase"	canary	→	"parrot"
gnome	→	"pixie"	liberty	→	"freedom"
ill	→	"sick"	ancient	→	"historic"
city	→	"town"	bush	→	"tree"
cattle	→	"animals"	cheer	→	"laugh"

Source: Marshall and Newcombe, (1966).

this book to illustrate particular patterns of performance and highlight the nature of case study analysis.

The third reason that the Marshall and Newcombe (1966) paper was significant was that it started a trend, albeit one that was initially very slow to gather speed. Further case analyses of the reading and spelling systems using a similar methodology became prevalent through the 1970s and 1980s. Analyses also spread to other cognitive domains: naming, auditory word recognition, syntax, calculation, object and face recognition, motor action, and memory (McCarthy & Warrington, 1990; Parkin, 1996).

This book discusses the application of cognitive neuropsychology to children. This is an approach which is increasingly popular in Europe, particularly in the UK and Italy, but which differs from the dominant approach to child neuropsychology in North America. Whereas adult cognitive neuropsychology builds models on the basis of the disorders seen following functional lesions to a pre-existing system, developmental cognitive neuropsychology builds models on the basis of disorders reflecting functional lesions within developing systems. Like adult cognitive neuropsychology it has two broad aims. The first is to expand models of normal function, using data from children with neuropsychological disorders. Such data is also used to test and contrast different types of developmental model. As with adult cognitive neuropsychology, the aim is to construct a single model of a cognitive domain, or part thereof, against which all childhood cases of disorders of that domain can be explained. In principle, such models, when divided at the seams appropriately, should function in such a way as to generate patterns of cognitive impairment observed in developmental disorders. The second aim has clinical relevance, since there is also interest in the identification of intact subsystems within the developing cognitive framework, which could be utilised in an educational or remedial context.

The most helpful cases in this endeavour are children for whom there are selective deficits, whose dissociation of skills may highlight elements of underlying structure. At its simplest, where one skill has failed to develop and another has developed normally, the development of the normal skill can not be seen to be dependent upon the failed skill. Such information both constrains the possible underlying models and may enable the identification of routes around a selective deficit. In areas where there is limited theoretical background and structure from studies of children, the more detailed models of adult cognition and adult cognitive neuropsychology may provide a useful starting point and background framework to develop new areas of developmental cognitive neuropsychology. There is interest in the success of the initial models as explanatory backdrops for the developmental disorders, since similarities between the developmental and acquired disorders place constraints on the extent to which the developing brain may be capable of reorganisation.

MODULARITY

Current attempts within cognitive neuropsychology to subdivide cognitive processes are based upon a belief in what Fodor (1983) had termed *modularity*. The idea of modularity derives, in part, from the arguments of Marr (1976) that it would make evolutionary sense if cognitive processes were composed of subparts, with mutual independence, in order that a small change or improvement could be made in one part of the system without the need for there to be consequences extensively throughout the rest of the system. In Fodor's (1983) writing, the term modularity is used in a very specific sense. The concept has subsequently broadened significantly and as employed in current developmental cognitive neuropsychology it bears only a limited resemblance to the original Fodorian proposals.

Following Marr, it had been argued that it would make evolutionary sense if cognitive processing depended upon separable modules, with each module carrying out its processing, without communicating or overlapping with other modules. Fodor (1983) has termed this property *informational encapsulation*. However, a slightly more flexible interpretation permits the possibility of some degree of communications between the modules. In such discussions modules are referred to as semi-independent (e.g. Temple, 1991, 1997). Certainly the strict view of information encapsulation as proposed by Fodor has to be abandoned in order to account for studies within experimental psychology indicating cross-module priming effects (e.g. Rhodes & Tremewan, 1993).

Fodor (1983) also argued that modules are *domain specific* and can only accept one type of input. Modularity, in Fodor's terms, was therefore not applicable to higher order processes, which may not be subject to such constraints. Others consider that Fodor (1983) was unduly restrictive in the application of the modularity concepts and that these can be applied with just as much success to higher order processes, arguing that executive systems may fractionate (e.g. Ellis & Young, 1988a; Shallice, 1988; Temple, Carney, & Mullarkey, 1996).

Fodor's (1983) modules are also *mandatory* and function outside voluntary control. He considered this to be a defining feature of modules. If the operation of a process was not mandatory then it was not modular. However, the ideas of modularity have more recently been applied to systems over which there is voluntary control. For example, the system of retrieving people's names has many of the required properties of modules, yet is under some degree of voluntary control (e.g. Ellis & Young, 1988a).

The divisions between modules which may arise as a consequence of brain injury reflect fractionation of systems, where selective modules may be impaired while others are left intact. These fractionations are used in the model building of cognitive neuropsychology. Developmental cognitive neuropsychology, uses the same principles when applied to disorders in children. It seeks to explore the concept of modularity within development (Temple, 1991, p. 174):

> The advantage of their (modules) semi-independent state in adulthood would be reduced in evolutionary terms, if it had to be acquired through a preceding phase of mutual interdependence and reliance.

There would be an evolutionary advantage if modularity was a principle of the development of systems, since abnormality or malfunction in one aspect of the developing system would not necessarily lead to a reduction in the quality of performance of all other aspects of the system.

A further property that Fodor (1983) proposed for modules was that they are of necessity *innate*. This view has important implications for developmental cognitive neuropsychology. For if modules are innate, there should be direct parallels between the modular fractionations which can be seen in adult and child disorders and similar underlying models may be used to explicate both areas. This issue is discussed further below in the section on plasticity.

Belief in modularity in development does not necessarily require the nativism of Fodor's view of modularity. Modules could become established and emerge overtime, with learning as well as, or instead of, innate specifications involved in their delineation. Karmiloff-Smith (1992,p. 5) distinguishes between Fodor's notion of pre-specified modules and a process of modularisation. In her view:

> nature specifies initial biases or predispositions that channel attention to relevant environmental inputs, which in turn affect subsequent brain development ... development involves a process of gradual modularisation.

With this view of development, the issues within developmental cognitive neuropsychology concern the ways in which disordered development impinge upon the process of gradual modularisation. Do disorders have a module-specific effect or is Karmiloff-Smith's system of modularisation so flexible that the end system, in a child with a disorder, will be of fundamentally distinct structure from normal? As Karmiloff-Smith herself points out, her theory relates to the timing of the appearance of modularisation and the degree of pre-specification evident in the neonate. She suggests that biological activation scans may ultimately be able to indicate the degree to which focal specialisation is present at birth. The debate between a pre-specified innate view of modules and a part learning, gradual process of modularisation is relevant whatever the interpretation of the concept of modularity itself. Thus it applies in equal measure to the strict modules of Fodor and to the looser conceptions of modularity which are more pervasive today, within which there may be some degree of communication between modules, more than one type of input may be incorporated (as in the executive disorders) and where processing may have some element of conscious control.

INDIVIDUAL DIFFERENCES

Developmental cognitive neuropsychology is also interested in exploring individual differences between subjects. It is interested in whether there is a single developmental pathway, to the acquisition of a system, or whether there may be parallel routes to accomplishing certain tasks, which may develop across individuals at different rates and with differential strength, thereby generating both considerable individual variation in acquisition patterns and also potentially individual differences in adult cognitive states. The idea of individual variation in acquisition patterns, arising from variation in the development of the parallel routes, differs significantly from traditional developmental descriptions, within which development is often described as developing in a series of stages which are in a fixed order and invariant in sequence. In relation to such stage models individual variation and impairment can only be accounted for in terms of delay in the acquisition of stages. Within developmental cognitive neuropsychology there is the potential for a considerably richer tapestry of accounts of individual variation. The interest in variations in the final adult state achieved differs from much of adult cognitive psychology, which aims primarily to identify areas of invariance across subjects, and works with the premise that single models are applicable to all adult subjects without fundamental differences between people in the architecture of underlying systems. Individual differences are merely perhaps in the databases upon which the systems operate and the nature of the stores which individuals may have established, and which are available during the implementation of a computation. Other individual differences could arise if there are differences in the degree to which components of the functional architecture become established.

These discussions of individual variation assume that there is nevertheless a common end-goal cognitive architecture for the child becoming an adult. A more fundamental account of individual differences would be that the wiring diagrams of the functional architectures achieved may also vary across subjects. If some brains had a fundamental organisational structure which differed from others, then the enterprise of cognitive neuropsychology applied to adults or children could be under threat (Temple, 1990b). The models would become untestable and irrefutable because any pattern of data could be fitted with the proposal of a further variation in architecture. Data would therefore have no constraining characteristic upon the possible models. There would be too many degrees of freedom. This would not be a problem unique to developmental cognitive neuropsychology; the whole field of cognitive neuropsychology would be threatened.

However, not all hypothetical individual variations in the structure of the systems need have such gloomy consequences. A possibility, which has been explored in neither adult nor developmental cognitive neuropsychology, is that a major biological marker could be associated with a difference in cognitive architectures. Candidates could be gender or handedness, two variables which repeatedly generate individual differences in group performance within experimental and neuropsychology, or within the clinical spectrum disorders such as autism or even dyslexia. From a more classical neuropsychological perspective, there could be a difference between the language systems of those with left hemisphere language and those with right hemisphere language. In the latter case, for example, many of the cases of phonological dyslexia in the literature would be inappropriate for the constraining of generalised theories of reading.

In such a world, for cognitive neuropsychology to continue to be viable, there would need to be a restriction in the final number of cognitive architectures, and it would be necessary to be able to correctly and unambiguously classify an individual to an architectural group. There could then be a cognitive neuropsychological analysis of each identified subgroup of the population. Models would continue to be restrained by the need to account for all the individual patterns of behaviour of the members of that subgroup. The analysis of an individual would constrain the model for the subgroup to which that case belonged but would have no impact upon the models for other subgroups. In this hypothetical world cognitive neuropsychology would be a much more complex discipline but would not be impossible. Though were there to be evidence of such differences, for example in relation to handedness, one can only imagine the debates that would surround the attempts at unambiguous group classification: on the basis of hand preference, or strength, or relative skill between the hands, or hand writing posture, or familial inheritance, etc? In such circumstances cognitive neuropsychology might become a discipline reliable only in the study of the right-handed, male, non-dyslexic, non-autistic, with left hemisphere language. The vast number of studies in experimental psychology which address just such subjects suggest that even then it might survive. However, at present such debate is mere speculation. As yet, there is no irrefutable evidence that differences in underlying architecture exist.

CASE STUDIES

Given the importance of individual differences within developmental cognitive neuropsychology, case studies are the most common form of analysis employed. As has been discussed, currently the data from all case studies of a particular system must be explicable against a single model of the system which it constrains. Averaging across subjects might mask the most relevant aspect of performance since it is dissociations in performance both within individuals and between individuals which is of interest. From a clinical perspective, a case study emphasis is helpful as it provides a framework for the analysis both of atypical patterns of performance and of change in performance over time. In relation to children the framework enables quantitative and qualitative monitoring of the progress of a disorder.

The dominance of a case study perspective within both adult and developmental cognitive neuropsychology does not preclude the interest of group studies in cases where there is reason to believe that a specific pattern of skill dissociation may be a consistent feature of members of the group. Thus for example, in certain genetic disorders such as Turner's syndrome, one may argue that certain elements of the functional architecture are impaired across individuals, whereas others are intact or enhanced (e.g. Temple & Carney, 1995, 1996). Such disorders may be associated with a specific pattern of skill dissociation which can be interpreted in relation to the common functional architecture. The claim for a deficit in a "theory of mind" module in autism (Baron-Cohen, 1992; Leslie, 1987) is a further example, though others argue that a disorder of executive skill is more pervasive (e.g. Ozonoff & McEvoy, 1994).

DYNAMICS

It could be argued that a cognitive neuropsychological analysis is valid for an adult, in a way that it is not for a child, because the adult system is static but the child's system is in a process of dynamic change. There are a number of problems with this assumption. First, adult systems may not be static. There have been a number of successful cognitive neuropsychological analyses of progressive degenerative disorders, such as semantic dementia which have yielded information of interest and utility (e.g. Hodges, Patterson, Oxbury, & Funnell, 1992). The cognitive neuropsychological framework has also been used successfully to explore improvement and recovery, whether spontaneous or in response to targeted remediation. Here, a merit of the framework is seen in its capacity to provide systematic analysis of snapshots in time, with which subsequent patterns of performance may be compared.

The second reservation is the perception of the child's system as being dynamic. It is of course true that most children are developing and acquiring skills and expanding their cognitive repertoire. However, even normal children pass through phases where skills may plateau over a period of time and certain components of cognitive skills may peak relatively early in development. It is therefore of importance that if extensive studies of individual children are conducted, without knowledge about the plateau or ceiling of their skills, then they should take place within a narrow time period, to ensure that previously assessed skills have not advanced, at the time of administration of comparison tests. Where assessments are conducted over extended periods, reassessment of certain skills may be necessary to ensure comparisons at the appropriate level. A further aspect relates to the extent to which children with developmental disorders have underlying cognitive systems, which are as dynamic in the area of difficulty as those of other children. In Chapter 4, the case of Dr S who has a developmental difficulty with face recognition will be discussed. Her difficulty was severe as a child and remains a profound deficit. She is now in her sixties. Dynamic development within her face recognition system is hard to discern. Thus, in some cases of severe and selective developmental deficit, the level of performance is not only slow but the rate of any development is so reduced as to virtually eliminate dynamic aspects in the system. Profound developmental disorders may therefore persist into adulthood, sometimes being resistant to remediation (e.g. Temple, 1988a).

In less profound developmental disorders, the dynamic rate of change in the skills within the problem area is usually slower than normal. Thus, as time passes, what in the early years may have appeared a minor delay in relation to peers can become more marked, as the relative lag becomes greater and greater (e.g. Temple, 1987, 1990c). Awareness of this element of system dynamics can be important in order not to underplay manifestations of developmental disorders at an early age.

A further issue in relation to the dynamics of the developing system is the potential impact of downstream effects upon development. An impairment in one aspect of skill may have knock-on effects upon the acquisition of other skills. In such cases, the impairment in the subsequent skill may be considered to be caused by the initial deficit rather than resulting from a selective impairment in the module for the latter skill. To provide a more concrete example, Tallal (Tallal & Piercy, 1973; Tallal & Stark, 1981; Tallal, Stark, Kallman, & Mellits, 1980; Tallal et al., 1996) argues that an impairment in processing speech sounds characterised by rapid transitional information may have a knock-on effect upon other areas of language. Thus, without the requisite input related components of the system develop abnormally. Downstream effects do not preclude a modular organisation within a developing system, but the impact upon related components may make it difficult to attain some of the classical double dissociations which are the hallmark of much of adult cognitive neuropsychology.

A positive advantage of the case study analyses of developmental cognitive neuropsychology is that they enable the testing of downstream theories. Downstream theories such as Tallal's (e.g. Tallal et al., 1996) propose that a particular initial defect has a specific consequence. Such a theory can be refuted if cases are identified for whom there is the initial defect but not the subsequent impairment. Thus the case studies of developmental cognitive neuropsychology have the potential to generate data to refute theoretical suggestions regarding general population effects. Case studies can also help to distinguish between theories with differing integral downstream elements. Indeed, it is difficult to propose how relevant data could be gathered, which was capable of leading to the rejection of a downstream theory, if a case study methodology, exploring different elements of a system's function, were not deployed.

There are some areas where downstream effects may have comparable effects upon behaviour in both adult and developmental cognitive neuropsychology. In the most commonly used model of face processing (Bruce & Young, 1986), structural encoding is an essential precursor to the access of face recognition units and analysers for expression, lip-reading, and making judgements about the appearance of unfamiliar faces. Young and Ellis (1989) (see Chapter 4) describe a developmental case of disorder in structural encoding for faces. As a consequence the other elements of the face processing system fail to develop normally. With adults a comparable disorder arises. An acquired disorder in the structural encoding of faces (e.g. Young, 1992) renders the remainder of the face processing system inaccessible. It may be that it has developed normally but since none of it can be utilised there is in practice a comparable downstream effect to that seen in the developmental cases. Such downstream effects are a feature of all those areas where one component of a processing system is an essential step before activation of a later stage and where the initial stage may be selectively impaired by brain injury. Thus downstream effects affect studies of both adults and children in cognitive neuropsychology and reduce both the expression of double dissociations and the degree of transparency of the effects of the disorders in determining that a specific module of a system is selectively disrupted.

PLASTICITY

A further problem for developmental cognitive neuropsychology would arise if the developing brain demonstrated plasticity and reorganised in the face of deficit (Lenneberg, 1967; Rasmussen & Milner, 1977). Thus, the developing brain would violate the assumptions of transparency and subtractivity, which are fundamental tenets of adult cognitive neuropsychology. The assumption of transparency requires that the abnormal pattern of performance will provide a basis, to determine the component of the system that is disrupted (Caramazza, 1984). The assumption of subtractivity, requires that the abnormal performance reflects the full cognitive system, minus those components that are disrupted (Saffran, 1982). If the brain can reorganise and generate new modules, these assumptions will not hold. As Ellis and Young (1988a) discuss, there is no evidence that the mature brain is capable of generating new modules after brain injury. Equally, I would maintain that there is no evidence that the developing brain is capable of generating new modules, if its system is deficient. As Ellis and Young (1988a) point out, it is not problematic if new strategies are developed in response to disorders, so long as pre-existing structures are employed. Equally, in development it is not a problem if different areas of the brain become involved in compensating for a developmental deficit so long as the structural organisation of the functional system is not different from normal, merely defective in components and potentially utilizing new strategies within these, or new anatomical substrates for these.

Traditional views of developmental plasticity do not suggest that new structures develop but do suggest that new areas in the brain may be able to take over functions that would normally be subserved by other areas, enabling a relocalisation of function and thereby compensation. In some cases, this might drive out the function normally subserved by the new area, but again, this would not necessarily be associated with the development of new structural systems that operate upon radically different components from normal. This traditional view of plasticity involving relocalisation is based in part on the dominating observation that whereas adults who sustain left hemisphere injuries are often left with severe and pervasive aphasias, young children who sustain head injuries, which initially lead to a regression of language skill, frequently recover linguistic skills and have appeared then to develop normally.

Lenneberg (1967) argued that even though the left hemisphere may show early signs of speech dominance, if there is an early lesion to this hemisphere there is the potential for the right hemisphere to develop language. Lenneberg (1967) argued that the basis for this was a lack of early polarisation of function so that the right hemisphere retained an involvement in language which could subsequently be strengthened, if the left hemisphere was injured. The potential of the right hemisphere to take over language function in this way has been demonstrated in cases of injury prior to the age of five or six years (Rasmussen & Milner, 1977), though the efficacy of this reorganisation has been questioned (e.g. Aram, 1988).

Studies of hemispherectomy patients demonstrate that the right hemisphere can sustain language after the removal of the majority of the cortex of the left hemisphere (e.g. Carlson, Netley, Hendrick, & Pritchard, 1968). Some argue that the quality of the language is inferior to that of normal people, particularly in the area of syntax, and that the effectiveness of the plasticity is therefore restricted (Dennis, 1980; Dennis & Kohn, 1975; Dennis, Lovett, & Wiegel-Crump, 1981; Dennis & Whitaker, 1976; Lovett, Dennis, & Newman, 1986). However, Bishop (1983, 1988) argues that these studies have serious methodological flaws and cannot be taken as evidence of limitations of functional plasticity. Were the case for impaired syntax to be proven, it would not be problematic for developmental cognitive neuropsychology as it could be interpreted as reflecting the weaker development of certain modules, such as a syntactic processor in the right hemisphere. It does not require the postulation of a distinctly structured system. The cognitive neuropsychological framework is not concerned with where something is happening but how it is happening. In similar fashion, the discovery that if motor input is manipulated, the spatial positions of cortical somatosensory representations can shift significantly (Jenkins, Merzenich, & Recanzone, 1990), demonstrates the potential for the transfer of the biological substrate for certain cognitive functions, but need not mean that at a cognitive level the control systems for sensory or motor skill have a different functional architecture. The results from both the hemispherectomy studies and from the somatosensory studies are of interest to neuropsychology and the neurosciences more generally, but they do not necessarily impact upon cognitive neuropsychology.

According to Lenneberg (1967), a reciprocal strengthening of non-linguistic function could take place within the left hemisphere, following right hemisphere injury. The effects of right hemisphere injury have been less extensively explored than those of left hemisphere injury in childhood. Nevertheless, we know that early right hemisphere focal brain injury can lead to identifiable and persistent spatial deficits. (Stiles-Davis, 1988; Stiles-Davis, Janowsky, Engel, & Nass, 1988; Stiles-Davis, Sugarman, & Nass, 1985; Stiles & Thal, 1993). However, spatial deficits are also seen following left hemisphere injury. Stiles and Thal (1993) argue that those with right hemisphere injuries have a spatial integrative deficit (Stiles & Nass, 1991), whereas those with early left hemisphere injury are proposed to have a spatial encoding deficit. A critical role for the left hemisphere in spatial processing has also been recognised for some time within adult neuropsychology (e.g. Mehta & Newcombe, 1991).

Although the concept of plasticity of brain function in the developing child, has developed from the observation in children of the development of a specific process, despite the absence or ablation of the brain area usually viewed as the executor of that function, recent studies also question its effectiveness. Aram and Eisele (1992) have discussed how traditionally the capacity for compensatory reorganisation was explained as resulting from: (1) the substitution of one brain area to cover the functions usually subserved by another area; (2) redundancy in neural representations such that a function might have multiple representations; or (3) neural repair mechanisms enabling the resurrection of function within a previously impaired region. None of these mechanisms suggest a fundamental reorganisation of the cognitive system itself. As Aram and Eisele (1992) highlight, the proposed mechanisms of compensation are now seen to have evident limitations. For example, long-term sequelae are seen in the language systems of children, who have sustained left hemisphere impairment, even where that damage is sustained early in life and is more subtle than that sustained in a hemispherectomy (Aram, 1988; Aram, Ekelman, Rose, & Whitaker, 1985; Aram, Ekelman, & Whitaker, 1986; Marchman, Miller, & Bates, 1991; Riva & Cazzaniga, 1986; Stiles & Thal, 1993; Thal et al., 1991; Vargha-Khadem, O'Gorman, & Watters, 1985; though see Bishop, 1988, for a methodological critique of some of these studies). The proposed impairments extend beyond syntax to incorporate general expressive language and vocabulary (Stiles & Thal, 1993). Delays may be seen in the initial stages of lexical production in infancy but, by school age, for some children the effects may be relatively subtle (Stiles & Thal, 1993).

Even in those developmental disorders, which had been thought to be virtually asymptomatic, detailed analyses now reveal persistent deficits, for which there has not been plastic reorganisation. For example, pervasive midline disconnection effects are seen in callosal agenesis (Lassonde, Sauerwein, & Lepore, 1995). Further, whereas plasticity had been seen as being most effective following an early injury, it is now known that for some disorders, such as Landau–Kleffner syndrome, earlier lesions are associated with more severe disorders (Bishop, 1985; see Chapter 2, this book). Thus, the mechanisms of plasticity may have limited effectiveness.

For the truly developmental disorders, where the underlying abnormality predates birth, the mechanisms of plasticity have always been in doubt. If plasticity is operational, why are there children with developmental dyslexia? Why does the brain not reorganise to compensate for the deficit? One possibility is that the presence of other intact brain tissue has an inhibitory effect, prohibiting the activation of compensatory systems. Another possibility is that such compensatory systems are not triggered, when the basis of the difficulty lies with the growth and development of underlying brain regions or where genetic mechanisms are involved. My own belief is that plasticity, in so far as it exists, may normally be a response to injury or disease in infancy or childhood, rather than to an abnormal developmental process.

This plasticity has its most significant compensatory effects when lesions are postnatal and a direct consequence of injury or disease. Where the origins are genetic in whole or part or reflect some other influence of a normal antenatal process, the effects of plasticity are restricted or simply absent. It is evident from the forthcoming chapters that children may have focal cognitive abnormalities in a variety of cognitive systems. These include disorders of reading, spelling, naming, drawing, face recognition, and executive disorders (e.g. Temple, 1985c,1986a, 1986b, 1990c, 1991, 1992a, 1992b; Temple & Carney, 1995; Temple et al., 1996; Temple & Marshall, 1983). In each of these areas the mechanisms of plasticity have failed to compensate for the focal deficit. Yet, the pervasive view of plasticity means that some may find it hard to comprehend a child with such evidently competent skills in one area, yet conspicuous performance failure in another. In the absence of a known head injury or neurological insult, the child's deficient performance may be written off as related to motivational or adjustment difficulties, rather than reflecting a fundamental neuropsychological problem.

These arguments about the limitations of functional plasticity should not be taken to mean that improvement in performance is not possible and that remediation is not of benefit. Some children will learn strategies to deal with their deficits. Others will relearn lost skills or eventually learn problematic skills. However, for those children with pervasive selective cognitive disorders, it is necessary for there to be a means to systematically analyse and decompose their problems. This will enable an accurate identification of the components skills which are disrupted and those which are intact, of benefit both to understanding the nature of the disorder and thinking of routes to address it in an educational context. It will also provide information about the way in which the system has cleaved at the seams and the possible modular structure which should be incorporated into developmental models. Thus, rather than starting with an assumption of infinite plasticity, developmental cognitive neuropsychology starts with similar assumptions to adult cognitive neuropsychology, until clear evidence suggests that these assumptions should be revised.

One reason why there may be limits to developmental plasticity is that some of our cognitive systems may be preformed. This does not mean that the structure itself is formed before birth or experience but that the ultimate structure is constrained by a preset architecture which limits the potential variation within the developing system. Chomsky (1957, 1965) has argued for preformism in the innate language acquisition device and the structure of deep grammar. Marshall (1984, 1987) has argued that other cognitive systems are also preformed. Preformism is of particular interest in comparisons between adult cognitive neuropsychology and developmental cognitive neuro-psychology. The more preformed the system under investigation, the more similar the explanatory models which may be involved to address both systems. In some areas of developmental cognitive neuro-psychology, there is a working assumption of preformism, with the adoption of well-developed and well-formed models of the adult cognitive system (e.g. face recognition, De Haan & Campbell, 1991; Temple, 1992b; see Chapter 4, this book). The model can then be tested against the developmental disorders to determine whether it also provides a useful explanatory framework for this range of problems. Areas where such models do not provide an effective backdrop may highlight adult and developmental differences and thereby areas where preformism reaches limits.

WHAT IS A DEVELOPMENTAL DISORDER?

In the previous discussion, there was reference to disorders that are "truly" developmental. It may therefore be relevant to consider what is meant by a developmental disorder. Neuropsychological disorders in children are sometimes divided into those that are termed acquired and those that are termed developmental. *Acquired disorders* occur in children who have had a period of normal development, following which as a result of neurological injury or disease their developmental progress is disrupted with loss of previously established skills. Their systems have partially established in a normal fashion, but after the injury there may be difficulty in reacquiring the lost skills, or there may be difficulty in learning subsequent skills during later development. There are thus two features that are generally associated with acquired disorders: (1) development has been normal for a period of time; and (2) a neurological injury is sustained.

In contrast, *developmental disorders* are often considered to be those where there has never been evidence that a skill was previously mastered and has been lost. The disorders become apparent as the child grows and develops. In comparison to peers, they exhibit particular difficulty in acquiring certain skills or abilities. Developmental disorders are usually considered to be those in which no explicit pathology is known. They include developmental dyslexia, specific language impairment, and other subtle disorders of higher cognitive function. Thus, there are two features which are generally associated with developmental disorders: (1) that they emerge during the course of development; and (2) that there is no associated neurological injury.

In childhood, a cognitive neuropsychological analysis may be applied to both developmental or acquired disorders. Indeed it is not necessary to have resolved a distinction between the two in order to use the framework. The analyses do not require explicit knowledge about the aetiology of the disorder, nor specific information about the timing of the onset of the disorder. This makes the approach particularly well suited for the analysis of many developmental disorders where the aetiological basis and relative contributions of genetics, constitution, and environment can be difficult to tease apart. In practice, the distinction between developmental and acquired disorders in childhood is often blurred in a number of ways.

For example, in developmental dyslexia, post mortem analyses have revealed abnormal ectopias and dysplasias throughout the left hemisphere (e.g. Galaburda, Sherman, Rosen, Aboitiz, & Geschwind, 1985). There may thus be an explicit neurological basis to the disorder seen later in life. On the second developmental criteria though, the impairment is present from birth and its influence pertains throughout the developmental course. Normal cognitive development has not been disrupted at a specific point, except in so far as development which does not place demands upon the disrupted circuitry may be normal, with the deficit becoming evident only when specific demands are placed upon the deficient physiological substrate. There is now a range of other disorders, particularly within neuropsychiatry (e.g. Lewis, 1989), where it is thought that a prenatal lesion or insult, sometimes associated with a virus or infection, may perturb a system in a way that only becomes manifest much later in life. Such effects may be particularly marked where a genetic predisposition renders the system vulnerable.

In genetic disorders, there is also a clear and explicit aetiology, which may have effect throughout development but which may also be associated with physiological alterations. However, in some metabolic disorders, the impact of this physiological disruption may be modulated by the environment. In phenylketonuria (discussed in Chapter 8), the error of metabolism may disrupt the process of myelination, but the severity of impact will be affected by the degree to which there is adherence to dietary modification (Williamson, Koch, Azen, & Chang, 1981). Here, there is a developmental disorder, with the potential for pervasive postnatal neurological injury, but also with the potential for reduction of injury to leave residual but yet specific neuropsychological effects.

Another disorder, which can be a symptom of either a developmental or an acquired disorder in childhood is epilepsy. In some cases, epilepsy develops after a known head injury or neurological insult or disease and, in such cases, it is appropriate to consider it an acquired disorder. However, in the majority of cases of epilepsy there is no such prior event. There may be a family history of seizure disorders; there may have been an episode of prenatal or early antenatal concern; or there may be no known precipitating factor. In some cases, cognitive skills may deteriorate following the onset of epilepsy, as for example in the Landau–Kleffner syndrome, discussed in Chapter 2, though even here the language deterioration may predate the seizure onset, raising the possibilities that both are symptoms of a common underlying abnormality.

Any human brain can sustain a seizure or convulsion, and in electroconvulsive therapy (ECT), such an event is artificially induced. However, in the absence of ECT, some brains have a greater predisposition to be triggered in this direction. There may be genetic, and/or biochemical, and/or electrophysiological reasons for this predisposition; there may be something inherent about the organisation or dynamics of regions of the underlying neuronal networks of such individuals, which gives them this susceptibility, and this characteristic of these individuals may be present from the earliest days. The expression of this vulnerability as an epileptic disorder, may or may not occur at a subsequent date, dependent upon other events.

Ultimately, a distinction between developmental and acquired disorders in childhood is important if it is believed that there are fundamental differences between their underlying functional systems. The field is as yet insufficiently developed for the formulation of a conclusion on this issue.

As the different areas of neuroscience stretch their boundaries and impinge upon each other, it is likely that our understanding of the biological underpinnings of many developmental disorders will expand. Although such knowledge may blur further the developmental–acquired distinction, it also has the potential to highlight issues in the child–adult comparisons of cognitive neuropsychology and to further inform our ideas about preformism and plasticity.

In many cases, even with biological advances, it may be difficult to localise the anatomical basis for a developmental disorder and, certainly, currently this is true for many disorders. The absence of need for an anatomical localisation in developmental cognitive neuropsychology thus renders it particularly useful within the developmental field and enables a range of studies, which traditional neuropsychology could not encompass. A traditional exercise of mapping function to localisation is of limited utility, if there are no known ways of determining localisation. However, a functional localisation or specification of area of difficulty within a system is possible when a cognitive disorder is manifest, irrespective of known elements of its underlying biology.

DEVELOPMENTAL MODELS

A persistent theoretical issue within developmental fields relates to the most appropriate models for representing normal development. Traditional post-Piagetian models involve a series of stages, which are invariant in sequence. Each child must master one stage before progressing to the next (e.g. Piaget & Inhelder, 1958). Stages cannot be omitted, nor can their order vary from child to child. Piaget considered that many of these stages operated across cognitive domains, with conceptual development in one field being paralleled by conceptual development in apparently unrelated fields (e.g. Piaget & Inhelder, 1958). Much of post-Piagetian developmental study has involved modification of these hypotheses of Piaget. Developments in one area are not always paralleled by developments in other cognitive domains (e.g. Gupta & Richardson, 1995). The ages at which children acquire skills are in general earlier than was supposed by Piaget but are also dependent upon the domain at issue, certain processes being learnt much earlier in one domain, than in another. Karmiloff-Smith (1992) suggests that even within domains, the timing of acquisition of certain cognitive processes may vary according to the specific microdomain involved. For example, within language, the transition from implicit understanding to explicit understanding to verbal use occurs earlier in relation to understanding what a word is, than it does in relation to pronoun acquisition. She discusses recurrent phase changes at different times across different microdomains and repeatedly within each domain, rather than using a terminology of stages. Despite these modifications to Piaget's overall theory, the notion of an invariant series of stages, or recurrent phases, has been persistent. Similarities in the paths to acquisition are assumed across children, with individual differences related to the relative rates of progress or the particular information content acquired, at a specified stage or substage or phase.

From the perspective of developmental cognitive neuropsychology, such serial models are unduly restrictive. By permitting no parallel routes to acquisition and no stage-jumping, they leave open only the option to explain a developmental disorder as a delay in acquisition. The child has progressed to a certain stage and has then failed to progress further. This type of explanation may be adequate when disordered performance is identical in character to that of a younger normal child but it is problematic when the pattern of disordered development is atypical and an explanation that goes beyond mere delay is required. Thus serial stage models cannot account for what used to be termed deviant performance, which deviates from the typical developmental path.

Stage models are also problematic in accounting for one of the basic tenets of both classical and cognitive neuropsychology, the double dissociation. A dissociation in performance occurs when a subject is competent at process A, but deficient at process B. From this one can conclude that B is not an essential prerequisite for A, since A functions well despite B's absence. A double dissociation occurs when a second subject is competent at process B, but deficient at process A. From these two subjects, it can be concluded that B is not an essential prerequisite for A, and that A is not an essential prerequisite for B. Processes A and B therefore exhibit a degree of independence, which suggests that their modular underpinnings are distinct. The problem for simple serial models is that both subjects cannot represent a simple delay in acquisition. If A is mastered earlier in the developmental series than B, then the first subject could be delayed in development, but there is no explanation for the second subject. Equally, if B is mastered earlier in the developmental series than A, then the second subject could be delayed in development, but there is no explanation for the first subject. If both A and B are acquired at a similar stage in the developmental series, there is no clear explanation for either subject, the first or the second. Moreover, where double dissociations do occur in development, there is no evidence that their character changes in form over time. Thus even the explanation of one of the two subjects as delayed in acquisition can be questioned.

In conclusion, although stage models may have proved useful within normal developmental psychology, they are unhelpful in developmental cognitive neuropsychology unless more sophisticated representations, incorporating parallel routes, were present at each stage and substage.

The most frequent representational models used in both adult and developmental cognitive neuropsychology are information processing models. Here, the black boxes of cognitive psychology are fractionated and developed, incorporating information from both neuropsychological patients and normal subjects to generate testable models. Parallel routes account for double dissociations. They also permit individual differences within the normal developmental range. Learning involves the filling out of the requisite database and structure of knowledge upon which the system operates and may also involve the development of particular component modules themselves. Even in a system constrained by biological underpinnings, there may be failure to establish certain subcomponents in the absence of particular input during critical periods, or in the absence of appropriate instruction where cultural notational systems are involved.

Most recently, connectionist models have entered the arena of developmental cognitive neuropsychology (e.g. Snowling, Hulme, & Goulandris, 1994). Based largely upon principles derived from matrix theory, these models utilise distributed networks, with loaded weightings between connections to account for the storage of information to which the network has been exposed and its subsequent availability. Connectionist theories are sometimes referred to as being based upon parallel distributed processing models. Rather confusingly in relation to terminology, such systems may still be serial processors when considered at the level of information acquisition. The distributed nature of the system relates to the storage of information, but the acquisition of that information may have a strictly serial quality with exposure to a serial training set from which rules are extracted.

Connectionist theories have a number of appeals to psychologists. First, they build upon some ideas which were incorporated into learning theory. Second, if nodes in the networks are substituted by neurons or clusters of neurons, there can be the appearance of a direct biological parallel to neural networks, engendering an apparent biological underpinning to the systems and thus possible cross-integration with the other neurosciences. Third, they have properties which parallel the brain injured, in that lesions to the systems generally result in a degradation of certain skills rather than an absolute loss of skill. Fourth, they utilise computers, providing a novel outlet for those with both hardware and software enthusiasms. Fifth, their descriptions in mathematical language convey an impression of precision and intelligence, which makes a significant impact on the many psychologists who have less established mathematical backgrounds. However, their real utility will emerge if they are able to generate new testable theories, which provide a better account of current knowledge than past models.

This does not necessarily mean that connectionist models are incompatible with information processing models. The connectionist systems may be very helpful ways of conceptualising the acquisition, storage, and retrieval of information within component modules (or boxes) of certain models. For example, they may account for the storage and retrieval of the letter(s)–sound(s) rules incorporated within the phonological reading routes of some models (see Chapter 5), even if their mode of acquisition of such correspondences does not, as yet, have good ecological validity. They may also account for the build-up, storage and retrieval of face recognition units in face processing models (see Chapter 4). In these cases, the connectionist modelling combines with the information processing models to provide a more complete account of the system.

Alternatively, an information processing model may provide a description of the emergent properties from a connectionist model. Thus, a distributed network may be associated with critical steady states which effectively generate parallel or modular processing systems. In such cases the connectionist model underlies the information processing model and may provide an account at a different level of explanation, just as a neural network provides explanations at different levels to cognitive models. Emergent modularity can therefore develop in formal neural networks (Edelman, 1987; Goldberg, 1995; Jacobs & Jordan, 1992). There remains the final possibility that connectionist models will entirely supersede information processing models, which will be seen to be redundant or incorrect historical representations. However, the time for such a radical revision has not yet emerged. In the forthcoming chapters, information processing models dominate, but reference to connectionist models is made where possible; although these are gradually developing in the fields of both normal development and adult cognitive neuropsychology, their appearance within developmental cognitive neuropsychology is as yet relatively sparse, outside the field of reading.

FORTHCOMING CHAPTERS

The text of the book is organised around seven key cognitive areas, which are addressed in turn: language, memory, perception, reading, spelling, arithmetic, and executive skills. The first three may be considered the core areas of cognition. The second three are core areas, with key cultural transmission involved in their acquisition. The final area concerns higher order control processes. The major emphasis of the book is upon developmental rather than acquired disorders (see above), however, where relevant some information about acquired disorders is also provided. Equally, reference to both normal developmental studies and adult cognitive neuropsychological studies is included, with the proviso that multiple texts could be addressed to each and the detail of their discussion is therefore of necessity sparse. There is an attempt to highlight the range of the disorders within each cognitive domain and therefore the range of patterns of performance for which explanations must be provided. In some cases there is a well-established literature of multiple cases. In other cases the literature is only sparse and suggestive. Throughout, case studies are used to illustrate particular profiles of behaviour in the hope of conveying an impression of what the cases are actually like and how the dissociations in performance are displayed.

For some topics the assignment to a particular chapter is to some extent arbitrary as they may be considered to reflect disorders in more than one key cognitive area. This is inevitable since, for example, the semantic systems of memory impinge upon the cognitive systems of both language and perception. There are other interesting topics that are not addressed by this book but which nevertheless lie within the remit of developmental cognitive neuropsychology and may in time generate a more substantive number of relevant studies. These include cognitive studies of emotional disorders other than obsessive–compulsive disorders, attention deficit disorder, and autism, all of which are addressed at least in passing. Motor and apraxic disorders have also received little attention, outside the area of speech. With these provisos in mind, the first core chapter is inevitably one of the more substantive in the volume since it addresses language, a subject which has received extensive relevant investigation, even though not always from a targeted developmental cognitive neuropsychological perspective.

There is no convincing intrinsic reason why the analyses of developmental cognitive neuropsychology should be more complex than the analyses of adult cognitive neuropsychology. Further, I would argue that all those interested in adult cognitive neuropsychology should also have at least some interest in and knowledge about the developmental disorders which may be manifest within the systems that they explore in detail when fully established. For reasons of biology or functional structure, disorders may sometimes be seen in the child group which are not evident in the adult group but which nevertheless provide information pertinent to an understanding of the adult computational structure. Disorders may also be described in the child group, which exist in the adult group but which have not yet been described, thereby providing clues for future model building. It is therefore hoped that the following chapters will be of interest not only to those interested in disorders of childhood but also to the cognitive neuropsychological field more generally.

CHAPTER TWO

Language Disorders

INTRODUCTION

Language disorders in children encompass a broad range of specific problems and are manifest in at least 2% of children with a male–female ratio of approximately 3:1. In addition there are a variety of syndromes, such as autism, within which language impairments are cardinal features. In keeping with the general format of this text, language disorders will be discussed in this chapter in relation to specific aspects of the language system itself rather than within a series of syndrome descriptions. Where neuropsychological syndromes are discussed, the objective will be to use relevant components within the syndromes to illustrate cognitive deficiencies in selective aspects of language processing.

Developmental models of language in traditional post-Piagetian style tend to describe a series of stages through which the child progresses. Although these descriptions are informative in focusing upon the aspects of mastery which a normal child develops and the use which the child is making of the linguistic utterances produced, such descriptions are less helpful as the backdrop for explicating the range of language disorders to be discussed here. Many of the children to be discussed in this chapter do not represent simple cases of developmental language delay in which for example one might see the general language characteristics of a three-year-old child manifest in a child with a chronological age of six; rather, the children described are characterised by the unevenness of their linguistic development in comparison with normal children. Their atypical profiles are of interest in addressing a series of questions, some of the theoretical issues of relevance being as follows: What restrictions are there to developmental plasticity in language development? Are developmental neuropsychological disorders of language explicable against cognitive models? How independent are different components of language skills during development? And related to this question, how many routes are there to competence? Is there a single developmental pathway? These questions are variants within the linguistic domain of some of the general theoretical issues raised in the first chapter.

The standard clinical taxonomy employed by *DSM-IV* (American Psychiatric Association, 1994) for developmental language disorders is insufficiently differentiated to be used to form a core structure for the chapter. Although *DSM-IV* distinguishes between three disorders — expressive language disorder, receptive/expressive language disorder, and phonological disorder, each may encompass broadly varying difficulties in psycholinguistic terms. For example, as Bishop (1994a) points out, receptive problems include difficulties in decoding speech sounds, restricted knowledge of the meanings of words, problems in interpreting grammatical constructions, or over-literal language ignoring its pragmatics. Each of these difficulties relates to a different aspect of language. Comparable cases can be made for both expressive disorders and phonological disorders.

The general scheme of the chapter and the outline cognitive system which will be used as a backdrop to the disorders to be discussed is illustrated in Fig. 2.1. This figure depicts a simplified sketch flowing from auditory input to speech production. The figure leaves open the issue of the nature of the representations which underlie different components and the extent to which distributed networks are involved.

The range of problems to be reviewed will encompass the effects of intermittent hearing impairment in otitis media, disorders of phonological discrimination, developmental auditory agnosia, disorders of the semantic system, and the consequences for the language system of memory impairment, category-specific impairments, anomic disorders, disorders of grammatical and morphological development, dyspraxic disorders of speech, and pragmatic disorders.

Severe impairment of auditory input is obviously to be found in the deaf. Their language acquisition is impaired in a broad range of different ways. However, in this chapter, there is particular interest in disorders which may have focal impairments, and we will discuss the milder disorder of otitis media, in which there is often intermittent hearing

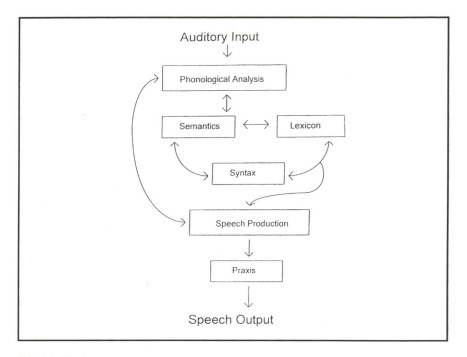

FIG. 2.1 The language system.

impairment which may have a selective effect upon auditory perception. Developmental disorders of phonological discrimination have also been discussed by Bird and Bishop (1992) and Tallal et al. (1980) and the hypothesised impact of such disorders upon grammatical understanding is articulated by Leonard (1989). Cases of developmental auditory agnosia are found in the Landau–Kleffner syndrome (Landau & Kleffner, 1957). In this syndrome it is believed that auditory perception is normal but that the speech sounds are no longer associated with the relevant meaning which provides the semantic content. Case reports of two identical twins with the disorder will be presented.

Impairments of the semantic system for language may have an impact on a broad range of cognitive systems. We will discuss here impairments of semantic access, the effects of memory impairment and consequent semantic deficit, and category-specific semantic disorders. The language problems which result from semantic deficit are associated with marked anomic impairments, which may be the most dominant presenting characteristic for a given child. A case report of such a child with semantic deficit and anomia will be presented. Anomic disorders may also result from other impairments and different types of disruption within the semantic system or lexicon; a selected literature on anomic disorders will be discussed, as will category specific disorders and their possible basis.

Disorders in the development of both the comprehension and production of grammar have been investigated by both linguists and psychologists and the theoretical accounts generated are sufficiently precise to enable predictions about observable behaviour. Whilst some work has addressed syntactic difficulties which concern the rules governing the combination of words in sentences, greater emphasis has been placed upon morphological disorders which concern the structure and form of words, including their grammatical markers. Contrasting theories about morphological disorders will be highlighted.

Disorders of language production may result not only from anomias or grammatical difficulties, but also from disorder in the control of speech movements. Whereas dysarthric disorders of speech may be part of a general disorder of all movements and may be evident in such syndromes as cerebral palsy or in disorders of the speech apparatus, developmental dyspraxic disorders of speech relate to disorders in the planning and organisation of purposive speech movements.

Associated with utilisation of the language system, we know that there are a variety of metalinguistic skills which are critical for interpersonal communication. One of the major elements of these is pragmatic skill, i.e. the use of language in relation to the constraints of social interaction and the communicative effects of language on other participants in a conversation. The pragmatic aspects of the language disorder of autism will be discussed and its impact upon general communicative abilities. The related disorders of Asperger's syndrome and semantic-pragmatic disorder will also be addressed.

IMPAIRED AUDITORY INPUT: OTITIS MEDIA

Otitis media is a form of conductive hearing loss, resulting from an inflammation of the middle ear. Within the middle ear the tympanic membrane and ossicles function as a mechanical transducer, transforming sound from the external air-filled auditory canal of the outer ear to the hair cells that rest upon the basilar membrane of the fluid-filled cochlea. The hair cells therefore transform the sound energy of mechanical origin into electrical energy which stimulates the nerve cells of the inner ear resulting in the transmission of auditory information to the brain. Normally, the Eustachian tubes equalise the pressure in the middle ear with atmospheric pressure by connection to the back of the nose but if the Eustachian tube does not open because of nasal obstruction or a cold there is a tendency for air in the middle ear to be reabsorbed and for fluid to accumulate. This fluid is an excellent culture medium for bacteria which may lead to the development of otitis media. Current use of the term otitis media refers to repeated infections of the middle ear over a defined period of time.

The effect of the otitis media is to impair the transformational chain such that sound has to be translated from air to fluid directly, requiring considerably more acoustic energy in order to stimulate the nerve cells of the inner ear. Effectively this leads to a conductive hearing loss usually in the range 15–40dB. This means that the stimulus must be considerably louder to achieve the same effect. Since otitis media most often affects infants and toddlers, episodes of middle ear infection may occur and recur while the children are learning language (Klein & Rapin, 1988). The distribution of sound in English is such that the fricatives, (consonants formed when the organs of articulation come so close that the air moving between them causes friction) and sibilants (fricatives which have a high frequency hiss characteristic) are particularly dependant upon high frequency information. It is not known the precise effect that altering early auditory input may have on the discrimination of speech sounds and the frequency changes in the acoustic energy bands that characterise consonants, referred to as formant transitions. However, the failure of children with recurrent otitis media to produce unvoiced fricatives such as /s/,/sh/,/th/, and /f/ has been argued by some to indicate that the children do not hear them clearly (Dobie & Berlin, 1979; Downs, 1985). If children with otitis media do fail to discriminate high frequency speech sounds (Fig. 2.2), this may have specific linguistic impact since these sounds mark tense, possession, number and also occur in key consonants in English (Downs, 1985).

Specific impact of otitis media upon auditory perception has been substantiated. In this regard the deficits in otitis media are seen as affecting the early processes of auditory speech perception. Eimas and Clarkson (1986) found that children with a history of recurrent otitis media were less able than controls to discriminate between consonant–vowel (CV) syllables when the voice onset time of the consonant was reduced. Thus for example, the major difference in the speech sound /p/ and /b/ is in the onset of voicing, with the vibration of the vocal chords starting earlier in the sound /b/ than /p/. Early studies in experimental psychology indicated that normal auditory speech perception is susceptible to an effect referred to as categorical perception. This means that if the voice onset time is artificially altered between the two sounds of /p/ and /b/, the experience is not to hear a sound intermediate between the two. Rather, at a particular point in the time there is a sharp transition, and the overall perception of the sound shifts dramatically. In other words, there is a tendency to allocate phonemic

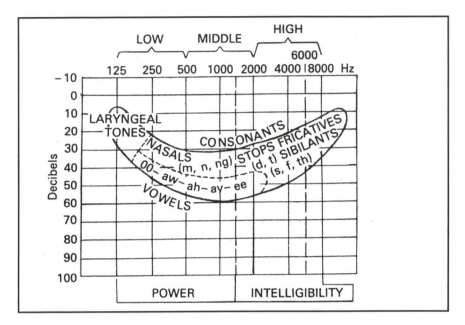

FIG. 2.2 The frequency components of English speech sounds (Ballantyne & Martin, 1984).

sounds into known categories. We impose this organisation upon the speech sound which we hear. The study of Eimas and Clarkson (1986) illustrated that the discriminative abilities of the children with a history of otitis media were poorer than normal on such tasks. The children had greater difficulty than normal in assigning a CV syllable to the correct category. Eimas and Clarkson (1986) also reported that these children were unable to discriminate between whole word stimuli manipulated in a similar way in respect to voice onset time, for example by using matched words such as bath and path. The speech sound discriminative abilities of the children improved when the volume of the stimulus was increased. Since these children only had a history of otitis media and did not have otitis media at the time of the experimentation, the results indicate long-term effects upon speech perception of the early hearing impairment.

Brandes and Ehinger (1971) studied children with otitis media and conductive hearing loss and found that they were impaired in comparison to controls only on the auditory perception of sound symbols within an auditory skills battery. Jerger, Jerger, Alford, and Abrams (1983) found greater than normal disruption in children with otitis media when they had to identify names and match them to pictures against a background of a competing speech message. This indicates an impaired ability to discriminate the picture names against other speech sound interference.

Teele, Klein, Rosner, and the Greater Boston Otitis Media Study Group (1984) found poor phonological comprehension in children with otitis media which was more marked when the infection had been bilateral rather than unilateral. Menyuk (1986) found children with recurrent middle ear infections to be poorer than controls at the age of seven on speech sound discrimination tasks.

In general, studies of otitis media indicate relatively intact processing of semantics, syntax, and expressive language but with impairment in auditory perception. There is no evidence of differences between children with otitis media and normal children in areas of vocabulary, semantics, or the lexicon. Syntactic comprehension also seems normal. The only suggestion of productive syntactic abnormalities is reported by Menyuk (1986). He reports that there is a reduced use of prepositional phrases, coordinate sentences, and morphological markers. However, other studies have not elaborated upon this suggestion.

Overall, in a review of over 50 studies of language performance in children with recurrent otitis media, Klein and Rapin (1988) conclude that the effects of otitis media on language development are relatively minimal, particularly if the children are of normal or above average IQ, with a school and home environment conducive to learning. Certainly, suggestions of more severe impact upon other aspects of language development are contradictory and earlier suggestions of depression of intellectual scores in children with otitis media have not been substantiated.

Bishop and Edmundson (1986) criticise the sample selection of some studies but agree with the conclusion that otitis media is unlikely to be a major feature in the aetiology of language disorders but that it may exacerbate the difficulties experienced by a child who is already vulnerable for language disorder.

PHONOLOGICAL DISORDERS

In a series of papers, Tallal and colleagues have demonstrated that some language disordered children are specifically impaired in both discriminating and sequencing speech sounds characterised by rapid transitional information (e.g. Tallal & Piercy, 1973; Tallal & Stark, 1981; Tallal et al., 1980). This cognitively based deficit is argued by Tallal to extend to non-verbal material and also to visually presented material. Within the language domain it has a specific impact upon phonological discrimination. The consistency and pervasiveness of such deficits has been much debated, but from a cognitive neuropsychological perspective it is not essential that all language disordered children show such deficits, it is simply of interest that a subsection of them may have a specific impairment in this area.

The potential association between difficulty in phonological discrimination and phonological problems in speech production is also unresolved. Bird and Bishop (1992) found that although some children with phonological problems in speech production also had difficultly discriminating between phonemes, many more had difficulty in perceiving the constancy of phonemes across different word contexts, where the form of the phoneme was influenced by the following vowel. They argued that rather than a simple deficit in phonemic discrimination there is a failure to identify the basic units necessary for the efficient perception and storage of the sounds of words, with each new word learnt as an unsegmented pattern. The absence of appreciation that words are composed of a small number of building blocks leads to protracted and inefficient language acquisition.

Leonard (1989; Leonard, Bertolini, Caselli, McGregor, & Sabbadini 1992) has argued that many of the expressive grammatical problems of language disordered children could be accounted for by downstream effects following perceptual limitations in the learning of specific features of language. According to this theory, the language input may be filtered, such that elements with low phonetic substance are unavailable to the language learning mechanism (Clahsen, in press). These would include grammatical morphemes within phonologically complex clusters (e.g. /ts/ in cats, /pt/ in helped) and unstressed syllables (eg. "is" in "he is big") (Bishop, 1992). However, the theory does not explain the greater ease of English children with grammatical difficulties in producing a noun plural s (e.g. dogs, cats) rather than a third person singular s (e.g. goes, walks). Thus, Leonard cannot account for the grammatical disorders on the basis of a phonological disorder alone and associated problems are therefore postulated by Leonard, in constructing paradigms to build morphology, which render the processing of the s in walks more difficult than the s in cats. He also argues for particular sensitivity to the degree of inflection of the language. Thus for example, a highly inflected language such as Hebrew enables greater ease in tuning in to the morphology and comparable language impaired children learning Hebrew are better able to produce present and past tense inflections (Rom & Leonard, 1990). Clahsen (in press) criticises the theory on the basis that the nature of the perceptual limitations and the concept of morphological building are insufficiently specified to be able to generate falsifiable predictions.

PURE WORD DEAFNESS/AUDITORY AGNOSIA

In adults, the syndrome of pure word deafness is associated with normal hearing and peripheral auditory perception but speech no longer retains meaning. The patients report that they are able to hear the speech that is spoken to them but they cannot work out its meaning. Some describe it as sounding like a foreigner speaking at a distance (e.g. Ziegler, 1952). Others report that the words appear to come too rapidly and run into each other (e.g. Albert & Bear, 1974; Klein & Harper, 1956). In this form of pure word deafness, it has been suggested that there is a difficulty similar to that which Tallal has proposed for auditory phonological problems in children with developmental aphasia. It has been suggested that these patients have difficulty making fine temporal discriminations about rapidly changing acoustic stimuli, associated with bilateral lesions of the temporal lobes (e.g Auerbach, Allard, Naeser, Alexander, & Albert, 1982). For this type of patient it is argued that a slowed rate of presentation of verbal material improves performance. For a number of these patients speech production is also normal. Some evidence suggests that a unilateral left hemisphere lesion may be sufficient to evoke a difficulty in the perception of word sounds (Faglioni, Spinnler, & Vignolo, 1969; Sitdis & Volpe, 1988).

A slightly different form of auditory agnosia is given the label word-meaning deafness. In these cases the patients are able to repeat spoken words and sentences that they are not able to understand. An early report of a syndrome of this sort is provided by Bramwell (1897/1984). For the patients to be able to repeat the word correctly, the word must have undergone adequate acoustic analysis. Furthermore, since these patients may often be able to understand speech presented in written form an adequate semantic representation must remain intact. Some theoretical accounts of this syndrome postulate a disconnection of an auditory input lexicon (store of all the known sound patterns of words) from the semantic system (a store which includes the associated word meanings) (see Ellis & Young, 1988a for a discussion).

A third form of auditory agnosia in neurological patients is described by Ellis and Young (1988a) as auditory phonological agnosia. They use this label in reference to the case of Beauvois, Derouesne, and Bastard (1980). In this case, although the patient was able to process familiar words perfectly, there was difficulty in both the repetition and writing to dictation of invented non-words. It was argued that this resulted from difficulty in transforming acoustic information to phonemic information. In Ellis and Young's (1988a) functional model the auditory analysis system has a direct connection to a phonemic production system and they postulate that disruption of the connection at this level means that only information mediated by a semantic system can be produced.

All of these cases of auditory agnosia occur in adults who have previously developed normal language systems and for whom an element of language production remains intact. However, any of these deficits would create severe problems at a developmental level if they were present from birth. An inability to process rapid transitional information (e.g. Tallal & Piercy, 1973; Tallal & Stark, 1981; Tallal et al., 1980) could have downstream effects upon other aspects of language (Tallal et al., 1996). Within development, word-meaning deafness, in which despite accurate analysis of the auditory input there was an inability to establish a connection to the word's meaning would have a very pervasive impact upon language acquisition. If present in extensive format in early life it might also prohibit productive language skills. It is this form of auditory agnosia as described in adults which seems most similar to the syndrome that has been described in children by Landau and Kleffner (1957) and which is generally referred to as the Landau–Kleffner syndrome, though it is sometimes called acquired aphasia of childhood.

In Landau–Kleffner syndrome both sexes are equally affected. The onset of the language disorder varies widely from 18 months to 13 years but has a peak incidence between 4 years and 7 years. The most common aphasic symptom is a profound receptive language impairment which may extend to total disappearance of auditory verbal comprehension (Landau & Kleffner, 1957; Paquier, van Dongen, & Loonen, 1992). Apart from a seizure disorder, which occurs in 80% of cases (Cole et al., 1988; Dugas, Masson, Le Heuzey, & Regnier, 1982), neurological examination and intelligence can be normal. Combination of the syndrome with some behavioural changes including aggression, restlessness, and inattentiveness are also reported and a co-occurrence of the syndrome with autism has also been documented. The long-term prognosis is severe. The syndrome co-occurs with bilateral EEG abnormality but with normal CT or MRI scan (e.g. Denes, Balliello, Volterra, & Pellegrini, 1986). Several authors have suggested that Landau–Kleffner syndrome results from unilateral or bilateral damage to Wernicke's area (e.g. Holmes, McKeever, & Saunders, 1981; Lou, Brandt, & Bruhn, 1977) but Rapin, Mattis, Rowan, and Golden (1977) have suggested that it is the processing of the auditory input to Wernicke's area that is disrupted rather than there being structural lesions. In this sense Landau–Kleffner syndrome is an auditory-verbal agnosia rather than a simple aphasia. The suggestion of an encephalitic aetiology to the syndrome has not been substantiated by post-mortem analysis (Cole et al., 1988). Otero et al. (1989) report a case of Landau–Kleffner syndrome in association with a case of parasitic cyst lying deep in the left sylvian fissure, which would support the view that the disorder could be explained in terms of a unilateral structural brain lesion in a particularly critical area. In this case speech was telegrammatic, with the omission of articles and prepositions in sentences (e.g. he said "el va casa" instead of "el va a la casa" [he goes home]), but with clear articulation and a severe comprehension impairment. Following recovery there remained a decrease in spontaneous speech and poor response to oral commands. High resolution rCBF imaging in a five-year-old boy with Landau–Kleffner syndrome demonstrated low flow areas in both the left middle frontal gyrus and the right mesiotemporal/ hippocampal region (Mouridsen, Videboek, Sogaard, & Andersen, 1992), indicating a bilateral aetiology in this case.

Landau–Kleffner syndrome is often described as an acquired aphasia of childhood since in some cases there is evidence of initial development of language which then recedes. However, Landau (1992) argues for the possibility of a genetic liability. The disorder has been reported twice in two siblings (Landau & Kleffner, 1957; Nakano, Okuno, & Mikawa, 1989) and in the case reports which will be presented below it was evident in twins. This supports the argument that the abnormality which generates the syndrome is present from an early stage in life but that in some cases its manifestations become evident and have impact after the initial stages of infant development.

In their original descriptions, Landau and Kleffner (1957) emphasised the association of speech impairment with seizures. For example, in case one of Landau and Kleffner (1957), they describe an aphasia appearing in a child with a convulsive disorder. On the first occasion the aphasia disappeared shortly after anticonvulsive therapy was started. On the second occasion, the speech impairment appeared without the onset of convulsions but with an electroencephalographic abnormality. As the electroencephalogram improved, with increased drug therapy, speech also improved. In other cases, improvement in seizures does not necessarily coincide with significant improvement in language (Zardini, Molteni, Nardocci, Sarti, Avanzini, & Granata, 1995). In some of the other cases reported by Landau and Kleffner (1957) the symptoms were more persistent and might extend for several years. In all cases they were associated with convulsive disorders. Later descriptions of Landau–Kleffner syndrome have described children for whom language never recovers to develop normally.

Although it is often argued that children recover more effectively from abnormalities that develop at a young age than from those that they acquire later, which would predict that children with Landau–Kleffner would have a better prognosis if the episode occurred earlier rather than later in life, an investigation by Bishop (1985) contradicts such a hypothesis. Bishop (1985) examined the relationship between age at onset of the language disorder in Landau–Kleffner syndrome and eventual outcome. She reviewed 45 cases, all of whom had been followed up to at least 12 years of age. In contrast to childhood aphasia in which the prognosis is better if the structural lesion affecting the left hemisphere occurs early, in Landau–Kleffner syndrome the older the child at onset the better the prognosis for language development. One interpretation of this is that the development of the convulsive disorder impairs the further development of the language system, but where that system was already partially established there may be retention or recovery of elements of the system or a sufficient substrate may have become established for a cognitive system to build upon. Thus, these cases of late onset may have characteristics more like those of acquired aphasia in adulthood whereas the early onset cases may be more similar to severe developmental aphasias in their impact.

In partial support of Bishop's (1985) observations, Gerard, Dugas, Valdois, Franc, and Lecendreux (1993) found that of five cases of Landau–Kleffner syndrome, with an age of onset for the language disorder of nine years or above, only one had a severe comprehension deficit, the remaining four being dysfluent with word finding difficulties but with relatively intact comprehension. Despite the late age of onset of the language difficulties, two of the cases who retained language comprehension skills had epilepsy with onset by five years. For these cases the development of the convulsive disorder has not in itself impaired further development of the language system. Rather the convulsions could reflect an underlying pathology potentially of genetic aetiology, and this pathology could generate a later expression of language disorder which would not in itself merely be a consequence of the seizures. Thus the relationship between the seizures and the language disorder may be to a related underlying cause, rather than in terms of a direct causal link between the two behavioural manifestations.

In an adult follow-up of seven cases of Landau–Kleffner syndrome, Deonna, Peter, and Ziegler (1989) report that none of their cases developed functional written language, indicating that the linguistic impact extends beyond oral language. Further, only one out of seven cases had developed any useful sign language. Four of the seven retained absence of language comprehension and lack of expressive speech. These cases had severe verbal auditory agnosia. For those with better verbal recovery, speech abnormalities included echolalia and restricted expression. Even for the best recovered patient who had good oral language, there remained a severe dyslexia. Thus, amongst the children who have Landau–Kleffner syndrome there are some who retain into adulthood a severe and global comprehension and expressive deficit despite intact auditory perception. These cases form pure parallels to verbal auditory agnosia.

In children with severe developmental agnosias, impairments on tests of receptive grammar have been reported in assessments of written as well as spoken language (Bishop, 1982). This suggests that failure to link the phonological analysis of words with their meanings has downstream "knock-on" effects on a system for encoding grammatical relations. These ideas integrate with those of Leonard, discussed previously, which argue that limitations in phonological processing have a specific impact upon the ability to process linguistic items of low phonetic substance such as grammatical markers, leading to downstream disorders in grammatical ability (Leonard, 1989; Leonard et al., 1992). Such downstream effects are consistent with the model depicted in Fig. 2.1, since phonological analysis feeds into both semantics and the lexicon and thereby to grammar, if specific semantic items within the lexicon or morphological markers within the lexicon are differentially affected. If the requisite input to a grammatical module is distorted, it cannot be expected to emerge, or develop efficiently. As discussed in Chapter 1, downstream effects to not preclude a modular organisation to the emerging language system, but they may reduce the potential for neat double dissociation to be evident within the specific language deficits. However, as discussed in Chapter 1, testable theories remain, since if auditory agnosias or phonological problems cause grammatical difficulties (Leonard, 1989; Leonard et al., 1992; Tallal et al., 1980) then all children with phonological problems or auditory agnosias should have grammatical difficulties, and there should be no children with one of the former difficulties but normal grammatical skills. Since the studies arguing for causal links have to date been largely group studies rather than case studies, the issue of the existence of children with the former problem but not the latter remains an empirical possibility. Such children could create problems for models such as Fig. 2.1, since the model either predicts downstream effects in all cases or in none, but does not permit a differential influence without some degree of further partitioning or fractionation of its components.

An explicit attempt to teach reading skills was included in the study of an eleven-year-old Landau–Kleffner boy reported by Denes et al. (1986). His deterioration of language began at the age of three, simultaneously with the onset of epilepsy. Language disappeared completely. However, at the age of six he was taught to match objects with written words and was subsequently taught reading and writing sufficiently to enable him to attend primary school. Phonemic discrimination, identification, and production remained absent despite the normal development of lexical–semantic abilities and comprehension of bound morphemes, tested through reading and writing. In visual short-term memory tasks, phonological mediation was also absent.

The authors confirmed that since pure auditory and brain stem auditory evoked potentials were normal, the severe auditory comprehension deficit could not be accounted for by peripheral factors. Their patient CS also showed almost normal performance in identifying meaningful non-verbal sounds. Further, although the discrimination of phonemes was totally absent, the patient was able to score above chance on vowel identification tasks and Denes et al. (1986) argued that this residual activity could be explained by the physical characteristics of the stimuli since vowels have a longer duration than the rapidly changing auditory stimuli associated with consonants. They thus argue for a basis of the deficit similar to that described in the first form of auditory agnosia above in relation to adults, i.e. pure word deafness. They propose that the patient's development of reading is mediated via semantic representations which bypass phonological processing.

Despite intact comprehension of bound morphemes, CS was also impaired in the production and comprehension of free morphemes, such as articles and prepositions, which Denes et al. (1986) argue supports the hypothesis of Caramazza, Berndt, and Basili (1983) that producing and understanding function words demands some form of phonological coding and decoding. It is not clear in this case whether the patient's early exposure to auditory material and initial acquisition of language contributed to his later reading abilities.

Papagno and Basso (1993) report a case of Landau–Kleffner syndrome in an eight-year-old child for whom oral language skills recovered within four months to a normal level but written language took seven months to recover. A more pervasive deficit in number processing and calculation remained.

In support of a genetic aetiology, the cases of Landau–Kleffner syndrome reported here describe the first cases of Landau–Kleffner syndrome appearing in twins. In one twin the disorder takes the form of a developmental aphasia with slowed language development. In this case there is no evidence of normal development of language which subsequently deteriorates. However, in the second twin initially normal language development is arrested at the age of 18 months. Associated with the subsequent deterioration, there are manifestations of autism. The ultimate linguistic pattern of the two children is similar with almost global comprehension impairment and expressive disorder.

Case Reports: Landau–Kleffner Syndrome, RD and MD

The twins are five-year-old boys from a professional family. Both parents are in good health. The maternal aunt had epilepsy following whooping cough at the age of six and has generalised language difficulties. The paternal uncle has a karyotype XYY which was associated with convulsions. Labour was induced at 39 weeks gestation. Slow progress led to the first twin (MD) being delivered in Keilands Rotation. The second twin (RD) was delivered as an assisted breach with forceps to the head, 14 minutes after twin one.

Twin: RD. Birth weight for RD was 3477g. He was the second twin to be delivered. No resuscitation was required nor was any special care. There was no significant early concern and no subsequent serious illnesses apart from a right hydrocele at the age of 3;5. Physically there are no dysmorphic characteristics except for a right single palmer crease. Height and weight have been consistently around the 95th centile but within the normal range. Head circumference has been consistently normal.

RD is reported to have smiled at four weeks but to have been a placid baby with little babble. He sat unsupported at five months and walked at 13 months. By 14 to 16 months, around 40 single words had become established with 15 intelligible to outsiders as reported by parents. Multiple word combinations had not developed.

From 18 months, RD was noted to become less affectionate, less cooperative and more inclined to cry. There was a loss of interest in toys. RD stopped kicking and throwing a ball and was reluctant to walk around outside. There was no imaginative play. Words appeared to decline from his vocabulary. Associated with the decline of speech there was a decline in the ability to follow instructions.

At the age of 2;10, RD was seen by his General Practitioner who reported few words and odd sounds. He did not answer to his name. He avoided eye contact, flapped his arms, and engaged in both head shaking and inappropriate laughter. The parents reported that such episodes of stereotypical movements, had had an onset around 2;6 years and were occurring up to 12 times a day. During the episodes, RD appeared to be in a world of his own but did not lose consciousness. At the age of 3;2, RD was seen by a clinical psychologist who gave a diagnosis of autism. The stereotyped episodes had declined to one every couple of months, although there had also been two episodes where the eyes rolled about. Holding therapy was instigated and this resulted by the age of 3;7 in improved eye contact and better interpersonal contact with parents. At the age of three computerised tomography was normal. X-ray of the spine and skull showed no specific features suggesting dysplasia. Two EEGs were recorded: Both were normal, including well-formed sleep phenomena.

Because of the similarity of the clinical features in the twins and a finding of an abnormal spike focus in the identical twin MD, RD was started at the age of 3;10 on tegretol. Following this he was reported as being more amenable, occupying himself for longer, being less obsessional, and taking more initiative. Temper outbursts increased replacing the previous rather diffuse sense of frustration. Hearing was tested as normal.

At the age of 4;2, it was commented that language did not appear to be meaningful, although there was responsiveness to tone of voice and facial expression employed by the parents. The decline and increase in language development is documented in Table 2.1. At the age of 5;1, two years after the period in which RD was producing no speech, only seven words had become established and these were used with low frequency. RD was able to respond to his name and could respond to simple instructions though this comprehension was facilitated when he was in a familiar context. Overall, language comprehension was profoundly restricted.

RD, at the age of five, was consistently right handed and could grasp and scribble with a pencil both straight lines and circular shapes. He continued to avoid eye contact but could communicate by action non-verbally. For example, if failing to enjoy the testing situation, he could indicate clearly that he wished to depart from the test room. Mother also reported that at this time RD no longer responded to music, consistent with a general deterioration in the meaning associated with auditory information both verbally and non-verbally. RD was also reported to like parallel lines. Particularly rows or trees in orchards and telegraph poles.

Twin: MD. Birth weight was 2978g. No resuscitation was required nor any special care. There were no serious illnesses. Height and weight are around the 95th centile, as for his twin.

TABLE 2.1
Single Words in RD's Productive Vocabulary

Age	
1;2–1;4	Banana, panda, traitor, cuckoo, quack, bubbles, down, bye, babies, clock, cuddle, car, shoes, tickle, M—, mama, dada, grandad, nana, teddy, cat, post-box, milkman, dog, rabbit, pat, apple, spoon, drink, biscuit, bus, dagger, mix, caravan, tree, R—, nose, bath, paper, fish, owl, hole, ball, key, bumble bee, umbrella, tick, hammer, amen, please, daisy, pooh, butterfly, kite, ladder, moon, chimney, more, again, puddle, rainbow. (n=61)
2;7	tractor, bubbles, down, bye, clock, car, M—, mama, dada, cat, post-box, pat, biscuit, digger, R—, key, amen, please, butterfly, moon, more.
2;11	moon, yes, dada, tree, teddy, mama, R—.
3;1	no words. [High pitched squealing]
3;11	daddy, I do.
5;1	car, biscuit, down, drink, ball, I did.

MD is reported to have smiled at 3 weeks, sat unsupported at 5.5 months and walked at 13 months. There was plentiful babble around 6 months. First words appeared at 15–18 months, with around 24 reported at this stage. Up to 18 months, parents thought that development was normal, but by 2 years speech was seen to be behind that of peers, despite comparable development in other areas.

At the age of 3;10, both comprehension and expression of language were at approximately a 2;3 level on the Reynell scales. No loss of language skills was reported but progress had become very slow. Speech was at the level of labelling with single words. In terms of general development, there was normal ability in some areas. Gross and fine motor skills were good. He was able to run, jump, and coordinate a tricycle. Vision and hearing were normal. Phobias of loud noises such as the vacuum cleaner were evident, although he did not turn away from speech. Other phobias included the sea which he had previously loved, and going out to play. When excited, hand flapping and eye squeezing occurred, with some noises. There were also temper tantrums. There had been no head injuries or ear infections.

There had been no overt seizures, but for a few months there had been twice daily attacks, during which MD would stand with his eyes closed, bring his hands up and open and close them. These lasted for two–three seconds. Subsequently blank spells were reported with vacant staring. An EEG at 3;10 revealed a very active spike discharge in the left mid-temporal area, spreading to the mid-central region of the same side and increasing with sleep. Cranial CT scan was normal. He was started on tegretol, with no daily attacks occurring subsequently.

By the age of 4;3, speech and comprehension were felt to have improved somewhat. He could distinguish within category words e.g. car/trailer/helicopter, but there was difficulty in understanding sentences with more than two concrete words. Articulation was impaired, making it difficult to determine on some occasions whether jargon was being employed or specific attempts to pronounce words. There was some use of gesture and an attempt was made to introduce Makarton signing but with little evident effect.

Temper tantrums had stopped although there continued to be mood fluctuations. There was also an increase of odd behaviours and head jerking, considered by the clinical psychologist to be displacement activities rather than seizure activity. He enjoyed jigsaws and repeatedly placing things into containers and taking them out again.

At the age of 5;1, MD had a productive vocabulary of words, some with clear articulation and some as phonemic approximations. Naming skills were well below age level but he could correctly name tree, boat, table, bear, and moon. He produced recognisable approximations for scarecrow, owl, snail, and goat. For a number of other items he could give one or two correct sounds. Comprehension of language was also well below age level but on Bishop's Test for the Reception of Grammar he could understand several nouns, verbs and adjectives and respond correctly to simple active sentences. Behaviour was much better and more cooperative than for his co-twin.

MD and RD are believed to be identical twins. Each has a developmental disorder of language but for RD initially good progress regressed, in association with increased behavioural disturbance, autistic features, but no seizures. For MD there is a developmental aphasia, with language development which may initially have been more rapid and then slowed in progress but for which there has been no regression. Seizure activity in the left mid-temporal area was recorded in one twin and both twins responded to anti-seizure medication. These two different manifestations of developmental language disorder seem to be varying phenotypical expressions of a common underlying abnormality.

SEMANTIC DISORDERS

Whereas some of the disorders described above may result from a difficulty in associating or analysing phonological input and integrating it with meaning, other developmental language disorders may result from impairment in the development of the semantic system itself, or in maintaining efficient access to it. In cases where the semantic system is established but there are access or retrieval problems in its utilisation, one may see relatively normal reception of language but anomia in expressive language with a preponderance of semantic errors (van Hout, 1993). Where the semantic system has failed to be encoded the presenting symptomatology might still be anomia but it would be accompanied by comparably severe receptive difficulty. Where severe receptive language disorders are associated with impairment in the development of the semantic system, they would actually represent specific forms of memory impairment rather than simply disorders of receptive language.

Denckla (1979) reported that a large group of children have developmental anomias. In her descriptions, such children talk a great deal and have relatively fluent comprehension but have trouble with word retrieval. Denckla (1979) distinguished between children with naming difficulties (aphasoid) and those with memory problems (amnesoid). The aphasoid was said to make better use of associative manoeuvres. The amnesoid tended to be a better reader and was more like a slow learner, needing many trials before registering new information.

Semantic Access Anomia

Van Hout (1993) classified two developmental anomics by the Denckla typology and compared their naming performance with both chronological and naming age controls as well as matched cases of acquired childhood anomia. The first developmental anomic, who was seven years old but with a naming age of three years, made 179 errors on a confrontation naming task. Ninety of the errors (50%) were semantic paraphasias (e.g. dog for cat). In contrast, only 20% of each of the naming age controls' and none of the chronological age controls' errors were semantic paraphasias. The second developmental anomic, who was nine years old, with a naming age of five years, made 150 errors of which 75 (50%) were semantic paraphasias. For this child the chronological age control was 98% accurate so an error comparison is of doubtful validity. The naming age control had a similar incidence of semantic errors, suggesting that limitations of semantic access can also appear in a normal developmental pathway. For both developmental anomic children, semantic paraphasias were the most common error category with twice as many errors of this type as of any other. This was not true for any of the naming age controls.

When a normal adult or child is able to activate the semantic representation for an item but has difficulty in using that to trigger the correct name, they may produce a circumlocution or description of use or location of the object (e.g. "has a nice fur and purrs for cat"). Van Hout included such a circumlocutory category in her error analysis. It is notable that the second developmental anomic made only 10% of errors of this type, whereas the matched naming age control produced 40% of errors as circumlocutions. For this anomic child there appeared to be few occasions when a descriptive semantic specification was available but no associated name was triggered.

Van Hout showed that the anomic performance did not reflect a general deficit in passive vocabulary knowledge by assessing receptive vocabulary. The ability to describe the meaning of aurally presented words was at age level on the WISC-R vocabulary test for both developmental anomics. A pointing task was also derived, in which ten items named wrongly in the naming tasks were presented one at a time with five foils (two semantic distracters, one visual, one phonological, and one unrelated). Both developmental anomics performed with greater than 80% accuracy.

In summary, these developmental anomics had normal passive vocabulary knowledge and significantly superior receptive vocabulary skills over naming skills, indicating good development of semantic representations for words. Yet, in naming tasks their severe anomias were marked by a dominance of semantic errors over other error types, suggesting restricted ability to access and utilise precise semantic knowledge efficiently in naming tasks. The disorders appear to be modality specific access impairments or activational difficulties, though the precise interpretation will vary dependent upon whether a model of a unitary or multiple semantic systems is adopted.

It is of interest that the two acquired childhood anomics also discussed by van Hout showed comparable performance to the developmental anomic cases. Their passive vocabulary was normal but naming was dominated by semantic errors, which were substantively the most common error category. The first acquired anomic, who was seven years old but with a naming age of four years, made 174 errors on confrontation naming. Seventy-two of the errors (41%) were semantic paraphasias. The second acquired anomic, who was nine years old with a naming age of five years, made 200 errors, of which 120 (60%) were semantic paraphasias. This format of naming disorder can thus occur in both developmental and acquired format in childhood.

Semantic Representation Anomia

Where there is a pervasive impairment of memory which appears in a developmental format and affects the acquisition of semantic representations it will inevitably also affect the naming skills of the child. Thus, developmental anomia may in some cases be a presenting symptom of impairments of the representations of semantic memory itself. One such case of memory impairment is discussed in detail in Chapter 3. In this section, we will discuss the nature of the naming impairment which results from this deficit.

Case Report: Julia

Julia was aged 12;8 and had temporal lobe epilepsy. She was born at 40 weeks. Delivery was by forceps and birthweight was 3745g. Julia smiled by six weeks, walked at thirteen months and dressed herself by two years. Within the family, Julia's father had night-time convulsions as a child. Her elder brother had articulation difficulties which responded to speech therapy. A cousin had learning difficulties which may have been developmental dyslexia. All of the family were right-handed, but Julia was left-handed. Delayed language development, including naming difficulties was recorded in the pre-school years; for example, at the age of 3;9, BAS naming was at the 1st centile for age. However, the seizure disorder did not become manifest until the age of six. CT scan at this time was normal but EEG indicated abnormal irregular slow discharges in the left hemisphere, especially the temporal region. The speech therapist's report noted "specific difficulty with word recognition and word-finding".

At the age of seven, Julia's classteacher reported that she "sometimes has difficulty remembering words or what a word actually means".

Julia was referred to the author for neuropsychological assessment when she was twelve and a half years old. She was taking phenytoin and there had been no seizures for the previous two years.

Intelligence.   On the Weschler Intelligence Scale for Children – Revised the following subtest scores were obtained:

Verbal Subtests		*Performance Subtests*	
Information	1	Picture Completion	5
Similarities	8	Picture Arrangement	6
Arithmetic	9	Block Design	6
Vocabulary	3	Object Assembly	7
Coding	10		

(An average subtest score is ten; Range 1-19; S.D.=3)

Calculating an average IQ score is misleading, since on some subtests performance is normal, whereas on others there are severe and selective difficulties. The two poorest subtests are "Information", which assesses factual general knowledge and "Vocabulary", which requires verbal definitions to be given to spoken words. Conversational speech was relatively fluent and comprehensible. With long words and under speed stress there were occasional misarticulations and her ability to explain and describe things was sometimes slow.

Naming.   On the Renfrew Word Finding Scale naming age was 5;3. Errors were predominantly semantic paraphasias or refusals. Some also shared visual similarity with the stimulus, e.g. *mountains* → "rocks"; *goat* → "cow"; *thermometer* → "ruler", but others did not have visual components, e.g. *coathanger* → "peg", *leaf* → "flower". There was one perceptual misidentification: *flame* → "leaf" and one phonemic paraphasia: *scarecrow* → "scrowman". Amongst the items refused, some were correctly identified in response to questions by indication of their function or use, e.g. apron; drill. Others were not recognised, e.g. anchor; screw; crutch .

On the Boston Naming Test 24/60 items were named correctly, a score at a five-year-old level. Of the items failed, 33% induced semantic paraphasias (some of which may also have had visual components), 31% were circumlocutions, 22% were refused, 6% were perceptual misidentifications, and there was one phonemic paraphasia. The Boston Naming Test was re-given after a delay of one month. On the repeat test 21/60 items were named correctly. Of the items failed, 38% induced semantic paraphasias, 28% were refused, 21% were circumlocutions, 8%

were perceptual misidentifications, and there were two phonemic paraphasias. The relationship between the errors to stimuli on the first and second presentation is indicated in Table 2.2.

Ninety-five per cent of responses were consistent in terms of being correct or incorrect across presentations. Of the stimuli which induced overt errors on both occasions, 96% induced errors which were consistent in type, in terms of the classifications employed above and 65% induced the identical error. If the stimuli which were responded to correctly and the stimuli which were refused are combined with those which induced overt errors, then of the full list of 60 stimuli, identical responses were generated to 48 (80%). Thus, the overall pattern is of highly consistent responses across presentations trials. Given that the delay between trials was one month, it is unlikely that memory of previous performance and responses contributed to this pattern.

Performance Across Semantic Categories. A selection of black and white line drawings, from those published by Snodgrass and Vanderwart (1980), were selected on the basis of membership of four semantic categories: indoor objects; animals; articles of clothing; and foodstuffs. Full listing of those employed and the criteria used for accepting a response as correct are given in Temple (1986a). Julia's performance is summarised in Table 2.3, where it is also compared with normal four-year-olds. Julia's performance with items of clothing does appear to be somewhat better developed than the young children and her performance in identifying foodstuffs is poor in comparison. The difference in performance between these two semantic classes is statistically significant for Julia (X^2=4.24, P<0.05, Yate's correction applied), but not for the four-year-olds.

On retest, the relative ordering of accuracy across semantic categories was consistent. Of the 144 targets, response type was consistent for 86%

TABLE 2.2
Consistency of Responses by Julia on the Boston Naming Test

R1	R2					
	SE	PE	PhE	CE	R	C
SE	12	–	–	–	2	–
PE	–	2	–	–	–	–
PhE	–	–	1	–	–	–
CE	1	–	–	7	3	–
R	2	1	–	–	5	–
C	–	–	1	1	1	21

R1 First Response; R2 Second Response; SE Semantic Error; PE Perceptual Error; PhE Phonological Error; CE Circumlocution; R Refusal; C Correct.

and actual response was identical for 85%. Examples of identical overt errors are given in Table 2.4.

Frequency Effects. The average frequency (Kucera & Francis, 1967) for stimuli which were correct on both trials was 29.72, although the average for stimuli correct on only one trial was 12.93. For stimuli that induced semantic errors on both trials, the average frequency was 5.56 and for those which were refused on both trials the average frequency was 3.71. These results suggest a relationship between frequency and response type. Items consistently correct, were of highest average frequency, with those correct on one trial of next highest average frequency. Items consistently refused were of lowest average frequency. It was noticeable that the items which induce semantic errors had a higher average frequency level than items refused but a lower average frequency than those read correctly.

Comprehension of Names. The 144 targets that comprised the semantic category stimulus set were spoken aloud and Julia had to select a matching picture from a picture array of 24 items, within the same semantic group. There was one array for each of foodstuffs and clothing. There were

TABLE 2.3
Performance Across Semantic Categories

	Rank Order				
	1	*2*	*3*	*4*	*Max. Difference*
Julia (1st test)	C 92%	I 73%	A 69%	F 63%	29%
Normal 4-year-olds	C 65%	I 65%	A 55%	F 50%	15%
Julia (retest)	C 83%	I 77%	A 73%	F 58%	

C: Clothes; I: Indoor Objects; A: Animals; F: Foods.

TABLE 2.4
Examples of Identical Overt Errors

Target	*First response*	*Second response*
zebra	horse	horse
bee	ant	ant
lamp	lampshade	lampshade
swan	duck	duck
thimble	bucket	bucket
pliers	clippers	clippers
hen	peacock	peacock
corn	fish	fish
potato	egg	egg

two arrays for indoor objects and two arrays for animals. Accuracy on this comprehension task was compared with accuracy on the naming task. There was no significant difference in Julia's ability to comprehend the names of clothes, animals and foodstuffs and her ability to name these items. The naming impairment was thus not a modality specific impairment.

Discussion. Julia had a developmental history of naming difficulty, which had been documented consistently since the age of four years, when she was first assessed because of concern over language development. The naming disorder preceded the development of the seizure disorder. The difficulties with naming were apparent as language began to develop and there was no evidence that naming was at one stage at a higher level and subsequently deteriorated. The evidence supports the view that the underlying neurological basis of Julia's disorder was already present in infancy.

Julia's naming difficulties were disproportionate to many of her other intellectual skills. Her arithmetical skills, her constructional skills (WISC-R Object Assembly subtest), and her ability to reason verbally (WISC-R Similarities subtest) were all entirely normal and within one standard deviation of the mean for age. Her naming difficulties were not therefore part of an undifferentiated developmental failure. Rather, there had been a dissociation between the cognitive skills which she has attained. Certain intellectual modules were established where other processing mechanisms were impaired. Thus, there was fractionation in her intellectual development, and fractionation within her language skills: Verbal reasoning was normal; reading and spelling were three–four years behind; naming was over seven years behind.

Performance over delays of a few hours or a month both revealed highly consistent patterns of responding, to the extent that the majority of errors were identical on retest. If the semantic system was established in the normal way but there was variable access, one would expect that the errors would vary from trial to trial. In contrast, the consistency data supports a storage deficit underlying the anomia rather than a retrieval deficit. Where semantic errors are dominant, it suggests that for some items a partial store of information is available, enough to access a semantically related item but insufficient for a precise specification of the target itself. The consistent patterns of responding, the dominance of semantic naming errors, and the difference in performance between semantic categories suggests failure in the establishment of the semantic representations themselves.

Ellis and Young (1988a) discuss the anomic disorders manifested in adults who have sustained brain damage. They suggest that word-finding difficulties can arise at one of two levels: the semantic level or the speech output lexicon. Patients with semantic level impairments, may have greater naming problems in some semantic domains than in others, thereby showing category specificity. They perform poorly on comprehension tasks that require precise semantic knowledge. They make semantic errors in both speech and in other tasks which do not require spoken responses. Patients with impairment of the output lexicon tend not to show category specificity, nor semantic naming errors, but neologistic errors or approximations are made to words which they cannot fully access.

If Julia was a patient with an acquired anomia, to be classified by these criteria, then she would fall within the semantic level anomic group. In favour of this, she showed a significant difference in performance between certain semantic categories (clothing and foodstuffs). She made semantic paraphasias in attempting to name items. She also made semantic errors on tasks that did not require a spoken response, but which required precise semantic knowledge (selecting by pointing, from a picture array). Against an output lexicon deficit, phonological approximations to target words were very rare.

The only behavioural feature which Julia displayed, which was not consistent with the criteria outlined by Ellis and Young (1988a) for semantic level anomias, was the frequency effect. Ellis and Young (1988a) argue that effects of frequency upon naming are evident in anomias arising from disorders of the speech output lexicon rather than the semantic system. However, Julia's disorder is developmental rather than acquired. It is not improbable that more common words, because of frequency of exposure, develop semantic representations more readily than lower frequency words. Thus in developmental disorders, a frequency effect might be predicted in disorders of semantic level representations. Words of high frequency might have sufficiently well-established semantic representations to be read correctly. Words of low frequency might have insufficient semantic specification to permit any guess as to the target name. Words of intermediate frequency might have partial semantic specification which enables a response in the appropriate semantic field but a response which is insufficiently precise to correctly specify the actual target, i.e. semantic paraphasias are induced. It should also be noted that the psycholinguistic dimensions of familiarity and age of acquisition are correlated with frequency and both may be contributing to the anomic effects.

Overall, the pattern of Julia's performance in naming suggests a deficit in the establishment of semantic level representations. The underlying cognitive cause of Julia's naming problem may be a memory impairment which affects the capacity to establish stored representations of word meanings. Julia's results are also consistent with the left temporal focus of her seizure disorder. It may be that when memory impairments occur in development they often induce anomic disorders. The nature of Julia's memory development and its similarity to classical amnesic syndromes will be discussed in Chapter 3.

Category-specific Semantic Anomia

In the adult cognitive neuropsychological literature there has been considerable interest in recent years in the category specific disorders which are manifest in a variety of different formats. Some of these relate to specific tasks or modalities of input and output with dissociability of some of the mechanisms underlying the frequently reported distinction between the processing of living things and animals (McCarthy & Warrington, 1990). Although this is not the only major categorical distinction that has been discussed, it is one of the most pervasively reported and there are a variety of different theoretical interpretations for its basis. One hypothesis is that the semantic system is actually organised in a categorical format and that selective brain injury might wipe out one category whilst leaving other categories intact. Another argument is that there are specific features associated with the information that is encoded in particular categories which makes these categorical distinctions emerge from the nature of the encoding process. Thus for example, it has been suggested that living things and animals tend to have a greater coding emphasis placed upon sensory features whereas non-living things and objects found inside a home may have a larger number of functional attributes associated with their identification (Warrington & Shallice, 1984). Thus, if the systems involved in encoding functional and sensory attributes differ, similar application of these overall systems could result in emergent properties which appear to have a categorical basis. It has also been argued that living things may have greater visual complexity than non living things, and may therefore be more vulnerable to disorders affecting the construction of knowledge about an object's visual form or linking perception from knowledge to meaning (Humphreys & Riddoch, 1987).

A case description of a child with a category specific disorder affecting living things is presented and then discussed in relation to the extent to which his disorder would be consistent with explanations proposed for adult neurological cases and the implications for the development of the semantic system underlying naming skills.

Case Report: Anomia for Animals, John

John (Temple, 1986a, 1995) was a 12-year-old boy who was the first of twins, born at full term. Developmental milestones were normal initially, and first concern did not appear until the age of six. At this time EEG showed high voltage spikes and waves confined to the right central area and brief spike outbursts bilaterally in the posterior of the region. Between the ages of three and six, John had two epileptic seizures but had none subsequently. At the time of his investigation he had an EEG abnormality which showed brief bursts of regular sharp and slow wave activity with a left hemisphere emphasis. CT scan was normal.

Assessed on the Wechsler Intelligence Scale for Children, Verbal IQ was 79, and Performance IQ was 75. Raven's Progressive Matrices generated a non-verbal intelligence score of 74. Digit Span was 5 forward and 2 backward.

Semantic System. At the time of John's neurological examination at the age of 12, the most obvious feature noted in the information gathered was his inability to report any current activities or to enlarge in a factual way on any topic. Similarly, school reports indicated that "John cannot carry information over from one minute to the next".

Story recall was deficient in detail for simple stories and absent for more complicated stories. Knowledge of factual information about the world was severely restricted. He was unable to provide his own date of birth, even in a forced choice situation where he was given four alternative dates to pick. He was unable to provide the Prime Minister's name, even though he was tested in the era of Margaret Thatcher. Non-verbal memory was also poor with a score at a five-year-old level on Benton's Visual Retention Test and the Figure of Rey. There was also immature grammar in speech production, and performance at a five-year level on Bishop's Test for the Reception of Grammar. Understanding vocabulary items was below the first centile for age on the Peabody Picture Vocabulary Test. Spontaneous speech was minimal and marked by severe word finding difficulties.

Naming. On the Renfrew Word Finding Vocabulary Scale performance was at a 4;5 level and on the Boston Naming Test at a 5;6 level. Semantic errors were the most common naming error and within these it was noted that animals appeared to create particular difficulties. For example the following errors occurred:

bear	→	"sheep"	*squirrel*	→	"mouse"
kangaroo	→	"goat"	*camel*	→	"bear"
goat	→	"cow"	*seahorse*	→	"octopus"
rhinoceros	→	"elephant"	*beaver*	→	"horse"

Category Naming. Pictorial stimuli were selected from the Snodgrass and Vanderwart (1980) pictures: 48 living creatures; 48 indoor objects; 24 food; 24 articles of clothing. Naming performance was compared to four-

TABLE 2.5
Naming of Indoor Objects

	Animals (n=48)	Indoor objects (n=48)
Control Mean	31.2	26.5
	(5.1)	(5.6)
John	18	41
Difference	−2.6SD	+2.6SD
	P<0.01	P<0.01

year-old naming age controls. Since the test has American norms, five normal adult speakers were asked to name the selected pictures and any of the responses produced by the adults were taken to be viable correct responses. Errors made by at least two of the ten control children were classified as non-dominant responses and were collated to form a non-dominant response list.

TABLE 2.6
John's Overt Errors (Adapted from Temple, 1986a)

Indoor Objects

chest of drawers → cupboard

rolling pin → rolling

broom → brush*

chest of drawers → cupboard

paintbrush → pencil

pliers → spanner

Animals

donkey → rabbit

camel → zebra

leopard → tiger

squirrel → mouse

sheep → cow

kangaroo → cat, lion

deer → goat

rhinoceros → cow

tiger → lion*

giraffe → zebra*

butterfly → spider

spider → wasp

frog → octopus

beetle → bee

eagle → blackbird

duck → goat

cockerel → chicken*

ostrich → goat

grasshopper → wasp

fly → wasp*

owl → lion

ant → wasp

crocodile → octopus

tortoise → octopus

snail → shell*

seal → lion

Food

peanut → potato*

grapes → plum

cherry → apple

pear → pineapple

strawberry → orange

tomato → orange

corn → leeks

celery → leeks

pepper → lemon

melon → sandwich

peach → orange*

Clothes

waistcoat → jacket

tie → knot

shirt → coat

crown → hat*

bow → butterfly

jacket → coat

*Non-dominant responses.

The results are summarised in Table 2.5. John was significantly better than the controls at naming indoor objects but was significantly poorer than the controls at naming animals. His accuracy in naming food and clothing did not differ significantly from control performance. In terms of the nature of errors, for animals, indoor objects, and food, the proportion of responses which were non-dominant responses was significantly lower for John than for controls. This indicates that when John makes an error in selecting a name for an item he is less likely to make a conventional selection. Typical control non-dominant responses to animals would be of the sort: *leopard* → "tiger"; *giraffe* → "zebra"; *beetle* → "ant"; *eagle* → "parrot"; *rhinoceros* → "hippo". Thus, they tend to be responses which share a broad range of semantic features, with the stimulus item. John's responses were frequently less closely related to the stimulus. They did generally preserve the overall grouping in the sense of an animal provoking an animal, a bird provoking a bird, and a sea creature provoking a sea creature, but within these, the items selected were less closely related than for the normal children's non-dominant responses. John's overt errors to indoor objects and animals are indicated in Table 2.6 with the non-dominant responses marked by an asterisk.

John was also given a task where the animal names corresponding to the pictures used in the naming task were spoken aloud and he was required to select from an array of 24 items the stimulus that went with the spoken name. On this task he was significantly better at pointing to indoor objects (44/48), than at pointing to animals (29/48) [X^2 =11.2, P<0.001]. Pointing to animals in response to their spoken names was however significantly better than naming of the animals had been: animal naming (18/48); comprehending animal names (29/48) [X^2 =4.1, P<0.05].

Discussion.   These results indicate that John does not simply have global and generalised developmental delay in naming skills. The profile and characteristics of his naming difficulties differ from those normal children whose overall performance is at a similar level to him. He finds certain classes of items significantly easier than the normal younger children and certain classes of items significantly more difficult. His severe difficulty with naming animals occurs despite the fact that animal names are commonly among the first words spoken (Nelson, 1973). Furthermore, the pattern of his errors suggests that the access to or organisation of his internal semantic system may differ from normal. Whereas errors that are provoked generally relate to the same overall category they are less closely related to the stimulus than typical non-dominant responses produced by controls. Pointing to pictures of animals in response to their spoken names, i.e. the comprehension of animal names, is significantly better than the naming of animals. It follows that for some items the naming difficulties must arise from a difficulty in accessing animal names which have been successfully encoded in some form. However, since the comprehension of animal names (as tested by the selection of items from an array in response to spoken names) remains significantly poorer than the comprehension of indoor object names, production access difficulties are insufficient to account for the degree of the disability.

One Year Follow-up.   After a year, John's performance, although it had improved slightly across categories, remained intrinsically unchanged in its qualitative pattern. Some further tasks were also given. John was read aloud descriptions of the target stimuli and asked to name the targets. Animals were named less well than indoor objects, with respectively 35% and 76% named correctly [X^2 =32, P<0.001]. The naming of line drawings was compared to naming of photographs and models. The percentage correct was similar for each group: 48% of black and white drawings; 45% of colour photographs; 43% of model animals. Finally, John was asked to describe 10 of the animals and 7 of the indoor objects. An insufficient number of stimuli were involved for a statistical analysis but overall the descriptions of the indoor objects appeared more detailed and effective than those of the animals. For example, an ashtray was described as, "It's glass. It's got a big round in it. You can put your ash in it." Similarly a kettle was described as, "for some water, can boil some water so you can have your cup of tea". In contrast a lion was described as "fat and eyes and ears and he's brown and black lines and eats apples". A donkey was described as "he walks and goes and finds something".

The significant difference between animals and indoor objects in naming to description as well as naming to pictures indicates that the effect is not modality specific and is not a simple input perceptual disorder. This supports the argument that the underlying basis of the name retrieval difficulty is at a semantic level. The pervasiveness of the deficit, independent of the nature of the stimuli that were presented, such that it is manifest both with photographs and models, indicates that the difficulty is not related to the reduction of perceptual stimuli found in a line drawing. Thus, it is not the degraded aspect of such representations that provokes the difficulty. This argues against some early perceptual aspect to the deficit. Finally, the verbal descriptions produced of animal and indoor objects indicate that, in some cases, John is unable to activate the relevant sets of semantic features associated with animals. For example, in questioning about a donkey, he indicated that a donkey had horns on it. He also suggested that a zebra had brown and black spots. Furthermore, a reindeer was white and black. The category-specific semantic impairment thus affects a multiplicity of tasks: naming of stimuli; comprehension of animal names; naming to description; and verbal description itself.

Theoretical Interpretations. The category-specific deficit manifested by John in confrontation naming is not merely the result of a basic perceptual disorder nor is it modality specific in effect. The dissociation between the ability to perform with animal names and indoor objects is pervasive across tasks. It is argued that this reflects a deficit at a semantic level.

One possibility is that the stimuli involved in the indoor object set are more frequently encountered than those of the animals. However, when a subset of items are selected from within each group, in order to produce a frequency balance slightly skewed in the opposite direction, i.e. in favour of animals, the significant difference between the two groups remains. Alternatively, it could be argued that John has led a life style in which he has had insufficient contact with animals and that the apparent category specific disorder is the result of differential or atypical learning experience. However, John lives on a farm and has if anything had more contact with animals during his development than many children might have experienced. Furthermore, his family home is very close to a wildlife park, which his family has also visited. He has therefore been exposed to a broad range of animals. Furthermore, his twin sister who has had a similar environmental experience does not show a marked discrepancy between her naming skills in different groups. At the time of the follow-up John's twin was tested on naming the animal and indoor object items and performed at an identical level on each category. She displayed no category-specific impairment and was significantly better than John at naming animals. Thus, environmental explanations may be discounted.

It is possible to argue that, for acquired category-specific disorders, neurological injury could have eliminated a category of semantic representations, if such representations were anatomically distinct from the representations for other groupings. This might seem improbable but is not impossible. However, in a developmental case it is difficult to imagine what type of underlying disruption to the biological substrate could produce a system that is attuned to the acquisition of one category of knowledge and not to another category of knowledge. It might seem difficult to argue that there are preformed boxes for indoor objects and animals, simply waiting to be filled and that one can be selectively disrupted without disruption of the other. Nevertheless, there is evidence that even early categorisation for animate and inanimate skills, at 12 months, is based upon conceptual similarity rather than perceptual similarity (Mandler & Bauer, 1988), with aeroplane being treated as a new category when it followed dog, horse, rabbit, and bird. This was despite the greater perceptual similarity of the plastic bird and aeroplane employed, than the bird and the dog. Mandler and Bauer (1988) suggest that this early conceptual categorisation is based upon an early fundamental representational distinction between animate and inanimate items. Other studies confirm a very early distinction between animate and inanimate objects (Carey & Gelman, 1991; Gelman, 1990; Gelman & Kremner, 1991).

Category-specific effects manifest in a developmental disorder could also be emergent properties if a critical distinction between the categories relates to some aspect associated with encoding or retrieval principles. For example, Warrington and Shallice (1984) have suggested that indoor objects and animals may be distinguished from each other on the basis of their functional or sensory characteristics. Animals tend to be identified more on the basis of visual or sensory characteristics whereas indoor objects may be identified on the basis of their functional significance. If the mechanisms involved in encoding, storing, or accessing sensory aspects were distinct from mechanisms involved in encoding, storing, and accessing functional attributes then more generalised disruption to one or other system could provoke an apparent category-specific disorder. Thus, if John had a developmental disability that affected the encoding, storage, or retrieval within the semantic system for information relating to sensory attributes then an apparent animal anomia could ensue, although strictly if the difficulty is at the level of either structural descriptions or visual semantics (Humphreys & Riddoch, 1987) the term anomia maybe less appropriate than agnosia.

Small, Hart, Nguyen, and Gordon (1995) argue that a category-specific organisation can emerge as a by-product of the representations of the perceptual features, function, and associations of objects. Employing a connectionist model, they encoded pictures in terms of their semantic features and argued that an inanimate–animate distinction emerged from the subsequent analysis of the network's characteristics, with the objects self-organising into categories. Goldberg (1995) has also argued that in relation to distributed representations of the lexicon somatosensory and motor dimensions are more integral to man-made objects thereby leading to emergent categorical distinction from animate objects.

GRAMMATICAL DISORDERS

Disorders of grammatical development are relatively common amongst the developmental aphasias both in the comprehension of grammar in receptive aphasias and in the production of grammatical structures within expressive aphasias. The most common measure of grammatical (morphological and syntactic) development in both normal and language impaired children is the mean length of utterance (MLU) which can be calculated in terms of words or morphemes (Rapin, Allen, & Dunn, 1992). MLU and syntactic development are highly correlated in development (Brown, 1973). Rapin et al. (1992) point out that in some language disordered children vocabulary development proceeds independently of grammar so that vocabulary size is not synchronised with mean length of utterance. The child may acquire lexical forms but may lack the means to express their ideas in multi-word utterances. With other children there may be evidence of grammatical construction but the application of the rules may be faulty. For example, Rapin et al. (1992) mention the case of a four-year-old child who described a picture of a boy blowing out candles on a birthday cake as follows: "that boy can't blow candles at hers birthday party next week because it too hard". This child has mastered some rules for grammatical construction. The child knows about negation (can't), infinitives (blow), plurals (candles), gender pronouns (hers), possession (hers), prepositions (at), and adverbs (next, hard). Yet, despite the acquisition of these morphological forms, this is not accompanied by an ability to use these in a grammatically appropriate way within long sentences. Such grammatical difficulties can create marked problems in communication since the grammatical markers indicate to the listener the interpretation that should be placed upon the other connecting words.

Studies of grammatical disorders in children indicate that such children do not simply reflect delayed development but the qualitative nature of the language is deviant in relation to a normal developmental pathway (e.g. Clahsen & Mohnhaus, 1987; Grimm & Weinert, 1990). A number of studies of children with grammatical disorders refer to children with SLI, specific language impairment. There is sometimes an implication in these studies that all children with specific language impairment have grammatical difficulty, whereas the perspective of this chapter is that grammatical disorders are merely one of a range of developmental language disorders, the others being addressed in the preceding and forthcoming sections of the chapter. In keeping therefore with the general organisation of the chapter, the term SLI will not be used to refer to children with grammatical disorders, rather we shall refer to the disorders simply as grammatical disorders.

Gopnik (1990a) described a case of what she referred to as feature blindness (Gopnik, 1990b), in which the language of an eight-year-old boy Paul, is interpreted as reflecting selective difficulty in constructing the linguistic morphological rules for grammatical features such as number, tense, or aspect. This case is also described informally in Gopnik (1992).

Case Report: Morphological Disorder, Paul

Paul's inability to use singular and plural is illustrated in his description of a picture book with a King and Queen (Gopnik, 1990a; 1992, p. 63).

> Once upon a time there is a dragon and they help on the Christmas time and the King decorate the Christmas and now there they put present under the Christmas trees. And then after everybody is going to bed except the dragon. He's looking to peek in the gifts. And now there the dragon's start to take one and the trees just fall down.

In spontaneous speech, Paul did not use the terminal *s* to demarcate plural in a consistent way in relation to the preceding words in a sentence. Thus, use of the article *a* always indicates a singular but in Paul's spontaneous speech a terminal *s* would sometimes be employed instead. Similarly, if a word or number is involved in the construction of a sentence indicative of a large number of items, Paul would not add a terminal *s* to the objects involved in order to match their plurality with the preceding words in the sentence. Detailed investigation of this difficulty by Gopnik indicated that it was a pervasive difficulty in the use of the terminal s but that this difficulty in marking the plural was not restricted to this particular grammatical form. There were also problems in expressing the difference between he, she, and they. Thus, the difficulty was in the expression of number within language rather than in any specific feature itself. Paul also failed to use the past tense marker *ed*. He had difficulty with demarcating past, present and future and bypassed his problems by the use of specific words incorporated into his sentences: "last time"; "now there"; "and after". His use of these expressions indicates that Paul has understanding of the concept of time and past, present, and future but he has difficulty in utilising these expressions in language. Similarly, he has excellent mathematical competence and is good at understanding numerical concepts. His inability to use the singular and plural grammatical markers within language does not reflect an inability to understand the concept of plurality itself.

A follow-up investigation of Paul at the age of fifteen years indicated that his pattern of difficulty with language development remained consistent despite intensive intervening remediation specifically targeted at those aspect of language which were problematic. Gopnik indicated that in addition to difficulties persisting with the terminal *s* and the terminal *ed*, the selection of grammatical words to indicate progressive aspect, that is the combination of the verb *to be*, before the verb and an *ing* after the verb was inappropriate. The selection of one or the other of the two necessary components or their combination together was random in its manifestation. It was argued that Paul was unable to construct the correct underlying rule for the progressive aspect. Further investigation indicated comparable difficulties in constructing the grammatical rules underlying tense and number. Paul's spontaneous speech indicated that he was able to construct basic sentences but construction of specific grammatical rules was more problematic.

Gopnik argued that when use of the past tense or plural is expressed by children of this sort it is because they have learnt the individual exemplars but have not derived the rule. With each new word, the inflected form has to be learnt rather than deduced by rule as there is no automatic extrapolation from previous cases to future cases.

This contrasts with the traditional account for normal children, in which there is a transition from early rote-learning to the systematic rule-governed treatment of verbs. For children like Paul, rote-learning appears to persist and the children do not extract the relevant rules for forming tenses, failing to make a transition to any systematic treatment of verbs. Some more recent connectionist networks also incorporate a transition from rote-learning to rule-governed behaviour, even though this is modelled within a single neural network mechanism (Plunkett & Marchman, 1993). With repeated rote-learning examples, reflected in a larger and larger training set, a critical mass of exposure is reached and the network reorganises, extracting the relevant rules (Plunkett & Marchman, 1993). For the children described by Gopnik, the appropriate reorganisation of the network does not appear to occur, despite exposure to a number of exemplars which should constitute a sufficient training set, to reach the critical mass of exposure for the shift to rule-governed behaviour.

An easier interpretation of the deficit in rule acquisition is possible in relation to Pinker and Prince's (1992) model in which normal children maintain two distinct inflectional mechanisms: a symbol manipulating rule system for regular morphology (e.g. walk—walked); and a memory based retrieval process for irregular morphology (e.g. fly—flew). The children studied by Gopnik are proposed to lack the symbolic rules of regular inflection and have knowledge restricted to an associative network, designed to process irregulars.

Gopnik's theory (1990a, 1990b, 1992) has been criticised in several areas. For example, it predicts similar feature errors across language but Leonard, Sabbadini, Leonard, and Volterra (1987) found different patterns of morphological errors in English and Italian children with grammatical difficulties. Lindner and Johnston (1992) also found different error patterns in English vs German. Another problem for the theory is that since it requires the absence of rule-governed morphology, children with grammatical difficulties should not show over regularisations but these are reported in several studies (Bishop, 1994b; Clahsen, Rothweiler, Woest, & Marcus, 1992; Leonard et al., 1992). Bishop (1994b) explores a number of the predictions for the feature deficit hypothesis and concludes that the results support a deficit in performance rather than competence.

Comparable impairments in children in the construction of rules to handle number, gender, and tense have also been reported in German children studied by Clahsen (1992). However, Clahsen proposes an alternative interpretation. His grammatical agreement theory (Clahsen, 1989, 1991, in press) argues that the children have problems in establishing agreement relations between two elements in phrase structure in which one element asymmetrically controls the other. Clahsen's theory differs from Gopnik's in the pervasiveness of the predicted areas of deficit. He argues that the impairments seen in these children are narrowly restricted to specific subareas of grammar, which he specifies, and do not encompass inflectional morphology as a whole. For example, he argues that difficulties with noun plurals are in practice very rare.

Much empirical evidence supports Clahsen's view and he uses his theory to make neat and specific predictions about both performance and remediation effects (Clahsen & Hansen, 1993, 1996). One of these relates to word order, a term used in grammatical analysis to refer to the sequential arrangements of words in a language. In both English and German, word order is a means of expressing grammatical relationships (e.g. "The small box is on the tray. The small tray is on the box"). In most areas, Clahsen's theory does not predict any particular difficulty with word order. However, there is an exception in the positioning of a particular group of verbs. In syntactic analysis of adult German, the basic pattern is placing the verb in the final clause position. However, there is a further specific rule, called V2, which moves certain verbs to the second structural position in main clauses. This V2 rule depends upon morphological features of the verb, as it applies only to finite verbs which are specified for person and number. These verb forms are therefore marked for subject–verb agreement. Clahsen (1991) has shown that German children with grammatical difficulties do not in general have word order problems, but do fail to acquire the V2 rule, which is consistent with his proposal that there are general difficulties with aspects of grammar dependent upon agreement relations. Clahsen and Hansen (1993) go one step further by predicting that if the difficulty in acquiring V2 is part of the same phenomenon as the difficulty with agreement relations, then remediation of one should help the other. They predicted that if systematic remediation was given, by teaching subject–verb agreements, then there should be a natural generalisation to also improve the word order skills for V2, without the need to explicitly teach V2. The results of their study upheld their predictions. Those children who acquired the ability to make subject–verb agreements also developed the correct V2 word order rule, without any additional effort. Evidence in support of their theory from other therapy experiments is discussed in Clahsen and Hansen (1996). Gopnik's theory has difficulty in accounting for such specific effects.

A further view of grammatical disorders is provided by Van der Lely (1990, 1994). She has studied the use of "canonical linking rules", which refer to the regular relationship found in the majority of languages between thematic roles, such as agent and patient, and syntactic functions, such as subject and direct object. For example, if a child knows that a verb involves an agent and a patient, she can infer that these arguments are expressed as the grammatical subject and object respectively (Van der Lely, 1994). Van der Lely (1990, 1994) argued that children with grammatical disorders can establish rules from semantics to grammar but cannot make the reverse links from grammar to semantics. To illustrate the ability to make rules from semantics to grammar, children were shown toys performing novel actions accompanied by novel words. For example, toy girl jumped up and down on the back of toy boy and the child was told "this is voozing". The child was then asked to act out sentences such as " the horse voozes the lion". The children with grammatical disorders could perform the task as well as controls. To illustrate the reverse ability, to establish rules from grammar to semantics, the child was asked to make up a meaning for a new word, and to act out sentences such as "the car rits the train". In this example, the child should have made the car perform an action on the train. The children with grammatical disorders had particular difficulty with this second group of tasks, which required the use of reverse linking rules from grammar to semantics.

Impairment of a specific module for grammar is therefore a possible explanation of the work of Gopnik (1990a, 1990b, 1992), Clahsen (1989, 1991), and Van der Lely (1990, 1994), but there are also other theoretical possibilities. Tallal and colleagues argue that grammatical relations arise as a consequence of the difficulties in auditory processing discussed earlier in this chapter (Tallal & Piercy, 1973; Tallal & Stark, 1981; Tallal et al., 1980). The recent finding that remediation involving acoustically modified speech, which altered its temporal characteristics, carried over positive effects to a test of grammatical comprehension (Tallal et al., 1996) adds further preliminary support for this view. As noted previously Leonard (1989; Leonard et al., 1987, 1992) has also argued that many of the expressive grammatical problems of language disordered children could be accounted for by perceptual limitations in the learning of specific features of language.

Thus, there is theoretical disagreement between the view that grammatical disorders arise as downstream effects of an earlier phonological or acoustic processing deficit and the view that they represent impaired development of a grammatical module. A cognitive neuropsychological perspective could distinguish between these hypotheses utilising case studies. If grammatical disorders are caused by phonological problems or problems with acoustic processing, then all children with grammatical difficulties should have processing problems. However, if on the basis of case study analyses children are identified who have grammatical difficulties but do not have difficulties with phonological discrimination of morphological features or with discriminating speech sounds characterised by rapid transitional information, then the arguments of Tallal, Leonard, and respective colleagues become insufficient and the possibility of a discrete grammatical module gains ground. If no such dissociation is identified then cognitive neuropsychology can not distinguish between the two groups of theories, since it cannot separate coincidental coexistence of an auditory/phonological problem and grammatical difficulties and causally linked coexistence of the two problems.

Whatever the correct theoretical interpretation of grammatical disorders, Gopnik argues that these types of developmental language problems are common amongst a large proportion of developmental aphasics and that in a proportion of developmental aphasic families there may be a genetic basis to the disorder. The basis of its manifestation and the distribution of developmental aphasia in certain families suggests that it could be a single gene disorder (Gopnik, 1990b; Gopnik & Cragow, 1991; Hurst, Baraitser, Auger, Graham, & Norell 1990; Tomblin, 1989). This would have direct implications for the notion that some critical element associated with deriving grammatical rules is genetically underpinned and would be consistent with Chomsky's (1965) notion of an innate language acquisition device. It would also account for how normal children are able to acquire language rapidly in the presence of a variety of conflicting linguistic inputs, and how aspects of language acquisition take place without explicit correction by adults. Rondal (1994) also argues that the SLI children with morpho-syntactic disorders form a double dissociation with the exceptional language development of some children with learning disabilities. For these children, there is advanced morpho-syntax but restricted cognitive development.

Neville, Coffey, Holcomb, and Tallal (1993) report that children who scored poorly on tests of grammatical understanding displayed abnormal hemispheric specialisation of an ERP component, specifically an anterior negative component elicited by closed class words. This supports a biological underpinning, though cause and effect in such correlations are difficult to distinguish.

VERBAL DYSPRAXIAS

Apraxic disorders of speech arise where there is difficulty in making the purposive series of coordinated movements required for the articulation of language. Apraxic disorders of speech may form part of a more general disorder of praxis which may affect the construction of organised movement in other domains. Crary (1984) defines verbal dyspraxia as "resulting from a breakdown in the ability to control the appropriate spatial/temporal properties of speech articulation". Developmental verbal dyspraxia is distinguished from a peripheral dysarthria in which all movements are affected not simply those which are planned.

The term dyspraxia was originally used by Broca (1861) in relation to acquired neurological disorders of language and was adopted by Morley (1965) for application to children with developmental speech difficulties. Verbal dyspraxia may occur in conjunction with intact ability to perform other purposeful movements of the oral musculature. Total inability to perform purposeful movements of the mouth and lower face in the absence of paralysis tends to be referred to as oral apraxia. In a study by Ferry, Hall, and Hicks (1975) about half of 60 developmental verbal dyspraxics studied also had oral dyspraxia. The authors note that conventional speech therapy had had limited success and that spontaneous improvement had only occurred up to the age of six. Geschwind's (1975) analysis of acquired apraxia stresses the multiple variants of disorder and in a developmental format a variety of different expressions may also emerge.

In cases of developmental verbal dyspraxia there are usually speech or learning difficulties in other members of the family (Crary, 1984; Lewis, Ekelman, & Aram, 1989; Morley, 1965). As with many developmental language disorders, the disorder is more common in males than in females (Stackhouse, 1992a). There is a history of delayed language development, rendering speech partially unintelligible (Macaluso-Haynes, 1985). Comprehension is usually significantly better than verbal expression and verbal expression is marked by a specific pattern of abnormality. The speech sounds articulated are often not valid within the native language. The problem is made more marked with increasing word length, and complexity of rapid change in the consonant patterns (Stackhouse, 1992a, 1992b), e.g. making *buttercup* more difficult than *daisy*. The flow of continuous speech can be disrupted and there can be a restricted use of complex syntax in the production of extensive prose, with mean length of utterance maintained by stringing sentences together (Ekelman & Aram, 1983). There is perseveration (repetition of component sounds or words) and metatheses (alteration of the sequence of sounds, e.g. *buttercup* → "bukertup"). Intrusive schwas may break up consonant clusters (e.g. *truck* → "tərəkə"). Sounds are often omitted, particularly in the final syllable position and there can be errors of voice, place, and manner. Vowels are frequently distorted. Prosody (variations in pitch, stress, loudness, tempo, and rhythm) is marked by inappropriate stress intonation, variable speed, and monotony. There can be fluctuating nasality. Together the incoordination of the vocal tract produces dysphonia, dysprosody, disorders or resonance, and inconsistent articulatory patterns. A word correctly articulated on one occasion may be incorrectly articulated on a subsequent occasion (Stackhouse, 1992a).

As noted previously, the dyspraxia may extend to include oral apraxia in which planned movements of the lips relate to non-speech activity. There may also be related feeding problems in chewing and sucking or drooling. Related apraxic disorders may lead to clumsiness and if there is a general constructional apraxia there may be difficulty with handwriting, drawing, dressing, and the organisation of sequencing of movements required for buckling of belts, tying shoelaces, and riding bicycles. Crary (1984) reported that 14/25 (56%) of children with verbal dyspraxia had motor incoordination difficulties. The developmental verbal dyspraxia itself is often resistant to therapy but tends to reduce in its significance and impact over time.

Stackhouse (1982; Snowling & Stackhouse, 1983) investigated reading and spelling skills of children with developmental verbal dyspraxia. They hypothesised that in order to conduct grapheme–phoneme segmentation of a word it may be necessary to pronounce it slowly, possible covertly in order to reflect upon each segment. The difficulties of verbal dyspraxics with voluntary control of oral speech movements might render this problematic. The use of a phonetic spelling strategy would also be more problematic than for reading age controls. Both predictions were upheld. In addition, spelling errors occurred more often on final consonants than initial consonants and also often incorporated voicing changes or place errors, the latter suggesting that dyspraxic subjects may fail to monitor their speech motor movements.

Case Report: Verbal Dyspraxia, Keith

Keith (Stackhouse, 1992b) had passed all the milestones apart from speech at the appropriate age. Although there were no obvious neurological or physical problems, he was clumsy in his movements and had had difficulty feeding. Head circumference was two standard deviations above the norm. Handedness was established late and both hands were used in the pre-school years. Tested at eight months and subsequently during the pre-school years, there were hearing problems. Keith was referred for speech therapy at the age of 2;6 because of concern over language development. There was a family history of minor speech difficulties and poor spelling.

Tested in the pre-school years, it was evident that Keith had oral dyspraxia as well as verbal dyspraxia. He had difficulty making any facial movements associated with putting his lips into a whistling position as well as making the facial movements associated with speech sound. Yet, if automatically blowing a kiss to his mother he could make broadly similar facial movements. The difficulty then was associated with planned movements of speech or the face. Between the ages of two and five years verbal comprehension was at an approximately normal level for age (see Table 2.7).

At the age of four Keith was unable to use any fricatives (f, v, s, z, sh) or affricatives (ch, j). He could not use "k" or "g", and a number of other sounds which could be used in isolation could not be used in continuous speech. He also replaced final consonants with a glottal stop. Stackhouse (1992b) describes Keith's production of the sentence "I played football in the garden" as sounding like "I day du-or I e dar-en".

Keith's interpersonal communicative skills were good and he made friends and got on well with staff.

By the age of eight, Keith was able to produce all sounds individually but could not use all of them in continuous speech. He used "p, b, t, d, m, n, l, f, v, and w" but "k, g, th, s, z, sh, ch, j, r, y" were seldom utilised. Distortions of sound produced the introduction of non-English sounds inappropriately into his flow of speech. By the age of eight, Keith had reduced rates of oral movements when asked to perform a sequence of movements at speed and he performed poorly on sound sequencing speech tests. For example, he had difficulty in producing the sound sequence "p — t — k" quickly. Stackhouse documents the different productions to the word buttercup as "buttertup, bukertup, butterpuk, bukerpup". Stackhouse emphasises that the difficulty is with the programming and coordination of sound sequences. This apraxic difficulty in organising movements was also evident in other tasks and was affecting

TABLE 2.7
Comprehension and Expression in Verbal Dyspraxia

Chronical age	Comprehension age	Expressive age
2;8	2;3	0;9
5;5	6;0	4;6

drawing, writing and the presentation of and layout of written material in school books. There was also a suggestion of a dressing apraxia.

At the age of fourteen, the dyspraxic difficulties persisted and Stackhouse provides the following errors as exemplars:

ambulance → "ambe, a-be-lance, abulance"
systematic → "sinsemakit"
classification → "classikekation"
bibliography → "biglegrafefi".

At this age, there were particular difficulties with consonant clusters and there were perseverative aspects within speech. The inability to repeat and articulate multisyllabic words affected his ability to produce written spelling for long multisyllabic words for which verbal rehearsal may have aided performance. The difficulty in planning and organisation also affected the flow of continuous speech production.

By the age of 17, performance had improved significantly. Speech errors no longer interfered with intelligibility and intrusive sounds occurred mainly on multisyllabic words. It was only long words that still showed the speech programming difficulties, for example:

hippopotamus → "hitopotanus"
chrysanthemum → "chrysanfefum"
preliminary → "plim, plewim, ple, pre, plelimewy".

Spelling had improved although some segmentation difficulties persisted. The constructional apraxia affecting handwriting had improved sufficiently to render his writing legible and his work tidy but the rate of output of written work was considerably longer than normal.

Stuttering

Stuttering is defined by Andrews, Craig, Feyer, Hoddinott, Howie and Neilson (1983) as "disorders in the rhythm of speech in which the speaker knows precisely what he wishes to say, but at the same time is unable to say it because of an involuntary repetitive, prolongation or cessation of sound." Other definitions emphasise, in addition, the disruption in the rate of speech output.

A possible association between stuttering and the organisation of the plan of speech output is suggested by the increased frequency of stuttering at syntactic locations where language is being formulated (Gordon, Luper, & Peterson, 1986) or at clause boundaries (Wall, 1980), with conjunctions and pronouns being disproportionately affected (Bloodstein & Gantwek, 1967). Aram, Myers, and Ekelman (1990) studied stuttering types of non-fluency in children with unilateral brain lesions. Both right and left hemisphere groups produced a higher percentage of stuttering non-fluencies than controls, with left lesioned subjects producing more prolongations and interjections than controls, and right lesioned subjects producing more part-word repetitions and low but enhanced rates of tense pauses, prolongations and broken words.

Analysing individual subjects, there was no specific association of these performance characteristics with lesion localisation nor did any of the children present stuttering behaviour as marked as in the developmental disorder. This suggests that either a bilateral abnormality underlies developmental stuttering or that the underlying neurological organisation in the developmental stutterer is in some ways atypical. Certainly, genetic studies indicate a high heritability for stuttering (Kidd, 1980). Rondal (1994) emphasises the dissociation between the difficulties with speech production in children who stutter and their lexical, grammatical, and pragmatic skills which may be intact.

PRAGMATIC DISORDERS

Pragmatic skills involve the use of language in relation to the constraints of social interaction and the communicative effects of language on other participants in a conversation. Rapin et al. (1992) point out that there can be a discrepancy in some children's developmental language disorders between vocabulary size and pragmatic use. Whereas normal young children having acquired words in the lexicon will use these in a communicative context for requesting, commenting, and protesting, there are language disordered children who develop large vocabularies, which are used only for labelling purposes. Specifically, they comment upon a two-year-old child who had an expressive and receptive (pointing) vocabulary of impressive size extending to several hundred words. These included the relatively low frequency word, "artichoke". Yet the same child was unable to use even simple words to express his needs. They also document another child with a comparable dissociation who could ask a specific labelling question "Is this a spatula or a slotted spoon?" Yet the same child was unable to answer the question "What do you do with the spoon?" (Rapin et al., 1992). A dissociation between semantic and pragmatic skill is also reported by Blank, Gessner, and Eposito (1978) who describe a three-year-old boy with normal levels of grammar and semantics but an inability both to initiate normal conversation, and to respond to questions.

Pragmatic skills also encompass a range of influential aspects of language that contribute to the metalinguistic aspects of communication (that is our linguistic inner experience, and the relationship of our linguistic system to other systems of behaviour in our culture). A variety of different types of pragmatic disorder could in principle be possible but a relatively restricted range of these have been documented. A pragmatic disorder is consistently reported in childhood autism (Tager-Flusberg, 1981, 1985). Although the pragmatic disorder is not the only aspect of language abnormality in autism, it is a consistent feature seen in each and every child with autism who develops language. In contrast, studies of the acquisition of phonological, grammatical, and lexical aspects of language in autism suggest that these formal aspects of language are not primary impairments (Bartolucci, Pierce, Streiner, & Epel, 1976; Cantwell, Baker, & Rutter, 1978; Pierce & Bartolucci, 1977; Tager-Flusberg, Calkins, Nolin, Baumberger, Anderson, & Chadwick-Dias, 1990). Major deficits in pragmatic aspects of language use have consistently been observed both in the range of functions autistic children express (Wetherby & Prutting, 1984) and in their ability to communicate in a discourse setting (Curcio & Paccia, 1987). Autism will therefore be used to illustrate pragmatic disorder here but the other elements of the linguistic performance of the autistic child will also be documented briefly in order that the pragmatic disorder can be seen in the context of the broader linguistic environment.

Autism

Serious abnormalities of language and communication form one of the core symptoms of autism, first described by Kanner (1943). The other major symptoms include an inability to form relationships with other people, a lack of spontaneous and imaginative play, and an obsessive insistence on specific routines or interests. In the *DSM-IV* (American Psychiatric Association, 1994) criteria for the classification of autistic disorder, gross deficits in language development are again a core feature. In addition, early onset before 30 months of age is emphasised and the absence of the delusions, hallucinations, or loosening of associations which would generally be characteristic of schizophrenia. The inability to form relationships extends to a lack of responsiveness to other people in many circumstances. The bizarre responses to the environment, including resistance to change, may also include peculiar interest or attachment to inanimate objects.

The incidence of autism is approximately 1 in 2000-2500 live births though estimates vary, and there is some trend to suggest a slightly increasing frequency in contemporary studies. The disorder is under a high degree of genetic control. Earlier theories of a major social component have largely been rejected in favour of a more biological model, partly because of the early onset and also because of the familial component. Of the siblings of autistics, 1 in 50 are diagnosed as autistic, a significantly higher rate than that observed in the normal population (Rutter, 1967). Folstein and Rutter (1977a, 1977b) analysed 21 pairs of twins for whom one was autistic. Of the 11 monozygotic pairs, in 4 sets of twins, each of the twins had autism, a 36% concordance rate. Amongst the children who were discordant for autism, many of the non-autistic twins had some other form of congenital abnormality with cognitive impairment, delayed speech or problems saying words. A concordance for some form of developmental disorder appeared in 82% of the twin pairs for the monozygotes. Amongst the 10 pairs of dizygotic children there was no concordance for autism. One child had a developmental cognitive impairment, so there was a 10% concordance for a developmental abnormality. The study suggested that heredity had a contributory role in autism, though the inherited abnormality might include but not be restricted to an autistic predisposition and in some cases appeared to encompass a linguistic element. Steffenberg et al. (1989) confirmed a high concordance rate for monozygotic twins (91%) for autism or cognitive deficit. There was no concordance for autism in dizygotic twins, but a 30% concordance rate for cognitive deficit. Combining the Folstein and Rutter (1977a, 1977b) sample and a new sample, Bailey et al. (1995) estimate heritability of the liability to autism at 91–93% using the statistical technique of structural equation modelling (Bentler, 1989).

Impairments in verbal skill have been reported in the parents of those with autism (Bartak, Rutter, & Cox, 1975). Plumet, Goldblum, and Leboyer (1995) failed to confirm a parental language impairment but found that brothers of autistic subjects were significantly impaired on language tasks.

An increased risk of autism in a number of childhood physical disorders has supported the suggestion of a physical basis for the disorder. An increased risk is seen following maternal rubella, cytomegalovirus, tuberous sclerosis, neurofibromatosis, untreated PKU, and though within less overlap than had been thought, fragile X; 25%–35% of autistic children have seizures. CT is most commonly normal though recent MRI investigations have suggested cerebellar or brain stem abnormalities. The pathological basis remains unresolved. More males than females are autistic, with a ratio of about three or four to one. Only a quarter to a third of autistic children attain IQ scores of above 70. For low functioning children, IQ is predictive of outcome but for high functioning children it is not. About 50% of autistic children remain mute all their lives. The overall prognosis for these children who remain mute is much less positive than for those who develop language.

It is suggested that even the early babbling patterns of autistic children may be abnormal with greater monotony and less variation in pattern. Ricks and Wing (1976) discuss a study by Ricks in which the noises made by autistic children between the ages of three and five in varying emotional situations were recorded. Amongst normal children there appears to be some universality in the depiction of these emotions as parents can identify their own child's messages and other children's messages. The autistic children appear to have a personal idiosyncratic way of expressing themselves in these contexts. Their parents were able to distinguish from hearing tape recordings of their children the emotion that was being conveyed and they were also able to distinguish the emotions of normal babies. However, the mothers of the normal babies could not distinguish the differing sounds of the autistic child.

When speech does develop in autism, it has a characteristic aspect (Wing, 1976). It may consist predominantly of echolalia (the verbatim repetition in part or in whole of recent heard utterances). Often the repetitions are with exactly the same inflection and accent as for the original speaker. Normal children imitate adults by modifying grammatical rules to those the child is able to utilise themselves by missing out complicated aspects of language. The autistic child echoes verbatim. The vocal delivery of speech often includes poor control of pitch and volume and abnormalities of intonation. Predominance of echolalia contributes to the prenominal reversal which is evident in the speech of many autistic children.

When words begin to develop they tend not to have the same definition of lexical and semantic content as normal. There may not be the rapid generalisation to the category, typical of normals. Thus the child may continue to associate a word with a very specific event or a narrow exemplar, for example using the word "cup" only in relation to one specific cup. Nor is there the rapid acceleration of naming skills which characterises normal child development. For the autistic child, it may require great effort to produce speech and the speech produced may be of immature or abnormal syntactic structure. There can also be a telegrammatic aspect to speech, with the omission of prepositions and connective words. Conversation is often linked to concrete pieces of information and there is an absence of colloquial speech. The use of inner language and imaginative play is absent. Autistic children's language may be distinguished from children who have developmental aphasic disorders by the absence of the use of spontaneous gesture and by the dominance of echolalic language in language production (Wing, 1976).

Even where vocabulary and grammar become established amongst the more able of the autistic children, pragmatic disorder remains. The tendency to engage in extensive conversation about a particular topic of interest, in the absence of an ongoing appraisal of whether the listener is interested in what is being communicated, indicates an insensitivity to the interpersonal aspects of language and communication. There is extreme literalness in the interpretation of speech and difficulty in the interpretation of any element of humour that requires a non-literal interpretation. Idiomatic and metaphorical expressions are not understood (Wing, 1976).

Autistic children have difficulty in using language effectively in a situation where they have to take account of the listener's emotion and the social context of language (Paul, 1987; Tager-Flusberg, 1981, 1989). As discussed in Chapter 8, contemporary theories of autism suggest a deficit in establishing what is referred to as a "theory of mind" (Baron-Cohen, Leslie, & Frith, 1985; Premack & Woodruff, 1978). This is a construct in which a child will reason about other people's reasoning and be aware that other people's perspective is different from their own. At a higher level, they will reason about the other person reasoning about their own reasoning. This ability to think about the emotional, motivational, and knowledge states of others and to be aware of the interpersonal complexities of these, contributes to the subtleties of human communication. According to Leslie (1987) this mode of interaction is impaired in autism. This inability to take account of the alternative person's perspective inevitably affects the nature of the linguistic communication which can take place between speaker and listener. According to this view, the areas of language that are particularly impaired, even in those who have developed relatively good language, are those elements which require metarepresentation (e.g. the understanding and use of metaphors and sarcasm; conversational discourse; lies and deception; indirect requests) (Leslie, 1987).

The proposal of a deficit in a "theory of mind" has been applied to many aspects of the language disorder. As an example of one such pragmatic deficit, Tager-Flusberg and Anderson (1991) contrasted discourse development in autistic, normal, and Down's children over the course of a year. They classified a contingent utterance as one which followed immediately after an adult utterance and maintained the topic without being simple imitation. A non-contingent utterance also followed immediately after the adult utterance but did not relate to the adult topic. Tager-Flusberg and Anderson (1991) pointed out that in the early stages of autistic language development turn-taking ability develops, and when MLU is less than 2.0 autistic children were similar to Down's and normals in contingent topic-related discourse. However, with growth in MLU, the autistic children did not show the normal increase in the use of contingent speech. Nor did they show the normal increase in the use of expansions or other modes of discourse which add new information to the discourse. Structurally their language became more sophisticated but its content did not change. Tager-Flusberg and Anderson (1991) interpret this impairment as stemming from absence of knowledge that people communicate by the exchange of information and that people have access to different information and knowledge states. In their view, development of this knowledge is contingent on the development of a "theory of mind".

The view of autism as caused by a deficit in "theory of mind" is complicated by the findings that 20% of the autistic children in Baron-Cohen et al.'s (1985) original study were able to understand that people could hold counterfactual beliefs; the reduced impairment in "theory of mind" seen with older autistic subjects (Leslie & Frith, 1988); and the less pervasive deficit in "theory of mind" observed in Asperger's syndrome (Ozonoff, Rogers, & Pennington, 1991). These issues are discussed further in Chapter 8.

As Bishop (1989) highlighted, Kanner (1943) himself documented the shift in the manifestations of the language disorder in autism with age:

> Between the ages of 5 and 6 years, they (autistic children) gradually abandon the echolalia and learn spontaneously to use person pronouns with adequate reference. Language becomes more communicative, at first in the sense of question-and-answer exercise, and then in the sense of greater spontaneity of sentence formation ... people are included in the child's world to the extent to which they satisfy needs, answer his obsessive questions, teach him how to read ... (Bishop, 1989, p. 111)

In these respects language develops but the absence of pragmatic competence means that normal communication or conversation is never attained.

In the American Psychiatric Association's *DSM-IV* (1994) autism is considered a severe form of pervasive developmental disorder. Less severe and prototypical cases are classified as pervasive developmental disorder not otherwise specified (PDDNOS). Both of these labels are unpopular in the UK. However, in recent years, there has been renewed interest in the syndrome described by Asperger (1944/1991), in which some autistic features are manifest. Frith (1991) suggests that Asperger's syndrome should be considered a particular form of autism which is not particularly rare. Indeed Gillberg and Gillberg (1989) reported that Asperger's syndrome was about five times as common as autism. Asperger's syndrome is sometimes considered to be high functioning autism. However, argument continues as to whether Asperger's syndrome should be considered within the autistic spectrum or as a distinct disorder. The pragmatic disorder in Asperger's syndrome is a dominant element of the language impairment (Wing, 1981).

Asperger's Syndrome

In Asperger's original paper (Asperger, 1944/1991), recently translated by Frith (1991), Asperger addresses and anticipates the element of language subsequently referred to as pragmatics. Asperger emphasises the elements in linguistic communication that express interpersonal relationships. For example, from the tone of voice in which the utterance is produced, the relationship people have to each other can be deduced. The listener derives from this information a view of what the speaker really thinks independent of the words that they are articulating. They also use such things to make judgements about the truth or falsehood of the utterance. Asperger argues that many of the linguistic pieces of information conveyed by volume, tone, and flow can contribute to those aspects of language which we appear to interpret intuitively and relatively automatically. Abnormalities of tone vary in Asperger's description of autism from a voice that is soft to a voice that is shrill or has excessive modulation. He argues that these changes have in common that they make the language seem unnatural and as a caricature. Further, the autistic language may be spoken into empty space and not directed to the addressee, in a similar form to autistic eye gaze.

Asperger highlights the newly formed or partially restructured expressions that autistic children may introduce into their speech. Frith (1991) points out that he stresses the originality of these abstruse utterances. She notes that Asperger tended to overlook the inappropriateness of much of the idiosyncratic language. The original words and phrases produced by autistic children are frequently characterised by disregard for the listener's ability to comprehend their meaning and the reason for their use. Thus, they are not constructive in a communicative context. As an example of linguistic utterance of this sort Frith (1991) translates the following: "I can't do this orally, only headily." "My sleep today was long but thin." "To an art-eye, these pictures might be nice, but I don't like them."

Asperger also points out that autistics do not understand the complexities of verbal humour. This observation has been confirmed subsequently (Frith, 1991) and is again attributed to the crucial dependence of a sense of humour upon the use of language within communication, that is in association with pragmatic aspects.

Tantam (1991) provides two examples of the pragmatic deficit in Asperger's syndrome. In one, a father described how distressing it was to him and his wife that although their Asperger's child would come and sit in the same room as them, he never brought his chair to be in the same group as theirs, so they never felt that he was with them. Another instance from the same family, which caused concern to the parents, occurred when the son terminated an interview with the headmaster of a private school to which he had applied, by asking the headmaster's age. In both of these situations the child failed to follow the recognised but not explicitly taught rules of social interaction. He transgressed social conventions relating to intimacy versus formality. These social conventions are closely applied to the social actions referred to as speech acts.

Asperger (1979) considered that the children he described had more normal language development than those described by Kanner. Tantam (1991) reports pragmatic abnormalities in two-thirds of an Asperger's group studied in relation to a variety of linguistic abnormalities. In contrast, syntactic errors were rare and always occurred in association with semantic errors. Although they were shown in 30% of the subjects, they were conspicuous in only 6%. Tantam (1991) considers that the syntactic and semantic abnormalities are not part of the essential autistic handicap in Asperger's syndrome but are expressions of a distinct language handicap. In other words, they are not a necessary condition for Asperger's syndrome though they may co-occur in some subjects. In Tantam's study, the pragmatic elements included such failures to respond to social convention as overfamiliarity with the interviewer, for example, by hailing a doctor at first meeting across a room by his first name. Abnormalities of perspective were observed, with lack of guardedness appropriate to the beginning of an interview with a stranger and a lack of curiosity about the purpose and consequences of the interview. Abnormal choice of topic was rated as idiosyncrasy or fanaticism depending upon how forcefully the topic was imposed upon the conversation. The interviewer also rated the assumptions by the subject of knowledge which the interviewer could not be expected to have.

The expressive pragmatic abnormalities of Asperger's syndrome were also investigated in a further study (Tantam, 1991) in which both experts and a general professional audience were played sections of a video of adults with Asperger's syndrome talking to normal volunteers; 89% of the general audience rated the Asperger's subject as "odd". Abnormalities of speech prosody, facial expression, gaze, and gesture made the largest contribution to the rating of abnormal non-verbal expression. Tantam argues that part of the impression of abnormality results from a lack of integration and coordination of expression, speech and gaze. This has the impact of making gestures seem incongruous or inexplicable.

Rapin and Allen (1983) incorporate a formal category of semantic-pragmatic syndrome within their framework of language disorders. This category overlaps with autism but 7 out of their 35 cases of semantic-pragmatic syndrome did not have autism (Rapin, 1987), indicating that there are children with a semantic-pragmatic impairment of language who do not necessarily meet the full range of other diagnostic criteria for autism, which include absence of imaginative play, excessive desire for sameness and routines and severely disordered social and affective development. Bishop and Rosenbloom (1987) specifically exclude autism from the developmental language disorder they call semantic-pragmatic disorder. In this disorder there is delayed language development, but the child then develops fluent, complex speech with clear articulation (Bishop, 1989).

> Although receptive difficulties may dominate the clinical picture when the child is young, leading to a diagnosis of developmental receptive aphasia, as they develop, such children might improve considerably ... however, in less structured situations, the children tend to give over-literal or tangential responses. (p. 115)

Bishop and Adams (1989) examined the conversational characteristics of 8, twelve-year-old children with semantic-pragmatic disorder. They identified points where the normal flow of conversation was disrupted because the child's utterance was inappropriate and then subcategorised these inappropriate responses. The children were similar to younger children, aged four–five in that they misunderstood the literal or implicit meaning of the adult utterances and violated some normal rules of exchange structure. However, they differed from normal children of any age in their provision of too much information with unnecessary repetitions, assertions, or denials of what is already known and the provision of over-precise and over-elaborate information. The difficulty was not simply one of stating too much or too little but in matching the conversation to the conversational needs of the partner, for which an understanding of their distinct knowledge state is also required, suggesting that "theory of mind" difficulties may also contribute to problems in this non-autistic group.

Bishop (1989) recommends that rigid diagnostic categories are loosened in this area and suggests that autism, Asperger's syndrome, and semantic-pragmatic disorder all have intersecting boundaries.

The long-term sequelae of developmental language disorders is likely to vary dependent upon both the nature of the original problem and the educational context in which the child develops. Haynes and Naidoo (1991) followed up 34, eighteen-year-olds who had attended a school for severe developmental language disorders, in those of otherwise normal intelligence and for whom there was no autism. In only three cases were no residual problems with spoken or written language reported. Persistent difficulties included problems in pronouncing long words, difficulties in filling in forms and in using the telephone, self-consciousness about odd sounding speech, and difficulty in following films (Bishop, 1994a).

IN CONCLUSION

This chapter has discussed a range of specific impairments in language development which affect different components of the language system. Starting with peripheral impairments of hearing, it was established that although otitis media has been suggested as creating downstream impairments in a variety of linguistic areas, it is unlikely to be a major feature in the aetiology of language disorders although it may exacerbate difficulties experienced by a child who is already vulnerable for language disorder.

Tallal and colleagues have argued that more substantive downstream effects are a consequence of an impairment in the discrimination and sequencing speech sounds characterised by rapid transitional information (Tallal & Piercy, 1973; Tallal & Stark, 1981; Tallal et al., 1980, 1996) with Leonard (1989; Leonard et al., 1992) arguing that perceptual limitations account specifically for impairments in grammatical acquisition. In contrast, Clahsen (1989, 1991), Gopnik (1990a, 1992), and Van der Lely (1994) all propose more specific theories of grammatical impairment which could be accounted for by a specific deficit in a grammatical module rather than their appearance as knock-on effects of a receptive phonological difficulty.

More extreme impairment in the reception of language is part of the auditory agnosia of the Landau–Kleffner syndrome. This language disorder is atypical in relation to other language impairments in a variety of ways. Both sexes are equally affected whereas for most developmental language disorders, the prevalence for boys is greater than that for girls. Early age of onset is also a negative prognostic characteristic of Landau–Kleffner syndrome (Bishop, 1985), an opposite pattern to that seen in other acquired aphasias of childhood for which early onset is generally a better prognostic feature. Bishop (1985) has suggested that this arises because of an arrest in the development of the language system at the time of onset of the disorder. Differing theories have suggested unilateral or bilateral abnormality of Wernicke's area or of the input to it. The relationship between the seizures which form part of the disorder and the language disorder itself may be due to a related underlying cause, rather than in terms of a direct causal connection between the two behavioural manifestations. A genetic basis for the disorder has been suggested and the case reports of developmental aphasia and EEG abnormality in one twin and a regression of language but no seizures in another twin, suggested that the two different manifestations of developmental language disorder might be phenotypical expressions of a common underlying abnormality.

Impairments in the development of the semantic system may have a specific effect upon language development. There are different forms of childhood anomia. The anomia may appear as a consequence of an impairment in semantic access (Van Hout, 1993), or the anomia may be a consequence of impairment in the semantic representations themselves, as reflected by consistency of performance, performance differences between semantic categories, semantic paraphasias in naming, and semantic errors on tasks not requiring a spoken response. This argued against an output lexicon deficit as a basis for the disorder. The context of generalised impairments in memory associated with the semantic representation anomic disorder, raised the possibility that memory impairments in development may often induce anomic disorders. Category-specific anomic disorders have also been described in development with varying theoretical interpretations possible.

Those who propose that the basis of grammatical difficulties within developmental language disorders lies in impairment of a grammatical system itself, differ in the precise formulation of the impairment. Gopnik (1990a, 1992) has suggested a selective difficulty in constructing the linguistic morphological rules for grammatical features such as number, tense and aspect and has described children with grammatical difficulties as being feature blind. However, Bishop (1994b) demonstrated that many of the predictions of the feature blind theory are not supported by recent data. Clahsen (1989, 1991, in press) has suggested that the basis of the difficulty lies in establishing agreement relations between two elements in phrase structure in which one element asymmetrically controls the other. On the basis of explicit predictions he also argues that remediation data support his theory (Clahsen & Hansen, 1993, 1996). Van der Lely (1990, 1994) proposes a more specific impairment in the use of canonical linking rules. Each of these theories would be consistent with the impaired development of components of a grammatical module. They contrast with the explanations of Tallal and Leonard, within which any impaired grammatical module is deficient as a consequence of earlier receptive difficulties. Cognitive neuropsychology cannot distinguish between coincidental coexistence of an auditory/phonological problem and grammatical difficulties, and causally linked coexistence of the two problems. However, if on the basis of case study analyses, children are identified who have grammatical difficulties but do not have difficulties with the phonological discrimination of morphological features or the discrimination of speech sounds characterised by rapid transitional information or vice versa then the Tallal and Leonard theories may be rejected and a grammatical module theory gains in strength.

Studies of developmental dyspraxia of speech suggest that they may fail to monitor the speech motor movements (Snowling & Stackhouse, 1983). The possibility that there may be multiple variants in the form of the disorder as is evident in the analysis of the acquired apraxias (Geschwind, 1975) is as yet unexplored within development.

Pragmatic impairments form one of the core elements of autism, which has been linked to discussion of their proposed impairment in theory of mind (Leslie, 1987; Tager-Flusberg & Anderson, 1991). Pragmatic impairment is also evident in Asperger's syndrome, even though theory of mind deficits are less pervasive in this group (Ozonoff et al., 1991). Bishop (1989) suggests that autism, Asperger's syndrome and semantic-pragmatic disorder all have intersecting boundaries.

A genetic basis to specific language disorders is supported by a number of recent studies (e.g. Bishop, North & Donlan, 1995) and in relation to children with a range of different types of difficulty: auditory agnosias; grammatical difficulties; verbal dyspraxias; stuttering; and autism with its pragmatic impairment.

The extent to which the patterns of developmental language disorders differ from those seen following unilateral lesions remains to be determined. Studies such as that of Van Hout (1993) highlight the striking similarity between the patterns of certain language disorders in acquired and developmental format when they are systematically compared on the same tasks. However, it seems that the mechanisms of compensation for language disorder following unilateral lesions are not activated in most cases of developmental disorders. If a structural lesion occurs in the left hemisphere, prior to the age of five or six years, language skills could develop in the right hemisphere (Rasmussen & Milner, 1977). Yet, the language disorders reported above are more marked than any reliable impairment of right hemisphere language skills (Bishop, 1988). More commonly, early focal left hemisphere lesions lead to reorganisation of language in the intact areas of the left hemisphere (Papanicolaou, DiScenna, Gillespie, & Aram, 1990). Why do such compensatory mechanisms not occur for the developmental language disorders?

There are several possibilities. The basis of some of the language disorders discussed earlier may be bilateral, so that there is no intact hemisphere to take over function (e.g. Lou et al., 1977) and the areas of the left hemisphere abnormality may be diffuse giving no opportunity for the ipsilateral reorganisation (Martins, Antunes, Castro-Caldas, & Antunes, 1995). The case report of Martins et al. (1995) is of interest since it suggests that in some cases of good recovery from developmental language disorder, the right hemisphere may indeed be involved in the recovery mechanism. They report a child with developmental language disorder whose language eventually developed to some degree, but for whom a subsequent right hemisphere gunshot injury induced aphasia. However, such cases appear to be rare. Another possibility is that these compensatory mechanisms are not activated when the basis of the disorder is under genetic control, but are instead responses to injury or disease. This could apply to both Landau–Kleffner syndrome (Landau, 1992) and specific language disorder more generally (Bishop et al. 1995; Gopnik, 1990b). Of particular interest, in the data from the twin study of specific language disorder by Bishop et al. (1995), there was a close concordance between identical twins for the type of language disorder, suggesting that genetic mechanisms may not only predispose to language disorder but may constrain the pattern of its expression. From a cognitive neuropsychological perspective, this would be consistent with the genetic specification of elements of the language system.

CHAPTER THREE

Memory Disorders

MEMORY AND FORGETTING IN NORMAL CHILDREN

As with many other areas of developmental psychology, recent research on children's memory processes has pushed back the ages for which certain skills are evident. For example, there had been a persistent belief that memories acquired in infancy were transient. However, Rovee-Collier's (1989) studies of young infants' memories for the kicking response required to activate a moving mobile have indicated that "when motivated infants have a reason to remember, they do so by orders of magnitude longer than previously thought". For example, after only 18 minutes of training, split into three sessions, two- to three-month-old infants exhibited excellent memory for the kicking response after a two-week delay (Enright, Rovee-Collier, Fagen, & Caniglia, 1983; Van der Linde, Morrongiello, & Rovee-Collier, 1985). Even when forgetting seemed complete and the memory no longer available, it could still be accessed by a context-specific retrieval cue, such as a distinctive crib bumper which had been present during initial acquisition (Greco, Rovee-Collier, Hayne, Griesler, & Earley 1986; Hayne & Rovee-Collier, 1985). Rovee-Collier (1989) termed such cued accessing of memory, reactivation. She found not only that early memories are highly organised but also that they are highly specific to the conditions and context in which they were acquired. She speculates that this context-specific requirement could constrain the probability that a response will be instantiated in an appropriate context.

In investigating young infants' responses after training with multiple perceptibly different mobiles, Rovee-Collier (1989; Greco, Hayne, & Rovee-Collier, 1986) also showed that there is evidence of early categorisation skill in the encoding and retrieval of the content of memories in the first few months. Such work has established that memory is not a system which emerges late in childhood. Memory systems are active in early infancy. Infants are able to code complex features of a stimulus and to make use of object categorisation. Moreover, even after relatively brief exposures, the memories can be retained over extended periods.

One reason why children's early memories may have been perceived as poor is the apparent childhood amnesia, whereby it is rare to find anyone who remembers a specific incident from before two years of age. Such autobiographical or so-called episodic memory has been studied extensively by Nelson and colleagues (e.g. Nelson, 1989, 1993). There had been a persistent belief that a major reorganisation of memory processes accounted for infantile amnesia, with memories in early childhood being coded and stored differently, such that they could not be retrieved with the cues available later. However, it now seems that although children may need more cues to access their memories, the cues themselves are not different from the cues used by older children. There is also no evidence of a discontinuous shift at some point in development reflecting reorganisation (Nelson, 1989).

Nelson (1989, 1993) has shown that children do have episodic memories prior to three years of age and can remember specific novel events for up to a year and longer. By the age of three years, at least some children can structure these episodes into well-formed narratives.

In infancy, when the same previously novel event is repeatedly experienced, it becomes harder to retrieve a specific instance of that event. Nelson suggests that a new experience leads the organism to set up a new schema which is like an autobiographical memory for a particular episode. However, with further experience of similar events, the memory becomes more standardised and script like. According to this view, the basic episodic system is initially a holding pattern which becomes script like if repeated but is forgotten over time if no comparable examples are experienced. Nelson also speculates that with the development of language, the functional significance of such memories changes. Memories can now be shared with other people and therefore have value in their own right for cultural social exchange. She argues that shared memory narratives establish the new social function of autobiographical memory and that this is facilitated by mothers who engage in narratives about past experience with the child. It is this which leads to the development of an episodic system which can be accessed in later life. According to this view it is not so much that the system of memory changes but that the significance of certain memories change. This could alter their encoding or ease of retrieval.

Amongst slightly older children, the literature on memory processes, in the 1970s and early 1980s, emphasised the minimal nature of developmental trends with report of nil or small effects, or effects reducible to associated factors. Thus, for example, Hudson and Nelson (1986) attribute age differences between three- and seven-year-olds in memory for autobiographical events to the length and degree of elaboration of the recall narratives. However, some argue that developmental trends of more substance are evident when stringent acquisition measures are utilised (e.g. Howe & Brainerd, 1989) and in some cases where recall measures are used rather than recognition.

Failure of memory in normal children could, in principle, result from deficiencies in encoding, storage, or retrieval. In relation to the first of these, the quality and structure of the encoding of material to be remembered is believed to be relevant to subsequent memory for that material. Improvements in children's recall are reported to relate to their ability to encode more and more features of stimuli at the time of acquisition (e.g. Bjorklund & Muir, 1988). In children with learning disabilities, the later stages of memory may be intact but the ability to code information for storage may be impaired (Clarke & Clarke, 1974; Estes, 1988).

The idea of forgetting as an alteration of information stored was discussed by Bartlett (1932). In relation to children, Piaget and Inhelder (1973) argued that, in normal development, improvement in memory over time was brought about by changes in the memory trace itself. Improved cognitive schema in relation to a task led to reorganisation of the memory for the original event. However, such an association between operative levels and reorganisation of memory stores has been disputed (e.g. Liben, 1981). Reorganisation of memory stores has also been discussed in studies of children's eye witness testimony. Here, susceptibility to misinformation has been variably interpreted as filling in a weakly stored trace, distorting an existing trace or emanating from a distinct trace (Cole & Loftus, 1987).

Retrieval theories of forgetting argue that memory storage remains intact but that there is difficulty in accessing or activating the relevant stores. Superior performance is often evident in recognition memory paradigms in comparison to recall. This is argued to provide evidence for more intact storage than suggested from simple recall. In the adult neuropsychological literature, where explicit memory fails, evidence for implicit memory may be derived from skin conductance responses to material claimed not to be recognised. In these cases, intact stores are being activated despite the overt retrieval difficulties. Similarly, in a study of memory for preschool classmates (Newcombe & Fox, 1994), children with little evidence of explicit memory for classmates were as likely to show differential skin conductance responding to faces of former classmates as were children with higher recognition scores. The authors argued that so-called infantile amnesia, for early childhood memories, may not always involve loss of the stores of encoded information.

Howe and Brainerd (1989) argue that storage-based and retrieval-based forgetting represent:

> different stages in the process of trace disintegration in which bonds that unite trace elements erode. Here, retrieval failures are associated with early stages of trace erosion and storage failures are associated with later stages ... storage-based failures are not associated with the absence of the concept from memory ... but are a function of the extent of dissolution of bonds that serve to integrate the conceptual elements together to form an active, unified trace structure. (p. 319)

They incorporate these ideas into a mathematical model.

The declarative memory system, which involves memory for facts and events may be dissociated from source memory, which involves the recall of when and where the information was learnt. The hippocampal complex is thought to underlie fact recall but the frontal lobes may underlie source recall. As will be discussed in greater detail in Chapter 8, two of the standard tasks thought to be sensitive to frontal lobe function are the Wisconsin Card Sorting Task (WCST) and verbal fluency. Craik, Morris, Morris, and Loewen (1990) found that in a population of healthy elderly subjects poor performance on a source memory task correlated with performance on the WCST and verbal fluency. They interpreted this as resulting from the differential effect of aging upon the frontal lobes. A similar study was conducted by Rybash and Colilla (1994) with children aged 10–14 years. The incidence of errors on the source recall task was also found to be related to WCST performance in this group. Source error rates did not relate to fact recall or age. The results suggest a distinction between the mechanisms which underlie the development of declarative and source memory and a possible frontal lobe substrate for source memory.

ACQUIRED AMNESIA IN ADULTS

Amnesia, in adult neurological patients, is characterised by memory impairment for events prior to injury or disease, retrograde amnesia, and also memory impairment in the acquisition of new knowledge, anterograde amnesia. Adults with amnesia may have intact intellectual skills, scoring at normal levels on some sections of intelligence tests. They may also have intact social skills and normal language abilities. Their anterograde amnesia, affects the acquisition of new facts about the world, but leaves intact previously acquired semantic knowledge about individual word meanings and knowledge of the function and appearance of objects (Parkin, 1996). Amnesic patients retain normal short-term memories and are also able to learn a variety of skills and automated behaviours (e.g. Brooks & Baddeley, 1976) which have been labelled as procedural. In contrast, declarative knowledge of explicit facts cannot be learnt.

The most commonly studied amnesic patients are alcoholics with Korsakoff amnesia (Korsakoff, 1887). They are sometimes referred to as diencephalic, since damage is thought to include the mamilliary bodies and the dorsomedial thalamus. However, their performance may be complicated by frontal lobe deficits (Leng & Parkin, 1989; Squire, 1982a). Patient NA, who sustained a penetrating paranasal injury as a consequence of an accident with a fencing foil, has also been studied extensively (Kaushall, Zetin, & Squire, 1981; Teuber, Milner, & Vaughan, 1968). It was thought that this patient had a left dorsomedial thalamic lesion (Squire & Moore, 1979). However, he was subsequently found to have a more extensive lesion involving multiple structures (Squire, Amaral, Zola-Morgan, Kritchevsky, & Press, 1989). Thalamic amnesia may also follow primary thalamic haemorrhage, particularly if the paramedian territory is affected (Parkin & Leng, 1993).

An alternative lesion location is implicated in the patient HM (Scoville & Milner, 1957), who had a bilateral medial temporal lobectomy, including the removal of the uncus, amygdala, and hippocampus. HM has a profound anterograde amnesia, prohibiting recall of new information. He will read and reread the same article again without recognition and has to be continually reintroduced to those working with him whom he fails to remember. Amnesia following localised medial temporal damage is also reported in other cases (Zola-Morgan, Squire, & Amaral, 1986). A hippocampal impairment has also been suggested in association with the memory deficit seen in patients who have had electroconvulsive therapy (Squire, 1982b). In a series of studies, Parkin has demonstrated that the characteristics of the memory impairment in the diencephalic amnesics differ from those with the hippocampal abnormalities (Hunkin, Parkin, & Longmore, 1994; Parkin, 1992; Parkin & Leng, 1988, 1993).

ACQUIRED AMNESIA IN CHILDHOOD

Cases of acquired amnesia in childhood have rarely been reported, but it is unclear whether this reflects the true incidence or simply frequency of report. The common cause of acquired amnesia in adulthood, namely Korsakoff syndrome, does not have a direct developmental parallel. The cause of amnesia in such chronic alcoholics is thiamine deficiency, which can also occur in children, but these children do not appear to develop an amnesic syndrome (Geschwind, 1974; Herskowitz & Rosman, 1982).

ECT has in some cases been given to children as well as adults, and Geschwind (1974) reported a child who had a course of ECT at the age of 10 years and who subsequently suffered from both a memory deficit and aphasia. He suggested that the aphasia resulted from a retrograde amnesia, which affected the time of language development.

Ostergaard (1987) reported the case of a child CC who became amnesic at the age of 10, following an episode of anoxia. CC remained of normal intelligence but had a persistent and severe impairment of declarative memory, encompassing both episodic and semantic aspects. Impaired areas of semantic memory demonstrated on laboratory investigation, included vocabulary, lexical decision, semantic classification, verbal fluency, reading, and spelling. In semantic classification, "anterograde" performance for items normally learnt after the age of eight was poorer than "retrograde" performance for items ordinarily learned earlier. Procedural memory skills were intact.

Wood, Brown, and Felton (1989) also presented a case report and long-term follow-up of an acquired amnesia in childhood. However, they argued that their case did not conform to the declarative–procedural memory distinction, since there was scholastic progress over the school years. Ostergaard and Squire (1990) disputed the Wood et al. (1989) interpretation. They argued that academic achievement may reflect the development of skills other than those of declarative memory, relying either on automated procedures or other conceptual development. In support of this view Brainerd and Reyna (1992) reported that in normal children logical, mathematical, and pragmatic inferences are not dependent upon memory as would intuitively be supposed, in the sense of activation of exact traces of background input. Ostergaard and Squire (1990) also argued that dissociations between components of memory are based upon relative severity of deficit not absolute loss and retention, and that the limited acquisition of declarative knowledge reported by Wood et al. (1989), may be explained by the residual level of day-to-day memory.

An unusual case of acquired amnesia in a child is reported by Vargha-Khadem, Isaacs, and Mishkin, (in press). Neil was a 14-year-old boy, who had received successful treatment the preceding year with chemotherapy and radiotherapy, for a tumour in the pineal region of the posterior third ventricle. His verbal intelligence was normal (Verbal IQ 111/109). Performance IQ was significantly impaired, though block design was normal. The Wechsler Memory Quotient was only 59. Retrograde autobiographical memory was virtually perfect but anterograde autobiographical memory was failed completely. He could copy a complex design well but delayed recall was significantly impaired. He was both agnosic and alexic, yet retained considerable skill in drawing, indicating intact stores for the visual appearance of objects, despite the agnosia. Writing was intact, and he was able to develop compensatory kinaesthetic strategies to use this intact ability to help with reading. Unusually, it was found that he was able to retrieve some memories through writing despite inability of oral recall and absence of apparent awareness of his responses. His ability indicated that he was able to learn and retain new information. He was able to store information that he was unaware of even when he was retrieving it. His capacity to accomplish this was limited but argues for the existence of two separate stores, and/or two separate retrieval modalities for verbal material, one oral and one orthographic. His ability to use orthographic output extended beyond information taught in verbal format at school, to the retrieval of day-to-day events, enabling enhanced communication with his family.

Carpentieri and Mulhern (1993) report memory disorders in children surviving temporal lobe tumours. The younger the age at diagnosis, the more severe the verbal long-term memory deficits. Children receiving radiation therapy were at greatest risk for both visual and auditory verbal memory deficits, relative to their intellectual levels. The risk of such deficits was high, even in the absence of general intellectual decline.

TEMPORAL LOBECTOMIES

The effects upon memory of unilateral temporal lobectomies have been studied by Milner (1966, 1970). Left temporal lobectomies are associated with deficits in the recall of prose passages and the acquisition of verbal paired associates. Right temporal lobectomies are associated with deficits in the recall of a variety of non-verbal materials: unfamiliar geometric figures; nonsense figures; tonal patterns; faces; and visual tactual mazes. These laterality effects are consistent with data from other sources indicating explicit functional asymmetry in the human brain. Patients with left temporal lobectomies also displayed neglect of detail in organised pictorial stimuli (Zaidel & Rausch, 1981) suggesting impairment of executive organisational components and memory.

Studies of temporal lobectomies in children are limited in number. Cavazzuti, Winston, Baker, and Welch (1980) report the effects of temporal lobe surgery for lateralised tumours in the temporal lobes, in subjects aged between 6 and 33 years, 60% of whom were aged between 13 and 19 years. Left temporal lobectomy reduced the verbal memory quotient and increased verbal dysfunction, but tended to improve non-verbal memory. Right temporal lobectomy improved verbal skills and verbal learning. Cavazzuti et al. (1980) interpreted the improvements in memory as resulting from the removal of the inhibitory preoperative influence of the tumour-infected lobe via the commissural pathways to the contralateral hemisphere.

Meyer, Marsh, Laws, and Sharborough (1986) report a study of temporal lobectomy for the treatment of epilepsy in 50 children aged less than 18 years. IQ was not significantly changed by the surgery. There were also no significant changes overall in memory quotient. However, when the group was divided by sex, it was evident that the girls were significantly more likely to show memory improvement after surgery than the boys, who were significantly more likely to have memory impairment. This difference was unrelated to side of resection or seizure duration.

A study of temporal lobectomy for seizure disorder, in adolescents and young adults, was also reported by Dennis et al. (1988). Those with left-sided surgery had poorer verbal recognition memory scores than those with right-sided surgery. The verbal recognition memory test employed required the subject to listen to serially presented words and indicate for each word, whether it had occurred previously on the list. A sequential memory test was also given. Here, the subject had to listen to a spoken word list and then place pictures representing the words in an identical sequence to that heard. There were no simple laterality effects but there were interactions of laterality and seizure type. Content memory (the association of words with their meanings) was also more impaired with extensive tissue resection in posterior areas.

Overall Dennis et al. (1988) reported that memory was affected by interactions between laterality, side of tissue removal, age at onset, and seizure type but not in a homogeneous fashion. Dennis et al. (1988) suggested that the memory scores were not only affected by laterality but also by the medical history as this might signal the structural and functional intactness of residual tissue.

MEMORY IN EPILEPSY

One reason that a discussion of epilepsy is particularly relevant to a chapter on memory disorders in children is that the most epileptogenic areas of the brain are those which are known to be intimately involved in memory. That is, the areas of the brain within which it is most probable that an epileptic seizure will be sustained are the temporal lobes. It was thought, that this was because of the proximity of the temporal lobes to the underlying hippocampus, and it has now been confirmed with invasive EEG monitoring that idiopathic temporal lobe seizures are predominantly of hippocampal origin (Spencer, Spencer, Williamson, & Mattson, 1990; Wyler, Walker, Richey, & Hermann, 1988). It is possible that, the underlying characteristics which make these regions susceptible to seizure are associated with the underlying characteristics which make them appropriate for memory encoding and/or storage. In both cases, distributed networks are involved and critical steady states are attained. Clearly, however, in epilepsy the mechanism is incorrectly tuned or specified such that seizures occur and in many cases memory is disrupted. Some characteristics of the underlying networks are relevant to both of these aspects. In addition, when the seizures are active they prohibit the generation of the steady states required for memory encoding or consolidation.

Epilepsy, is often associated with memory disorders (Loiseau, Strube, & Signoret, 1988). About one-third of all patients with epilepsy, suffer from temporal lobe epilepsy (TLE) and pathology or abnormality in the temporal lobes and underlying hippocampus may produce both the epilepsy and memory impairment. Seizures and sub-ictal electrical discharges in temporal lobes may also interfere with processes of memory consolidation (Glowinski, 1973). Anticonvulsant drugs, particularly phenobarbital, phenytoin, and primidone, may exacerbate memory impairment (Thompson & Trimble, 1982; Trimble & Reynolds, 1976). Repeated seizures may also cause further cerebral damage (Reynolds, Elwes, & Shorvon, 1983), though this is a less probable event, except in cases of status epilepticus.

Specific associations of memory impairment have been found with TLE, though Milner reported that in her patients the memory difficulties may be mild before surgery (Milner, 1975). Left TLE has been reported as associated with verbal memory impairment and right TLE as associated with non-verbal memory impairment (Delaney, Rosen, Mattson, & Novelly, 1980), though not all studies report lateralised effects (Glowinski, 1973) and some fail to show a disproportionate deficit in comparison to other patients with epilepsy. Hermann, Seidenberg, Haltiner, and Wyler (1992) reported that patients with left TLE performed significantly more poorly than those with right TLE on sentence repetition, the Token test, aural comprehension and reading comprehension as well as visual naming. They also pointed out that for both left and right groups, adequacy of language function related to learning and memory performance. This implied a directional causality but could also have been stated in reverse, as learning and memory performance relating to adequacy of language function.

Rausch, Boone, and Ary (1991) reported that for patients with left TLE but known right hemisphere dominance for language, comparable degrees of verbal memory loss were not shown either pre-operatively or after left temporal lobectomy, when compared with those with left temporal seizures and left hemisphere dominance for language. This indicated that the right hemisphere group had verbal memory functions as well as general language functions supported primarily by the right hemisphere. They noted that the right hemisphere dominant group had a more consistent history of brain involvement before the age of five years and also had a higher seizure frequency, both of which may have contributed to the reorganisation of language dominance.

The majority of studies of memory impairment in epilepsy have employed group analyses. It is not clear that each and every patient in these studies shows the overall pattern. Indeed the study by Loiseau et al. (1988) of a homogeneous group of 27 patients with epilepsy, included five patients who had normal scores on the memory tests. Thus, there are individual differences in the degree to which memory is affected in patients with epilepsy. Interestingly, the study of Loiseau et al. (1988 p.170) also shows a selective preservation of verbal recognition memory, despite other memory deficits:

> As a group the epileptic patients scored significantly lower than the controls except in one task (verbal recognition).

A comparable result is noted in the Delaney et al. (1980, p.110) study:

> recognition ... methods did not differentiate groups (epileptics and controls).

In this study the lack of difference was attributed by the authors, to ceiling effects.

In comparison to matched controls, general memory impairments have not been always been observed in children with epilepsy (Davies-

Eysenck, 1952; Epir, Renda, & Baser, 1984). However, a specific memory impairment has been found in children with TLE, contrasting with normal memory function in centrencephalic epilepsy. Children with left TLE perform more poorly than children with right TLE on memory for factual material (Fedio & Mirsky, 1969).

Beardsworth and Zaidel (1994) studied memory for unfamiliar faces in children and adolescents with TLE. Both before and after temporal lobe surgery, those with right TLE performed more poorly than those with left TLE, on delayed recall for the faces. These results support early right hemisphere specialisation for face processing and face memory.

DEVELOPMENTAL AMNESIA

Developmental memory impairments in children have been subject to few detailed case analyses. As noted in Chapter 2, Denckla (1979) distinguished between aphasoid children, who have naming difficulties, and amnesoid children, who have memory problems. She suggested that the aphasoid makes better use of associative manoeuvres, whereas the amnesoid tends to be a better reader and is more like a slow learner, requiring many trials before registering new information.

Maurer (1992) provided a brief clinical description of a child with congenital amnesia, for whom CT revealed low density regions in both temporal fossae, indicating absence of the left temporal lobe and the pole and mesial parts of the right temporal pole. These abnormalities were thought to result from prenatal events. Her memory disorder was said to resemble that of HM (Scoville & Milner, 1957). As classical amnesia is believed to result from a disorder in declarative memory, with intact procedural memory, Maurer (1992) attempted to teach their childhood amnesic new information by embedding it in actions, which were trained as habits. Information which they wanted her to learn was embedded in stimulus–response sets of pairings, which were then trained through repetition day after day. For example, she had been unable to learn the names of the people whom she met every day. She was cued to say "hello" and then the name of the person, every time she met them. Not only was she able by this method, to learn the names but she was also able to use the names correctly in other contexts. Using similar procedures, Maurer (1992) report, that they were able to teach her to read, though precise details of the training and its outcome are not given.

Maurer's (1992) patient also had lesions of the amygdala. He noted that Mishkin and Appenzeller (1987) had studied memory in monkeys with lesions of the amygdala. The monkeys were unable to select a member of a pair of objects, on the basis of whether the sample member of the pair had or had not been associated with reward. Maurer reasoned that his patient should be unable to learn stimulus-reinforcement association and that operant conditioning should not be effective. However, against prediction, some acquisition of stable approach-avoidance did occur on the basis of a small number of trials. Maurer (1992) then reasoned that, in line with the ideas of Mackintosh (1983), operant conditioning could be considered to be made up of two parallel processes: classical conditioning of drive states; and storage of information about stimulus response reinforcement relationships. The memory deficits of his patient would impair the storage of information but not the classical conditioning. Thus, instrumental conditioning would motivate her, but the information was not available to appropriately actualise the motivation. The conditioning which was observed was similar in quality to that originally reported by Claparede (1911) and more recently reported by Weiskrantz and Warrington (1979), in their classical conditioning study of an adult with acquired amnesia.

De Renzi and Lucchelli (1990) report an investigation of a 22-year-old man, MS, who had complained of memory difficulties since childhood. He was the second of two children, delivered after seven months of gestation and with a birth weight of 2500g. His developmental milestones were normal. A CT scan was also normal but EEG showed irregular and unstable alpha rhythms. There were bilateral bursts of theta and delta waves with a left frontotemporal prevalence. He was of good intelligence, with a verbal IQ of 110 and a performance IQ of 111. Attention, oral language, visual perception, and praxis were intact.

MS reported that foreign language words, historical and geographical names, proper names, and mathematical formulae were particularly problematic for him to remember and that he had never succeeded in learning by heart a poem or song, nor mathematical tables. He also claimed that he was poor at remembering faces.

Formal assessment indicated impaired scores, at an amnesic level, on both verbal logical memory and verbal paired associate learning. Memory for past general events was also impaired as was recognition memory for famous names. Both unfamiliar and famous face recognition was poor. Sequential memory was also poor. When memory for recurring stimuli was tested, MS was severely impaired for verbal items, but surprisingly quite unimpaired with non-verbal figures. Reading was slow and laborious.

De Renzi and Lucchelli (1990) discuss the case as a developmental amnesia, suggesting that there is no apparent relationship to acquired brain disease but a congenital deficiency of the neuronal structures specific for memory.

The case reported below, involves memory impairment in a girl with temporal lobe epilepsy. Specifically, it addresses the issue of what type of memories are affected and how the memory impairment compares with the adult amnesic syndrome. In Chapter 2, the anomic difficulty of this case was discussed and the case history is not repeated here. Given the relative absence of case reports of developmental amnesia, the tasks and results are described in some detail.

Case Report: Development Amnesia, Julia

As noted earlier, at the time of the investigation, Julia was twelve years eight months old. She had temporal lobe epilepsy (TLE). Delayed language development was recorded in the pre-school years. The seizure disorder did not become manifest until the age of six.

Investigation of Memory

Memory Tasks Employed were as follows:

1. *Short-term Memory (STM).*   Short-term memory is thought to have both verbal and non-verbal components. In Baddeley and Hitch's (1974) terms, these two components are the articulatory loop and the visuo-spatial scratch pad and together with the central executive they form working memory. One method of assessing the capacities of these short-term memory constituent components is by span recall tests. Digit span was given as outlined by Wechsler (1974). The Corsi test (Milner, 1971) assessed span for spatial positions.

2. *Procedural Knowledge.*   Procedural knowledge is differentiated from semantic knowledge in a variety of ways. It is thought to comprise more highly automated behaviours and was assessed here by the generation aloud of automated sequences: the alphabet; days of the week; months of the year; counting from 1 to 30. Counting was done twice: once at the subject's own pace and once as quickly as possible.

3. *Established Semantic Knowledge.*   Semantic knowledge comprises both factual knowledge about the world and at a more fundamental level knowledge of individual word meanings. Both skills were assessed, the former with questions of general knowledge, and the latter by the production of word definitions and the ability to find and retrieve the correct name for presented pictures, naming skills being dependent upon the normal establishment of semantic representations for words.

The Information subtest of the WISC-R consists of a series of questions of general knowledge. In addition to this three factual questions were also asked: Who is the Prime Minister? Who is Princess Diana married to? What is the capital city of England?

Knowledge of individual word meanings was assessed with the WISC-R Vocabulary subtest (Wechsler, 1974). Naming tasks included the Renfrew Word Finding Scale and the Boston Naming Test (Goodglass & Kaplan, 1983), both of which employ a graded series of black and white line drawings.

4. Anterograde Verbal Memory.   The capacity to remember new information was assessed from both oral and written presentation. The Taylor Stories (Kimura & McGlone, 1979), which are short passages of text, were read to Julia for immediate recall. Unexpected delayed recall was requested after a 30-minute interval. The first three stories from the Neale Analysis of Reading were read by Julia (Neale, 1966). Any reading errors were corrected as she progressed. At the end of each passage, a short set of questions about the story was asked.

5. Acquisition of New Non-verbal Memory.   In order to investigate whether memory performance was dependent upon the type of new knowledge which had to be acquired Julia was tested on the acquisition of new non-verbal information. As a precursor to the non-verbal memory tests, Julia's ability to copy designs was tested.

The designs from Benton's Visual Retention Test (Benton, 1974) consist of a fairly simple central pattern and a smaller peripheral figure of a square, triangle or circle. A set of these designs was copied with no time restriction. A set of different Benton designs, matched for difficulty with the set copied, was given in the recall test. Each design was exposed for 10 seconds, following which Julia had to immediately draw the design. The Figure of Rey (Osterrieth, 1944) is a much more complicated non-verbal design. It was first copied. Unexpectedly, after a delay of 30 minutes, Julia was requested to recall details of the design.

6. Recognition Memory.   Where information has been encoded but their is difficulty in accessing it, recognition memory can be superior to free recall. This is true of most normal performance and is also observed in many cases of amnesia, where specific cues may also aid recall.

Warrington Recognition Memory Battery (Warrington, 1984) contrasts recognition memory for words and faces. A series of stimuli was presented with an approximate exposure period of three seconds, per item. For each stimulus, Julia had to make a forced choice to decide whether it was pleasant or unpleasant. Immediately after the series presentation, the subject was shown a series of stimulus pairs. For each pair, the subject had to select the member which was in the previously shown pack.

Results

1. Short-term Memory. Auditory STM , as assessed by the recall of a sequence of digits was 4 forward and 3 backward. In relation to the WISC-R, Digit Span subtest, Julia attained a scaled score of 4 which was 2 standard deviations below the mean for age (P<0.05). Recall span, of a sequence of spatial positions on the Corsi blocks, was 5. In general Corsi span is expected to be one below verbal span, rather than one above. These results indicate poor auditory–verbal short-term memory.

2. Procedural Knowledge. Requested to produce the specified automated sequences of information, Julia generated the sequence of letters that make up the alphabet in 13 seconds; the names of the days of the week in 4 seconds; and the names of the months of the years in 10 seconds. There were no errors in any of these sequences. She counted steadily from 1 to 30 in 22 seconds. When requested to count more quickly, she rapidly counted from 1 to 30 in 9 seconds, thus attaining a speed of at least three numbers a second. This increased speed did not reduce accuracy. Julia had efficiently established and could accurately access a variety of automated sequences. In relation to this measure, procedural knowledge had become established.

3. Established Semantic Knowledge — Facts. Julia attained a score of only 1 on the Information subtest on the WISC (3 SD below mean for age, P<0.01), indicating a significant impairment in her general knowledge. On this subtest she was unable to give the name for a baby cow. She did not know the animal from which bacon is obtained. She did not know how many things make a dozen and when asked what the four seasons of the year were, she said "What do you mean by seasons?"

In response to the three extra general knowledge questions, Julia said she did not know the name of the prime minister (at the time, Mrs Thatcher had been Prime Minister for a decade). Asked whether it was a man or a woman, she picked a man. She was then asked "Do you know who Mrs. Thatcher is?" Julia said that she did, but could not be more specific. Asked whether she was an actress, Julia replied "Yes". Thus, Julia appeared to have some capacity to recognise the name Mrs. Thatcher, but she could not access any more specific semantic information about her, nor could she access her name from a semantic description. She was unable to indicate to whom Princess Diana was married (this preceded the Royal divorce). She also suggested that the capital of England was Oxford, her own town of residence.

3b. Established Semantic Knowledge—Vocabulary. On the vocabulary subtest of the WISC-R, Julia attained a scaled score of three, the second lowest of the subtest scores and over 2 SDs below the mean for age (P<0.05). This significant deficit in knowledge of word meanings was also apparent on some other subtests. On the Similarities subtest, she showed comparable failure, for example failing to understand the word "anger".

On the Renfrew Word Finding Scale, a naming age of five years three months was attained, representing a deficit in naming skills of seven years five months, in relation to chronological age. On the Boston Naming test, naming age was at a comparable level to the Renfrew. As indicated in Chapter 2, consistency of naming responses and failure to show better recognition than retrieval of names suggests a failure to establish semantic representations rather than an access problem underlying the anomic disorder.

Overall, performance on tests of established semantic knowledge revealed both deficiencies in semantic knowledge about individual word meanings and deficiencies in knowledge about factual information about the world.

4. Anterograde Verbal Memory.   Julia was read the two short Taylor Stories, for both immediate and delayed recall. Norms for nine-year-olds on this task predicted a recall score of 10–11 items per story with no loss of information over a 30–45 minute delay. Julia's score on the first story was at an approximately normal level for age (11 items) but the score on the second story was significantly impaired (2 items). On delayed recall the score for the first story dropped to six, whilst the floor score of two remained unchanged. Thus, on one story, the immediate recall was normal but there is an abnormally rapid decay in the memory, half of the information being lost with delay. On the other story, the initial registration of the information was ineffective, but with retention over time of the minimal facts encoded.

The first three stories from the Neale comprise, in total, 149 words. Only six words induced reading errors (which were corrected for the subject, by the tester). Of the 20 questions about the stories, Julia answered only 4 (20%) correctly, attaining a score significantly below that expected on the basis of her reading accuracy. In terms of reading ages her accuracy score was 8;7 months, whereas her score based on ability to answer questions was 6;9 months. Of the questions answered correctly, three were the first question asked about each story, and one was the second question asked about one story, which required as its answer, the selection from three given alternatives.

Thus the position of the questions in the question series seemed to affect performance. There are two possible interpretations. The first questions related to events early in the story. Thus, it could be argued that the registration of the initial events in each story was better than the registration of latter events and the effect of question position relates to primacy effects in recall. Alternatively, it may be relevant that the first question was asked earlier than the other questions. All the events in the story may have attained comparable registration but if there was abnormally rapid decay, then by the time the first question had been answered, the rest of the story may have degraded.

When Julia was unable to answer questions, she sometimes confabulated. Thus, one of the principal features of the second story was that it was foggy. When asked what the weather was like in the story, Julia said that it was a nice day.

Julia had impaired anterograde verbal memory. The differential effect of question position may suggest abnormally rapid decay.

5. Non-verbal Memory. With the simple geometrical designs from Benton's Visual Retention Test, Julia could copy 8/10 correctly. This is a normal level for age. On the matched set of designs, to those used for copying, Julia could immediately recall only 3/10. This is well outside the normal range and significantly below the mean level for age. On both copying and recall of the more complex Figure of Rey, scores below the 5th percentile for age were attained. It was noticeable in the style of her recall, that she was relatively accurate in conveying the external shape of the overall design but was very poor in depicting any of the detailed information about the features of the design.

Although Julia could analyse and copy simple non-verbal designs at a normal level for age, she was significantly impaired in the immediate recall of such designs. She had comparable levels of difficulty in the delayed recall of a more complex design, though she also had difficulty in the initial copy of this figure. There was no evidence that Julia's memory difficulties were restricted to verbal areas.

6. Recognition Memory. Julia's performance on the word recognition section of the Warrington test was almost perfect (49/50) and entirely normal. In contrast, performance on face recognition was entirely random (25/50). There was a significant dissociation between these scores (X^2=27.49, P<0.01, Yate's Correction Applied). Julia's recognition memory deficit was material specific. It did not affect recognition memory for words but did affect recognition memory for faces.

Discussion. Julia was a child with TLE who displayed memory impairment. She had a clear developmental history of memory problems which were documented consistently since the age of four years. The memory disorder preceded the development of the seizure disorder. The difficulties with memory were apparent in the earliest clinical reports with no evidence that memory had once been normal and had subsequently deteriorated. The evidence supports the view that the underlying neurological basis of Julia's disorder was already present in infancy.

Julia's memory difficulties were disproportionate to a number of her other intellectual skills. As noted in Chapter 2, her arithmetical skills, her constructional skills, and her ability to reason verbally were all normal. Her memory difficulties were not therefore part of an undifferentiated developmental failure. Rather, there has been a dissociation between the cognitive skills which she has attained. Certain intellectual modules were established, where other processing mechanisms were impaired. Thus, there was fractionation in her intellectual development. Severe memory impairment in development does not therefore necessarily impair the acquisition of all other intellectual skills.

Julia had a clear impairment of long-term memory which included deficits in semantic memory and the acquisition of new information. This is comparable to an adult with an acquired amnesic disorder. However, whereas adult amnesics have preserved semantic knowledge about words and word meanings, Julia also had an anomic disorder. Adult amnesics have had normal memories at the time when they were acquiring language. In contrast Julia had an impaired memory during the stage of language acquisition. This memory impairment may have affected the establishment of semantic representations, and thereby also had an effect upon language development. This may be a feature of certain types of children with severe memory disorders.

In common with amnesics, Julia appeared to have preserved procedural memory skills. This suggested that the acquisition or recall of highly automated information involves distinct memory systems in children from those involved in memory for semantic information.

Unlike amnesics, Julia did not show preservation of all aspects of short-term memory. Verbal short-term memory was below expectation for age. The literature on developmental disorders suggest that disorders of short-term memory are not uncommon in children but that these may co-occur with normal long-term memory. Verbal short-term memory impairments are not sufficient to produce either the anomia or the semantic memory disorder manifested by Julia.

Although the temporal lobe focus of the seizure disorder is on the left, there is no evidence of the restriction of the memory impairment to verbal material. Clear deficits are observable in the acquisition of memory for non-verbal material. In this developmental case material specific laterality effects were not apparent, except for recognition memory, where in agreement with the group study of Loiseau et al. (1988), there was selective preservation of recognition memory for verbal material. The verbal preservation occurred despite the left TLE. Parkin, Dunn, Lee, O'Hara, and Nussbaum (1993) report a case of acquired Wernicke's encephalopathy in an adult amnesic for whom recognition memory was remarkably well preserved, despite other memory impairments typical of classical amnesia. They point out that in Korsakoff syndrome, recognition memory is usually extremely defective. It can become close to normal levels of performance but only when initial exposure times of the target stimuli are greatly lengthened. Parkin et al. (1993) attempted to explain the deficit in their Wernicke's encephalopathy case, primarily in terms of a frontally based retrieval deficit but such an explanation seems less parsimonious in Julia's case, where temporal lesions are emphasised and the intact recognition memory is only demonstrated for verbal material comprising single words after a brief delay. More extended delay before test might have produced a quite different pattern. The material specific effect might also argue against generalised retrieval difficulties.

In summary, in this case of TLE there is a severe memory impairment for semantic knowledge of both facts and word meanings and anterograde memory impairment for the acquisition of new information. The memory deficit does not involve predictable laterality effects as it also affects non-verbal material. However, procedural memory appears intact as does recognition memory for single words. The general pattern of results suggests an overall organisation of memory in the child comparable to that of the adult. Julia may be described as having developmental amnesia. However, as a child, one consequence in this case is that she also displays an apparent anomia.

It is of interest to compare Julia's amnesia with that of MS (De Renzi & Lucchelli, 1990). In each case a pervasive memory impairment has been evident through childhood, with no known acquired neurological injury. Both cases have severe impairments in verbal memory and memory for semantic knowledge. However, whereas MS has established a normal level of vocabulary, Julia's amnesia is associated with memory difficulties in building up the lexicon. In contrast whereas Julia has been able to learn automated sequences of information, such as days of the week and months of the year, MS has difficulty in acquiring these series. Julia's verbal recognition memory is also better developed than that of MS, though both are impaired in face recognition memory. The two cases indicate that developmental amnesia is not a homogeneous disorder but may take different forms. In each case, there is severe impairment of memory but there are differences in the selective components of memory which are preserved. An exploration of the potential range of such dissociations, and the links between memory and language development, awaits the description of further cases of developmental amnesia. However, the cases described to date highlight both the dissociability of memory from a number of other cognitive systems in development and the structural divisions between components of memory in acquisition which enable certain elements to be mastered whereas others are impaired.

CONTENT-SPECIFIC MEMORY DISORDERS

The case of Dr S, discussed in the following chapter on spatial and perceptual disorders (Chapter 4) concerns a developmental disorder in face recognition. Although, Dr S (Temple, 1992b) had an excellent verbal memory, a well-developed vocabulary, and high academic attainments in areas requiring the mastery of large banks of factual information, she neverthless had a severe impairment of visual memory, and although this is predominantly discussed and has predominantly been investigated in relation to her consequent face recognition difficulties, the memory impairment did extend to other classes of visual material, including houses, buildings, and visual patterns. It is perhaps of interest here, to illustrate in passing the marked dissociation in her skills by contrasting her verbal story recall and her recall of the Figure of Rey. The contrasting quality of her performance is illustrated in Table 3.1 and Fig. 3.1A and 3.1B. The consistency of the visual memory disorder is indicated by the pattern of her recall of the Figure of Rey, on two separate occasions, three years apart. The memory disorder of Dr S is content-specific and affects non-verbal material.

In Chapter 2, a child John (Temple, 1986a, 1995) who had particular anomic difficulties with animals but not with indoor objects was discussed. Although comprehension was somewhat better than production, suggesting aspects of access difficulty, the fundamental disorder was evident irrespective of the modality of investigation and the store of semantic entries associated with animals was considered to be deficient. The semantic store within language systems is a memory based store and John's difficulties could therefore be considered a developmental category-specific memory impairment. Fundamental semantic memory disorders in children may have impact on other systems, in a way which is not seen in their adult counterparts, for whom cognitive development is established prior to semantic loss. Thus, in cases such as John's, the distinctions between a language based category-specific anomia and a semantically based category-specific amnesia merge.

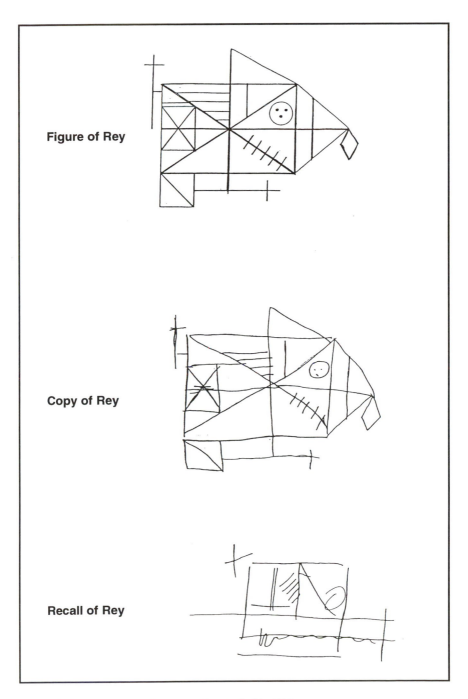

Figure of Rey

Copy of Rey

Recall of Rey

Fig. 3.1A Copy and recall of the figure of Rey by Dr S in 1987.

103

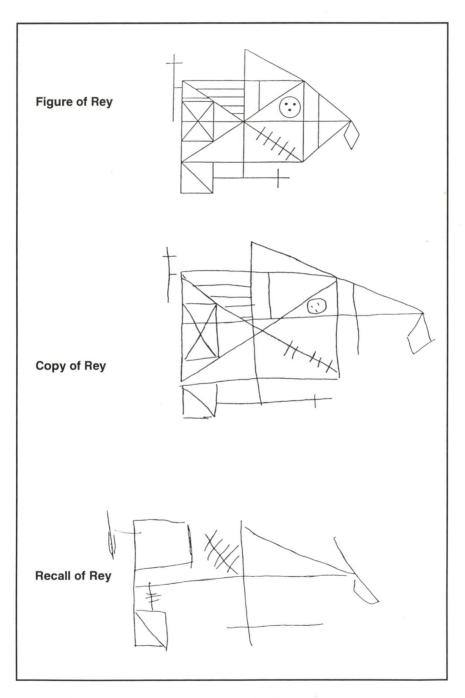

Figure of Rey

Copy of Rey

Recall of Rey

FIG. 3.1B Copy and recall of the figure of Rey by Dr S. in 1990.

TABLE 3.1
Verbal Recall of a Story by Dr S

Story employed (adapted from the Weschler Memory Battery)
Anna Thompson of South London, employed as a charwoman in an office building, reported at the City Police Station that she had been held up on Bond Street the night before and robbed of fifteen pounds. She had four little children, the rent was due, and they had not eaten for two days. The officers, touched by the woman's story, had a collection for her.

Verbal recall by Dr S
"Anna Thompson of South London was employed in an office in an office building. She reported at the police station in South London, that she had had fifteen pounds stolen. Her four children hadn't eaten for two days. The officers, moved by her story, did a collection there and then for her."

Further material-specific semantic disorders are also discussed in later chapters. Thus any specific difficulty for which there are problems in learning a particular class of material could be seen as an impairment of memory for that material without specifying whether the problem is in encoding, storage, or retrieval. Within reading, surface dyslexics fail to encode, store, or retrieve the appropriate visual input logogens or their linked semantic representations (see Chapter 5). Within spelling, surface dysgraphics have comparable difficulty with the recall or access of the relevant graphemic outputs (see Chapter 6). Within arithmetical disorders, those with number fact disorders who have difficulty in mastering tables are having a material-specific difficulty in establishing an accessible long-term knowledge base for these abstracted pieces of information (see Chapter 7). However, to describe these difficulties as category-specific memory impairments is in some respects simply a rearticulation of the evident difficulties. There is more theoretical interest in discussing the disorders beside the contrasting impairments, seen to affect related components of the relevant cognitive systems, as is done in following chapters.

DISORDERS OF SHORT-TERM MEMORY

The Baddeley and Hitch (1974) model of working memory incorporates three elements: an articulatory loop, a visuo-spatial scratch pad, and a central executive. Without doubt, the first of these components has received the most detailed and systematic investigation in both the adult and child literature.

Some children with reading difficulty may have poorly developed articulatory loops. This is not true for all children with reading difficulty and the degree to which there is a causal or merely a correlational association is also unknown. However, in group studies, poor readers are found to have poorer memories for strings of written or spoken letters (Shankweiler, Liberman, Mark, Fowler, & Fuscher, 1979). They are also poorer at recalling strings of spoken words and at recalling the words of spoken sentences (Mann, Liberman, & Shankweiler, 1980). This has been interpreted as reflecting the impoverished development of the articulatory loop used for the rehearsal of verbal material in working memory. The linguistic speci- ficity of the short-term memory differences, between good and poor readers, are evident from studies which indicate no differences in short term memory between good and poor readers when abstract shapes, nonsense designs, photographs of unfamiliar faces, or CVC nonsense syllables are involved (Hulme, 1981; Liberman, Mann, Shankweiler, & Werfelman, 1982; McDougall, Hulme, Ellis, & Monk, 1994).

Since the articulatory loop uses an articulatory code, its quality of performance can be disrupted when material with phonetic similarity is employed. Thus, when phonetically confusable items are involved, such as letters with rhyming names, or words that rhyme with one another, the memory performance of normal adults and children who are good readers declines sharply. However, when children who are poor readers are tested as a group, with phonetically confusable items, their performance remains unchanged from their performance with the other types of verbal material (Liberman et al., 1977; Mann, Liberman, & Shankweiler, 1980). This has again been interpreted as reflecting the under-involvement of an articulatory loop in their memory processes. However, more recently it has been shown that if the level of task difficulty is equated for good and poor readers, the effects of phonetic confusability upon short-term memory are the same for both groups (Brady, Mann, & Schmidt, 1987; Hall, Wilson, Humphreys, Tinzman, & Bowyer, 1983; Holligan & Johnston, 1988; Johnston, 1982).

Hulme, Maughan, and Brown (1991) have proposed a two-component theory of short-term memory span. The first component relates to speech rate, which has been interpreted as a measure of how quickly words can be encoded and rehearsed within the articulatory loop. Hulme et al. (1991) consider that their first component reflects the "speed and efficiency of some time-limited, speech based memory mechanism" (McDougall et al., 1994, p.127). Hulme et al. (1991) were also interested in the possibility that another component of memory span reflected the operation of long-term memory mechanisms. Their second short-term memory component was proposed to reflect the use of long-term memory representations of the phonological forms of the words that had to be recalled. Such representations might help in the retrieval of the partially decayed traces of words held in the articulatory loop.

McDougall et al. (1994) studied good and poor readers on measures of memory span, speech rate, and phonological skills. Their results supported a difference between the groups in the efficiency of the speech based components of short-term memory span but no difference in the long-term component of short-term memory span. Moreover speech rate, rather than short-term memory span per se, was the most important predictor of reading skill. One possible conclusion they proposed was that short-term memory capacity itself had little effect upon learning to read, although a closely related process tapped by speech rate was relevant. Certainly, when speech rate was taken account of, short-term memory failed to account for any independent variance in reading ability.

Another measure which is sometimes taken to reflect phonological short-term memory is non-word repetition, even though other factors may contribute to non-word repetition skills (Gathercole & Baddeley, 1993). Snowling (1981) demonstrated that children of low reading ability were impaired in repeating non-words, but had comparable levels of performance in repetition of real words, and this result had been confirmed in other group studies (Brady, Shankweiler, & Mann, 1983; Snowling, Goulandris, Bowlby, & Howell, 1986). Gathercole and Baddeley (1993) reported that in a longitudinal study non-word repetition skills, taken as a measure of phonological short-term memory, were found in pre-readers to be predictive of later reading skill on an early reading test that encouraged the use of letter–sound correspondences. However, there was no association with the rate at which a sight vocabulary was established. There was also no important developmental relationship between phonological memory and reading between the ages of six and eight years. Ellis and Large (1988; Ellis, 1989), also on the basis of longitudinal data, argued that at the age of six years, reading stimulates phonological memory skills, and the two skills then develop in a reciprocal relationship. Gathercole and Baddeley (1993) argued that the Ellis studies also support the view that sight vocabulary may proceed independently of phonological memory factors.

An impaired short-term phonological memory might therefore be most likely for those readers for whom phonological difficulties predominate in reading (see Chapter 5), though even here they are not seen in all cases, for example, the phonological dyslexic HM had a normal digit span (Temple & Marshall, 1983). Similarly, implied causal connections are rendered problematic by those children for whom verbal short-term memory is severely impaired, yet reading development is normal. One such child, Paul (Temple, 1989, 1992b), is discussed in Chapter 7, in relation to his number processing difficulties. He had a digit span of only two, and a word span and letter span of only three.

Yet his reading of both long regular and relatively low frequency irregular words was excellent, and reading skills were at age level. Examples of accurate reading of long regular words included *hectographic, chitterling,* and *integral.* Examples of accurate reading of irregular words included *orchestra, physics, colonel,* and *antique.* There was therefore excellent development of both phonological and lexical aspects of reading, despite the evident deficiencies in short-term memory.

Disorders of the visuo-spatial scratch pad have received little study amongst either adults or children. This may be in part, because this aspect of working memory has been less well specified than the other components. It is therefore harder to predict the potential developmental consequences of a congenital deficiency in this area.

The potential association of the actions of the central executive control system and frontal brain regions has received recent discussion. It is possible that a disorder of the central executive is relevant in some of the attentional disorders of childhood in which there is particular difficulty in sustaining attention on task. However, this is speculative. The influence of higher order control systems potentially subserved by the frontal lobes is discussed further in Chapter 8.

IN CONCLUSION

The lack of description of cases of developmental amnesia in the literature might have suggested that the syndrome does not exist. It could have been that memory systems in children are quite different from those of adults and following a period of reorganisation, adult systems emerge. In this case the selective impairment of memory might simply not have been possible. However, there are a number of instances in the history of neuropsychology where an apparently rare or non-existent disorder becomes of interest and subsequently a large number of cases are described. For example, deep dyslexia was treated with some scepticism when it was first described by Marshall and Newcombe (1966). In fact, many cases of deep dyslexia have been described subsequently and historical searches have also revealed early neglected cases, e.g. Low (1931). The same may be true of developmental amnesia. There may have been an assumption that the condition did not exist, simply because it had not been described in detail. However, it is possible that developmental disorders of memory are very common.

Another complicating factor in their identification may occur for those cases where the most obvious presenting characteristic of the amnesia is a naming difficulty, so that the disorder is perceived as principally that of another system, i.e. language. There is a tendency to focus upon aspects of language more than aspects of memory in routine investigations. For example, the most commonly used international battery for the assessment of intelligence, the WISC, contains a number of measures of language but does not assess memory other than digit span, except indirectly in relation to vocabulary and general knowledge. Recent expansion of the standardised tests available for the assessment of children's memories and increased interest may widen the number of childhood disorders identified in the future.

Despite the difficulty that we have in recalling early events in our childhood, it is now evident that memory systems are active from earliest days. Further they are capable of long lasting storage. They are structured and access is improved with cued retrieval (e.g. Rovee-Collier, 1989). A system ultimately becomes established or emerges which contains clearly differentiated subcomponents. Studies of adult amnesia highlight the different components of memory in adulthood. Short-term memory is intact and procedural memory active, despite the deficits in both retrograde and anterograde memory.

In amnesia in childhood, there is also preservation of procedural skill. The case of Ostergaard (1987; Ostergaard & Squire, 1990) reports this retention of skill in a case of acquired amnesia in childhood. A similar preservation of the mastery of procedural memory is reported in the case description earlier of developmental amnesia. In both the acquired case descriptions and the developmental case, Julia, there were deficits for generalised semantic information. In the developmental form this extended to an impairment in the establishment of semantic representations for individual words and a consequent anomia. This suggests that developmental amnesia may impact upon language development itself. In contrast to cases of adult amnesia, Julia also has an impairment of short term memory, though in a material-specific form. It remains to be seen whether the STM/LTM distinction holds up in other cases of developmental amnesia.

In the case of developmental amnesia reported by De Renzi and Lucchelli (1990) the pattern of impairment differed slightly. Here, despite severe impairments for verbal memory and semantic knowledge, there was normal development of vocabulary. In contrast procedural memory was also impaired. These contrasts in the pattern of the memory impairment reported in the case of Julia and in the case of De Renzi and Lucchelli (1990) raise the interesting possibility that developmental amnesia may take several forms. Further case descriptions of developmental amnesia should enable identification of the range of possible dissociations in terms of preserved and impaired components of memory and enable exploration of the links between memory and language development.

Content-specific memory disorders indicate a modular element in developing memory systems. For Dr S, there is a dissociation between excellent verbal memory but impaired memory for faces, buildings and visual patterns (Temple, 1992b) (Fig. 3.1 and Table 3.1). In the category-specific disorders, there is further division of memory. Such cases illustrate that the different types of memory processes active in children are similar to those seen in adults, with apparent compartmentalisation of some components, leaving open the issue in children as for adults as to whether the compartments are emergent properties of an underlying distributed system or reflect fundamental distinctions between the processes involved in the encoding, storage, or retrieval of the different content areas. Nevertheless, these content-specific disorders are forceful evidence arguing in favour of a structured internal organisation of memory systems in children.

Finally, it is evident from some of the cases described in this chapter that memory and intelligence may be distinct. Processes which we consider to be intelligent can develop in the child with a severe memory disorder. In acquired amnesia, we may find it unsurprising that intelligence can be preserved since the systems of intelligent thought are established prior to the deterioration of memory. In children, it appears that some elements of intelligence do not require memory to become established. This is considerably less self-evident and raises issues about the mechanisms of learning involved in developing, acquiring, or expressing intelligent behaviour.

CHAPTER FOUR

Perceptual and Spatial Disorders

INTRODUCTION

Perceptual and spatial disorders in children have been much less extensively investigated than language disorders. Yet, this does not necessarily reflect differential incidence but may reflect the more salient characteristics of many language disorders, since it may be easier to notice them without explicit testing. Further, the critical role of verbal communication within our culture may lead to the preferential study of such problems. Nevertheless, spatial and perceptual problems may also have significant impact upon a child's development in all spheres of operation: school, home, and social interaction.

This chapter will discuss perceptual and spatial disorders, in relation to the selective impairment of specific aspects of perceptual and spatial systems. The chapter will also discuss syndromes, within which perceptual and spatial disorders are cardinal features. The key questions of interest are similar to those raised in previous chapters. What restrictions are there to developmental plasticity in perceptual and spatial development? Are developmental neuropsychological disorders of perceptual and spatial skill explicable against cognitive models? How independent are different components of perception and spatial skill during development? These questions are variants within a perceptual or spatial domain of the general theoretical questions raised in Chapter 1.

Standard clinical taxonomies such as *DSM-IV* (American Psychiatric Association, 1994) do not recognise perceptual or spatial disorders as self-contained and specific impairments in the way that language disorders are identified, as are reading, writing, arithmetical, and motor disorders. Thus, there is thus no available taxonomy of perceptual and spatial disorders against which to discuss them. In order to provide a background theoretical framework, it is therefore relevant to consider some of the principles about the operation of perceptual and spatial systems accepted within cognitive psychology.

There is evidence that location, form, and motion are processed in separate parallel channels simultaneously. These three areas can be referred to as the "where", "what", and "how" of perception. The anatomical substrates for these channels are complex and potentially overlapping. Studies which have addressed perceptual and spatial disorders in children have focused predominantly upon disorders of the systems involved in the processing of form, e.g. object and face identification and abstract judgements about shape and spatial relationships. However, there are some studies which may be relevant to the issue of location and the processing of "where" an object is positioned and there are new indications of interesting difficulties in the perception of motion, an area for which, even within adult neuropsychology, case reports are sparse.

The range of problems to be reviewed will encompass disorders of visual sensation, disorders in the perception of location, disorders in the perception of movement, and disorders of objects identification and recognition. The perception of location, movement, or form could be impaired by a low-level visual disorder in the processing of visual sensation. The issue of "downstream" effects (see Chapters 1 and 2) may be relevant here. The chapter will therefore begin with a brief discussion of disorders linked to visual sensation: congenital blindness, transient ictal blindness, visual hallucinations, and blindsight. It will then address potential disorder of location: object localisation, navigational disorder, and visual neglect. A necessarily brief section will address disorders in the perception of motion. Included here will be recent studies of the long-term effect of early strabismus. The chapter will then discuss recognition disorders, both for objects and in more detail the analysis of face recognition disorders. Finally, two syndromes will be discussed, within which perceptual and spatial disorders are considered to be dominant characteristics: Turner's syndrome; and Williams syndrome. In relation to these syndromes, there will be particular interest in attempting to identify whether the perceptual and spatial disabilities are generalised or have task-specific impact, and in the latter case whether this integrates with impairment to any particular component of perceptual and spatial skill. Throughout this chapter, the emphasis will be upon disorders of *visual* perception, since, as yet, there has been limited investigation of perceptual and spatial disorders in childhood within other sensory domains.

A brief summary of the physiology and anatomy of the visual pathways will precede the discussion of disorders, since it is relevant to some of the accounts which follow, though this description represents a considerable simplification of current knowledge. The majority of the fibres from the retina project via the dorsal lateral geniculate nucleus (DLGN) to the visual cortex (V1). Within these fibres, one pathway derived from alpha cells in the retina projects to layers of the DLGN that contain large cells, so-called magnocellular layers. From here there is a further projection to specific layers of V1, which is the first area in the cortex to receive visual information. Information from V1 then projects forward to V3, which processes information about form and V5, which is selective to direction and movement. V5 is also sometimes called MT. These sources of information can combine in areas sensitive to dynamic motion in the parietal lobes. A second major pathway is derived from beta cells in the retina. These project to the parvocellular layers of the DLGN, which have smaller neurons than magnocellular areas. There is a further projection to different layers of V1. Information from these layers of V1 projects to layers of V2, which signals form and V4, which signals colour.

There is evidence that the substrate for the alpha pathway in the retina involves Y-cells. These have large receptive fields, respond very quickly and occur more on the periphery of vision. They are sensitive to rapid movement and insensitive to colour. They are sensitive to low contrast and movement. They are attuned to the analysis of low spatial frequency. In contrast 85% of the cells in the fovea are X-cells and these may provide a substrate for the beta cells. They have a slower speed of response and smaller receptive fields and are attuned to the analysis of structure. The Y-cell system may be specialised to make judgements about movement and the X-cell system to make judgements about form.

One per cent of geniculate neurons are intermediate in size between the magnocellular and parvocellular neurons and survive the removal of the visual cortex as they project to other areas. Other cells in the DLGN may project to layer 1 of the cortex, and have properties like W-cells, with large receptive fields and slow speed of activation. There is also a pathway from the retina to the superior colliculus, which may be sensitive to location. There are many other, more minor pathways whose function is not well established (Temple, 1993).

DISORDERS OF PERCEPTUAL SENSATION

Congenital Blindness

In general, children who are congenitally blind have normal intelligence, indicating that visual sensory input is not an essential prerequisite for the development of fundamental intellectual processes. On most measures of verbal function, scores are comparable to those from sighted children, though a number of studies find elevated scores on verbal memory in the congenitally blind (Dekker & Koole, 1992). In contrast, spatial skills are impaired, with poorer performance attained than for those with acquired blindness. Both groups score more poorly than those with partial residual vision (Dekker, Drenth, & Zaal, 1991; Warren, 1974, 1978). The impairments described in those with congenital blindness and those with low vision encompass impairments in the perception of location, movement and identity, suggesting that early vision may be important in the establishment of mental representations for spatial systems, which may be involved in making judgements about the "what", "where", and "how" of objects (Barraga & Morris, 1980; Warren, 1974).

However, Landau (1991; Landau & Gleitman, 1985; Landau, Spelke, & Gleitman, 1984) argues that although the systems for establishing spatial representations of objects may be somewhat less efficient in the young blind child, they are established. Any relative weakness in relation to the sighted child may result from the intrinsic reduction in efficiency of encoding spatial information from the input of the other sensory modalities, rather than arising as a consequence of an impairment in the construction of mental representations themselves.

In a series of experiments, Landau (1991) demonstrated that blind toddlers of 18 months actively explore objects with their hands like sighted children. Their patterns of exploration were similar in that they fingered new textures and both rotated and handled new shapes. They became familiar with the objects, as shown by habituation and then responded to novelty created by a change in shape or texture with increased exploration. Although they took longer to habituate than sighted children and their patterns of shape exploration were more diffuse, perhaps because haptic skills are more biased towards the exploration of texture than shape, their naturally developed exploratory activities could enable the extraction of enough information to construct and transform spatial representations. Landau (1991) showed that by 2;6 the blind child could integrate the haptic exploration with an established system of mental representation, to enable the rapid identification of familiar shapes, distinguishing squares, triangles, and circles, as well as the textures rough, bumpy, and smooth. Some of the geometric figures used in the shape items were too large for the child to explore the entire object at once, yet the blind child was still able to identify them, presumably by building up the geometrical figures from the limited information conveyed by the exploration of critical segments such as corners and circle segments. By the age of three years, the blind child could construct a mental representation of a novel object sufficiently well to recognise that object when it was rotated 180°, either top to bottom or right to left.

Thus, Landau (1991) attributes the reported weakness in the spatial skills of blind children to the differential efficiency of the haptic system, which may be designed to extract texture rather than shape, whereas the visual system may be designed to extract shape (Biederman, 1985). This might lead to representations of shape which are more fragile in the blind than in the sighted person (Landau, 1991).

Pring (1987, 1992; Pathak & Pring, 1989; Pring & Rusted, 1985) has explored both drawing and tactile picture recognition in blind children. Pring and Rusted (1985) found that blind children had significant difficulty in recognising tactile pictures, with a tendency to substitute objects which share a prominent perceptual feature (e.g. a flower for a toothbrush, which both share a "stalk" and a "head"). However, if the children were given a cue, such as being told that a chair was a piece of furniture, their object recognition improved significantly (Pring, 1987). The blind child Sally, reported in detail by Pring (1992), who became blind at the age of 15 months, performed like the blind children described earlier, having difficulty with tactile pictures unless she was given a cue. However, she could match a spoken verbal label to a picture with ease. Sally was also able to draw many items successfully. However, her descriptions of these drawings were dominated by their structural appearance, whereas a control subject produced descriptions of her drawings which contained more functional elements, integrating her knowledge of the objects. Thus, Sally appeared to process drawings by their structural appearance and when this was not precise enough to enable an exact identification, her performance was restricted. Her conceptual knowledge did not seem to be able to compensate for the limitations in the perceptual input. Pring (1992) suggested the extraction of tactile information demands the allocation of considerable attention, which may lead to neglect of semantics and context. It may lack sufficient precision without a guided search in a known context. Further feedback from continual perceptual analysis is less available. This may lead to a more fractionated mental activity where the effortful perceptual analysis is less well integrated with semantic and contextual processing.

Transient Ictal Blindness

Transient ictal blindness refers to the loss of visual sensation, with sudden onset, associated with an epileptic fit. Such disorders are of interest as they present a sort of transient global blindness on a par with the transient global amnesia described in adulthood (Hodges & Ward, 1989). The theoretical interest is in the impact of such sudden sensory impairment upon a perceptual system which has in principle developed normally.

In adults, visual phenomena are sometimes experienced before, after, or during seizures. Before a seizure, these usually consist of an aura of positive sensations of light, colour, or pattern. Visual loss is less common, though occasionally reported. Penfield and Kristiansen (1951) found that in a study of over 200 patients with epilepsy, only 4% had a visual aura as an initial symptom of a seizure. Where subjects are restricted to those with EEGs implicating the occipital lobes, the incidence of a visual aura becomes much higher, reaching 47% in the study of Ludwig and Marsan (1975).

In children, EEG abnormalities of the occipital lobes are more common than in adults and visual auras have also been reported in childhood epilepsy. Smith and Kellaway (1963) studied 452 children with occipital epileptic foci and reported a pre-ictal aura of either flashing lights or blindness in 9.1%.

In adulthood, post-ictal blindness in all or part of the visual field has been reported more frequently than blindness as an aura. It may last from a few hours to a few days (Harris, 1897; Sadeh, Goldhammer, & Kuritzky, 1983; Skolik, Mizen, & Burde, 1987). An early report of post-ictal cortical blindness in children is given by Ashby and Stephenson (1903). The blindness was prolonged but reversible and occurred following severe febrile seizures in which there was generalised status epilepticus, followed by coma. More recently, Olurin (1970) has also reported cortical blindness after severe febrile convulsions in childhood, though the phenomena is not restricted to this type of convulsion and has been reported following other types of seizure (Kosnik, Paulson, & Laguna, 1976). The duration may vary from a few hours (Kosnik et al., 1976) to a few weeks (Pritchard, 1918) and the basis for the longer lasting effects is not known.

Blindness during seizure activity has also been reported occasionally, in association with occipital lobe EEG abnormalities. Ayala (1929) reported the case of a 13-year-old girl for whom blindness was triggered by photic stimulation which also induced EEG spiking. Strauss (1963) found occipital lobe abnormality in the EEG of an 11-year-old boy with ictal blindness and preserved consciousness. The blindness lasted for only a few minutes. Zung and Margolith (1993) describe a seven-year-old boy with ictal blindness. The seizure activity had a bilateral occipital focus on EEG, but the behavioural effects did not include any motor or postural alterations, nor headache, nor disturbance of consciousness. There was however a sensation of loud noise, fear associated with the loss of vision, and "pain in the eyes". There was no family history of migraine or epilepsy, nor any such history for the child. Both CT scan and ophthalmological examinations were normal. Post-ictally there was abrupt and complete visual recovery with no post-ictal phenomena.

Thus, young children may experience transient global blindness before, during, or after seizure activity as a result of the localised disruption of visual circuitry. It appears that such transient disruption has no long-term impact upon the development of perceptual and spatial systems. The possible restrictions in the degree of spatial skill which follow congenital blindness therefore either relate to the sustained absence of visual information or the severe reduction of visual input during a critical period.

The studies of ictal blindness are also of interest as they directly implicate the occipital lobes and not other areas. This confirms that cortical specialisation for visual processing in the occipital lobes is established early in childhood.

Blindsight
Patients who have damage to the primary visual areas, the striate cortex, report that they are blind in a region of the visual field and have no conscious awareness of being able to see anything in this portion of the visual field. Nevertheless, some of these patients are able to detect and localise targets within their area of subjective blindness. This phenomenon is referred to as blindsight (Poppel, Held, & Frost, 1973; Weiskrantz, 1987).

Braddick, Atkinson, Hood, Harkness, Jackson, and Vargha-Khadem (1992) report a similar phenomenon in two infants who had each had one cerebral hemisphere removed, in an attempt to control intractable myoclonic epilepsy caused by congenital abnormality of one hemisphere (megalencephaly). PP was four months old when the right hemisphere was removed and testing was conducted 3–7 months later. LAH was eight months old when the left hemisphere was removed and testing was carried out 8–10 months later. In both cases surgery included removal of both striate and extra-striate visual cortex.

Post-operatively, the infants were visually alert, had a full range of eye movements and had normal visual acuity for their ages. Informally both children ignored a toy presented in the "blind field". Nevertheless, single conspicuous targets in the "blind field" could elicit fixations. The authors suggest that, just as in blindsight in adulthood, a subcortical visual system including the superior colliculus could be involved in enabling the detection and orienting responses. As Braddick et al. (1992) note, the presence of these responses in such young children argues against their being a response reflecting the acquisition of a special strategy or the impact of plasticity.

Visual Hallucinations

The following description of visual hallucinations in childhood represents both a reciprocal of blindness and of blindsight. In both blindness and blindsight (assuming that infant subjective experience here is similar to adults), there is no subjective awareness of a stimulus that is present. In visual hallucinations, there is subjective awareness of a stimulus that is not present. In blindness or blindsight, there is inability to "see" what is present because of reduced sensory input or impaired visual cortical mechanisms. In visual hallucinations, objects are seen that are not present, possibly because of increased activation of critical circuitry, resulting from the effects of invasive surgery to the occipital lobes.

Charles Bonnet syndrome normally involves visual hallucinations in elderly subjects following deterioration of vision. In this syndrome there is no psychiatric disorder and intellect is intact (Bonnet, 1769). Lepore (1990) studied over a hundred cases of retinal or neural visual loss and found reports of visual phenomena in 57%.

White and Jan (1992) reported Charles Bonnet syndrome in a child of 3;6, following surgery to debulk a tumour involving the optic radiation, which was detected on CT at 11 months. The surgery resulted in complete blindness. CT showed reduction in tumour size. There were no seizures or episodes of fever and no medication was taken. Nevertheless one week post-operatively, visual hallucinations were experienced of people, including the child's brother and Santa Claus, animals, and other familiar objects. The hallucinations were experienced in both visual fields and moved about. They thus affected both the "what" and the "how" systems of perception. They lasted for three days, disappearing only when the child was asleep. For this child, the hallucinations were complex, continuous and occurred in the context of sudden total loss of vision. The authors interpret them as "release phenomena", similar to those seen in normal adults following sensory deprivation (Heron, Doane, & Scott, 1956). However, this explanation might lead to the expectation that the hallucination would become more severe and disturbing as the sensory deprivation (blindness) continued. In contrast, after three days the hallucinations disappeared completely. It is therefore more probable that the surgery led to a residual increase in stimulation of the network circuitry underlying the mental images associated with the child's brother, Santa Claus, etc. PET studies indicate that for adults the superior occipital cortex is specifically involved in the generation and maintenance of visual mental images (Mellet, Tzourio, Denis, & Mazoyer, 1995). In the White and Jan (1992) study, the surgery involved the occipital lobes, suggesting some similar region specialisation for mental images has been established in children by the age of 3;6.

White and Jan (1992) note that visual hallucinations in childhood could be more common than reports suggest since if they occur in infancy the child may not be able to describe clearly or articulate their presence and adults may misinterpret their complaints.

DISORDERS IN THE PERCEPTION OF LOCATION

Object Localisation

A case study of a developmental deficit in localising objects from vision has recently been described (McCloskey et al., 1995). AH was a 20-year-old right-handed college student. Her EEG and MRI showed no neurological abnormalities. Visual acuity, visual fields, and contrast sensitivity were all normal. In copying designs, she would depict all of the component parts of the figures but made many errors of location or orientation. As a consequence, her performance was significantly impaired, in relation to standard norms. Reproducing figures from memory did not produce any further decline in performance and the authors suggested that short-term memory for location and orientation was intact.

As part of an art class, AH visited a gallery and copied Renoir's *The Luncheon of the Boating Party*, which depicts a number of people wearing straw hats. Her placement of a centrally located hat was correct but all the hats appearing on the left-hand side of the painting were drawn on the right and vice versa.

In formal testing of visual localisation, AH had to move a computer mouse to indicate the location of an X which had been presented on the monitor for 250msec. The control error rate was 0.6%, but AH's error rate was 36–57%. All the errors were left–right or up–down confusions. In a ballistic reaching task (i.e. without changing direction mid-movement), the error rate of 66% reflected reaches to the wrong side of the midline. Performance was significantly worse than chance. The vast majority of the errors, preserved the correct distance and eccentricity, but simply erred in the left–right direction. Thus, the visual system was systematically computing the incorrect location. McCloskey et al. (1995) suggested that this indicated mental location representations have an internal structure with discrete components. The component representing the direction of displacement from the reference axis may be represented independently of the other components such as eccentricity and in this case the displacement component is impaired, whilst other components remain intact.

When permitted to change direction during the movement, AH could reach with accuracy, so that the deficit did not significantly impair her day-to-day life. Moreover, in contrast to her performance with visual stimuli, her localisation from auditory, kinaesthetic, and tactile information was intact. Her identification of the object for which she showed the impaired ballistic reaching was also intact. The impairment is thus selective for location but not identification; for vision but not for other modalities; and for ballistic but not corrected reaching.

Interestingly, although detection of location was poor with high contrast, stationary stimuli of longer duration, it was better with brief, moving, or low contrast visual stimuli, suggesting that there may be a dissociation between visual subsystems, with greater impairment in parvocellular circuits than magnocellular circuits.

Navigational Disorder

Whereas object location requires the identification of a single spatial area, with possible reaching to that location, navigational skill requires the ability to orient one's self in space in relation to an established spatial map. On the basis of animal studies, septal areas appear to be implicated in navigation.

Septal lesions in rats lead to a disturbance of their navigational ability (Miller, Innes, & Enloe, 1977). In contrast, septal transplants for rats with damaged septal-hippocampal connections lead to improvements in navigational skill (Segal, Greenberger, & Pearl, 1989). Congenital disorder of septal systems in children is found when optic nerve hypoplasia (underdevelopment) is combined with congenital absence of the septum pellucidum, a pairing first reported by Reeves (1941).

Griffiths and Hunt (1984) describe a blind adolescent with optic nerve hypoplasia and congenital absence of the septum pellucidum, for whom egocentric spatial skills were investigated, i.e. his knowledge of spatial location in relation to his own position. They argued that their case demonstrated a substantial impairment in both the retention and implementation of patterns of body movement, impairing navigational performance. However, Groenveld, Pohl, Espezel, and Jan (1994) studied 17 children with optic nerve hypoplasia, 12 of whom had a septum pellucidum and 5 of whom did not. They assessed navigational ability on the basis of response to a 10-item questionnaire regarding spatial ability, which was given to caretakers. On this relatively crude measure, the authors report no differences in spatial navigational abilities between the group with and the group without the septum pellucidum. However, their subject data are complicated by the inclusion of several children with limited intellectual ability and, as the authors themselves note, those with poorest navigational scores also have the lowest verbal IQ scores. When subjects with IQs below 80 are removed from their data, there is a trend in favour of greater disruption of spatial skills in those without the septum pellucidum, in relation to those with the septum pellucidum. More detailed cognitive analyses of individual cases will be required to clarify the issue.

Potentially, navigational skills could be disrupted by either an impairment in egocentric orientation or an impairment in establishing and using an internal spatial map of the world. The role of the hippocampus in any developmental disorder of navigational ability has been neither determined nor to my knowledge discussed. Yet, the suggestion that the hippocampus forms a cognitive map incorporating a geometrical representation of the world was made by O'Keefe and Nadel (1978). It is known that neurons sensitive to place and direction are present in distinct regions of the hippocampus. Further, there is an allometric relationship between place learning and hippocampal structure. Damage to the hippocampal formation also impairs place learning (Morris, Garrud, Rawlins, & O'Keefe, 1982). Together, this evidence indicates that allometric spatial learning is subserved by the hippocampus. The stability of markers in the real world is critical in order to establish such a representation (Biegler & Morris, 1993). Amongst those children who have had unilateral temporal lobectomies for the relief of intractable epilepsy, there should be cases with hippocampal damage who could be investigated in relation to their navigational skill, though the presence of general memory problems in such groups (see Chapter 3) might mask any such specific effects.

Both clinical and day-to-day experience suggests that impairments in navigational skill may be relatively common. It awaits a more systematic analysis of these disorders to determine whether they take a similar form or whether there is evidence of a modular organisation within the components of navigational skill itself. For example, hippocampal abnormality might lead to an impaired ability to establish a spatial map, whereas septal abnormality might lead to impaired ability to guide oneself along a route through space in relation to the spatial map.

Visual Neglect
Judgements of location, in relation to a spatial frame, may be impaired if disproportionate weighting is given to part of the frame. In adults,

overemphasis and underemphasis in relation to areas of visual space is associated with a series of behaviours called visual neglect. The syndrome of visual neglect has been the focus of considerable interest, within adult cognitive neuropsychology. However, case studies of children exhibiting neglect have been sparse. The syndrome has been described following intracerebral haemorrhage in childhood (Ferro, Martins, & Tavora, 1984). The three cases described by Ferro et al. (1984) all had right hemisphere lesions.

Case 1 was six years old. She failed to respond to threatening gestures from the left side, and failed to notice people coming or talking to her from the left. When writing, she neglected the left half of sentences or words and used only the right part of the paper. On Benton's Visual Retention Test, in which a series of designs with a main and peripheral figure have to be copied and recalled, she often omitted or distorted the figures appearing in the left periphery. In a cancellation task, in which a large set of small lines scattered randomly across a page at varying angles have to be crossed out, she missed lines on the left-hand side. On simultaneous tactile stimulation, she failed to notice stimuli on the left, and on dichotic listening she demonstrated left-channel extinction. Two weeks after the onset of her neglect symptoms, they had resolved.

Case 2 was a nine-year-old boy who displayed left hemi-spatial inattention on a line cancellation task, performed at the bedside. One month later, neglect was no longer evident.

Case 3 was a five-year-old boy who displayed left hemi-spatial neglect on cancellation and line bisection. On a task of repeated movements, with both hands, the left hand would gradually stop moving. There was left-channel extinction on dichotic listening. Surgery was performed for a right hemisphere meningioma. One month post-operatively, the neglect on line cancellation and bisection had resolved, although left-channel extinction continued on dichotic listening.

Such a syndrome of neglect had not been reported following left hemisphere injury in childhood and since their cases all had right hemisphere lesions, Ferro et al. (1984) interpreted their results as indicating right hemisphere control over the direction of selective attention, in parallel to some interpretations of neglect following right hemisphere lesions in adulthood. They noted that this apparent specialisation of the right hemisphere had appeared by the age of five years. They also noted the rapid recovery seen in each case and speculated that the sparse report of the syndrome in childhood may result from such rapid recovery, the usual absence of testing for neglect in childhood, and the potential to attribute the behavioural effects of neglect to an impairment of visual fields.

Thompson, Ewing-Cobbs, Fletcher, Miner, and Levin (1991) describe left unilateral neglect in a pre-school child, BL, following a relatively early right hemisphere injury, at the age of 3;8. The injury was sustained in a car accident. CT revealed right frontal and right posterior temporo-parietal contusions. There was also diffuse cerebral atrophy. Evaluation took place two weeks after the accident.

There was a marked tendency to attend to objects presented in his right visual field, but to neglect those presented in the left. When the child was asked to point to a body part, for example, an ear or an eye, he consistently pointed to those on the right. If he was then asked to point to his other ear or eye, he failed to respond. On drawing tasks, drawings were also displaced to the right.

The authors designed a test to assess attention in the pre-school period. They used 12 line drawings of animals, eight of which were selected as targets. The child was presented with a target picture individually and asked to name it. He was then presented with an array of all the items arranged in three rows of four columns and asked to find the animal that had just been named. The target presentation was randomised so that the targets appeared with equal frequency on the left and on the right, within the array.

Five normal children aged between 3;4 and 4;10 acted as controls. All the control children, except one, were correct on all trials. One child made a single error. The average control time to locate targets on the right was 4.8s (range 2–10s) and on the left was 4.1s (range 2–9s).

BL correctly located all four of the targets on the right of the array. His average response latency was 35s (range 2–60s). However, he was unable to locate any of the targets on the left of the array, despite searching for an average of a minute and a half for each stimulus.

Four days later, performance had improved but neglect was still evident. BL was now able to locate all four targets on the right in an average of 9s. He was also able to locate two of the four left-sided items in 30 and 75s. Tested six months after his injury, his left neglect had resolved, although attentional and other cognitive difficulties persisted.

The authors point out that these results, following right hemisphere injury, in a pre-school child suggest that right hemisphere systems may subserve visually guided attention from an early age. Nevertheless, there was fairly rapid resolution of the disorder.

Weintraub and Mesulam (1983) discuss developmental learning disabilities which they consider reflect abnormalities of the right hemisphere. They suggest that in some cases the syndrome is genetically determined, as the characteristics of some of their patients also reported in other close family relatives. Amongst the specific disorders they discuss, they mention unilateral neglect. Thus, for example, case 2 tended to avoid the left side of the page when writing, leaving an unusually large margin, with successive movement to the right of the page and avoidance of the left, as the text progressed down the page. The same avoidance of the left side of the page was seen in a letter written by the mother of case 2. Case 3 described a 42-year-old former nun, who had a history of seizures, possible precipitated by a head injury after falling from her bicycle at the age of eight. She had a tendency to be inattentive to the left visual field. When presented with an array of letters and asked to find all the As, she omitted 8/30 targets on the left but only 2/30 on the right. Case 2 is suggestive of developmental neglect. Case 3 could reflect developmental neglect or an acquired disorder of neglect in childhood which has been sustained into adulthood.

Left hemispatial inattention has also been documented in congenitally hemiplegic children, for whom brain injury precedes birth (Heller & Levine, 1989). Thus, left neglect is not simply evident as a consequence of acquired right hemisphere lesions in childhood.

However, in contrast to the view that right hemisphere systems dominate in the control of guided attention, right hemispatial inattention after extensive left parieto-occipital injury has also been documented in a child of 14 years of age, following injury in infancy (Johnston & Shapiro, 1986). This case exemplifies the potential long-term attentional sequelae, from an early injury but also suggests that each hemisphere has control over attention in the contralateral field and that right neglect can occur as well as left neglect. This parallels the picture in adulthood, though in adults neglect following right hemisphere lesions is much more common. Amongst children there may be too few cases as yet to reach a clear conclusion but the majority of childhood cases with a unilateral basis have sustained right hemisphere lesions.

Behaviour which could be interpreted as mild visual neglect, which appears as a consequence of bilateral lesions but is explained in terms of a right hemisphere attentional system is reported by Craft, White, Park, and Figiel, 1994. Craft et al. (1994) studied 33 children who had bilateral perinatal injury, in a follow-up at an average age of six–seven years. The task employed was a visual orienting task (Posner, 1980) in which subjects responded to the appearance of a target, following a cue. Children with bilateral anterior lesions were significantly slower than normal children, and reaction times to validly cued targets in the right field were slow. Children with bilateral posterior lesions were generally slower than normal. Craft et al. (1994) argue that their results suggest that anterior brain areas have a significant role in the development of visual attention. However, they also argue that their results integrate with the view that there is an early dominance of right hemisphere attentional processes, noting that such biases have been reported in normal infants. A bias to orient to the left could lead to inattention to right visual field cues and thereby produced slowing of right field responses.

Developmental visual neglect following a midline abnormality has been described in a child with callosal agenesis (Temple & Ilsley, 1994). A line bisection paradigm was employed. When normal subjects carry out this task, they tend to make a slight error bisecting the line a little to the left of the true centre. One interpretation of this effect called "pseudo-neglect", again relates to a greater involvement of the right hemisphere in the control and orientation of attention, than the left hemisphere. This, right hemisphere dominance could cause slightly greater significance to be attached to the left-hand side of the visual field, thereby leading to an overestimation of the size of the left-hand side of the lines and a pattern of bisecting slightly to the left of the true centre.

The pattern of pseudo-neglect in normal 14-year-old children when asked to bisect lines presented horizontally across the midline, with their centres in the middle of the visual field, is illustrated in Fig. 4.1A. This shows the performance of eight control children, each of whom participated in eight trials of line bisection per line length, using the right hand. The lines varied in length from 2cm to 20cm and were randomly ordered. If there was a similar proportion of error on each line, then the connecting line through the responses would be straight. Errors consistent enough to appear in the averaged data, show a trend to bisection to the left of centre, thereby exhibiting "right pseudo-neglect".

In comparison, for the acallosal MJ, tested at the age of 14, instead of right pseudo-neglect, there is evidence of left neglect (see Fig. 4.1B). The lines are bisected to the right of the midline rather than the left and the magnitude of the error is greater than for controls. If the right hemisphere is controlling the orientation of attention, Temple and Ilsley (1994) speculate that when the right hand is employed under the control of the left hemisphere, the deficient callosal connections might prohibit full integration with these right hemisphere attentional systems. They hypothesised that if the lines were presented in the right hemispace, this would make the neglect worse, by increasing still further the proposed disconnection from the right hemisphere, since in right hemispace the lines would at least initially project to the left hemisphere. In contrast, if the lines were presented in the left hemispace it would reduce the neglect, since the lines would be in the space more directly controlled by the right hemisphere. They found that with lines in the right hemispace the neglect did become more exaggerated, as predicted (see Fig. 4.1C), supporting the interpretation of an increased disconnection from the right hemisphere attentional system. In left space, with lines up to 10cm in length, the neglect reduces, as predicted, to the normal size and direction of "pseudo-neglect". These results substantiate an interpretation based upon disconnection of attentional mechanisms. However, with longer lines in the left hemispace, a clear right neglect becomes evident, which lies outside the control range (see Fig. 4.1D). Although this could also reflect disrupted attentional mechanisms, it is harder to interpret in relation to the simple mechanisms. The results therefore only partially substantiated a disconnection in attentional control mechanisms, though they indicated abnormality in the development of mechanisms involved in the control and orientation of attention in space.

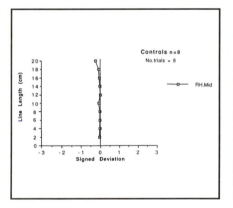

FIG. 4.1A.

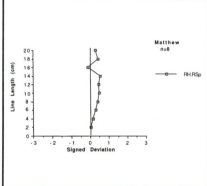

FIG. 4.1C.

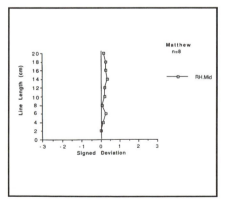

FIG. 4.1B.

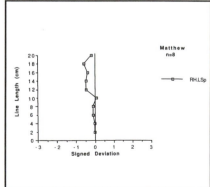

FIG. 4.1D.

This discussion of visual neglect in childhood has considered only attentional explanations. For a discussion and integration of alternative theories of neglect in adulthood including perceptual, representational, intentional, and premotor, see Halligan and Marshall (1994). They suggest that neglect in adulthood can be accounted for in relation to two conceptually independent properties: the bias of each hemisphere to orient to contralateral space; and the association of focal processing strategies with the left hemisphere and global processing strategies with the right hemisphere. There has been an insufficient range of testing of the childhood cases of neglect to enable a theoretical integration of the Halligan and Marshall (1994) ideas within development.

DISORDERS OF MOTION PERCEPTION

A recent case report of a child with good binocular visual acuity but a severe impairment in the perception of movement is given by Ahmed and Dutton (1996). Looking at the garden, she could see a stationary cat or rabbit but not a moving cat or rabbit. When her school taxi arrived she could only see it when it stopped. She appears to have akinetopsia, similar to that described by Zihl, Von Cramon, and Mai (1983), and Zeki (1991).

Strabismus

Strabismus (heterotropia) is the formal term for a squint, i.e. any abnormal alignment of the two eyes. Most often the misalignment is horizontal. When strabismus occurs early in infancy, there are permanent deficits in both binocularity (Mohindra, Zwaan, Held, Brill, & Zwaan, 1985) and visual motion perception, with difficulty in judging the speed of moving targets (e.g. Hess & Anderson, 1993; Schor & Levi, 1980; Tychsen & Lisberger, 1986). Specifically, targets moving in a temporal-nasal direction are perceived as moving faster than in reality, whereas targets moving in a nasal-temporal direction are perceived as moving slower than in reality (Tychsen & Lisberger, 1986). Adults with strabismus also perceive unilateral motion when viewing counterphase gratings, that remain stationary but reverse in contrast several times per second (Wang & Norcia, 1992). Normal subjects do not perceive such motion.

In normal adult primates, the visual cortex contains balanced and antagonistic populations of directionally selective neurons (Albright, Desimone, & Gross, 1984; Levinson & Sekuler, 1975; Maunsell & van Essen, 1983) and the perception of motion in viewing the counterphase gratings experienced by humans with early onset strabismus could reflect an imbalance in the responsiveness of opposing sets of such neurons. The possibility that these deficits reflect maldevelopment of directionally sensitive neurons was explored by Tychsen, Rastelli, Steinman, and Steinman (1996). They note that magnocellular neurons, which provide major input to motion sensitive pathways, develop earlier than parvocellular neurons (Burkhalter, Bernardo, & Charles, 1993) and may therefore be more susceptible to disruption in infancy. They predict that, on this basis, those with early onset strabismus should have greater abnormalities in motion perception than those with late onset strabismus. They also predict that since motion sensitive neurons are sensitive to low rather than high spatial frequencies (van Essen, Anderson, & Felleman, 1992), the deficit in motion perception should be more apparent with low spatial frequencies. Further, since the neurons underlying motion detection also underlie eye movements, stimulation of the directionally biased motion neurons should also generate directionally biased eye movements. All three predictions were upheld in studies using counterphase gratings: the motion perception abnormalities were greater for those with early onset strabismus than for those with late onset strabismus; the deficit was more marked with low spatial frequencies; and directionally biased eye movements were induced by some of the gratings.

They conclude by suggesting that the strabismus affects the binocular driven, direction sensitive neurons of lamina 4B and 6 in striate cortex, which are known to be abnormally connected in primates who have infantile strabismus (Tychsen, Lisberger, & Burkhalter, 1995). In relation to the visual channels discussed previously, those with stabismus have intact channels for establishing identity and recognising objects but an impaired channel for motion detection. Perception of location is thought to be intact except where binocularity is required.

RECOGNITION DISORDERS

Visual Object Agnosia

Following brain injury or disease, adult neurological patients may experience visual agnosia, which is a difficulty in recognising objects by sight which cannot be explained on the basis of visual impairment or intellectual difficulties. Reports of developmental visual agnosia in children have been rare. However, whether this reflects the rarity of the condition or its tendency to be overlooked or misclassified as a peripheral visual impairment is unclear. Gordon (1968) describes two children with object recognition disorders associated with convulsive disorders. One of the children, with occipito-temporal EEG abnormalities, had no difficulty with object recognition if pictures were presented individually, but had difficulties if several pictures were presented simultaneously. The case resembles descriptions of simultanagnosia in adults. The other child had bilateral occipital EEG abnormalities and had object recognition skills that were impaired if the objects were large. Neither of these cases is a particularly convincing example of a pure object agnosia (Young & Ellis, 1992). More clear-cut cases of developmental face recognition disorders have been documented.

Prosopagnosia

Prosopagnosia was described by Bodamer in 1947. It involves an inability to recognise familiar people from their faces. The prosopagnosic is able to indicate that a face is a face, but is not able to indicate the identity of the face. In severe cases, the problem may extend to a disorder in recognising close family and friends. The difficulty with recognition is restricted to problems in identifying faces. The ability to use other cues to identification such as a person's voice, gait, or clothing, is usually preserved. Prosopagnosia is a relatively unusual disorder following neurological injury. The anatomical basis is disputed, but bilateral occipito-inferotemporal lesions have been implicated. The necessity for a bilateral lesion is still under debate. There is also argument about the specificity of the disorder, with other forms of visual recognition often also impaired. Nevertheless, the case described by De Renzi (1986) appears to have recognition difficulties, specific to faces.

Recognition disorders including prosopagnosia have been described by cognitive neuropsychologists, in relation to information processing models of object and face recognition. These models incorporate elements of the theory of visual perception proposed by Marr (1976, 1980, 1982), within which objects are recognised using at least three levels of description. At the first level, texture, gradations of light, and discontinuities are coded in a primal sketch. The second stage incorporates descriptions of the structures of objects which are said to be viewer-centred. This is called the "2½D" level, and it is dependent upon the angle of the viewer. When the viewer moves, the "2½D" representation also changes. The third level in Marr's model is independent of the viewer's position. It is called the 3D level of representation and is said to be object-centred. At the 3D level there must be stored descriptions of the variable appearance of objects. This level of representation is essential for object constancy and to enable us to recognise unusual or partially obscured views of objects.

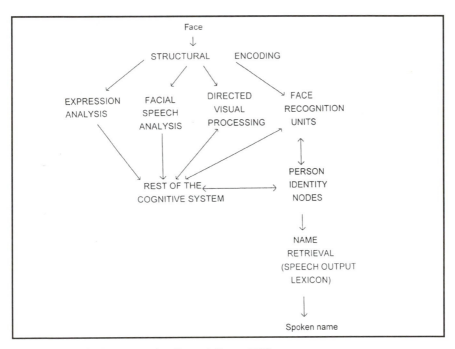

FIG. 4.2 Model for face processing (Bruce & Young, 1986).

A Model of Face Processing

A structural model of face processing, against which face recognition disorders can be interpreted, has been proposed by Bruce and Young (1986) (see Fig. 4.2). This model does not make explicit the distinction between initial representations, viewer-centred representations, and object-centred representations. Instead it described a general process of structural encoding which includes these processes and which gains access to established face recognition units. Face recognition units are established during the course of our everyday life and each unit corresponds to a particular person's face. The units have thresholds of activation. When a face is seen, there will be an increase in activity in all the units representing faces which resemble it but only the unit which corresponds to the viewed face will be fully activated. This unit should reach threshold and "fire", triggering a corresponding person identity node, containing personal information about an individual which identifies them. This includes their personal characteristics, and factual pieces of information about the person such as their occupation or nationality. In order to retrieve the name of someone, their person identity node must first be activated, which should then trigger the name, though it is possible that partial activation of this knowledge may be sufficient for name retrieval (Brennen, David, Fluchaire, & Pellat, 1996).

Following structural encoding, parallel systems to those activating the face recognition units are utilised for the simultaneous extraction of information about expression and therefore the mood and affect of the person viewed, and for directed visual processing, which may make judgements about the similarities and differences between the faces of unfamiliar people. Facial speech analysis, employed in lip-reading, is also extracted in parallel.

The Development of Face Processing
In the first minutes of life, when no prior experience of learning faces has occurred, infants show preferences for faces over other visual stimuli. This suggests that faces are special and that at birth the infant has available some structural information relating to the broad characteristics associated with faces, possibly programmed within a primitive pathway linked to the control of orienting (Johnson & Morton, 1991). Such a system would provide a stimulus to the development of face processing skills, ultimately resulting in the highly specialised mechanism seen in adulthood, as an emergent property of the preferential face looking, and anatomical and environmental constraints. Such a view would be compatible with emergent modularity. Developmental prosopagnosia would then arise if "something" precluded the effective development of face processing modules. In this case, one might expect developmental prosopagnosia to always coexist with some other hypothetical problems in visual analysis. A more preformist view, would suggest that a region in the right hemisphere around the superior temporal sulcus is genetically programmed to form a dedicated face processing system. Damage or malfunction of this area at or pre-birth, or to similar bilateral areas if there is bilateral involvement in face processing (e.g. Damasio & Damasio, 1986) could then result in developmental prosopagnosia (e.g. Campbell, 1992; de Haan & Campbell, 1991; McConachie, 1976; Temple, 1992b) discussed below. In support of more preformist views, PET studies reported by Mancini, de Schonen, Deruelle, and Massoulier (1994) indicated that face stimuli but not other visual stimuli activated the external temporal cortex and parts of the inferotemporal cortex in two-month-old infants. In infants aged 4–10 months, the right hemisphere is also more efficient than the left hemisphere at face recognition (de Schonen, de Diaz, & Mathivet, 1986; de Schonen & Mathivet, 1990).

The Fodorian view would require that a modular system for face processing used specialised neural machinery, without the influence of a central semantic system or other modules, i.e. it should be information encapsulated. However, Rhodes and Tremewan (1993) found that semantic priming across modalities eased the decision process for famous/non-famous face discriminations. For example, names primed face targets which could not arise from associative links within a strict face module. Thus, factors from the cognitive system influence the sensitivity of face recognition units (Bruce & Young, 1986). The sensitivity priming effects of Rhodes and Tremewan (1993) would also be consistent with spreading activation effects within a network of face representations. With the variations in the contemporary usage of the concept module, a network of face representations could itself be considered a module.

Fodor's concept of domain specificity may also be violated with regard to face processing. It has been argued that other homogeneous classes of stimuli use the specialised computational processes for faces, as expertise develops. For example, the recognition of birds by ornithologists might use this system (Diamond & Carey, 1986; Rhodes & McLean, 1990). This does not mean that the system did not develop as a dedicated face processing system but simply that it is capable nevertheless of processing other forms of complex visual information for which considerable expertise has become established.

Face recognition skills in children are said to improve to the age of 10 years, plateau to the age of 14 years, with a possible decline at the age of 12 years, and then increase again in competence to an adult level. The existence, timing, and possible theoretical explanation for this plateau, dip, and rise have been debated. Carey and Diamond (1977; Carey, 1978) claimed that face recognition improved up to the age of 10 years because young children encode predominantly piecemeal details from unfamiliar faces, whereas older children and adults rely mainly on configuration information. Flynn (1985) has disputed such a conclusion, claiming that floor effects in Carey's data contaminate the results and that the tendency of young children incorrectly to select paraphernalia cues as a basis for identity judgements is dependent upon the similarity of faces paired in each trial. The precise timing of the putative "dip" in performance varies across studies. Its earliest maximum is reported between 11 and 12 years (Flynn, 1980). In contrast, Carey, Diamond, and Woods (1980) report the dip between the ages of 12 and 14 years. Investigating encoding and storage effects in memory for faces in children, Ellis and Flynn (1990) suggest that improvement of 10-year-olds over 7-year-olds,may relate to differences in the degree of initial encoding. Young children may encode only a small amount of basic facial information which is relatively resilient to decay or interference, whereas older children may encode more information and utilise better strategies in encoding. Such improvement could result as discussed earlier, from the maturation or development of a face processing module, albeit one without the strict domain specificity specified by Fodor. One could also propose that the improvement results not from any development in a face recognition module per se but from the influence of improved executive processes upon memory more generally, leading to better strategic encoding.

Acquired Prosopagnosia in Childhood

Amongst adults with neurological injury, prosopagnosic disorders have been described in relation to failures at several different stages within the Bruce and Young (1986) model. A case of acquired prosopagnosia in a child has also been documented by Young and Ellis (1989). The child's disorder followed meningitis and hydrocephalus, at the age of 14 months. She was unable to recognise familiar faces, even her own mother, but used voices effectively as an aid to recognition, so a person identification system had become established. She knew that a stimulus was a face, could match photographs of faces using a feature by feature strategy and could comprehend facial expressions to a reasonable degree.

The difficulties did not occur in isolation. There were also difficulties with object recognition. Her object recognition showed excessive reliance on particular features and was particularly disturbed by foreshortening of the stimulus. Thus, although not globally agnosic, KD did have an impaired recognition system, reminiscent of the adult parietal lobe patients described by Warrington and Taylor (1973). Young and Ellis (1989) suggested that the basis of her difficulties lay in an impaired ability to form the abstract three-dimensional representations depicting object-centred descriptions of items. According to Marr's theories (Marr 1976, 1980, 1982), this is important for recognition of items depicted from a variety of angles and positions, for whilst the associated visual stimulus may change significantly, the identity of the item does not. Marr argued that an effective recognition system required the construction of 3D representations that were object-centred and unaffected by viewing angle. For faces this disrupted the process of structural encoding. Their attempts to reteach face recognition skills were unsuccessful (Ellis & Young, 1988b). Despite these deficits, reading skills were acquired, confirming the distinctions between the brain mechanisms underlying the perception of the complex visual configurations which comprise words and the complex visual configurations which comprise faces. In a similar triad to many adult prosopagnosics, KD had topographical difficulties and a disorder of colour perception in addition to her prosopagnosia.

The early age of the illness which resulted in the face recognition difficulties supports the early establishment of a face recognition module, rather than its appearance as an emergent property following a process of gradual modularisation. Although associated visual difficulties and object recognition suggest a lack of specificity in the face recognition disorder, Young and Ellis (1989) established that controls whose basic visual abilities were comparable to KD had no problems with face recognition. Further, the degree of difficulty with faces vastly surpassed the degree of difficulty with objects. KD could not recognise even the most familiar faces such as her mother's. However, she could recognise real objects (19/21 correct) presented in prototypical views. This could suggest a distinction in the underlying processes which are impaired. However, Young and Ellis (1989) argued that the object and face recognition difficulties do have a common basis in the failure to establish 3D representations. They point out that the 3D structure of individual faces is particularly important in face recognition (e.g. Ellis, 1986; Sergent, 1984) and also that KD's object recognition difficulties became very marked when tested with visually homogeneous stimuli, for which individual features were insufficient for successful recognition. So despite the severity of KD's recognition difficulties, the case does not require an innate face processing module for explanation but does require the importance of 3D representations within perceptual processes.

Developmental Prosopagnosia

Dissociations in face processing skill are reported by Mancini et al. (1994) in a study of six children with pre- or perinatal unilateral lesions, who were assessed when they were between 7 and 11 years old. Subject 3, who had a right hemisphere lesion, was able to sort faces on the basis of facial expression and sort faces on the basis of grimaces vs speech-related facial gesture, but was impaired in sorting faces on the basis of identity and on the basis of lip-reading (photographs of faces of people forming specific vowel sounds). Subject 11, who had a left hemisphere lesion, displayed a different dissociation of skills, being able to categorise both emotional expression and lip-reading photographs but being impaired in sorting grimaces vs speech-related facial gesture. Thus, the performance with grimaces vs speech-related facial gestures and the performance with lip-reading photographs forms a double dissociation. These results support the early development of independence between the channel for lip-reading and the channel for directed visual processing described within the model of Bruce and Young (1986).

Although none of the subjects were overtly prosopagnosic, as they were all able to recognise famous faces from photographs, performance on some measures of face processing were extremely poor. Two of the three right hemisphere lesioned children and one of the three left hemisphere lesioned children were significantly impaired in sorting photographs on the basis of the identity of the person. Further in a visual field study, in which an unfamiliar face was presented on one or other visual field and the child then had to select the same face from an array of four faces, performance in each visual field was very poor in relation to controls. Only one of the six subjects (who had a left hemisphere lesion) performed above chance in the LVF. All six of the controls performed above chance in both fields.

Kracke (1994) describes a probable case of developmental prosopagnosia in a young man, HD, aged 19 years. On Warrington's Recognition Memory Test, performance with faces was random, although performance with words was normal. When asked to recognise colour slides of his family, HD initially identified 14/15 correctly. However, when their hairstyles and clothing were covered, he recognised only 2/15, the picture of his father who had a beard and his grandfather who wore glasses. He also appeared to have severe difficulty in grouping together pictures showing the same famous person, though no quantitative details are given. In a task requiring the identification of facial expression, he had a success rate of 60% compared to the control success rate of 92%. There was apparent difficulty in making judgements of age, since he claimed that photographs of people aged 20–90 years were all "about 40". No control data was given. HD's father was also reported to have some face recognition difficulties in everyday life. HD also had some social difficulties, which Kracke argues were of a sufficient degree to merit a label of Asperger's syndrome, Kracke goes on to propose, controversially, an intrinsic link between the two disorders. However, McConachie (1995), the author of one of the case reports of developmental prosopagnosia described below, disagrees with this suggestion. Certainly, in relation to our own case of developmental prosopagnosia (Temple, 1992b), Dr S, there is definitely not Asperger's syndrome. Indeed, Dr S (described later) was an affectionate and charming lady, with a large circle of friends.

Two contrasting cases of developmental prosopagnosics have been described (Campbell, 1992; de Haan & Campbell, 1991; McConachie, 1976; Temple, 1992b), both of which have been interpreted in relation to the Bruce and Young (1986) model. The first appears to have a difficulty at the level of structural encoding of faces. The second has difficulty in accessing person identity information from faces, though the same information can be accessed from the names of people. These two cases will be described in more detail below.

Case Report: Developmental Prosopagnosia — A Structural Encoding Deficit, AB

The developmental prosopagnosic AB was first described at the age of 12 years 9 months (McConachie, 1976) and was then studied subsequently when she was a young adult (Campbell, 1992; de Haan & Campbell, 1991). AB was born at 37 weeks' gestation and there was no concern in the neonatal period, although subsequent milestones are reported as somewhat delayed. At the age of 12, AB was right handed. She had no visual field defects. Neurological examination was normal except for a posterior right hemisphere EEG abnormality. However, there had been no overt seizures, nor unexplained episodes of loss of consciousness. There appeared to be right–left confusion and topographical disorientation.

AB explained that she recognised people by their clothing, voice, and mannerisms. She reported that she had never been able to recognise faces except for the most familiar ones. AB's mother was also reported to have similar difficulties.

There was a significant difference between AB's verbal and performance IQ, with the former scoring at a very high level at 144, but the later at an average level of 100. This level of difference between the two scales is statistically highly significant, indicating a reliable difference in underlying cognitive skills. Nevertheless the scores are more indicative of verbal talents than of perceptual deficiencies, since a performance IQ of 100 is entirely normal. Generalised difficulties with fundamental perceptual skills were further ruled out by normal performance on a test of embedded figures and by intact ability to copy simple line drawings. Further, there were no generalised agnosic difficulties since object recognition appeared intact. AB could both name objects and indicate their use. Performance was poor on Benton's Visual Retention test, suggesting poor visual short-term memory for unfamiliar patterns.

Reference to a reassessment of AB in her teenage years by Dr Maria Wyke, is given by de Haan and Campbell (1991). A CT scan at this time was normal. On the Wechsler adult intelligence scale, a verbal IQ of 140 and a performance IQ of 102 were obtained, scores highly similar to the earlier test results. Colour perception and judgements of distances were normal. Matching of shapes and overlapping figures was accurate but slow. Discrimination of line drawings and photographs of objects was also accurate but slow. Tachistoscopic measures of response times confirmed the lengthened response times for recognition of pictures. There was particular difficulty with pictures of unusual views of objects.

AB was tested again in young adulthood by de Haan and Campbell (1991). In relation to visual sensory abilities, they found that colour vision was normal on the Farnworth–Munsell test, but that there were some idiosyncratic responses on a grey discrimination task. Contrast sensitivity was normal on Wilkins and Robson's (1986) test. Judgements of line orientation were normal as were shape matching abilities.

Face Processing/Face Perception.   AB was asked to make judgements about whether stimuli depicted faces or were non-faces containing jumbled face features. Her performance was normal. Thus, she did know when a stimulus is a face.

In order to recognise that a face is a face, it is necessary to integrate features. Sometimes this must be done under conditions of poor lighting or when the face is partially obscured. The processes involved in integrating aspects of perceptual stimuli are sometimes referred to as gestalt processes and AB's gestalt skills with face stimuli were investigated with the Mooney faces (Lansdell, 1968) (see Fig. 4.3). These present patterns of light and shadow, in black and white, depicting faces for which sex and approximate age judgements are requested. The subjects are told that all the stimuli are faces, but they will need to integrate the patterns of black and white correctly, if they are to be able to make the age and sex judgements. AB attained a score of 27/40 on this task, compared to mean control performance of 34.8 (SD=2.5). Thus, although AB has some abilities on this task, she is significantly impaired in relation to matched controls.

FIG. 4.3 A mooney face.

Face Matching.   AB was given Benton's Face Recognition task (Benton, Hamsher, Varney, & Spreen, 1983). This involves matching a target face with an identical face, photographed in the same or a differing orientation. The faces are photographed partially in shadow. AB performed at a borderline level in comparison to control subjects. On a second task, two faces were back projected onto a screen for 4s each, with an interstimulus interval of 1s. AB had to indicate whether each pair of faces were of the same person. She was impaired on this task.

Recognition Memory for Faces.   AB was taught a set of new faces on the Warrington Recognition Memory Battery (Warrington, 1984). The test is in two matched sections. In the first section, the subject is shown a pack of 50 words, each of which is exposed for 3s. The subject must make a judgement about whether or not the associations of the word are pleasant. This encourages some degree of encoding of semantics. Immediately after the stimulus cards have all been exposed, the subject is required to make a forced choice judgement between pairs of words, one of which has appeared in the stimulus pack and one of which is novel. The faces section is identical, except that the stimuli consist of unfamiliar faces of men. The forced choice responses are made to pairs of faces, one of which has been shown in the stimulus pack. AB was severely impaired with the face stimuli but had a perfect score for word recognition. The specific recognition memory difficulties for faces were confirmed on a second test.

Face Recognition.   AB was presented with a series of slides of famous and unfamiliar faces and asked to indicate whether the faces were familiar. The same procedure was employed with famous and unfamiliar names. AB performed at a normal level of accuracy in making judgements about the names but was severely impaired in making judgements about the faces.

Other Face Processing Tasks.   AB was able to match facial expressions but she had difficulty in recognising emotional expressions. Lip movements appeared not to affect speech perception, in a normal way and she was unperturbed by anomalous movements which were incompatible with the speech sounds heard. She did not therefore use facial speech analysis in a normal way.

Finally, AB also has some difficulties with object recognition and naming. She had difficulty in recognising silhouettes of familiar objects, when they were presented in unfamiliar orientations. She also had difficulty on Warrington's test of recognising photographs of objects, taken from unconventional angles. Further, she had difficulty naming within categories. For example, she had difficulty in naming common flowers. She was also unable to recognise any make of car.

Theoretical Interpretation.   In relation to the information processing model of face recognition (see Fig. 4.2), AB has problems at the level of structural encoding. She can discriminate that a face is a face, and can to some extent match faces on expression and identity but she is poor at identifying expressions, speech, age, familiarity, and identity of the person from their face. De Haan and Campbell (1991) speculate that the same basic high-level perceptual impairment may account for the object recognition difficulties.

In some studies of prosopagnosia in adulthood, there has been evidence that although patients may report that they are unable to identify faces, they nevertheless appear to have some recognition without awareness. For example, Bauer (1984) found increased GSR to familiar faces over unfamiliar faces, in the absence of overt ability to make judgements discriminating the two sets.

Other studies address the issue in a different way. De Haan, Young, and Newcombe (1987) retaught famous faces to a prosopagnosic who had been unable to identify them. They found that relearning correct names linked to famous faces was significantly faster than learning the famous faces linked to incorrect famous names. De Haan and Campbell (1991) were therefore interested to try to find evidence of covert recognition in their developmental case. However, in a series of studies they were unable to find any evidence of covert recognition skills for AB. Her overt recognition skills appear to be an accurate reflection of her face recognition abilities.

Case Report: Developmental Prosopagnosia — Impaired Access to Person Identity Information, Dr S

A contrasting report of developmental prosopagnosia is given by Temple (1992b). She reports the case of Dr S, a lady in her 60s, who had face recognition difficulties from her earliest years. Dr S was highly intelligent, with a Verbal IQ of 136 and a Performance IQ of 147. She was a doctor of medicine but also had a BA in Psychology. She had travelled widely and was multi-lingual. Her four children all had university degrees. A cousin also had difficulty in recognising faces. Dr S was in good health. She had had no seizures nor any accident associated with loss of consciousness. Dr S's difficulties with face recognition were severe, and over the multiple appointments involved in our assessments of her, she never developed the ability to recognise me despite our many hours of contact. She knew that I had blonde hair, but could be seen to move expectantly at our meeting point towards any person with blonde hair who happened to pass. Her problem created marked difficulties for her in her day-to-day social interactions.

Dr S had exceptional fluency with language. For example, on an oral fluency task for animals, a typical healthy control in her 60s generated 14 animal names in one minute. In contrast, Dr S generated 35 animal names on one occasion and 42 on another.

A series of tasks were given to Dr S which overlap with those used by de Haan and Campbell (1991) for AB, enabling a direct comparison of the two cases. Throughout, Dr S's performance was compared with that of 12 other healthy, alert, non-dementing, women in their 60s.

Visual Perception. Dr S's ability to make judgements about line orientation was assessed with a modified version of the Benton, Varney, and Hamsher (1978) line orientation task. In our version, 30 different line orientations are employed and the lines to be matched, vary in length. The test is therefore considerably more difficult than its clinical predecessor.

Dr S performed at a normal level on both this task and a parallel tactile version. Thus, she has no unusual difficulty in making basic perceptual judgements about the orientation of lines.

Dr S was given a shortened version of a mental rotation task (Vandenburg & Kuse, 1978), requiring the internalised spatial rotation of 3D structures depicted by 2D drawings. The drawings appear to represent 3D structures composed of multiple cubes. The subjects are told that they may mentally rotate the structures in any direction and they must then select, two identical structures from an array of four.

Dr S performed slightly better than the control subjects on this task. Thus, she can perform this complex spatial manipulation and can recognise shapes from different angles. There is no evident perceptual basis, at least in terms of mental rotation skill, for any difficulty in establishing the viewer-centred or object-centred representations which Marr has discussed. However, other aspects may be involved in establishing these representations and ability on mental rotation does not necessarily imply that the 3D representations are normal.

Face Processing/Face Perception. Dr S was given the Mooney faces task, which was described earlier (an example is given in Fig. 4.3). She had to integrate the patterns of black and white and then make an age and sex judgement about the face. She was able to make these judgements as easily as the control subjects. Thus her Gestalt integrative skills with face stimuli are normal.

Face Matching. Dr S was given Benton's Face Recognition task, described previously. She had to match the black and white photographs with identical photographs of the same person or with alternatively angled photographs of the same person. Both in comparison to the controls and in comparison to the test norms Dr S performed normally. She is able to match unfamiliar faces seen at different angles. The good face perception and face matching performance indicated that Dr S's structural encoding of faces and directed visual processing (see Fig. 4.2) have developed normally.

Registration of Face Recognition Units.   Dr S was given Warrington's Recognition Memory Battery for faces and words (described above). On the word section, Dr S attained a perfect score. On the faces section, she was slightly better than controls with 43/50 items correct. This contrasts with AB's performance of only 28/50 on this task.

Face Recognition.   Dr S was presented with 45 pictures of famous people. She recognised only 14, a score significantly lower than that of the control subjects. When presented with a matched set of 40 famous faces and 40 famous names, she was able to give the occupation of the person in response to only 12 of the faces but to 28 of the names. Thus many faces failed to elicit person identity information, which we knew that Dr S possessed.

A further set of famous faces was employed in a familiarity decision paradigm (de Haan, Young, & Newcombe, 1991). On this task, Dr S performed at close to chance levels with the famous faces. No such problems were experienced in making familiarity judgements about objects or names (see Table 4.1).

Whereas AB also had difficulties with object recognition, Dr S's object recognition skills were intact (see Table 4.1), supporting the view that the recognition mechanisms disrupted in her case are specific to face recognition. She did however have difficulty with visual memory for designs on the Wechsler Memory Battery and on the Figure of Rey. Further, she had difficulty in recognising the appearance of her own home. Thus, visual memory difficulties may have been more broadly based.

Theoretical Interpretation.   Dr S appeared to have intact structural encoding skills and normal abilities in the initial registration of face recognition units. Nevertheless there was significant impairment in accessing person identity information from faces in order to recognise them. Either the face recognition units have failed to consolidate over time or there is difficulty in using the units to activate person identity information. In terms of the model in Fig. 4.2, the failure in the face processing system is at a later stage than that proposed for AB. Thus, although Dr S and AB both have developmental prosopagnosia, each has a different type of disorder.

To summarise, there a number of critical distinctions between the two cases of developmental prosopagnosia. Dr S could match faces differing in their angle of orientation on the Benton test; AB could not.

TABLE 4.1
Scores on Familiarity Decision for Dr S

	% Correct
Familiar faces	44
Unfamiliar faces	100
Familiar objects	100
Unfamiliar objects	88
Familiar names	82
Unfamiliar names	94

Dr S could register at least briefly, new face recognition units, as assessed on the Warrington recognition memory test; AB was unable to register and retain new face recognition units, even for the few minutes required by this task. Dr S could make judgements about the age of faces as required by the Mooney faces task. AB could not. Since Dr S is able to perform well with the Mooney faces her Gestalt skills are intact. This is a task which could not be accomplished successfully by a piecemeal analysis, so her success on face tasks is not simply being accomplished by making intelligent use of small details of faces, a strategy which could generate competent performance on the Benton test and which may give rise to the misleading degree of competence seen on this task in Williams syndrome (see later). Neither AB nor Dr S can discriminate familiar and unfamiliar faces with accuracy.

AB has an impairment in structural encoding (see Fig. 4.1). Dr S has intact structural encoding and seems able to initially register face recognition units. However, she either has difficulty in maintaining the face recognition units over time and/or using them to activate person identity information. As de Haan and Campbell (1991) point out, this suggests "that different components of the face processing system may be separately and independently affected in disorders with a developmental aetiology, as has been convincingly demonstrated for acquired deficits" (p. 506).

Dr S does not have any other known visual impairments. Nor is she agnosic for objects. She performs normally on object recognition tests and experiences no difficulty with recognising objects in day-to-day activities. On the de Haan et al. (1991) familiarity task, Dr S performed randomly in making familiarity decisions about faces yet had a perfect score for familiarity decision about objects. Dr S could therefore be a case for whom an innate face processing module has been partially impaired. The fact that she has topographical difficulties and is unable to recognise her own house leaves open the possibility that she uses the same system for recognising buildings, but in itself this does not preclude the system being principally designed for face stimuli.

Autism and Face Processing.   Face recognition abnormalities have also been reported in children with autism. Langdell (1978) showed that when autistic children recognise their classmates, they attend to the lower facial features. This contrasts with the normal pattern, where upper facial features are more important. Further, whereas normal face recognition is disrupted if faces are inverted, autistic children are unaffected by this manipulation. One interpretation is that children with autism employ a strategy in face recognition where there is greater dependence upon the component parts of the face rather than analysis of the whole (Tantam, Monaghan, Nicholson, & Stirling, 1989).

Boucher and Lewis (1992) demonstrated that there were difficulties in recognising new faces. These difficulties with unfamiliar face recognition do not extend to other complex material. Relative to verbal ability matched controls, recognition of buildings was found to be normal (Boucher & Lewis, 1992). Autistic children may also have difficulty in interpreting emotional expressions (e.g. Hobson, Ouston, & Lee, 1988; Tantam et al., 1989), but the primacy of a perceptual, emotional or reasoning disorder (see Chapter 8), in relation to such difficulties is unclear. Not all face processing skills are impaired in autism. Despite difficulties with face identity recognition, they are comparable to controls in lip-reading (de Gelder, Vroomen, & van der Heide, 1991), which, as de Gelder et al. (1991) discuss, supports the parallel channels for these face processing systems within the Bruce and Young (1986) model.

SPECIFIC SYNDROMES

There are a number of specific developmental syndromes in which disorders of perception and spatial cognition have been documented. In the majority of these studies, a group study methodology has been adopted and the results have therefore been less informative from a cognitive neuropsychological perspective. Nevertheless in some syndromes there is sufficient similarity across cases for specific aspects of fractionation in the development of spatial cognition to be evident. The syndromes also provide areas where future developmental cognitive neuropsychological analyses may yield further information of theoretical relevance.

Turner's Syndrome (TS)
Turner (1938) identified a syndrome in which there was sexual infantilism, small stature, and skeletal abnormalities. A specific genetic abnormality was found to be associated with the syndrome, with absence

or abnormality in the second X chromosome (Ford, Jones, Polani, De Almeida, & Briggs, 1959). On genetic analysis, in approximately half of cases, the TS genotype appears to be pure 45XO, in all sampled cells (Jacobs et al., 1990). Among other cases of TS, some have an isochromosome of X, in which there is duplication of one arm of the X chromosome with loss of the other arm (45Xi(Xq)). In other cases, there is partial deletion of the second X or a ring chromosome of X. Mosaicism, with more than one cell line, is found in 30–40% of cases, with 10–15% of the total group being mosaics of 45XO and the normal chromosomal complement of 46XX.

The incidence of TS is 1 in 2500 live female births. Approximately, 1% of conceptuses have a genotype of TS, but at least 99% are spontaneously aborted. It is thought that the pure genotype 45XO may be lethal and that in those who survive to term there may be a small number of normal cells, even if these are not detected.

The children are of short stature, which is sometimes treated with growth hormone. The children have broad chests, short necks, sometimes with posterior webbing, and a low hair line. There may be an abnormal carrying angle of the elbow, multiple pigmented naevi, and dysplastic nails. Additional medical problems may include ear, nose, and throat disorders, cardiac disorders, and renal tract anomalies.

The condition results in gonadal dysgenesis, where the ovaries are absent or merely vestigial streaks. The majority of cases of TS are therefore infertile and hormone replacement therapy is usually necessary to enable the onset of puberty. However, during foetal development, the brain grows and develops in the absence of the normal exposure to endogenous sex hormones. A well-established animal literature (e.g. Goy & McEwan, 1980) has documented the influence of sex hormones on brain growth and development across species, from rats to primates. Sex differences between males and females in both behaviour and cognitive skill are often attributed to the activating effects of gonadal hormones during foetal development, which may lay down circuitry, some of which is active from birth and some of which is not activated until sexual maturity. Since children with TS develop without the normal exposure to both the masculinising and defeminising effects of brain hormones, it has been argued that they may reflect the female end of a male–female continuum.

In 1962, Shaffer suggested that TS was associated with a particular cognitive profile and that there was low performance in perceptual organisation, a factor derived from factor analysis of the Wechsler Intelligence subtest scores. Low performance on perceptual organisation, reflected poor scores on block design and object assembly. Overall, Shaffer documented a lower Performance IQ than Verbal IQ, reporting a difference of 19 points between the two scales. Money and Alexander (1966) adopted the term space–form blindness to refer to the difficulties in perceptual organisation, described by Shaffer (1962) in girls with TS.

Recent, studies of children with focal prenatal or perinatal brain lesions, have confirmed that although left hemisphere lesions depress both Verbal IQ and Performance IQ to a similar extent, right hemisphere lesions depress Performance IQ significantly more than Verbal IQ (Ballantyne, Scarvie, & Trauner, 1994). In both groups, IQs remain within the normal range (Aram & Ekelman, 1986; Ballantyne et al., 1994). The hypothesis of a right hemisphere or right parietal lobe abnormality in TS has been repeatedly discussed (e.g. Alexander & Money, 1966; Bender, Puck, Salbenblatt, & Robinson, 1984; Kolb & Heaton, 1975; Silbert, Wolff, & Lilienthal, 1977). Shucard, Shucard, Clopper, and Schacter (1992) argue that their electrophysiological results support a right hemisphere hypothesis. A study of regional cerebral glucose metabolism has suggested decreases in metabolism bilaterally in both parietal and occipital cortex (Clark, Klonoff, & Hayden, 1990). Bilateral parieto-occipital involvement in terms of reduced MRI measures was also found by Murphy et al. (1993), though their study also suggested subcortical involvement.

Following Shaffer's study, the pattern of depressed Performance IQ in relation to Verbal IQ in TS has been consistently documented (e.g. Buckley, 1971; Christensen & Nielsen, 1981; Cohen, 1962; Downey et al., 1991; Garron, 1977; Pennington, Heaton, Karzmark, Pendleton, Lehman, & Shucard, 1985). The degree of the documented discrepancy has varied across studies. In Shaffer's (1962) report there was an 18–19 point discrepancy, for a sample of 20 cases aged 5–30 years. Netley and Rovet (1982) reported an average discrepancy of 11 points, in a study of 35 cases, aged 6 to 24 years. Only one of their 35 cases had a Performance IQ higher than Verbal IQ. In a sample of 10 children with TS, Lewandowski, Costenbader, and Richman (1985) found a 20 point discrepancy and in a study of adolescents, McGlone (1985) reported a 12.5 point discrepancy. Rovet (1990) reviewed 19 IQ studies of TS and found an average discrepancy of 12 points across the combined total of 226 females with TS, spanning childhood and adulthood. They concluded that the size of the Verbal–Performance discrepancy was unrelated to the age of the subjects and also unrelated to the karyotype of the TS.

In contrast, Temple and Carney (1993) found karyotype to be significant in a study of 19 girls with TS, with a restricted age range of 8–12 years. They found significant genotype-phenotype relationships, in that the nine girls with 45XO TS had an average discrepancy between Verbal and Performance IQ of 14.6 points but those with mixed genotypes (mosaicism, isochromosomes, and partial deletion of X) had an average discrepancy of only 2.3 points. There were also considerable individual differences, with the discrepancy between Verbal and Performance IQ being as high as 43 points in one case of 45XO TS, yet there also being a case of 45X0 with equal scores on both scales. In several of the cases of mosaicism and in one case of an isochromosome of X, Performance IQ was higher than Verbal IQ

In relation to specific subtests, Shaffer (1962) emphasised weakness on block design and object assembly, both of which are within the Performance scale. Block design is a constructional task in which cubes with white, red, or mixed faces are arranged to construct target abstract two-dimensional patterns. Object assembly is also a constructional task, but involves the assembly of jigsaws of real objects.

However, impairments on these two spatial constructional subtests have not been consistently reported. Block design has been found to be unimpaired in comparison to controls in several studies (Lahood & Bacon, 1985; McGlone,1985; Silbert et al., 1977; Waber, 1979). Waber (1979) and Lahood and Bacon (1985) also failed to find any deficit on object assembly. Temple and Carney (1993) wondered if the wide age range in some studies, and the variation in genotypes, might have contributed to some of the inconsistencies across studies, in addition to other individual differences between the subjects.

In their 19 cases of children with TS, they found a characteristic profile across subtests, and variation in relation to genotype (see Fig. 4.4). When all the subjects were combined, the lowest subtest score was found on arithmetic. However, when the TS cases were divided on the basis of genotype, particular weakness of the 45XO children was evident on object assembly. Scores for object assembly were significantly lower than those for block design. The 45XO TS children also had significantly lower scores on object assembly than the other TS children. Both groups of TS subjects had significantly lower scores than controls on object assembly. This was true even though the controls were girls, and girls have been found to be weaker than boys at object assembly. Thus, in relation to the object assembly subtest, the TS girls show a significant exaggeration of a normal sex difference. In relation to block design, the 45XO TS subjects were impaired in relation to controls, which is also an exaggeration of a normal sex difference (Temple & Cornish, submitted 1996) but the other mixed karyotype TS subjects were not impaired in relation to controls. On the verbal scale, the 45XO TS subjects also had consistent trends in favour of better performance than the mixed TS group, but none reached significance.

In a relatively early study of TS, Alexander, Ehrhardt, and Money (1966), also reported performance on Benton's Test of Visual Retention

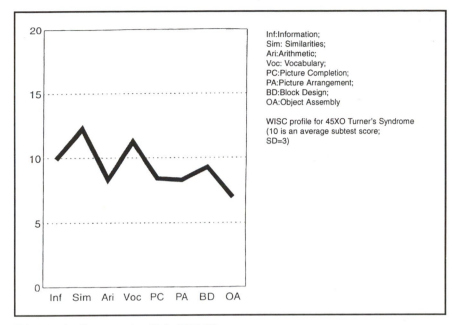

FIG. 4.4.   Intelligence test profile in 45XO TS.

and on Harris's revision of the Goodenough Draw-a-man test (Harris, 1963). They comment that "visual memory is less implicated than visuo-constructional recognition and performance". This is one of the first suggestions that certain aspects of spatial cognition may be affected more than others and that the deficit may not generalise to all aspects of spatial cognition. The greater impairment, found previously, with object assembly than with block design, despite both being constructional tasks, confirms the potential dissociability of spatial skills within TS.

The pervasiveness of the spatial deficits has been explored by Temple and Carney (1995). They tested 15 girls with TS, of normal intelligence, aged 8–12 years across a range of spatial tasks encompassing perceptual and spatial judgements, constructional tasks, and visual and tactile modalities. There was a significant main effect of group, indicating that spatial cognitive skills were dependent upon the karyotype of the subjects. Best performance was found in the control 46XX group, intermediate in the group of mixed karyotype TS, and weakest performance in the 45X0 TS group. However, there was also significant group by task interaction, indicating a task-specific nature to the group effects. There were individual main effects of group on only four of the eleven tasks employed: the Street task; Object Assembly; Draw-a-man;

and Draw-a-bicycle. The first of these tasks is visuo-perceptual requiring Gestalt integrative skill. The latter three are visuo-constructive and all require the construction of known objects. There were no significant differences between the groups on any tasks of tactile spatial skill, nor were there any group differences on tasks of visuo-spatial judgement such as line orientation and mental rotation. Interpretation of the mental rotation results was tempered by poor performance on this test by controls, which may have masked greater difficulties in the TS subjects, as previously reported by others (e.g. Rovet & Netley, 1982).

The marked deficit in drawing substantiates the proposal first postulated by Alexander et al. (1966) and supported by Nielsen, Nyborg, and Dahl (1977), Waber (1979), and Lahood (1981). It is also of interest in view of the similarities and contrasts between TS and Williams syndrome, which is discussed later. The deficit in Gestalt perception refutes the proposal of Waber (1979) that spatial deficits are secondary to poor visual memory and to motor incoordination.

The absence of impairment on several classical spatial tasks and on all the tasks of tactile spatial skill emphasises the fractionation of the spatial deficit and the potential modularity in the acquisition of these skills. As recently as 1985, Lahood and Bacon stated that "a specific spatial deficit is not present in TS patients who have average or above average intelligence" (p.358). These results contradict this view, indicating significant impairment in both visual Gestalt perception and in the integrative spatial constructional skills required for assembling jigsaws and drawings.

Williams Syndrome

Background. Williams syndrome (WS) has only been identified as a specific entity since the 1950s (Fanconi, Girardet, Schlesinger, Butler, & Black, 1952; Williams, Barratt-Boyes, & Lowe, 1961). It occurs in 1 in 25,000 to 1 in 50,000 live births. It is associated with a characteristic facial appearance, sometimes described as "elfin", and abnormalities of many of the major systems, including cardiac and renal. There is also delayed growth and low ultimate height. Early studies of aetiology emphasised abnormalities of calcium metabolism, which led to its earlier description as idiopathic infantile hypercalcaemia. Vitamin D was also suspect, but no clear role for vitamin D in the hypercalcaemia which can occur in WS has been established. A genetic aetiology now seems probable, with autosomal dominant inheritance, and most cases representing new mutation (Morris, Thomas, & Greenberg, 1993). MRI studies have revealed no space occupying lesions but have found decreased posterior width and elongated posterior to anterior length in comparison to normal. There is also decreased myelination and reduced cerebral volume (Bellugi, Birle, Jernigan, Trauner, & Docherty, 1990; Jernigan & Bellugi, 1990).

Cognition. Udwin, Yule, and Martin (1986, 1987) reported that 95% of cases have moderate to severe mental retardation. Impairments in the acquisition of basic Piagetian principles are also reported (Bellugi et al., 1990). There is also delay in the acquisition of motor skills.

However, in contrast to autism, there is relative preservation of theory of mind (Karmiloff-Smith, Klima, Bellugi, Grant, & Baron-Cohen, 1995) (see Chapter 8 for a further discussion of theory of mind in autism).

Behaviour. Children with WS have particular behavioural difficulties. They are overactive, with poor concentration. There is a prevalence of eating and sleeping difficulties, excessive anxiety and fearfulness, and uninhibited approach of adults (Udwin & Yule, 1991).

Language. There has been interest from linguists in the language development of children with WS because of the apparent dissociation between cognitive and linguistic development. A number of theories have suggested that specific cognitive abilities are prerequisites for linguistic development. Yet, in WS it is suggested that aspects of language development exceed that expected on the basis of intellectual level, supporting the view that language may be a domain-specific faculty that can develop with little input from other areas of cognition (Cromer, 1981). During development language is delayed in acquisition, with single words often not evident until two or three years (Lopez-Rangal, Maurice, McGillivray, & Friedman, 1992). Nevertheless, subsequent mastery exceeds that seen in other forms of mental retardation. Udwin and Yule (1990) report that 84% of children with WS have fluent and well-articulated speech. Expressive language skills have been found to exceed comprehension scores on the Reynell Developmental Language Scales (Arnold, Yule, & Martin, 1985). So-called "cocktail party speech" is used by about 40% of children (Udwin & Yule, 1990). It is characterised by verbosity and contains many social phrases, fillers, and cliches. However, the content is not as has been suggested simply meaningless, repetitive, and superficial, as a significant proportion serves an elaborated communicative purpose such as the expression of personal evaluations and explanations. The utterances are communicative in intent. The WS children also have an overfamiliar manner and use more adult vocabulary. They perform well on fluency tasks but tend to include low frequency, non-prototypical category members (Bellugi et al., 1990).

Perceptual and Spatial Cognition. Hypersensitivity to auditory stimuli is frequently noted in WS. This may take the form of an exaggerated startle response to certain everyday sounds, such as vacuum cleaners and lawnmowers, and in some cases even laughter above a certain pitch (Udwin, 1990).

Depth perception may also be abnormal. Difficulty in stepping off kerbs is reported in older preschoolers. Climbing up ladders and playground slides are commonly feared activities. Both children and adults, with WS have greater difficulty in walking down than up stairs (Dilts, Morris, & Leonard, 1990). There is also fear of heights and unsteadiness when negotiating uneven surfaces (Udwin et al., 1987).

WS children are said to have visuo-spatial difficulties. Performance IQ has been reported as lower than Verbal IQ (Kataria, Goldstein, & Kushnick, 1984; Udwin & Yule, 1990; Udwin et al., 1986, 1987), although exceptions are reported (Arnold et al., 1985).

Within, the Wechsler Intelligence Scale subtests, severe impairment on block design is reported (Bellugi, Sabo, & Vaid, 1988). Difficulties with more simple copying tasks of block construction and copying shapes have also been described (Thal, Bates, & Bellugi, 1989).

With perceptual stimuli, contrasting patterns of performance are found dependent upon the task demands. There are impairments on simple judgements of line orientation on the Benton Line Orientation Task. Yet, on Benton's Face Recognition Task, performance is superior to that of controls and close to adult levels (Bellugi et al., 1990; Bellugi, Sabo & Vaid, 1988). The latter task assesses the ability to discriminate and match unfamiliar faces photographed partially in shadow. Superior performance on face recognition has also been found with the face recognition subtask of the Rivermead Behavioural Memory Test (Udwin & Yule, 1991). However, the good performance on the Benton and Rivermead Task could be accomplished by adopting a piecemeal strategy, with attention to small local features rather than deriving an integrated percept of the faces. As such the Benton score would be at normal level but accomplished by an abnormal strategy. As yet unpublished studies by Karmiloff-Smith suggest various abnormalities in face processing.

Udwin and Yule (1991) also studied memory for spatial location, employing a task in which tokens, each of which depicts a different design, are displayed on a blackboard and shown to the subject for 10s. The tokens are then removed and the child is asked to replace them. The procedure is repeated for four further trials to assess the ability to learn over repeated trials. The WS subjects performed less well than matched controls on each of the five trials, with the difference reaching significance on two of the trials. This suggests that the spatial difficulties of children with WS encompass the perceptual systems involved in making judgements about the positions of items.

The drawings of children with WS often exhibit great attention to the detail of component parts but with an inability to make a coherent representation of the integration of the parts and depict their relative positions correctly. Bellugi, Marks, Bihrle, and Sabo (1988) asked children with WS to draw an elephant and a bicycle freehand. Examples of the responses are given in Fig. 4.5A and 4.5B. Bellugi, Marks et al. (1988) noted that often the child would verbalise before and during the task, providing a commentary on the drawing. The children were able to label the parts which they had depicted. They could also explain the parts. In some cases the details were drawn in the correct position relative to other features, though the individual features remain fragmented. In other cases, the features were placed haphazardly without maintenance of the correct spatial relationships.

This pattern of drawing performance has been contrasted with that of children with Down's syndrome, with comparable mental age. The children with Down's syndrome also have impaired drawing skills but the character of their depictions is significantly different from that of the WS children. The Down's syndrome children depict an overall Gestalt of the object but then incorporate little internal detail (Bihrle, Bellugi, Delis, & Marks, 1989) (see Fig. 4.6).

Bihrle et al. (1989) noted that a similar contrast in style of drawing has been reported in studies of adult neurological patients, following left or right hemisphere injury. Patients with right hemisphere lesions have drawings which lack an overall spatial organisation and integration but which are nevertheless replete with details. Patients with left hemisphere lesions are more accurate in the general configurations which they produce but incorporate little internal detail (Gainotti, Misserlie, & Tissot, 1972; Warrington, James, & Kinsbourne, 1966). A similar dissociation in drawing styles has been reported in children following unilateral brain injury (Stiles-Davis, 1988).

Bihrle et al. (1989) investigated this global and local processing in more detail. They studied 14 children with WS, aged between 9 and 18 years. The tasks employed were drawing from memory and copying hierarchical stimuli. The stimuli consisted of large letter-like forms which were composed of smaller letters. Thus, for example, a large letter D might be composed from smaller Y or an arrow of smaller dashes (see Fig. 4.7). Each stimulus was presented for 5s. There then followed a 5s delay, immediately after which the child had to draw the figure from memory. In the copying condition the stimulus remained in view, whilst the child copied it. The performance of the children with WS was compared to that of children with Down's syndrome. The WS subjects

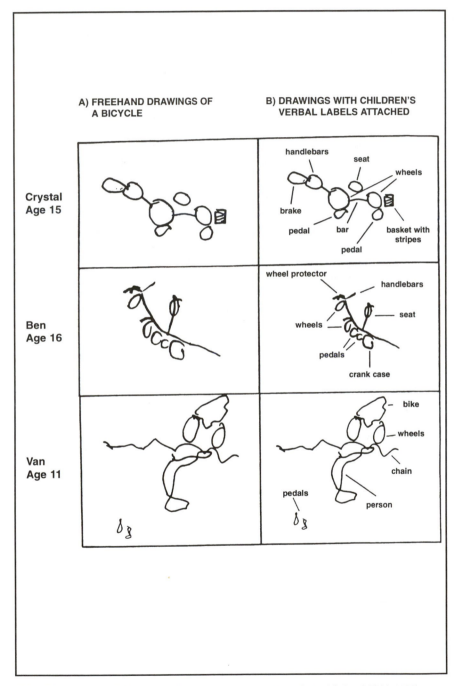

FIG 4.5A Drawings of a bicycle by Williams syndrome children (Bellugi,Sabo, & Vaid, 1988).

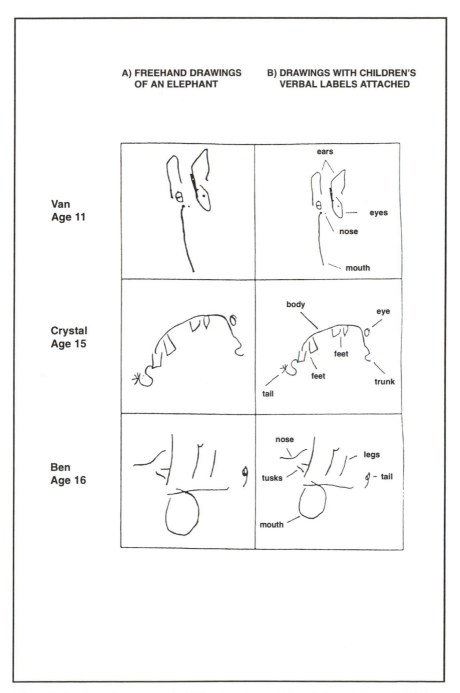

FIG. 4.5B Drawings of an elephant by Williams syndrome children (Bellugi, Marks et al., 1988).

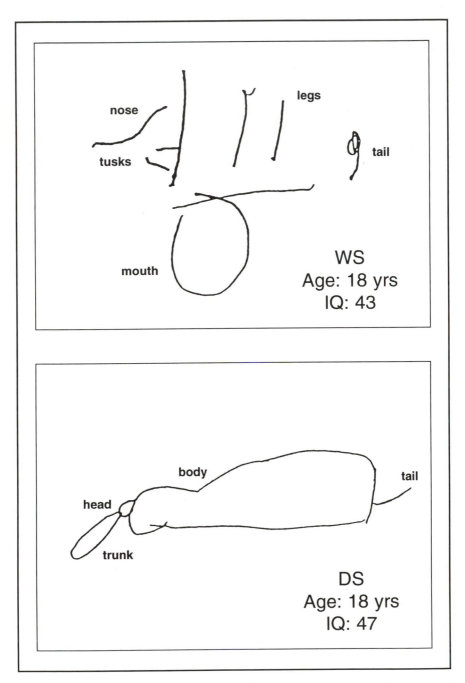

FIG. 4.6 Drawings of an elephant by a child with Williams syndrome and a child with Down's syndrome (Bihrle et al., 1989).

were more accurate in drawing the local forms relative to the global forms, whereas the Down's syndrome subjects were more accurate in drawing the global forms relative to the local forms. Examples of their drawing responses are given in Fig. 4.8A and 4.8B. A similar pattern of performance was found in the copying tasks, with the WS children more accurate at copying local forms and the Down's syndrome children more accurate at copying global forms. These different patterns of performance emerged despite comparable levels of overall accuracy in copying and memory.

Bihrle et al. (1989) point out that these results are also comparable to those obtained with adult neurological patients who have sustained unilateral lesions (Delis, Kiefner, & Fridlund, 1988; Delis, Robertson, & Efron, 1986). The right hemisphere damaged patients, in similar fashion to the children with WS, depicted the local elements of the hierarchical stimuli but made poor representation of the global forms. The left hemisphere damaged patients, in similar fashion to the children with Down's syndrome, depict the global structures but omit the local components' features of the hierarchical stimuli. These results suggest that the two groups of children with learning disabilities have acquired distinct components of spatial skill, which are therefore evidently dissociable during development. Each skill, however, is inadequate in enabling efficient performance of drawing and copying, without the counterbalancing influence of the other.

This distinction between global and local structure has now been discussed in a variety of contexts. In normal subjects, there is an advantage of global processing over local processing, such that global

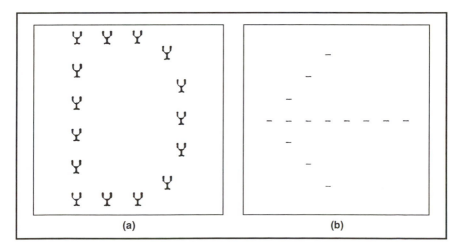

(a)   (b)

FIG. 4.7 Stimuli used in Bihrle et al.'s (1989) experiments.

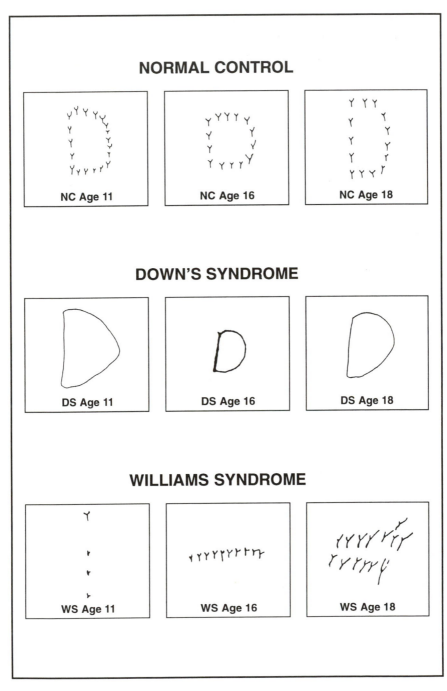

FIG. 4.8A Responses to the Bihrle et al. (1989) "D" stimulus.

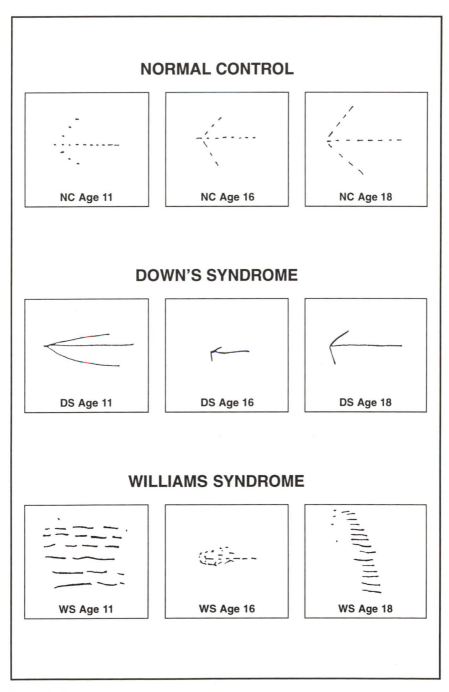

FIG. 4.8B Responses to the Bihrle et al. (1989) "arrow" stimulus.

processing is usually quicker and more accurate than local processing (Navron, 1977). When a pattern diverges in relation to its local and global elements, interference of one level over the other occurs and usually the global level interferes with the local level (Lamb & Robertson, 1989). In normal subjects the interference effects and advantage effects can vary independently (Navron & Norman, 1983). From the results with the hierarchical stimuli in Williams syndrome, it appears that interference favours the local level over the global level, in contrast to the normal pattern. The relevant experiments have not been carried out but it may be that the normal advantage of global over local processing is also reversed in Williams syndrome and that all of their perceptual skills are dominated by a local analysis.

IN CONCLUSION

This chapter has explored developmental disorders of perception which affect either basic sensation, or one of three putative channels of visual perception: location, movement, and form. In each case selective impairments were identified.

Absence of visual sensation associated with blindness does not preclude the establishment of internal spatial representations of objects. Blind children explore novel objects in a similar way to other children, habituate to them, and have renewed interest in novel objects. They can recognise and discriminate between simple shapes in infancy and can perform mental rotation in order to identify novel objects in rotated positions (Landau, 1991). However, the system of spatial representation that is established in the congenitally blind may be less resilient than normal and less well integrated with semantic and conceptual systems (Pring, 1992). The congenitally blind appear to have weaker spatial skill than those who have acquired blindness later in life and both groups have poorer skills than controls. This applies to judgements of location, movement, and identity. In contrast transient global blindness associated with seizures does not appear to have any long-term implications for perceptual skill.

Two syndromes were discussed where visually related behaviour occurred in the presence of blindness. In one case, there was subjective awareness of a stimulus which was not present. In the other there was no subjective awareness of stimulus which was present, but behaviour indicated that detection was occurring. In the former, the visual hallucinations may have been a consequence of residual activation resulting from recent occipital lobe surgery, with potential stimulation of superior occipital cortex, the probable anatomical substrate for visual images (Mellet et al., 1995). In the latter, characteristics of blindsight appeared to parallel adult reports of the condition, suggesting that their physiological basis is established early in infancy, and is not a consequence of the development of an atypical strategy or plastic reorganisation.

The selective disorder of location perception described by McCloskey et al. (1995) suggested that the mental location representations have an internal structure with discrete components. The component representing the direction of displacement from the reference axis may be represented independently of the other components such as eccentricity, and in the McCloskey et al. (1995) case the displacement component is impaired, whereas other components remain intact. There has been no attempt at a cognitive decomposition of navigational disorder in childhood but there are suggestions of possible links to septal abnormalities in parallel to adult studies. The role of the hippocampus as a spatial map has also not been explored within development, despite the probable availability of suitable case material from within samples of temporal lobectomy groups.

One group of theories relating to visual neglect suggests that it arises from a disorder in a right hemisphere based system for the control of attention in space. There are several case reports of neglect in childhood following right hemisphere lesions Behaviourally, neglect has been reported amongst these children on many tasks derived from adult studies of neglect: line cancellation, drawing and copying, letter cancellation, pointing to body parts. It is also manifest in modalities other than visual, with for example, extinction of left side stimulation, on simultaneous bilateral tactile stimulation (Ferro et al., 1984). Results from reaction time analysis of those with bilateral lesions would also be consistent with the right hemisphere theory (Craft et al., 1994). An analysis of visual neglect in a child with callosal agenesis was also partly compatible with a right hemisphere basis for the dominant control of attention (Temple & Ilsley, 1994). However, the report of right neglect after a left hemisphere lesion (Johnston & Shapiro, 1986) and the performance of the acallosal subject with long lines in left hemispace (Temple & Ilsley, 1994) indicates that a more sophisticated explanatory model is required.

A selective disorder of movement perception is reported for those who have had early onset strabismus. The effect is to perceive temporal nasal targets as moving more rapidly than they are and to perceive nasal-temporal targets as moving more slowly than they are. This may reflect the abnormal development of the relative strengths of motion detecting neurons (Tychsen et al., 1996) and thereby disrupt the anatomical substrate for the putative movement detection channel of vision. A recent case report of selective impairment in the perception of movement, with intact visual acuity and object identification has also been described (Ahmed & Dutton, 1996).

A convincing case of developmental object agnosia has not been described but both acquired prosopagnosia in childhood and developmental prosopagnosia have been identified. There are several critical distinctions between the two cases of developmental prosopagnosia which have been discussed in relation to the Bruce and Young (1986) model (de Haan & Campbell, 1991; Temple, 1992b). One has an impairment in structural encoding for faces, which also creates downstream effects for all the channels of face processing. The other case appears to have intact structural encoding but has an impairment later in the face processing system. There is either difficulty in maintaining face recognition units over time and/or using them to activate person identity information. Thus, different components of the face processing system are affected in different cases of developmental prosopagnosia.

It could be argued that the downstream effects which occur as a consequence of the deficit in structural encoding weaken the potential for double dissociations within development and therefore weaken the power of the cognitive neuropsychological perspective. However, a similar problem arises in the analysis of the acquired prosopagnosias. For adults structural encoding is required in order to access face recognition units and other channels in the face processing system. Those adults with structural encoding deficits will be unable to access the rest of the face processing system, even though it is conjectured that it remains intact. The possibilities for double dissociation within the adult prosopagnosias are also therefore restricted. However, the cognitive neuropsychological perspective cross-linked to cognitive psychology has been successful in analysing the acquired prosopagnosias (e.g. Bruce, Cowey, Ellis, & Perret, 1992) and the paucity of current studies of prosopagnosia in childhood leaves scope for further productivity in this domain also.

Both Turner's syndrome and Williams syndrome represent genetic disorders within which selective aspects of spatial cognition are impaired. In Turner's syndrome, the suggestion of an impairment in perceptual organisation was proposed by Shaffer (1962). Children with Turner's syndrome are of normal intelligence but have selective impairments and talents within the scatter of their cognitive skills. The impairment in perceptual and spatial skills is greatest for those with the karyotype 45XO, and less severe for those with other mixed karyotypes. However, there is a task-specific nature to the impairment. Temple and Carney (1995) found greatest impairment in constructing simple jigsaws, Gestalt integrative skills, and drawing. Other studies have found problems with mental rotation (e.g. Rovet & Netley, 1982). Tactile spatial skills appear intact (Temple & Carney, 1995).

In Williams syndrome, intellectual skills are compromised more generally. There is also hyperacuisis. Visuo-spatial difficulties include difficulties with block design and also severe problems with copying and drawing. Details of component parts may be represented but with an inability to integrate these into a whole and with greater emphasis upon local forms than the global structure, a reverse dissociation being seen in some cases of Down's syndrome (Bellugi, Marks et al., 1988; Bihrle et al., 1989). A dominance of local over global processing may pervade many aspects of their perceptual and spatial skill.

CHAPTER FIVE

Reading Disorders

HISTORICAL PERSPECTIVES: THE GLASGOW VIEW

In 1877, Kussmaul coined the term word-blindness to refer to acquired disorders of reading resulting from brain damage. Kussmaul had noticed that "a complete text-blindness may exist, although the powers of sight, the intellect and the powers of speech are intact."

Nineteen years later, Morgan (1896) adopted the term word-blindness to refer to cases of reading disability which occur developmentally as a selective impairment and without recognisable aetiology. He modified the term to incorporate the developmental aspects and referred to these disorders as *congenital word-blindness*. It was not simply the adoption of similar terminology that suggested a relationship between the two groups of reading disorders. At the end of the 19th century, the similarities between the behavioural format of the reading disorders of acquired and congenital word-blindness were described. Word without letter-blindness was described within both congenital word-blindness and acquired word-blindness (Dejerine, 1892; Kerr, 1887). It was known that the angular gyrus was damaged in many cases of acquired word-blindness, and in 1910, Fisher speculated that a congenital aplasia of the angular gyrus might underlie problems in learning to read. Thus, not only were cognitive aspects associated with the expression of the acquired and developmental disorders postulated to be similar but a similarity in underlying neurological substrate was also postulated.

Morgan (1896) described a 14-year-old boy who was bright and intelligent and good at games. He was of a similar intellectual level to the other children of his age but had specific difficulty in learning to read. He had by constant application learnt to know what letters were, but though at school for seven years and though he had persistent remedial help, he could only with difficulty spell out words of one syllable. Written or printed words conveyed no instant impression to him and it was only after laboriously spelling them that he was able, by the sounds of the letters, to discover the identity of the word. In this description, the boy resembles contemporary cases within the adult neurological literature of acquired letter-by-letter reading. The boy's schoolmaster said that he would have been one of the most intelligent children in the school if his instruction had been entirely oral. Thus, in this early description, Morgan emphasises the good intelligence of the child and the selective impact of the disorder.

Both acquired and congenital word-blindness were studied in detail by James Hinshelwood, a surgeon at the Glasgow Eye Infirmary and a lecturer on ophthalmology in the Glasgow Western Medical School, who worked at the end of the 19th and in the earlier part of the 20th century. Following a series of publications in the *Lancet*, Hinshelwood (1900a) published his book on acquired word-blindness, which described the distinct disorders of letter-, word-, and mind-blindness. This taxonomic classification system was based upon the performance of the patients when attempting to read. In this regard, Hinshelwood's formulations and methodology resemble those of contemporary neuropsychology. Although Hinshelwood was concerned about the anatomical substrates to the different components involved in the reading process, he also discussed in some detail his conceptual formulation of visual word memory and the visual word centre. Seventeen years later, in 1917, Hinshelwood published his book on congenital word-blindness. In the foreword to this book he noted that he had:

> devoted considerable space to the subject of acquired word-blindness, without an adequate knowledge of which, in my opinion, congenital word-blindness cannot be properly understood. My aim has been first to furnish the reader with the chief facts regarding acquired word-blindness and then to employ this knowledge in the interpretation and explanation of the various phenomena of congenital word-blindness.

Within the text of the book Hinshelwood made his thesis even more explicit:

the complex processes involved in vision proceed smoothly and harmoniously during health in the region of the unconscious cerebration, but when disease disturbs the delicate mechanisms of the brain, there are revealed to us glimpses of its intimate working, a knowledge of which we would not acquire otherwise. It is for this reason that we have studied at such length the symptoms of acquired word-blindness, the knowledge of which will enable us to interpret and explain the phenomena of the congenital form. An adequate knowledge of the former condition is an essential preliminary to the proper understanding of the latter. (p. 40)

Hinshelwood's interest in congenital word-blindness pre-dated the publication of his congenital word-blindness book. Within a fortnight of Morgan's publication in 1896 of the description of the 14-year-old child with congenital word-blindness, Hinshelwood had published a critical note about the paper explaining some of the symptoms in the light of his studies with acquired word-blindness. Morgan was already aware of Hinshelwood's work and in private correspondence with Hinshelwood had pointed out that:

it was your paper — may I call it your classical paper? — on word-blindness and visual memory published in 1895, which first drew my attention to the subject, and my reason for publishing this case was that there was no reference anywhere, so far as I knew, to the possibility of the condition being congenital.

Hinshelwood's first report of his own cases of congenital word-blindness came in 1900 (1900b) and he attempted not only to record the cases but also to analyse and explain the symptoms. Five further cases were described by Nettleship in 1901 and two further by Hinshelwood in 1902. By 1903, interest had spread to the continent and there were case reports in different languages.

Hinshelwood (1917) proposed a three-stage model of learning to read. He pointed out that his comments refer to his "old-fashioned" (p. 53) method of learning to read which he distinguished from more recent training on "look and say" systems. The first stage in the old method was to store up in the memory, the individual letters of the alphabet. It was by comparison with this permanent visual image of the letters and the words in the cerebral centre that Hinshelwood proposed we were able to recognise printed letters and words on the pages of a book. He argued that in normal circumstances, this first stage was accomplished with comparative ease since there are only 26 letters in the alphabet, or taking both capitals and small letters, 52 visual images in all to be acquired. Thus, Hinshelwood dealt with the issue of recognition of different cases by postulating two different sets of recognition systems that are acquired for upper and lower case letters. (He did not discuss the issue of how handwriting and other permutations and alterations of the standard format are recognised.)

Hinshelwood was aware that normally we learn to read material which relates to words which we have already learnt in oral form. He proposed that the memory for words is first registered in our auditory memory centre which he located in the temporal sphenoidal lobe. This was proposed to have close connections with the visual memory centre and strong interconnections with other centres involved in language.

Traditional instruction in reading at this time involved reciting the individual letters involved in words and Hinshelwood argued that we are able to spell words before we are able to recognise them by sight. When the individual has stored up both the visual memories of the individual letters of the alphabet, in the left angular gyrus, and the spelling of words, in the auditory centre, then the individual can proceed to the second stage of reading. This formulation clearly differs from our contemporary ideas, in which although we expect that some abstract letter identification system has become established before we are able to read; it is not expected that we are able to spell words. Hinshelwood emphasised letter-by-letter analysis within the second stage of reading. He argued that in this stage, words are read by spelling them aloud letter-by-letter and appealing to auditory memory to identify the word. However, he also pointed out that sometimes children are simply seen to move their lips, spelling silently each letter, and appealing, in his view, to the memory of speech movements or glosso-kinaesthetic memory. Alternatively, the child may trace the letters with his fingers on the table and appeal to memory of the kinaesthetic movements of writing.

Contemporary formulations of reading development tend to emphasise the mastery of individual sounds associated with specific letters. In Frith's (1985) model this alphabetic phase is the second stage of reading development. In the preceding model of Marsh, Friedman, Welch, and Desberg (1981), it is the third stage of reading development. In these formulations, there is a letter-by-letter analysis but the processing of the word comes from combining the individual sounds. Hinshelwood appears to be referring to individual letter names but there is some ambiguity in his description. It is possible that one of the three aspects he described at this stage is a form of sounding out. However, he also proposed alternatives to access the word's identification by appealing to either speech movements or the writing centre. These modes only appear in contemporary models, in descriptions of circumventory strategies adopted by acquired dyslexics to bypass their fundamental reading disorder. Contemporary remedial systems attempting to improve children's reading difficulties also often incorporate multi-modal aspects associated with reading despite the absence of the other modalities in the models of normal child acquisition. In Bradley's remedial spelling system there is the involvement of speech movements, spelling aloud, and kinaesthetic hand movements (Bradley, 1980).

Hinshelwood considers his third stage in reading development to be the hardest and to require a longer period of acquisition than the preceding stages. He described it as "a formidable task" (p. 54). The third stage in Hinshelwood's model involved the acquisition and storage of visual memories for words and this involved not reading or analysing by individual letters, but recognising each word as a separate picture. In this formulation, Hinshelwood was suggesting that in order to identify a word, it is not necessary to evoke the sound characteristics associated with the word prior to activation of its meaning. Such a stage of formulation of phonological activation prior to meaning extraction is evident in many reading models in the 1960s and 1970s. However, Hinshelwood's formulation ties in more closely with the formulations proposed in the late 1970s and 1980s in which it is possible to recognise and identify a word prior to identifying the sound characteristics associated with it.

In relation to this recognition process, Hinshelwood suggested each word is regarded as an idiogram, picture, or symbol that suggests a particular idea. This conception of the evocation of an idea seems close to what we would consider to be the activation of an item within the semantic system. According to Hinshelwood, a word is recognised at this stage just as an individual would recognise a landscape or a familiar face, by its general outline and form without resolving it into its constituent details. This emphasis upon the outline and form activating an idea, comes close to aspects of contemporary models in which input logogens or word recognition systems activate semantic systems or face recognition units access personal identity information. Thus, Hinshelwood proposed that when we look at words we compare them with abstract visual word memories of symbolic form, which suggest particular ideas. He explicitly stated that there is no need for further appeal to the auditory memory or writing centres. By Hinshelwood's final stage in reading development, the reader has attained the power to read by sight alone.

Hinshelwood pointed out that there are individual differences in the efficiency with which we acquire this final stage of reading and that there are differences in reading speed, with some people able to skip over the pages of a book with great rapidity and ease and others only able to proceed slowly and with effort. Although he considered that practice and training may be relevant to these differences, he also suggested fundamental congenital distinctions between people and argued (Hinshelwood, 1917) that the degree of development of the visual memory centre may be relevant: "We are not all furnished at the start of life with visual memories of the same capacity, and this influences us more or less throughout our whole existence" (p. 55).

Since, in his other work and discussions, Hinshelwood emphasised the distinctions between visual memory for different kinds of material such as words, letters, and numbers (see Chapter 7) it is unlikely that in this discussion he is referring to a generalised visual memory process. Rather, since the discussion occurs at the end of a paragraph discussing visual word memories, one could argue that he is suggesting individual differences in this aspect of memory processes.

Hinshelwood described a series of cases of congenital word-blindness and then attempted to explain the symptomatology which they displayed in relation to his model of reading development. Case three, in which a child had taken nine months to acquire the letters of the alphabet, following persistent effort from his mother, was interpreted as a difficulty in acquiring the first stage of reading acquisition. It was interpreted as a grave defect in the visual memory centre, since there had been difficulty in acquiring the registration, even for the 26 basic letters (or 52 if one includes upper and lower case). Hinshelwood pointed out that most of the cases observed with congenital word-blindness are able to acquire basic letter identification skill and have difficulty with a later stage in reading development.

Hinshelwood emphasised that for most of his children auditory memory was good. In this regard, he placed very different emphasis upon the congenital reading disorders than is seen in current analyses. In the 1990s, studies tended to emphasise potential phonological processing disorders associated with developmental reading disorders (see later discussion). The only case for which Hinshelwood described specific difficulty in spelling out words, despite mastery of the identity of most of the letters, is a case where reading instruction has been based on "look and say". In this mode of reading instruction, Hinshelwood emphasised that individual letter spellings were not taught. However, since the child was able to identify individual letters but not spell them out, we may perhaps assume that there is an aspect associated with sounding out which reflects a deficiency of instruction. Hinshelwood argued that whereas for most normal children it would not be problematic if they were not taught these explicit letter spellings, since they have good visual memories and they may acquire reading by this means, for children who have weakened visual word memories, aspects of auditory processing become more critical.

Hinshelwood described a remedial system for the boy who had been taught "look and say" which is consistent with current phonemic remedial ventures. He was to be taught to spell and then to read simple words by spelling them out letter-by-letter and appealing to his auditory memory. According to Hinshelwood (1917), if there is a case of a defective visual centre but other cerebral centres are intact, the method of instruction which will be most successful is to appeal to centres other than the visual:

> this condition is fulfilled by the old-fashioned method of learning to read, in which simultaneous appeal is made to visual centre, auditory centre and the centre for the memory of speech movements. (p. 105)

Hinshelwood argued that this mode of acquisition is also employed by normal people when they try to learn passages of text, and that if trying to learn a piece of prose by heart, normal individuals will do so more rapidly if they are allowed to read it aloud, than if they are compelled to read it silently. He claimed that the reason for this increased success is that there is simultaneous appeal to three centres: the auditory; speech movements; and the visual.

Hinshelwood's cases five and six had difficulty in acquiring the final stage in reading, which requires reading by sight alone. He claimed that in order to accomplish this proficiently, a very large number of visual memories for words have to be acquired. In this fairly commonly documented disorder, the children show a frequency effect in that short, familiar words are easier to acquire than more rare words. Hinshelwood suggests that these children have been unable:

> unlike the other children to furnish their visual memory centre with the visual memories for words, and it is the great and persevering efforts which are necessary to repair this failure and to remedy this defect which make their educational career so different from that of the ordinary child. (p. 57)

In addition to his cognitive discussion of these congenital disorders, Hinshelwood also made a variety of observations which are relevant to our current conceptions of these disorders. He emphasised that in many cases there is a hereditary aspect to the congenital disorder. The suggestion of congenital word-blindness as a hereditary entity was first proposed by Thomas in 1905. Hinshelwood himself studied six cases of congenital word-blindness spanning two generations and Stephenson (1905) described six cases spanning three generations. Although it is known through current clinical observation that specific reading disorders frequently have familial components, there are still relatively few analyses of reading disorders affecting more than one member of a family and few analyses of the nature of the reading disorders manifest across generations.

Hinshelwood was also aware of methodological issues. He noted (1917) that the incidence of congenital word-blindness would depend upon what the writer meant by the term congenital word-blindness.

> Nothing has been more misleading in medicine than the use of statistics. Figures and percentages are worthless, unless we know precisely the basis on which they have been drawn up. (p. 76)

Hinshelwood considered that the term congenital word-blindness should not be used for every child who experienced difficulty in learning to read, but that there were two important conditions: (1) the defect should be very severe; and (2) the symptoms should be pure. Hinshelwood suggested that where children lag behind others in acquiring reading skills but have a level of deficit which can be overcome relatively easily by remediation, then the term congenital dyslexia should be applied. The term congenital word-blindness should then be reserved for more serious cases of disorder. He suggested that whereas the early descriptions referred to grave cases, the writers who subsequently described cases extended the term to include slight degrees of defect in the visual word centre, rather than the more marked degrees of deficit in the centre which he had described. Hinshelwood also argued that the terms should be restricted to children who have neither generalised intellectual defect nor generalised memory impairment. The specificity of the nature of the memory impairment is emphasised. Hinshelwood is clear that memory for the written word is distinct from other memories. Where the reading difficulty is combined with low intelligence, Hinshelwood proposed the term congenital alexia. He thus distinguished between three different types of disorder, the first two of which would be referred to as developmental dyslexias in contemporary classifications. The distinction between congenital word-blindness and congenital dyslexia is based on the severity of the disorder. The distinction between congenital dyslexia and congenital alexia is based on the other intellectual skills of the child.

TWENTIETH-CENTURY DEBATES

Labelling and Classification

Throughout the rest of the 20th century, there has been continuing discussion and debate regarding both the nature of the labelling of the disorder and the aspects which are most important for diagnosis. This continues even today with the term developmental dyslexia not being accepted in educational circles and the term specific learning difficulties shifting to 'and from' specific learning disabilities. During the 20th century a variety of other terms have been applied to the condition. Amongst these are strephosymbolia (Orton, 1928), specific dyslexia (Hallgren, 1950), constitutional dyslexia (Skysgaard, 1942), and developmental alexia (Orton, 1937). It was not until 1975, that the medical neurological fraternity formally recognised the condition which Hinshelwood had discussed in such detail, in the earlier part of the century. The World Federation of Neurology defined developmental dyslexia as follows:

> a disorder manifested by difficulty in learning to read despite conventional instruction, adequate intelligence, and socio-cultural opportunity. It depended upon fundamental cognitive disabilities which are frequently of constitutional origin. (Critchley, 1970)

This type of definition differs greatly from diagnosis of most medical conditions which will occur on the basis of positive symptomatology. This definition is a definition by exclusion. Dyslexia occurs where there is difficulty learning to read once several things are eliminated: poor teaching; poor intellect; poor socio-economic possibilities. The definition does however recognise the potential constitutional basis of the disorder.

In the 1970s, prevalence statistics were also proposed. Rutter, Tizard, Yule, Graham, and Whitmore's (1976) Isle of Wight study suggested an incidence of 3.5% and the inner London study of Berger, Yule, and Rutter (1975) suggested an incidence of 6%. More recently, Lewis, Hitch, and Walker (1994) tested an unselected sample of children, composed of the population of 9- and 10-year-olds in a single education authority district in England, and found that 6.2% had specific reading difficulties. It remains debated whether these children represent a group who are distinct from the main distribution of children, as suggested by the Isle of Wight study, or represent the lower tail of a normal distribution (e.g. Shaywitz, Escobar, Shaywitz, Fletcher, & Makuch, 1992).

Rutter and Newell led the way for a more mathematical definition of the disorder proposing a specific equation in relation to which one could make a formal definition of whether or not a child was dyslexic. The formal equation is documented by Yule, Lansdowne, and Urbanowicz (1982) and is as follows:

$$Predicted\ reading\ accuracy = -\,38.86 + 0.63 \times \text{FSIQ} + 0.78 \times \text{Age}$$

This equation is considered appropriate for use in the age range 6–12 years. Tabulated discrepancies between actual and predicted reading scores considered to reach statistical abnormality are of the order of 21 months for significance at a 5% level. In clinical practice, this precise equation is seldom formally applied and a child is often diagnosed as having a specific reading difficulty if the distinction between what might be expected as an appropriate reading level and what is attained is of the order of 2–3 years. Children of high intelligence with reading levels well below their other intellectual skills but nevertheless at an average level for age often fail to be identified as having specific difficulties.

From a cognitive neuropsychological perspective it is not clear that the models or systems which we should use to explain and understand reading disorders must be formally different depending on the degree of impairment in a child's reading. If we are to interpret reading difficulties in relation to a disorder of normal development, or the partial attainment of an adult system, then it ought to be possible to explain all reading disorders, regardless of the severity of the deficit. Similarly, Siegel (1989) has questioned the use of IQ in classifying the developmental dyslexic. The child's intellectual ability may not be relevant in that at all levels the disorders should be explicable in relation to the same model. Yet, in current formulations, it is not possible to describe a child as having a specific difficulty with reading if the child is also intellectually impaired. Children may have a variety of intellectual levels and not have reading difficulties and children with reading difficulties may also have a variety of intellectual levels (Siegel, 1988). We have no documentary evidence that the nature of the reading difficulties manifest in children of limited intellectual ability differ from the nature of the reading difficulties exhibited by the child with specific impairment.

From a cognitive neuropsychological perspective, one would wish to see descriptions of the different types of manifestation of reading disorder in children of normal intelligence and then descriptions of the different manifestations of reading disorder in children of limited intellectual development, in order to determine whether there is anything different in the formal expression of the two groups of conditions. In particular, although group studies have discussed phonological skills in what are called garden variety poor readers (those who are poor at reading and have low IQs) (Stanovich, 1988), there has been no systematic cognitive neuropsychological analysis of individual cases of garden variety reader and there is therefore no evidence about the patterns of reading impairment and their relationships to the pattern of the developmental dyslexias as discussed later.

Biological Bases

Arguments about labelling and classification have unfortunately led to the implication that there is some doubt about whether or not these specific reading disorders exist. However, there is now broadly based biological evidence to support the existence of developmental dyslexia as a specific entity, whatever we may wish to call it. Firstly, it has already been noted, that there is a heredity aspect to some of the conditions and, although the precise mechanism is unclear, familial trends are evident. Vogler, DeFries, and Decker (1985) reported that the risk to a son of having an affected father was 40% and of having an affected mother was 55%, a five- to seven-fold increase in risk over sons with no affected parent. The risk to a daughter of having an affected parent of either sex was 17–18%, a 10–12 fold increase over the risk with no affected parents. In a study of dyslexic twins, Olson, Wise, Conners, and Rack (1989) found significant heritability for a measure of oral non-word reading accuracy. In a minority of families, a linkage between dyslexia and chromosome 15 was reported, with autosomal dominant transmission (Smith, Kimberling, Pennington, & Lubs, 1983). However Pennington (1990) also emphasises that there is genetic heterogeneity in the transmission of dyslexia and no clear convergence on which different modes of transmission are operating. This could account for the failure to find linkage to chromosome 15 in other studies (e.g. Bisgaard, Eiberg, Moller, Niebuhr, & Mohr, 1987). Pennington et al. (1991), in a review of four independent familial samples, concluded that in three a major gene locus was the most likely mechanism of transmission with polygenetic transmission in the fourth.

Secondly, there are the electrophysiological studies, indicating specific EEG abnormalities associated with specific reading difficulties which moreover, indicate that the nature of these abnormalities is not consistent across all subjects but rather, some have more focal abnormalities in temporo-parietal areas and others include a specific frontal focus (Duffy, Denckla, Bartels, & Sandini, 1980; Duffy & McAnulty, 1985).

A series of post-mortem analyses of developmental dyslexics who have died as the result of other illness or accident, has been conducted by Galaburda and colleagues in Boston (Galaburda, 1985; Galaburda & Livingstone, 1993; Galaburda et al., 1985). Although there is some debate about the significance of certain cases for whom there were other neurological complications, there have nevertheless been fairly consistent striking architectonic abnormalities in the majority of the cases that have been investigated, which are not easily explicable. These have taken the form of foci of ectopic neurons and focal microgyria constellated particularly in areas of the left hemisphere with minor representation in the right hemisphere. The locations of these abnormalities within the left hemisphere have been fairly broadly distributed but have included those centres which we would classically consider to be involved in language and reading: the perisylvian cortex, inferior frontal cortex, the parietal operculum, parietal lobe, and temporal gyri (Galaburda, 1994).

The basis for the abnormalities is unknown and, although the Geschwind and Galaburda (1985) theory has remained controversial in suggesting that the abnormalities result from hormonal anomalies during foetal development, the basic post-mortem results nevertheless remain striking. One difficulty in interpreting these cases is the limitation in the number of comparable detailed analyses of non-dyslexic subjects, the time scale and effort required to conduct such analyses providing part of the explanation for limitation in studies. The specificity of the abnormalities is also unclear as abnormalities of cell migration have also been postulated to be associated with a broad range of other developmental disorders.

MRI studies have reported increased symmetry of the planum temporale in subjects with dyslexia (Hynd, Semrud-Clikeman, Lorys, Norey, & Epiopulos, 1990; Larsen, Hien, Lundberg, & Odegaard, 1990) and symmetry in the superior surface of the temporal lobe (Kushch et al., 1993). A higher incidence of bilateral anomalies is also reported (Leonard et al., 1993). Studies reporting differences in the size of the corpus callosum between dyslexics and controls have been contradictory (Duara et al., 1991; Hynd et al., 1995; Larsen, Hoien, & Odegaard, 1992). PET studies have demonstrated abnormalities in cerebral blood flow in the left temporal parietal region in men with dyslexia when carrying out a rhyming task, with normal patterns of activation on non-linguistic tasks, and normal activation of fronto-temporal cortex during syntactic processing (Hagram et al., 1992; Rumsey et al., 1992, 1994). This argues for a left hemisphere dysfunction restricted to posterior language areas. Flowers, Wood, and Naylor (1991) report that when poor readers carry out a spelling task, which in normals activates classical Wernicke areas, the area in the immediately posterior temporo-parietal region is activated instead.

A further argument for a biological basis to developmental dyslexic disorders is the evident sex difference in incidence and, although precise proportions are unclear, the ratio of males to females with dyslexia is of the order of 2 or 3:1. In the recent study of Lewis et al. (1994) a ratio of 3.2:1 is reported.

It has also repeatedly been argued that the incidence of left-handedness is higher amongst people with specific reading difficulties. However, this supposition has been the focus of considerable recent dispute and Bishop (1990) has argued that such a view cannot now be substantiated. Nevertheless, in combination, the biological evidence from genetic, electrophysiological, and post-mortem studies supports the view of developmental dyslexia as a congenital neuropsychological disorder.

Unitary Factors

The principal research efforts addressed at the developmental dyslexias in the 1960s and 1970s concerned group studies with a quest for a unitary associated factor that might be causal in generating the disorders. However, there is a limitation to the amount of information that may be obtained within group studies if the group involved is not homogeneous with respect to the factor under investigation. Despite Hinshelwood's (1917) early documentation of the different formats of developmental reading disorders, the multiple syndrome nature of developmental dyslexia continues to be ignored in many studies. Some of the early attempts to categorise the developmental dyslexias described a variety of syndrome features which were believed to co-occur in particular dyslexic populations. A number of these features did not relate to the reading process itself. However, with increasing investigation of the disorders it has been difficult to substantiate these different syndrome groupings. While certain symptoms co-occur in some children, in other children they fractionate and dissociate, indicating that they are not intrinsically interrelated.

Contemporary psycholinguistic analyses of the developmental dyslexias adopt a methodology comparable to that which has been used with the acquired dyslexias. They echo aspects of the analyses conducted by Hinshelwood (1917) but with more systematic decomposition of the precise nature of the response evoked by the presentation of particular types of linguistic material. Before presenting specific case descriptions of these disorders some models should be proposed. The case reports will then be discussed in relation to these formulations.

MODELS OF NORMAL READING

Stage Models of Normal Reading

Within the neuropsychological literature there continues to be discussion of the stage models of Marsh et al. (1981) and Frith (1985). The stages in these models of acquisition are summarised in Table 5.1. The Marsh et al. (1981) model postulates four stages in reading acquisition. The first stage is referred to as *glance and guess*. In this stage of reading development, children are able to recognise a small set of words by sight. They have no phonic skills. They are unable to read unfamiliar words except by guessing within a story. The word guessed does not in any systematic fashion resemble the target word. If in reading the sentence *the boy went to the moon in a rocket*, the child guessed "spaceship" for rocket, this is a guess based on general context rather than the extraction of partial information from the word spaceship. A similar guess would have been proposed even if the written sentence had been *the boy went to the moon in a cauliflower*. Thus, meaning related guesses take place only in the context of the story and are not the true semantic errors of the acquired neurological literature.

Stage two in the Marsh model involves the acquisition of more *discrimination net guessing*. Normally, within the first year of reading acquisition there will be progress to this stage. Stage two begins the building up of sight vocabulary. Now when words which are unfamiliar are guessed at in context, known words are used to constrain the guesses. The children also look for overlap between the stored visual units and the new words. Thus the guesses now begin to resemble the target visually. At this stage, aspects of approximate visual access are employed.

In stage three, there is acquisition of *sequential decoding* with simple grapheme to phoneme correspondences. The child is taught or notices that certain letter groups are pronounced in the same way in different words and that it is therefore possible to work out a new word's pronunciation. Decoding is initially a simple left to right sequential process. Subsequently, digraphs and specific rules are mastered. The reader becomes more versatile. In stage four, skilled reading has been acquired, which is context sensitive and also incorporates aspects of reading by analogy. It involves *hierarchical decoding*. This stage is typically not reached until the middle years of childhood.

Marsh's model (Marsh et al. 1981) was modified by Frith (1985) who delineated a three phase rather than a four phase theory. Each phase follows the other in sequential order and capitalises upon the previous one. In the first *logographic phase* a sight vocabulary of instantly recognisable words is built up. Phonological factors are secondary, i.e.

TABLE 5.1
Proposed Stages of Normal Reading Development

Marsh et al. (1981)	*Frith (1985)*	*Ehri (1991, 1992)*
1. Glance and Guess	1. Logographic	1. Logographic
2. Discrimination Net Guessing	2. Alphabetic	2. Phonetic Cue
3. Sequential Decoding	3. Orthographic	3. Cipher
4. Hierarchical Decoding		

the child only pronounces the word after if is recognised. In the second *alphabetic phase* the analytical skill of decoding graphemes to phonemes in sequential order develops. In the final *orthographic phase* words are systematically analysed into orthographic units (ideally morphemes) without phonological conversion. These units are internally represented as abstract letter-by-letter strings.

Frith (1985) argued that the early logographic skills might lead to the formation of input logogens (Morton & Patterson, 1980) or word form analysers (Shallice & Warrington, 1980). Alphabetic skills might lead to the development of grapheme to phoneme conversion systems (Coltheart, 1978). Orthographic skill acquisition leads to word component analysers (Shallice & McCarthy, 1985; Shallice, Warrington, & McCarthy, 1983; Temple, 1985b). Thus, this model predicts a sequential basis to the acquisition of components of a normal adult reading system, a model of which will be discussed later. Morton (1989) also incorporates a single, universally applicable programme of stages in literacy development to attain the adult system. Seymour and MacGregor (1984) retain the three stages proposed by Frith (1985) but develop them within a model of the reading system in which there are two distinct lexicons. The logographic reader sets up a logographic lexicon; the orthographic lexicon develops out of an alphabetic lexicon. Once established, both lexicons remain throughout life. Later Seymour modified this view of the relationship between the alphabetic and orthographic lexicon (see the later section on hyperlexia).

A fundamental principle of these stage theories is that all children pass through the same stages in the same invariant order. In contrast, Stuart and Coltheart (1988) argue that there are individual differences in the patterns of acquisition. They report that children who are phonologically skilled use phonological skills from the beginning and do not go through a logographic stage. Ehri (1987) also argues that although pre-readers may use visual or context cues to identify words, as soon as children move into reading they shift to letter-sound cues. Wimmer and Hummer (1990) report that alphabetic strategies are also used from the beginning in German children who are learning a language which is phonologically transparent. However, they argue that this gives the German children an advantage in reading nonsense words over English children for whom such a strategy is less common (Wimmer & Goswami, 1994).

Stuart and Coltheart (1988) do not argue that all children use phonological skills from the beginning. Children who are not phonologically skilled may initially treat reading as a visual memory task, and may become logographic readers. In Stuart and Coltheart's view, children use whatever skills they have available when learning new words, and the available skills differ between children.

Multiple Route Models of Reading

In the late 1970s and through the 1980s, a series of different dual or triple route models of normal adult reading were proposed. They incorporated a variety of similar principles but there are slight variations in the features incorporated from one research group to another. I will discuss my own formulation here (Temple, 1985c) but this derives in large part from previous work (Coltheart, 1978; Morton, 1969, 1979; Newcombe & Marshall, 1981; Shallice et al., 1983). Further, although the case reports presented later will be discussed in relation to this model, they could easily be discussed in relation to other similar formulations and a discussion of this sort is not dependent upon the acceptance of the precise features of the specific formulation presented here.

In the late 1980s and early 1990s, parallel distributed processing models and other network models have become popular in discussions of the underpinnings of cognitive systems. Some argue that these should supplant the modular information processing models. Others argue that they merely depict mechanisms to represent the acquisition of information within the modules of previous models. Whichever stance is valid, and these models will be discussed further later, a detailed understanding of the multiple route models of reading and their implications clarifies the developmental thrust of the field, some of the focal theoretical issues, and outlines the psycholinguistic distinctions of relevance to a developmental cognitive neuropsychology of literacy.

The early dual route models (see Fig. 5.1) indicated two routes by which a word might be read aloud. When reading occurs via route 1, the *semantic route*, the following stages occur. Following preliminary visual analysis, abstract letter representations are extracted. The system which is involved in determining these aspects is not sensitive to whether the letters are lower case, upper case, or hand written. The result of this process feeds into a system of representation which in Morton's models are referred to as *input logogens*. In Shallice et al.'s (1983) formulations the system is referred to as a *visual word form system*. In my own model, the system contains *word detectors*. The system contains representations of words which are activated by visual input. The words have thresholds of activation, such that a word of higher frequency is more easily activated than a word of low frequency, since words of high frequency have lower thresholds. There is a biological analogy employed in this recognition system, which is similar to the activation of neuronal responses. Evidence is summated and if it reaches the critical threshold the word detection is activated. Thus, the

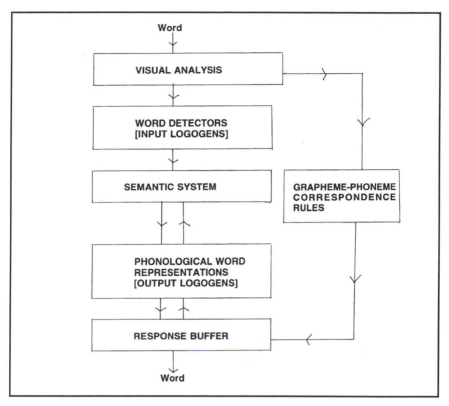

FIG. 5.1 A dual route model of reading.

triggering or not of an item within the store resembles the all-or-none firing of classical descriptions of neuronal transmission. (Such classical views of neural transmission no longer remain valid (Temple, 1993).

The word detection system contains stores of words based upon morphemic representations. Thus, the word *tree* and the word *trees* activate a similar morpheme tree within the system. The processing of affixes, or other bound morphemes, is represented differentially across models and will be discussed further later. Subsequent to activation of the logogen, a representation is triggered within the *semantic system* which provides information about the meaning of the word and its associations. This meaning then activates a representation which is phonologically based and which is referred to as an *output logogen* in Morton's model, and a phonological representation in other models. This pronunciation can either be spoken aloud or can be held in a *response buffer*. The crucial element of dual route models is that the systems employing whole word recognition via the semantic system are distinct from the *phonological reading route* which is marked as route 2 in Fig. 5.1.

The phonological reading route involves a system within which following visual analysis, words are broken down into components. These are then associated via a system of rules with the words' pronunciation. The initial formulations of this rule system were based upon grapheme to phoneme rules (e.g. Coltheart, 1978). Subsequent models suggested that the orthographic unit upon which the conversion rules were based may be variable in size. Shallice and colleagues (Shallice & McCarthy, 1985; Shallice & Warrington, 1980; Shallice et al., 1983) suggested that correspondences could be based upon larger orthographic segments and suggested that there were translation rules for graphemes, consonant clusters, sub-syllabic units, syllables and morphemes. They postulated a visual word form system, composed of orthographic units for letter groups, which exist in at least one English word to which the subject has been exposed. Such units might be restricted to letter groups with functional phonological or semantic correspondence. The orthographic units would activate corresponding units in a phonological system. Orthographic units with more than one possible pronunciation would have the distinct pronunciations represented by separate correspondence rules, differing in strength. This system which links the word form system to a phonological data base is labelled by Shallice and McCarthy (1985) as "phonological correspondence processing" (p. 364).

The ambiguity and disagreement in the precise way in which such a system should operate is reflected in the model that adorns the cover of Patterson, Marshall, and Coltheart (1985) (see Fig. 5.2). Here the phonological reading route becomes described ambiguously as a system of "orthography to phonology (sub-word level)". Its point of exit and entry in relation to other reading routes is sufficiently uncertain to warrant representation by a dotted line. The model adorning the cover of this book also depicts a third reading route labelled as orthography to phonology (word-level). The third route is generally referred to as the direct reading route. In a more simply depicted triple route model of reading (see Fig. 5.3) the direct route passes directly from input logogens to output logogens or from word detectors to phonological word representations.

The direct route was introduced into reading models following the description by Schwartz, Saffran, and Marin (1980) of a dementing patient who remained able to read irregular words aloud correctly, at a point when comprehension of their meaning had been lost. Irregular words do not conform to spelling to sound pronunciation rules and therefore cannot be read aloud correctly by the phonological route. Such words had previously therefore been believed to be read by the semantic reading route (route 1 as depicted on Fig. 5.1 and Fig. 5.3). However, reading via the semantic reading route involves activation of the meaning of a word prior to its pronunciation. For the patient described by Schwartz et al. (1980) this meaning was not accessible as a result of the deterioration associated with the dementia. The patient was therefore described as having direct dyslexia, in which direct access from word detectors to phonological representations bypasses semantics. This form of dyslexia is relatively common in patients with dementia of Alzheimer's type. The reading disorder is not consistent in its format throughout the process of deterioration but is evident at a particular stage and has been further explored by Hodges et al. (1992). As the cover picture of Patterson et al. (1985) illustrates (Fig. 5.2) the relationship of the direct reading route to the phonological reading route is vague. In Shallice and Warrington's formulations (e.g. Shallice et al., 1983) the

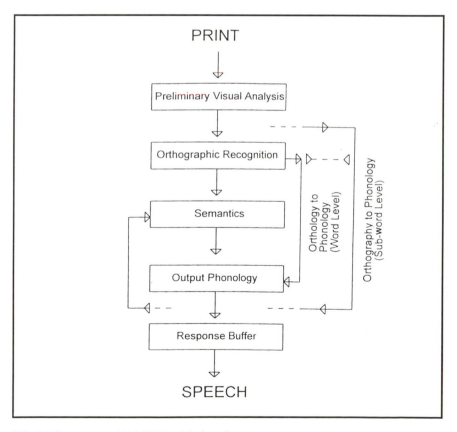

FIG. 5.2 Patterson et al.'s (1985) model of reading.

direct reading route is abandoned altogether in favour of the expanded phonological route. Temple's (1985c) formulation retains all three routes.

Temple (1985c) makes the relationship between the alternative reading systems more explicit (see Fig. 5.4). A further modification to the early depiction of the phonological reading route is also represented. Prior to the rule based translator a *parser* is activated in segmenting the words into chunks. A chunk is defined as the written representation of p phonemes where $0 < p < n$, and n is the number of phonemes in a word. The preferred parsing depends upon the experience of the reader. Treiman (1992, 1993) provides evidence that children must use multi-letter units within any phonological translation system. The *translator* also contains representations of more than one translation possibility. Thus, a chunk like *ead* would have available a translation rule parallel to that in *dead* and that in in *bead*. More translation rules are internalised as contact with the written word increases. Although in

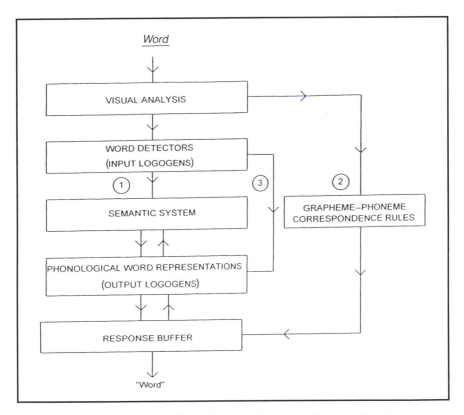

FIG. 5.3 Triple route model of reading: 1. The semantic route; 2. The phonological route; 3. The direct route.

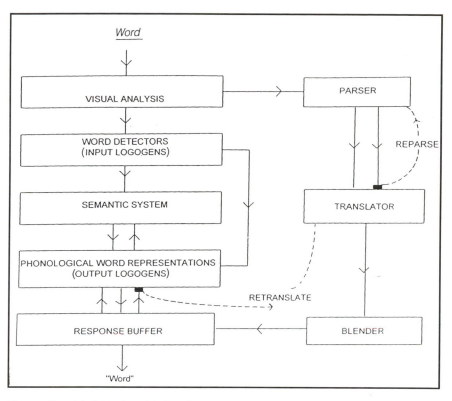

Fig. 5.4 Temple's (1985c) model of reading.

Temple's (1985c) formulation it was proposed that young beginning readers parse into smaller chunks than experienced readers, more recent studies suggest that in some normal children the reverse pattern operates, i.e. children parse words into larger chunks prior to attending to smaller chunks (e.g. Goswami & Bryant, 1990). The issue of the development of the parser therefore remains open. Acquired surface dyslexia may be explained as a malfunction of the parser, in which parsing operates on chunks below the optimum level. Acquired phonological dyslexia may result from a malfunction of the parser in which parsing operates on chunks above the optimum level. These interpretations will be discussed in more detail below in relation to developmental abnormalities. Normal young children, may also sometimes parse into chunks which are non-optimal, if their experience with the written word has not yet been sufficient to internalise more substantive parsing rules. In such cases, their reading performance may resemble surface dyslexia, a comparison first noted by Marcel (1980). Though as Seymour (1986) notes, even when patterns of performance are similar, dyslexics and normals may be differentiated by their speed of response.

Subsequent to the translator, Temple (1985c) depicts a *blender*, which combines phonological segments and produces an integrated phonological output. Malfunctions of the blender produce emissions or repetitions of phonological segments in the overt responses. The translator itself is capable of rejecting an input. If it has no representation of any chunk resultant from prior parsing, it may trigger a re-parse operation. Thus, Temple's model incorporates feedback routes. Once the translator has accepted an input it selects between valid alternative translations by attempting that of higher token frequency first. If this ultimately produces a neologistic response, a mismatch with known words is detected and a retranslation will occur. This system is frequently under conscious control and may prevent the production of neologistic responses. The translator may malfunction by mismatching orthographic and phonological chunks. As discussed later, surface dyslexia may be used to investigate malfunctions at different levels of this system.

Connectionist Models

An alternative to the multiple route models is the single route analogy model (Glushko, 1979). In this model, there is a single procedure which is used to read aloud both non-words and irregular words. The model in its initial formulation was difficult to test but it was then incorporated into an explicit connectionist model by Seidenberg and McClelland (1989). In this model, a set of hidden units connects an orthographic store, which codes the visual properties of words, and a phonological store, which codes their phonological properties. The connection weights, via the hidden units between the two stores, are established by training using the back propagation algorithm of Rumelhart, Hinton, and Williams (1986). The model establishes correspondences between English words and their pronunciations, which are stores in the connection weights. Regularity effects emerge as a consequence of the probabilities of exposure to particular types of word. The network was also able to "pronounce" non-words on which it had not been directly trained.

There were however, a number of criticisms of the model. One problem related to non-word reading. For example, Besner, Twilley, McCann, and Seergobin (1990) showed that the network was much poorer than normal adults at both reading aloud non-words and at lexical decision. Coltheart and Leahy (1992) demonstrated that young children also read non-words with better accuracy than the model predicts. The model also had difficulty in accounting for the range of patterns of acquired dyslexia which may follow brain injury. In particular it was unable to offer an account of the double dissociations evident within the acquired dyslexias (Castles & Coltheart, 1993), and for cases where non-word reading may be better than word reading (Coltheart, Curtis, Atkins, & Haller, 1993). This limitation is also relevant for the cases of developmental dyslexia which will be discussed below.

More recently, in response both to the difficulties in accounting for the patterns of the acquired dyslexias and the skill of normal subjects in reading non-words, revised connectionist models have been proposed which are better at reading non-words and which incorporate dual routes (Plaut & McClelland, 1993; Plaut, McClelland, Seidenberg, & Patterson, 1996; Seidenberg, Plaut, Peterson, McClelland, & McCrae, 1994). Thus, connectionist models have become multiple route models.

One of the distinctions between connectionist and some non-connectionist models of normal reading now lies in the number of routes involved. Both types of model have a semantic reading route. However, the connectionist models have a route which incorporates elements of both the phonological and direct reading routes of triple route models, whereas triple route models retain a distinction between the two. Note however, that the non-connectionist model of Shallice et al. (1983) also incorporates the phonological route into the direct route. Thus, for many theorists the two groups of models have become close. Nevertheless, Besner (in press) argues that the three route model continues to provide a better account of the data, and there remains some degree of division between the McClelland/Seidenberg/Plaut view and the Coltheart/Besner view, albeit with considerable overlap between the two previously opposed perspectives.

Recent PET studies also support the multiple route hypotheses. For example, Bookheimer, Zeffiro, Blaxton, Gaillard, and Theodore (1995) report activation of an inferior temporal pathway in silent reading and object naming where there may be direct access to a lexical entry. In reading aloud there is activation of a superior temporal-inferior parietal route which may involve the sequential transcription of visual elements into phonological sounds.

Developmental Connectionist Models

Both Ehri (1980, 1984, 1991, 1992) and Perfetti (1992) have attempted to incorporate analogy theory and the older version Seidenberg and McClelland (1989) model into a developmental model. Ehri argues that in order to establish a sight vocabulary (the lexical or semantic route[s] of multiple route models) phonological recoding is required. Ehri believes that phonological recoding is a prerequisite for learning to read and that dual route models do not explain this. Over time, as a word is established in sight vocabulary, the need for phonological recoding is eliminated. In Ehri's model the use of phonological recoding leads to the establishment of a visual-phonological route. Spelling units become linked to pronunciation units. Readers find words in lexical memory via connections linking spelling to pronunciation, rather than links between spelling and meaning, although connections between spelling and meaning are also formed. However, the access to pronunciation is not like that in the phonological reading route. Access to lexical memory to locate pronunciation is not via grapheme–phoneme conversion rules but via the word's spelling. In Ehri's theory, letters in spelling symbolise the phonemes used to pronounce words leading to the visual–phonological connection. Spelling and pronunciation are therefore merged in visual–letter analysed representations. These representations are then amalgamated to meanings and this amalgam is activated in sight reading, via the visual–phonological connection.

Ehri goes on to incorporate these ideas into a stage model. In the logographic phase rote memory is used to link visual cues and word meaning as there is no letter–sound system knowledge. In a phonetic cue reading phase, readers use a basic knowledge of letter names or sounds to form partial connections between spelling and pronunciations. Finally, in the cipher phase, phonological segmentation and recoding skill enables the formation of complete connections between the entire spelling of the word in memory and the phonemic units in its pronunciation.

Perfetti (1992) proposes a restricted interaction model of reading within which there is interaction of information within the lexicon and reciprocal activation between letters, words and phonemes, as well as multiple letter and multiple phoneme units. At the same time, there is restriction on the influence of information from outside the lexicon. In particular, general knowledge and expectancies have little or no influence on the initial access of a word, so that the lexicon is itself autonomous or modular. Perfetti (1992) claims to be merging the interactive principles of McClelland and Rumelhart (1981) and the autonomous principle of Foster (1979). In the Perfetti (1992) model, phonemic activation occurs as an intrinsic part of lexical access. There is also a single representation which serves both reading and spelling.

In the acquisition of this system, rules have a minor role and the major development is in the acquisition of individual word representations which as skill develops increase in number and quantity. Within the lexicon, there are two subsections. The beginning reader develops a functional lexicon which is not autonomous and has contributions from knowledge, expectations, and context. The representations within this are under-specified. A second autonomous lexicon is also established which has fully specified and redundant representations. Specific words change status to join this lexicon. Speed of correct spelling is taken as an index of a representation within the autonomous lexicon. Although computational phonemic knowledge is required to develop the functional lexicon, the explicit reflective phonemic knowledge required by most tests of phonemic awareness, such as rhyming and phoneme deletion, develops through experience with alphabetic stimuli.

In this model speech codes are part of the lexical representation. Thus phonemic information is activated during lexical access. There are qualitatively no differences in the representations of words, and regularity and irregularity have no bearing on representation. The stronger the context-sensitive rules, the more entries a learner can acquire. The more entries, the more powerful the decoding rules. Lexical learning is therefore highly interactive. Perfetti argues that he finds the existence of Boder's (1973) dyseidetic dyslexics who use only a visual strategy unconvincing. There appears to be a confusion over terminology here, since Boder's dyseidetics are children who have both surface dyslexia (see later) and surface dysgraphia (see Chapter 6). Such children use phonological not visual strategies, which Perfetti could accept. Non-phonemic spelling strategies are a feature of phonological dysgraphia (see Chapter 6) and Boder's dysphonetic dyslexics. Perfetti's model (1992) has difficulty in accounting for the patterns of the developmental dyslexias, just as the earlier connectionist models did in accounting for the acquired dyslexias (see later discussion).

We turn finally to the cognitive neuropsychological analyses of the developmental dyslexias and their theoretical interpretations. In historical terms, developmental surface dyslexia (Holmes, 1973) was described before developmental phonological dyslexia (Temple & Marshall, 1983). It will therefore be discussed first amongst the dyslexic disorders.

DEVELOPMENTAL SURFACE DYSLEXIA

The suggestion that a pattern of reading performance which has been labelled developmental surface dyslexia might be found amongst developmental dyslexias was first proposed by Holmes (1973) in her doctoral thesis and by Coltheart, Masterson, Byng, Prior, and Riddoch (1983) who described the case of an 18-year-old girl CD, of average intelligence but with a reading age of 10 years. CD displayed a significant regularity effect in reading words aloud, in that words that conformed to spelling to sound rules were read more easily than those which were not consistent with such rules. Her errors showed the application of a rule based system, e.g. *bear* →"beer"; *subtle* →"subtill". She also displayed homophone confusion, in that words with the same pronunciations but different spellings were confused. For example, she defined *pane* as "something which hurts". Prior to the discussion of the features of developmental surface dyslexia in relation to models proposed earlier, a case description will be presented upon which to base the discussion.

Case Report: Developmental Surface Dyslexia, RB

RB was first described at the age of 10 years (Temple, 1984b, 1986b). Further aspects of her performance are expanded upon here. There were no features of concern during pregnancy or the early months of life. Early motor milestones and language development were satisfactory with plentiful, clear speech well before the third year. There were no early illnesses nor injury of any significance. Concern at slowness in learning to read started around age seven.

On examination by a paediatric neurologist, RB was reported as an alert, cooperative, attentive child of good intelligence. Skull, spine, stance, gait, visual acuity, and hearing were all within normal limits. There was minor dyspraxia apparent in ocular motor movements and sequential finger movements with slight impairment of imitative movement but overall RB was presented as a healthy child whose development appeared normal. The report concluded that there was "no evidence of neurological defect". There was a family history of literacy difficulties.

At the age of 10, the Wechsler Intelligence Scale for Children was given to RB. A full scale IQ of 115 was obtained. The following subtest scores were attained:

Verbal Tests		Performance Tests	
Information	11	Picture Completion	10
Similarities	12	Picture Arrangement	12
Digit Span	14	Block Design	12
Vocabulary	17	Coding	8
Verbal IQ	122	Performance IQ	104

(mean subtest score = 10; range 1–19; SD = 3)

On the Peabody Picture Vocabulary Test, RB attained a raw score at the 99th percentile for age. These tests indicated that RB was of at least average intelligence with an extensive vocabulary. At the time of assessment RB was 10;10 and had a reading age for accuracy on the Neale Analysis of Reading of 8;7. The progress of her reading and change over time is discussed later.

Non-word Reading.   Three lists were presented to RB. On each list, half the stimuli were words and half were matched to pronounceable non-words made from the words by altering one letter. The first list contained stimuli three letters in length, and the second contained stimuli five to six letters in length. The third list consisted of the shortest stimuli taken from an unpublished list of Coltheart's, normally used as a lexical decision task. On these lists RB read respectively, 13 words and 12 non-words; 12 words and 11 non-words; and 23 words and 20 non-words. There was no significant difference between her performance in reading words and in reading non-words. Thus, she displayed one of the fundamental characteristics of surface dyslexia, in that non-word reading is as good as word reading. In Castles and Coltheart's 1996 study of the surface dyslexic MI, it was also emphasised that in surface dyslexia, non-word reading is at age level and unimpaired in relation to peers.

RB was also presented with Temple's homophonic non-word list (Temple & Marshall, 1983). Of her errors, 11 were to stimuli homophonic with real words and 10 to stimuli non-homophonic with real words. For RB, being a homophone with a real word was not a determinant of whether a non-word would be read more easily. Her ability to read aloud non-words was independent of whether the pronunciation is identical to a real word. There was thus no evidence of any interaction with established lexical stores.

Reading Words Aloud.   RB's reading analysis was based on her reading of 434 words, 181 of which she read correctly. 64% of errors were neologisms and 36% were paralexias. Of the neologistic error responses, 36% were valid, in that they conformed to the application of a rule based pronunciation system, e.g. *anchor* →"/ænt∫ɔɪ/"; *dumb* →"/dʌmb/".

These two examples are classic regularisation errors. There are other valid errors which are not classic regularisations but which do conform to the application of a rule based system if lower frequency correspondences are permitted, e.g. *break* →"/brɛk/"; *host* →"/hɒst/"; *teach* →"/tiæt∫/". Although there were fewer paralexic responses than neologistic responses, a number of the paralexic errors are also valid, e.g. *baker*→"backer"; *aide* →"eyed"; *sweat* →"sweet"; *sour* →"sore".

The majority of paralexic errors (75%) were visual paralexias where the response shared at least 50% of the letters in common with the stimulus, or vice versa. However, since paralexic errors were very much less frequent than the neologistic errors, these visual paralexias represent only 24% of the total error responses. Examples of the visual paralexic errors are *orchestra* →"orchard"; *mattress* →"matters"; *metal* →"mental"; *steak* →"shark".

Only 1% of RB's errors could be classified as morphological paralexias, in which the base of the word is read correctly but an affix is dropped, added, or substituted. As will be discussed later, this error type is very common in developmental phonological dyslexia but is virtually absent from the error corpus of a relatively pure surface dyslexic. Within the error corpus of RB there were also no errors of the pseudo-derivational type which will be discussed later in the section on developmental phonological dyslexia.

In addition to these general error types, RB was also somewhat unusual as a developmental dyslexic of this age, in persisting in showing letter orientation confusions, particularly u–n confusion. Thus, for example, she made the errors, *soul* →"/sʌnl/"; and *doubt* →"/dʌnt/". This feature of performance is not known to be characteristic of other surface dyslexics.

Regularity Effects.   RB was presented with 78 words on the Coltheart, Besner, Jonasson, and Davelaar (1979) list. Half these words are regular and half irregular; they are matched for frequency, number of letters, number of syllables, and part of speech, but not for imageability. RB read 24 regular words correctly but only 10 irregular words. Whereas such regularity effects are also seen in normal children learning to read, in surface dyslexia they persist beyond the normal age at which they would reduce in evidence.

Investigations involving the presentation of matched lists which explored effects of frequency, imageability, length, and word class were all non-significant with RB. The only linguistic dimension which clearly affected reading performance was spelling to sound regularity, with irregular words being read more poorly.

Homophone Reading.   40 words on Temple's homophonic word list (Temple, 1984c) were presented in random order for reading aloud. The homophonic stimuli on this list are all regular. After reading each word, RB was asked to define it. Of the 21 words read correctly, 10 appropriate definitions were given and homophonic definitions. Examples of these responses are as follows:

male: "chain mail or mail in the mornings"
dye: "kill yourself"
heel: "cut my knee and it heals"
steal: "a kind of metal"
peace: "a piece of paper"

Thus, when RB read a homophone correctly, her ability to assign meaning to it was random with respect to the word itself and its homophones. Meaning was derived not directly from the appearance of the word but indirectly from its phonological recoding.

Typescript Distortions. In four different test sessions RB was presented with 25 words written in one of four formats: normal typescript, handwriting, reversed lower case typescript, and reversed upper case typescript. Her performance is summarised in Table 5.2.

Reversing the order of the letters in the words did not impair performance. For RB distortions of the global characteristics of words did not impair the ability to read them if the individual letters remained distinguishable.

Theoretical Explanations. RB's pattern of reading performance may be explained in relation to the Marsh et al. (1981) model of reading development as an arrestment of acquisition which has produced a pattern of reading performance characteristic of stage three of reading acquisition, sequential decoding, but which has failed to progress to stage four, hierarchical decoding. RB had mastered some simple grapheme–phoneme correspondences and was able to implement these in a simple right to left fashion but she had not been able to become a versatile, skilled reader with context sensitivity, analogical reading, and whole word recognition.

Similarly, in relation to Frith's (1985) model of reading development, developmental surface dyslexia can receive a relatively straightforward explanation in relation to arrestment at the second stage, the alphabetic stage of reading development. There is mastery of grapheme to phoneme rules and some other correspondence rules but there is a failure to proceed to the sophisticated, orthographic reading that characterises normal adult reading performance. This has particular impact in a language like English in which there are a large number of irregular words and appropriate orthographic reading is required for effective reading of the language. In a language such as Italian or Spanish where the correspondence rules are significantly more regularly invoked, a child with developmental surface dyslexia would be significantly less impaired. In these languages, mastery of alphabetic routes may be sufficient to provide the child with a code to decipher words. This may be slower in its application than instant recognition of the word, but should nevertheless be effective in enabling activation of the pronunciation and thereby the meaning of the word.

TABLE 5.2
Reading of Distorted Typescript by a Surface Dyslexic

Stimuli	Example	Number correct
Normal typescript	e.g. large	10/25
Handwritten		6/25
Reversed lower case	e.g. egral	12/25
Reversed upper case	e.g. EGRAL	13/25

It was noted above that there is some debate about whether the series of stages, as outlined by Frith (1985) are followed for all children. In particular, it was noted that some children appear to start with an alphabetic stage. In such interpretations, RB would be arrested at this initial phase of reading. If it is accepted that there are different routes to reading acquisition then RB is placing greater emphasis upon alphabetic strategies (Stuart & Coltheart, 1988).

Just as acquired surface dyslexia may be interpreted in terms of an impairment of semantic route reading and direct route reading, with preservation of phonological route reading, so RB the developmental surface dyslexic may be interpreted in a similar fashion. It can be argued that the direct and semantic reading routes have failed to become established properly, and that there is therefore over-reliance upon phonological reading. This explanation can account for the main characteristics of the disorder. The good reading of non-words in relation to words results from good development of phonological reading route mechanisms, which enable, by the application of a system of rules, the pronunciation of unfamiliar stimuli. The presence of a marked regularity effect can be explained in a similar fashion. The over-reliance placed on phonological reading means that this route is used to read and pronounce a number of irregular words that would normally be dependent upon semantic or direct route reading for their word-specific pronunciation to be activated. The application of a logical system to these irregular stimuli produces errors, and in many cases these errors are regularisation or valid errors as illustrated earlier. In RB's case, the presence of a large number of neologistic errors further confirmed that reading is not resulting from the activation of phonological representations of words, stored in relation to the whole word. It is also evident that the feedback mechanism which would normally prohibit the activation of these neologistic responses in Temple's model (see Fig. 5.4) is not effective in RB's case.

Homophone confusions can be seen to arise because meaning is being activated after the activation of pronunciation. The semantic representations associated with lexical entries, in Fig. 5.4 are triggered after the phonological representation for the word by feedback up the lexical route. The representation that activates semantics therefore has no information about the original visual representation of the word, and the child is unable to distinguish between alternative meanings associated with identical pronunciations.

This analytical reading system, upon which the surface dyslexic depends, is not itself dependent on the overall visual characteristics of the word. It therefore works as effectively when the words are written in the normal direction as when the letters are written in the reverse order. RB's performance is unaffected by such reverse type distortions. When the distortion applied to the typescript is sufficient to reduce the clarity of individual letters, the performance declines. Thus, handwritten text is more problematic, since the individual letters and graphemes to which the translation rules are to be applied may be difficult to abstract. RB is not able to use the overall visual characteristics of the word to activate word recognition units, a mechanism which could function relatively effectively independent of specific information about each and every constituent letter.

If RB is to be interpreted as a child who reflects an impairment in the acquisition of semantic and direct reading systems, but with relative preservation of phonological reading routes, she does not represent an absolute dissociation. If her phonological reading route was perfectly established there should be no examples of errors that are not entirely valid. Thus, for RB we must also postulate some impairment within the phonological reading route itself.

Suggestion of impairment at the level of the parser is evident in the translation of some digraphs, with the assignment of a pronunciation to each of the component letters within the digraph. For example, the word ashamed is read as "as.hammed". The letters "s" and "h'" should have been parsed together as one unit, "sh". Separate parsing produces the two sounds /sə/ and /hə/ rather than the combined /ʃ/. The pronunciation of the "a" in shortened form as /ae/ (rather than /e/) also results from a misparsing. The "a" should have been parsed with the unit that contains the following "e" so that a lengthened translation would occur utilising the "rule of e" in English. Since the "e" was parsed separately, it received its own phonetic translation. There are many other examples amongst the error corpus of comparable misparsing errors from RB, though in relation to certain words she was able to parse above a single letter level. For example, the letter string "tion" was often read correctly. However, in general parsing decomposed into units which were too small. This may be a common feature in surface dyslexia.

In addition to the incompletely developed parser, RB has an incompletely developed translator. For her translator to be perfectly developed there should be no invalid errors within the error corpus. However, not all errors were valid and there were mismatches between orthographic chunks and phonological segments. Also, within the translator, in selecting from valid alternatives, RB would sometimes select a lower frequency alternative rather than a higher frequency alternative. This resulted in a valid error, though not strictly a regularisation error. Amongst RB's errors, there were few examples of blender errors, in which there would be omissions or missequences in the component sounds of target words. The large number of neologistic responses however, does suggest an impoverished lexical check system.

Other surface dyslexics have been described who have even better development of the phonological reading route. In these cases, the dissociation between the development of the routes is clear and crisper. An explicit example is Temple's (1984c) description of a case of surface dyslexia in a child with epilepsy. The child, NG, was able to read regular words whether familiar or unfamiliar with perfect accuracy. Irregular words frequently provoked regularisation errors. However, all of NG's reading performance could be accounted for by the strict application of a rule-based system. His phonological route performed excellently. Control children of a similar reading age to NG showed small trends in favour of regularity effects but none showed the degree of regularisation effect that NG displayed. NG was also significantly poorer than the control children at reading irregular words. Finally, NG displayed homophone confusion. Eleven out of twenty-two words read correctly were defined as their respective homophones. NG's performance resembled the performance described by Bub, Cancelliere, and Kertesz (1985) at a particular stage in the reading deterioration of their Alzheimer's patient. More recently, Hodges et al. (1992) have investigated such literacy deterioration in more detail.

Shallice and Warrington have argued that acquired surface dyslexics are using a small orthographic unit as a basis for processing in the phonological route and have lost the ability to process larger segments. Applying a similar interpretation to developmental surface dyslexia, it could be argued in relation to their model and to Temple's (1985c) model that small orthographic units are being used as a basis for processing and that there is failure to establish the ability to process larger segments. This was seen within the corpus of errors made by RB, when discussing some of her errors in processing digraphs and her impairment in parsing.

The Seidenberg and McClelland (1989) connectionist model which represents the relationships between orthography and phonology in a series of distributed connection weights was able to produce a moderate parallel to surface dyslexia. Regularity effects were emergent properties and the model was also able to produce readings of unfamiliar non-words (van Orden, Pennington, & Stone, 1990). We have suggested that RB's inability to process segments above a phonemic level contributes to her difficulty, and van Orden et al. (1990) showed that the availability of phonological representations at the phonemic level allows the generalisations to non-words and the apparent regularity effects. However, as Besner et al. (1990) emphasised the Seidenberg and McClelland (1989) network was not very good at reading non-words. It therefore provided a poor model of those surface dyslexics with well established phonological reading routes, for whom non-word reading is better than word reading. The Plaut et al. (1996) model, which incorporates dual routes, has much better skills at reading non-words and can therefore provide a better model of surface dyslexia.

As mentioned earlier, Marcel (1980) has suggested that the reading performance of normal children often resembles that of developmental surface dyslexia. However, in the reaction time studies of Seymour (1986), it is clear that surface dyslexics (whom he refers to as morphemic dyslexics) have response times which lie outside those of normal children. Thus, although the overall qualitative pattern of surface dyslexia resembles the pattern of some normal children they are nevertheless distinguishable from them in quantitative measures. Furthermore, the discrepancy between the developmental surface dyslexic and the normal child becomes more apparent as development proceeds. The surface dyslexic's strategy remains in comparable format but the normal child's repertoire develops into an orthographic processing system or other theoretical equivalent.

In relation to Ehri's (1992) model, RB would have acquired phonetic cue reading but failed to acquire cipher skills. The connection between a word's spelling and its pronunciation would be partially established. There is some difficulty in explaining why this skill has not developed further. There is no evidence of any phonological impairment for RB (see further discussion later), so there is no obvious reason why the full links to phonological representations could not be derived. In relation to Perfetti's (1992) model the strength in non-word reading despite limitations in irregular word reading require explanation.

Long-term Effects

The increase in RB's reading age over time is given in Table 5.3. Subsequent to the analysis of her performance as presented above, RB was incorporated into a remedial year of intensive tuition outside mainstream schooling. Remediation began at the age of 10;8 and was maintained for a year. The first column of Table 5.3 indicates performance prior to the remedial academic year and the fourth column indicates progress at the end of it. A change in reading age over time is

TABLE 5.3
Sustained Dyslexia, Despite Remediation, for RB

	Year 1	Year 2	Year 3	Year 4	Year 5
Chronological age	10;6	10;11	11;3	11;6	14;6
Neale reading age (accuracy)	7;8	8;7	8;11	9;11	10;1

also documented in this table. However, despite the increase in reading age the character of reading remained unchanged. RB continued to display surface dyslexia with impoverished ability to read by non-phonological systems.

Underlying Disorders Relevant to Impaired Lexical Reading

Some authors have suggested that a phonological processing disorder underlies developmental dyslexia (Stanovich, 1988; Wagner & Torgeson, 1987), in that all developmental dyslexics have phonological processing problems (Wilding, 1989, 1990). However, analyses of phonological problems have tended to be based upon group studies which mask variation in performance pattern within the dyslexias. It now seems clear that, in the form of developmental dyslexia called developmental phonological dyslexia (Temple & Marshall, 1983), there is also an oral phonological processing deficit and the nature of this deficit will be discussed later, following the discussion of phonological dyslexia itself. However, in many cases of surface dyslexia, there is no evidence of a phonological processing impairment.

It is unfortunate that the first detailed published case description of surface dyslexia (Coltheart et al., 1983) was a rather impure case and did also have phonological processing problems. For RB previously described, there were also some abnormal aspects to the functioning of her phonological reading route. This has raised the question of whether in surface dyslexia there is always an abnormality in the phonological reading route and indeed, whether there is always an abnormality in the phonological reading route in developmental dyslexia. If this were the case the distinction between the different developmental disorders might simply relate to differences in the development of the semantic reading route. However, the available evidence indicates that surface dyslexia is not always associated with impaired development of the phonological reading route.

The case of surface dyslexia in NG (Temple, 1984c) answers this issue. NG is a surface dyslexic but here the phonological route has developed perfectly but with marked impairment in lexico-semantic mechanisms. The surface dyslexic NG (Temple, 1984c), is no poorer than control children of a comparable reading age in reading non-words, so there is no impairment in his phonological reading route. Yet, he is dyslexic. The existence of children like NG enable rejection of the theory broadly held by developmental psychologists that reading disorders always result from phonological disorders and requires an amendment permitting the view that reading disorders often result from phonological disorders.

Often, the phonological discussions are based upon performance on phonological tasks outside the reading domain itself. Most frequently rhyming tasks are employed. In our studies, one such test of performance is assessed on the basis of a rhyme fluency task. In this task, 12 different individual words are dictated. Each contains a different central vowel. The child is asked to generate as many words as possible that rhyme with the target word, and is given one minute for each word. RB's fluency performance was assessed when she was aged 14 and had a reading age of 10;1. Control children with an average reading age of 10;6 were also assessed. On the rhyme fluency task, controls attained a mean score of 45.6 rhymes. RB produced 49 rhymes on this task, indicating no impairment on rhyme fluency.

Similar results are reported for other cases of surface dyslexia. Allan, the surface dyslexic studied by Hanley, Hastie, and Kay (1992), performed well on a series of tests of phonological ability including making rhyme judgements and constructing spoonerisms on Perin's (1983) test, showing intact phonemic awareness and ability to parse and manipulate phonemes. The case of surface dyslexia described by Goulandris and Snowling (1991) had no impairment in phonological awareness. MI, the surface dyslexic described by Castles and Coltheart (1996), had normal performance on auditory rhyme judgement scoring 40/40 compared to a control mean of 38.5 (SD=1.18) and 28/30 on a phoneme deletion task also compared to a control mean of 27.8 (SD=1.14). The intact phonological skills in these cases of developmental surface dyslexia are further evidence of the need to revise the view that phonological problems are a consistent feature of developmental dyslexia. Lexical reading problems are not necessarily associated with problems in phonological awareness. Thus, surface dyslexics do not have impaired performance on oral phonological tasks.

It is generally assumed that reading was introduced into our civilisation after the end of the evolutionary processes which produced *homo sapiens* and the apparently superior cortical development. In this case, the reading mechanisms which have been discussed must be parasitic upon mechanisms which previously evolved within the brain to carry out alternative processes. If there is no underlying abnormality in general phonological processes, the question arises as to the nature of the abnormality of non-phonological processes that might underlie the impairments of surface dyslexia. What is the system whose impairment has led to these difficulties with non-phonological processes?

Marshall (1984, 1987) gets around this type of discussion by suggesting that reading might have entered our cognitive repertoire far earlier than we had realised, but the absence of preserved written records has left us with no evidence of this early mastery. He suggests that the reading process is "preformed" and that experience in education merely fills out the system's content. Ellis (1985, 1987) has suggested that the reading skills required for lexical semantic processes are dependent upon systems which are adapted for analysing complex visual patterns. In support of this view, Goulandris and Snowling (1991) report impairments in both recognition and retention measures of visual memory in JAS, their case of surface dyslexia, though as Castles and Coltheart (1996) point out their case is a more convincing report of surface dysgraphia than of surface dyslexia. Castles and Coltheart (1996) found intact visual memory in their case MI, of surface dyslexia in a nine-year-old boy. Recognition memory was normal on the Warrington Recognition Memory Battery. Recall of patterns was normal on Benton's Test of Visual Retention and sequential memory was normal on the IPTA sequential memory test. Indeed on the latter, performance was in the top 1%. Furthermore, Dr S (Temple, 1992b), who has been discussed in Chapters 2 and 3, had severe impairment in visual memory but had intact reading skills, supporting a double dissociation between memory for complex visual material and word recognition skills.

Naming Deficits

Margolin, Marcel, and Carlson (1985) have discussed a possible association between one form of acquired surface dyslexia in adults and anomic difficulties. They have suggested a common deficit in the output lexicon which disrupts both processes. Naming difficulties in children with developmental dyslexia were discussed by Rudel (1985), who spoke of a subtle dysnomia. It has been found that dyslexics, as a group, respond less accurately and more slowly than chronological age controls on tasks which involve rapid automatised naming and the retrieval of verbal labels from the lexicon (Denckla & Rudel, 1976; Denckla, Rudel, & Broman, 1981). Wolf (1991) has shown that this deficit extends to comparisons with reading age controls as well as chronological age controls when letter and number naming is involved. Fourth grade dyslexic children were slower than second grade average readers in speed of naming letters and numbers. Thus, exposure to print is not an adequate explanation of the difference.

Ellis and Miles (1981) argued that naming speed reflected lexical encoding mechanisms. In their view the difficulty is prior to articulatory encoding and lies within the connection or translation of visual to lexical codes. Bowers and Wolf (1993) emphasised that processes underlying naming speed should not be subsumed under phonological processes, as occurs in some discussions, but should be more closely aligned with processes involved in establishing the automatic induction of good quality orthographic codes. Speeded naming is therefore believed to reflect the automaticity of name retrieval. Murphy, Pollatsek, and Well (1988) speculate that breakdown in the establishment of dyslexic readers' orthographic codes may be linked to a breakdown in the establishment of visual input logogens. These studies therefore emphasise the failure of input processes rather than the output processes discussed by Margolin et al. (1985).

Some support for an association of reduced naming speed and patterns of dyslexia with intact phonological skills, also comes from Wimmer's (in press) study of German children. The German dyslexic subjects studies had adequate phonemic decoding skill yet had digit naming speeds which were slower than reading age controls.

The specificity of the processing difficulties have been explored in several studies. Dyslexics perform at a similar level to average readers in processing stimuli that are difficult to name such as Hebrew letters. It is only with nameable stimuli that differences arise (Ellis & Miles, 1981). Griffiths (1991) compared dyslexics and reading age controls on three different cued retrieval tasks: graphemic, phonemic, and semantic. In the graphemic task, words had to be retrieved on the basis of a lower case letter cue projected onto a screen. In the phonemic task, the cues were initial letter sounds. In the semantic task, the cues were spoken words and the subject had to produce another word which was partially defined by the cue. Examples of cues were *big*, *noisy*, *soft*, and *sweet*, and examples of acceptable responses to these were *elephant*, *tractor*, *quilt*, and *toffee*. Performance with graphemic cues, was poor for dyslexic readers in relation to both control groups. However, although performance with the phonemic cues was also poor in comparison to chronological age controls, it was at a comparable level to that of reading age controls. Performance with the semantic cues, was actually better for the dyslexic group than for either of the control groups. Relative to good readers, dyslexics had impaired retrieval at a word form level, but enhanced retrieval at a semantic level. Katz and Shankweiler (1985) have also argued for the specificity of the naming deficit to orthographic material, finding no relationship between reading ability and naming when objects, colours, or animals were employed but a significant relationship with letters.

Wolf has attempted to explore the individual differences in naming skills, in relation to patterns of reading ability. In contrast to the Shankweiler studies, she has argued that name retrieval difficulties are evident in dyslexics even when picture naming is involved, although the effects may not be as strong as with orthographic material. Using the Boston naming test, Wolf and Obregon (1992) examined naming skills and comprehension of the same lexical items on a multiple choice test in eight dyslexic subjects. They also looked at reading of regular words, irregular words, and non-words. Several subjects had global reading difficulties which affected both irregular, regular, and non-word reading.

These subjects also performed very poorly on the Boston naming test but performed well on the multiple choice comprehension test, indicating unambiguous retrieval deficits.

Wolf and Obregon (1992) also described a subject with preserved accuracy in reading phonologically regular and nonsense words but impaired accuracy in reading irregular words. Latencies exhibited the same pattern and were twice as long for irregular as for regular words. They note that this pattern of performance conforms to that of surface dyslexia. However, this subject performed at a normal level on the naming task, and did not display evident lexical retrieval difficulties in naming. It is possible that the confrontation naming task emphasised phonological skills more than the automaticity of retrieval required for speeded naming and conclusions are also tempered by the superior vocabulary knowledge of this subject, which averaged three years above his grade level. Thus, although naming was at an average level for age, it could be argued that it indicated a subtle retrieval deficit when compared with the actual levels of vocabulary knowledge.

However, support for Wolf and Obregon's (1992) apparent dissociation between surface dyslexia and naming impairments comes from our recent study of both executive skills and hyperlexia in Turner's syndrome (Temple & Carney, 1996; Temple, Carney, & Mullarkey, 1996; see also Chapter 4 for a syndrome description and analysis of spatial skills and Chapter 6 for a discussion of executive skills in Turner's syndrome). Nine- to 11-year-old girls with Turner's syndrome were found to be significantly impaired in comparison to controls in the rapid automatised naming of colours. Yet, despite the impairment in speeded naming, the children with Turner's syndrome were hyperlexic, according to the original definition of hyperlexia proposed by Silberberg and Silberberg (1967, 1968), in that they read at a level significantly above what would be predicted by their intellectual level and also at a level significantly higher than their peers both for material requiring phonological skills and, more importantly for the arguments here, for material requiring word specific knowledge, i.e. irregular words. So despite the impairment in speeded naming of colours, they do not have surface dyslexia. The pervasiveness of their automatised naming deficit in relation to other classes of material remains to be explored.

The specificity of any association between deficits in rapid automatised naming or confrontation naming and the impaired development of the lexical reading route in surface dyslexia therefore remains to be substantiated.

A variety of other earlier visual processes have also been suggested as being impaired in dyslexia (e.g. Lovegrove, Martin, & Slaghuis, 1986). However, they are not suitable as potential underpinnings for surface dyslexia as they fail to account for the material specific nature of the difficulties. Specifically, peripheral visual deficits could not account for the intact processing of non-words and regular words. In general, peripheral visual accounts of developmental dyslexia fail to explain the variation in reading performance in relation to the nature of the stimulus material to be read (Hulme, 1988). Hulme (1988) argued that when low-level visual impairments are reported, they are irrelevant correlates of the developmental dyslexias. Rare dyslexias arising from high-level visual impairment remain a possibility. Such a case is reported by Valdois, Gerard, Vanault, and Dugas (1995). Their 10-year-old dyslexic girl made reading errors dominated by visual paralexias. Significantly, the typical psycholinguistic dimensions did not affect the quality of her reading. There were neither regularity nor lexicality effects. The impairment was common across all stimulus material, with simply a frequency effect upon overall accuracy. Words could not be read automatically. The case of Valdois et al. (1995) was clearly not that of surface dyslexia.

Precise case descriptions of children with surface dyslexia have been limited in number, although the syndrome has now been described in relation to a variety of different European languages. It would nevertheless appear that developmental surface dyslexia is less common than developmental phonological dyslexia, which will be described next. Castles and Coltheart (1993) examined the lexical and sublexical reading skills of 56 developmental dyslexics and 56 normal readers. Eighty-five per cent of the dyslexic subjects showed a dissociation between their irregular word reading (lexical processes) and their non-word reading (sublexical processes). Of these 46% showed a surface dyslexic pattern (poor irregular word reading), whereas 64% showed a phonological dyslexic pattern (poor non-word reading). Of the total sample of dyslexics, 30% showed a surface dyslexic pattern, a rate higher than the case reports in the literature might suggest. Castles and Coltheart (1993) note that in some subjects for whom there is a dissociation, both skills are impaired with one being markedly more impaired than the other. Nevertheless, of particular interest, one in three of the dyslexic children had particular difficulty with one reading procedure in the absence of any difficulty with the other.

Overall, these results indicate that the patterns of surface and phonological dyslexia are not rare, spurious, and atypical anomalies but are encountered frequently within dyslexic populations. The results are consistent with those of Olson, Wise, Conners, and Rack (1990) who found greater independence of phonological and orthographic skills in a sample of disabled readers than within normal readers. Notably, Olson et al. (1990) found significant and strong heritability only for the phonological coding contribution to word recognition. It is impairment of these processes which are relevant to the discussion in the following section on developmental phonological dyslexia.

DEVELOPMENTAL PHONOLOGICAL DYSLEXIA

In contrast to developmental surface dyslexia, the major characteristic of developmental phonological dyslexia is a selective impairment of phonological reading processes.

The term developmental phonological dyslexia was first utilised by Temple and Marshall (1983), to apply to a case of a seventeen-year-old girl HM with a specific difficulty in reading. HM had normal speech, no known neurological abnormalities and was of good intelligence. However, she had significant difficulty in reading non-words aloud. Moreover, the pattern of her reading errors was dominated by paralexic responses and a substantive number of morphological paralexias. Rather than discussing this previous case in detail, a further case report will be presented which describes the teenager, JE. JE was briefly documented by Temple (1984a) but more extensive details are given here.

Case Report: Developmental Phonological Dyslexia, JE

JE was a 17-year-old, right-handed girl with no known neurological abnormality. There is a family history of reading and spelling difficulties. Administration of the Wechsler Intelligence Scale for Children revealed the following subtest profile for JE:

Verbal Tests		Performance Tests	
Information	9	Picture Completion	15
Similarities	16	Picture Arrangement	9
Vocabulary	10	Block Design	10
Comprehension	15	Object Assembly	13
(10 is an average subtest score, range 1–19, SD = 3)			

Verbal IQ	15	Performance IQ	112
Full Scale IQ	116		

JE had fluent and articulate speech. She attained five "O" levels at school in Biology, English Literature, English Language, History, and Art. Subsequently, she went on to attend Chelsea Art College. In a discussion about Braque and Picasso, she made the following comments which give some minimal indication of her intact intellectual and vocabulary skills:

They became very friendly and some of their early work, you can't tell the difference between; it is very difficult. Cubist painting tends to have much more life and much more feel about it. It can express anger with much more power than a conventional painting can. Cubism was criticised by the futurists in Italy and they said it wasn't art. But the cubists said that futurism wasn't art, while the constructivists said it all wasn't art.

At the time of assessment presented, JE's single word reading age on the Schonell Single Word Reading Test was 12;4. Tested one year later, in the absence of repeated daily practise in reading, while she was attending art college, performance had declined slightly and a Schonell reading age of 11;8 was attained. Performance has plateaued at this level.

Non-word Reading. JE was presented with the same three lists described for RB previously. In each case the non-words differed from the words by the alteration of only one letter. Overall, JE read 53/54 words correctly but only 30/54 non-words. Thus, JE displayed the major characteristic of phonological dyslexia, which is that non-words are significantly harder to read aloud than words i.e. there is a significant lexicality effect (X^2 = 27.53; P<0.001). Some errors to non-words were lexicalisations, e.g. *zan* →"tan"; *fip* →"flip"; *chait* →"chart"...."trait". Such lexicalisations are relatively common responses amongst developmental phonological dyslexics. JE was also given non-words to read aloud, which were either homophonic or non-homophonic with real words. Unlike other cases of both acquired and developmental phonological dyslexia (e.g. Temple & Marshall, 1983), she derived no benefit in the reading of non-words, if they were homophonic with real words.

Word Reading. Although JE was unable to read correctly the non-words *zan* and *fip*, she was able to read correctly words such as *disproportionately, overconfident,* and *categorically*. In contrast to her poorly established phonological reading skills, her lexical reading mechanisms were well established.

JE was presented with 434 words to read aloud. She made 49 errors. Of her errors, only 10% (i.e. five) were neologisms and the remainder were paralexias. Of the paralexias, 55% were morphological, in that the base of the word was read correctly but an affix was dropped, added, or substituted. The remaining errors were either visual paralexias in which stimulus and response shared at least 50% of letters in common or were visuo-semantic paralexias in which there was similarity between stimulus and response in both visual characteristics and meaning. Examples of JE's morphological paralexias were as follows:

weigh →"weight"	*instance* →"instant"
choir →"choirs"	*image* →"imagine"
jumper →"jump"	*banishment* →"banished"
sickness →"sicken"	*political* →"politician"

Visual paralexias included the following items:

adjective →"abject"	*archer* →"anchor"
fight →"fright"	*furnish* →"finish"
couch →"cough"	*chassis* →"chase"

It is evident from these visual paralexias that JE often produced irregular words as responses. It was not the case that she was producing a simplified regular word in response to an item which she did not recognise.

JE was also given the long words and non-words from Coltheart's Lexical Decision Task to read aloud. It was clear that in deriving pronunciations, JE did not simply apply a rule based system, rather, there was activation of whole word items. Thus, for example, in attempting to read the word *belligerently*, JE produced the response "belly.gravely". The word *miscalculations* was read as "miscellaneous.shun". The word *undemocratic* was read as "under.macratic". Similarly, in relation to non-words, the non-word *laborcolator* was read as "labour.curator". The non-word *ramifationic* was read as "ramification.inic". The non-word *electrifationic* was read as "electrification.onic". And again, *dimeocrities* was read as "dimo.critic". The generation of large word subcomponents within incorrect responses was also noted by Temple and Marshall (1983) in their original case description of phonological dyslexia.

Psycholinguistic Dimensions. On Coltheart et al.'s (1979) regular and irregular words, JE displayed no regularity effect, reading 36 regular items and 35 irregular items. In the case description of the developmental phonological dyslexic HM, Temple and Marshall (1983) pointed out that her reading was significantly influenced by the psycholinguistic dimensions of both imageability and frequency. For JE no such differences were evident, she performed equally well on high and low imageability items and on high and low frequency items. On all sections performance was relatively high. In this regard, developmental phonological dyslexics are like acquired phonological dyslexics in that the effects of psycholinguistic dimensions are somewhat inconsistent. JE was presented with the 40 items on the homophonic word list (Temple, 1984b) to read aloud and to define. She read and defined all stimuli correctly, displaying no homophone confusion.

Distorted Typescript. JE was presented with a set of 80 words written in four different formats: normal typescript; handwriting; reversed lower case script; and reversed upper case script. The results of her performance are summarised in Table 5.4.

JE was not significantly impaired when handwritten stimuli were presented but was significantly impaired, when the stimuli were presented with the component letters typed in the reversed order. (Lower case, $X^2 =$ 14.7, P<0.001; upper case, $X^2 =$11.38, P<0.001). It was the distortion that requires a sequential, analytical strategy to be activated, that created greatest problems for JE. This impairment in performance is relatively consistent across developmental phonological dyslexic cases, although it was less marked in the original description of HM (Temple & Marshall, 1983). It is relatively resistant to change over time and is a mode of detecting subtle reading impairments in apparently recovered adult phonological dyslexics (e.g. Temple, 1988a).

Many further cases of phonological dyslexia have been described in children in a number of different languages. Examples of detailed case descriptions are to be found in Snowling, Stackhouse, and Rack (1986), Campbell and Butterworth (1985), and Seymour (1986). Developmental phonological dyslexia is a pervasive form of developmental dyslexia (Castles & Coltheart, 1993).

Theoretical Explanations. Developmental phonological dyslexia is not easily explained in relation to stage models of normal reading development, in which stages must be passed through in an invariant sequence. Whereas surface dyslexia can be described as arrestment of reading development at the alphabetic stage, phonological dyslexia cannot be explained in relation to arrestment at a particular stage of the Marsh et al. (1981), Frith (1985), or Ehri (1992) models, since in phonological dyslexia there appears to be development of orthographic reading skills, despite the failure to master alphabetic skills effectively. The only alternative is to suggest that phonological dyslexics have a significantly expanded logographic reading system which is able to incorporate thousands of words. However, no such logographic reading system has ever been described in normal children.

TABLE 5.4
Reading of Distorted Typescript by a Phonological Dyslexic

Stimuli	Example	Number Correct
Normal typescript	e.g. large	71/80
Handwritten		67/80
Reversed lower case	e.g. egral	49/80
Reversed upper case	e.g. EGRAL	52/80

A further alternative, is to suggest that there are different pathways through which children proceed in the acquisition of reading. Although the majority might go through the traditional routes described by Frith, Marsh, or Ehri and colleagues, for some children there may be greater emphasis upon orthographic mechanisms with less mastery of alphabetic stages. This general argument is similar in principle, though opposite in direction, to that discussed by Stuart and Coltheart in relation to the individual differences in the first phase of reading. Stuart and Coltheart (1988) argued that not all children start with a logographic phase but some go directly to using alphabetical principles. Here, we argue that there are also children who may start with a logographic phase but never develop into an alphabetic stage, proceeding directly to orthographic skill. Thus, in relation to the standard developmental models, the alphabetic skills of some children have been underemphasised at the start and for others they have been over-emphasised in later development.

This view also echoes the type of arguments proposed by Baron and Strawson (1976) in their discussion of Chinese and Phoenecian readers. The normal, adult Chinese readers described by Baron and Strawson (1976) show greater strength in the reading of whole words than in the mastery of non-word mechanisms. Such individual differences in the normal population may be relevant to discussions of alternative modes in the acquisition of information. Certainly, if a modular organisation is postulated in both child and adult reading systems, there is a priori reason why a specific module should have to be essential as a precursor for another module, if the two relate to semi-independent parallel reading systems.

In discussing phonological dyslexia in relation to adult models of normal reading, the disorder receives a relatively straightforward explanation by postulating relatively normal development of semantic, lexical, and direct reading systems but with impairment in the acquisition of the phonological reading route. This would represent a deficit in the functioning of the route marked as "3" (in Fig. 5.4) of Temple's (1985c) model. Temple (1988a) has suggested that the abnormality in the phonological reading route could relate to an inappropriate parsing or translating mechanism, such that the units on which the systems operate are too large. Insufficient decomposition of the stimulus leads to the responses documented earlier in which whole words or morphemic components are found within responses, when trying to read aloud long unfamiliar words or non-words. Thus, whereas in surface dyslexia we see evidence of the system parsing at too small a unit level, in phonological dyslexia we see evidence of parsing at too large a unit level (Temple, 1988a).

The proportion of morphological errors amongst the error corpus for JE is substantial. These errors are a core and substantive element of overall performance. The morphological errors made by developmental phonological dyslexics are explicable in two alternative ways in relation to models of adult reading. One explanation postulates that affix-like endings are dependent upon processing in the phonological reading route (Patterson, 1982). This argument is based on the notion that such endings have low semantic content and meaning and are therefore more similar to non-words than to other morphemic entries. A parsimonious explanation can therefore be produced for the appearance of morphological errors in developmental phonological dyslexia by merely arguing that a well-established phonological reading route is essential for the correct reading of such items in a consistent fashion. In developmental phonological dyslexia, the prevalence of morphological errors and function word substitutions tends to increase in text reading (Temple & Marshall, 1983), just as it does for acquired phonological dyslexics. In normal adult readers, there is some suggestion that text reading reduces the involvement of normal phonological reading mechanisms. Normal subjects also begin to make occasional morphological errors, if reading text rapidly.

An alternative explanation for morphological errors is that in parallel with the morphemically based logogen system in the semantic reading route, there is a second channel which is processing affix-like components. This system is also argued to be impaired in acquired phonological dyslexia (Caramazza, Miceli, & Villa, 1986). With this explanation, it is necessary to postulate two deficits within the reading system in phonological dyslexia, both acquired and developmental, one to explain the non-word deficit and a second to explain the morphological errors.

Morphological reading errors create practical difficulties for phonological dyslexics in examination situations, since they may lead to paragrammatic misreading of examination questions which can result in inaccurate interpretation of examination questions.

Initial attempts to model phonological dyslexia within connectionist networks were limited in their success. It was possible to model the emergence of phonological skills in these systems. However, in phonological dyslexia, it was the failure of phonological skills to be mastered in a normal fashion, which had to be modelled. Besner et al. (1990) suggested that since the connectionist model of Seidenberg and McClelland (1989) was poorer than normal at reading non-words, the model's performance actually resembled phonological dyslexia rather than normality, but this hardly provides an account of phonological dyslexia in relation to a model of normal reading. Perfetti's (1992) connectionist model within a developmental framework faces similar problems.

In relation to Ehri's model (1992), there is only a visual-phonological route to reading. Phonological recoding is essential to develop this, and an amalgamation of spelling and pronunciation. In Ehri's terms the phonetic cue reading phase is not properly established. Thus, Ehri (1992) would have to predict a marked impairment in reading development in developmental phonological dyslexia. Yet, reading attains high levels. The model is not able to account for these high levels of word recognition skill but the simultaneously poor performance in non-word reading. Ehri argues that with any partial connection the reader will be slow and inaccurate. The nature of the inaccuracy is not specified and if it relates to a low level of errors within which there are morphological and visual paralexias, it has some validity, but overall in developmental phonological dyslexia such as JE's, word recognition is quick and accurate, which cannot be accommodated within Ehri's theory.

In relation to the revised connectionist model of Plaut et al. (1996), phonological dyslexia could be explained as reflecting impairment of their direct route, which maps orthography onto phonology through a set of hidden units, but with development of their semantic route, which maps orthography to semantics, through a different set of hidden units and then to phonology via a further set of hidden units. The semantic route can read words but not non-words. Besner (in press) notes that there are difficulties in explaining the acquired phonological dyslexics, who have impaired comprehension and a damaged semantic system but for whom there are no semantic errors, arguing that a triple route model is needed to account for such cases. Amongst developmental phonological dyslexia, such cases have not yet been described so, at present, the Plaut et al. (1996) model could account for the major characteristics of developmental phonological dyslexia. As yet, the dual route connectionist model has not been assimilated by a developmental psychologist into a more articulated model of reading development.

Long-term Effects.   AH, a developmental phonological dyslexic (Temple, 1984b, 1985b, 1990c), has been followed up for six years since the original description of his case. At the age of 10, the proportion of paralexic errors in different categories was as follows: visual paralexias 60%; visuo-semantic paralexias 5%; morphological paralexias 15%; pseudo-morphological paralexias (in which letters resembling affixes, but which are not actually affixes, are substituted) 5%; valid paralexias 6%. At the age of 16, the distribution of error types had shifted to look more similar to the pattern described for JE above. The distribution of paralexic responses was now: visual paralexias 27%; visuo-semantic paralexias 19%; and morphological paralexias 54%. There were no regularisations.

In summary, as AH became older, there was no suggestion of his error distribution becoming more like that of a surface dyslexic. Instead, it resembled the picture of other described phonological dyslexics. Overall reading age did improve. On the Schonell reading test, a reading age at the age of 10;2 of 8;2 improved by the age of 16;3 to a reading age of 13;8. However, AH was still impaired in the reading of non-words, despite what appeared to be an almost adult level of competence in the recognition of real words. Thus, a significant lexicality effect also persisted with age. Errors to short non-words included both lexicalisations and non-word responses. As noted for JE, neologistic responses to long, low-frequency words or non-words included substantive word subcomponents (e.g. *existentialism* →"extentionolism"; *imparsonious* →"impassionous"; *cirsumicular* →"cirmycircular").

The stability of the pattern of reading seen in phonological dyslexia over time has also been observed in other studies. Hulme and Snowling (1992) reported a follow-up study of a case of developmental phonological dyslexia. Their case, first seen at 8 years was followed through to 13 years. He showed a "highly stable form of dyslexia characterised by a slowly expanding sight vocabulary in the face of massively deficient non-word reading skills" (p. 63).

Persistence of this overall pattern of developmental phonological dyslexia into middle age was described by Temple for a 47-year-old, right-handed man, JR (Temple, 1988a). JR was a self-employed man who ran his own building firm but recalled having difficulty with reading from the start at school. Mathematics and woodwork were unproblematic. After school he attended a technical college for carpentry and joinery. He obtained an intermediate level and went into the army. However, he continued to experience difficulty with reading and spelling. He had had no serious illness, head injury or neurological disorder. He had four children, two of whom had difficulties at school with reading and spelling. A third child was autistic.

JR was found to be of normal intelligence with fluent and articulate speech and no anomia. He displayed the characteristic symptomatology of developmental phonological dyslexia with an impairment of non-word reading in relation to word reading and with reading errors dominated by morphological paralexias, neologistic responses containing large word components and some visual paralexias. Presented with 25 items in lower case typescript, he was able to read 96% correctly but when these same items were presented in reversed typescript, he was able to read only 24% correctly. Thus, the major features of developmental phonological dyslexia may be sustained throughout the life span and what is observed in a 10- or 12-year-old child is not necessarily a delayed and deviant development that will simply resolve with time.

Nevertheless, in the longer term, the developmental phonological dyslexic may be less impaired by their pattern of deficit than the developmental surface dyslexic. At the age of 10, RB and AH were compared by Temple (1984b). RB, as described earlier, was a developmental surface dyslexic and AH, as also mentioned previously was a developmental phonological dyslexic. At the age of 10, the children were of comparable ability, with a similar reading age and a similar spelling age. Indeed had these children been being assigned to some type of remedial trial, it would have seemed that they were well matched on conventional test results and that one could validly have been assigned to one condition and one to the other. A detailed analysis of the nature of their reading though, showed up the numerous, sharp double dissociations in performance that there are between surface and phonological dyslexia.

Retested at the age of 14 (Temple, 1987), it was evident that AH had made more substantive progress than RB, despite the intensive remediation which RB had received for one year in the earlier portion of the intermediate period. At the age of 14, AH had a reading age of 11;8 but RB had only progressed to a reading age of 10;1. One possible explanation for the difference is that, as the demands made upon the reading system increase in a language like English, the lower frequency items which are expected to be incorporated into the vocabulary include a larger number of irregular items. For a developmental surface dyslexic, these produce particular difficulties, whereas for a developmental phonological dyslexic, they are no more problematic than other items and indeed, if it is argued that irregular words are more visually distinct from other words than regular words, then it may even be easier for the developmental phonological dyslexic to add such items into their vocabulary. Thus, while the developmental phonological dyslexic continues to be hampered by the grammatical aspects and affixes associated with words and has difficulty in working out unfamiliar scientific terms, unfamiliar technical terms, or unfamiliar names, they are nevertheless able to build up a large repertoire of recognisable items within their recognition system for words. The surface dyslexic is constrained by the laborious requirements of decomposing words and applying a rule system to attain their pronunciation which may reach a plateau in the possible level of attainment and effectiveness.

Underlying Disorders Relevant to Impaired Phonological Reading?

As mentioned earlier, there has been much contemporary interest in the possibility that a basic phonological processing deficit may underlie developmental dyslexia. As argued previously, we do not have evidence for a phonological processing deficit in cases of surface dyslexia. Nevertheless there is evidence for such an impairment of this sort in cases of developmental phonological dyslexia and since these cases represent the more common pattern of developmental dyslexia (Castles & Coltheart, 1993) this may account for the group effects which are seen on group analyses.

JE, described earlier, was tested when her reading age was 12;4, with a fall a year later to 11;8. Temple, Jeeves, and Villaroya (1989) document control results from normal children age 11 with a reading age of 11;11 on the rhyme fluency task. They report a mean fluency score of 61.25 with a standard deviation of 2.8. JE attains a score of 47 on rhyme fluency. She therefore clearly has an impairment in producing rhymes. An impairment in rhyme fluency is also documented for AH, who with a reading age of 11;8 produces only 33 rhymes (Temple, 1987). Other researchers have also documented rhyming impairments in developmental phonological dyslexia.

The theories about the relationship between reading disorders and phonological or phonemic difficulties have been expressed in a number of formats. As has been discussed previously, our view is that if present at all, they may be characteristic of only a subsection of dyslexics. Nevertheless, since there is considerable current interest in this issue, the different theoretical formulations will be discussed, despite the dominance of group studies, in their investigation.

Impaired Phonological Awareness as a Cause of Dyslexia. Bradley and Bryant (1983) argued that the ability to categorise sounds is causally related to reading ability. In a further study, they found that sensitivity to rhyme was linked in development to awareness of phonemes and that both of these skills influenced later reading development (Bryant, MacLean, Bradley, & Crossland, 1990). Snowling (1980) has also argued that a deficit in phoneme awareness would hinder reading development, though she is more explicit by proposing that it would be the development of grapheme–phoneme skills which would be impaired, a proposal more in keeping with the data and models discussed above.

This view is also compatible with the evidence from cases of callosal agenesis, a disorder in which there is congenital absence of the corpus callosum. Jeeves and Temple (1987) suggested a consistent deficit across acallosal adults in explicit phonological processing as reflected in initial letter fluency tasks and rhyming tasks. Temple et al. (1989) confirmed such deficits in children with callosal agenesis. Despite these problems with phonological awareness, their reading ages and word recognition skills were at a normal level for age (Temple, Jeeves, & Villaroya, 1990). However, further analysis of the nature of reading performance indicated preservation of lexicality effects beyond the normal age and an impairment in non-word reading, reflecting deficiencies in the acquisition of orthographic–phonological correspondences (Temple et al., 1990). Thus, these children display relatively pure phonological dyslexias, if the term can be applied to children who are actually reading at age level. Their data are consistent with the view that impairments in phonological awareness may lead to impaired development of the phonological reading route.

For some children, training in phonemic segmentation skill is said to lead to improvements in learning to read (e.g. Bradley & Bryant, 1983; Brown & Felton, 1990). However, the evidence that training in phonological awareness leads to selective improvement in reading skills is in doubt (Bryant & Goswami, 1987; Hulme, 1987, 1988). The effectiveness of such training in severe cases of phonological dyslexia is even more debatable, as these disorders may be resistant to substantive improvement in phonological skills, proceeding instead by an ever expanding sight vocabulary as discussed in the follow-up studies mentioned earlier (Hulme & Snowling, 1992; Temple, 1990c).

Hatcher, Hulme, and Ellis (1994) found that in a remediation study of poor readers, intervention involving training in phonological awareness only generalised to a significant improvement in reading when training in reading had also been involved in the intervention. They conclude that "intervention to boost phonological skills needs to be integrated with the teaching of reading, if they are to be maximally effective in improving literacy skills". Training in phonological awareness alone did not produce a significant improvement in reading skill.

Reading as a Cause of Phonological Awareness.   Other theorists have argued that phonological deficits are not a cause of reading problems but are a consequence of them (Morais, Bertelson, Cary, & Alegria, 1986; Morais, Cary, Alegria, & Bertelson, 1979). Their case is that learning to read in an alphabetic system provides the training which enables phonological awareness to develop. In the absence of an alphabetic writing system, phonemic segmentation skill may not be acquired naturally (Read, Yun-Fei, Hong-Yin, & Bao-Qing, 1986), though for children learning a syllabary, the skills may emerge later in school development, well after the time of their appearance for readers of alphabetic scripts (Mann, 1986).

However, dyslexics may not develop phonological awareness as a consequence of reading development. Bruck (1992) reports that dyslexics do not develop the same level of phonological awareness as younger normal children matched for reading level. Even adult dyslexics with fairly high levels of word recognition skill show phonemic awareness deficits. For normal subjects, phonological awareness increased with age and reading ability. For dyslexic subjects there was no systematic association.

Phonological Awareness as a Cause of Reading as a Cause of Phonological Awareness. Goswami (1991) suggested that the associations may differ dependent upon the type of phonological awareness being addressed. She argued that there are two critical levels of phonological awareness. The phonemic level of awareness, where words are broken into their smallest constituent sounds, may be a consequence of reading development. However, an intrasyllabic level of awareness, at which single syllables are broken into onset (initial consonant or consonant cluster) and rime (vowel and final consonant or cluster) may be predictive of reading ability. Goswami (1986) reported that pre-readers could form analogies between the ends of words. Fox (1994) pursued the issue of phonological discriminations in relation to positions within words, and found that dyslexics have much greater difficulty in processing the phonological characteristics of the ends of words in cross-modal tasks, than the beginnings of words.

Bruck (1992) found that dyslexics do eventually acquire onset–rime awareness following reading development but fail to develop phonemic awareness. Despite the onset–rime skills they remain dyslexic and despite the development of word recognition skills they remain impaired at phonemic awareness. It is not clear how these results, are compatible with Goswami's (1991) view. Despite, the development of onset–rime skills, there is not a disappearance of their dyslexia, and an impairment in this aspect of processing is therefore insufficient to account for their reading difficulties. However, although Goswami argues that onset–rime skills are predictive of reading ability in the normal population, it remains possible that an extension of the prediction to dyslexics is inappropriate or that the degree of onset–rime skills of Bruck's (1992) adult dyslexics provide the basis to enable their reading skills to improve, even if they are insufficient to eliminate the dyslexia. The impairment in adult dyslexics in the development of phonemic awareness (Bruck, 1992) indicates that the development of phonemic awareness is not a necessary consequence of improvement in reading skill.

With some similarity to Goswami (1991), in the Perfetti (1992) model some computational phonemic knowledge is needed to develop the initial functional lexicon but explicit phonemic awareness develops through experience of alphabetic stimuli.

Stuart and Coltheart (1988) argue that the conflicting views on the direction of causality can be resolved without the need to postulate different levels of awareness. They argue that phonological awareness and reading acquisition have a reciprocal interactive causal relationship not a unidirectional relationship. They see nothing contradictory in the notion that teaching phonological awareness accelerates reading acquisition but that learning an alphabetic script also causes people to be more phonologically aware than those learning other scripts or no scripts.

However, there remains a critical issue as to whether phonological awareness accelerates reading development or is an essential prerequisite. It is simply beneficial or is it necessary? Or expressed another way, is a deficiency in phonological awareness necessarily causal in producing reading disorder?

Bishop and Adams (1990) explored literacy skills in children who had had impaired language development at four years. They found only weak links between expressive phonological disorders and later ability to read either meaningful text or non-words. Cossu, Rossini, and Marshall (1993) argue more explicitly that phonological awareness is not a necessary prerequisite for reading development. They report that adequate reading of words and non-words, at least to a level characteristic of normal seven-year-olds, can be established by children with Down's syndrome despite their failure on tests of phonological awareness. They also report that, in children of limited intellectual abilities, advanced reading skill can be found in children without phonological awareness skills (Cossu & Marshall, 1990). They conclude:

> not all children depend upon phonological awareness in order to learn to read. If it is agreed that different children learn to read in different ways and that phonological awareness may play little or no role with some children, then we have no quarrel with assigning some importance to phonological awareness in the reading development of other children. (Cossu, Rossini, & Marshall, 1993, p. 135)

Further, the ability of their cases to read non-words as well as words counters the suggestions of deficits in phonological awareness as causal in even a restricted component of reading acquisition, namely grapheme–phoneme correspondences or the phonological reading route (Snowling, 1980; Temple et al., 1990).

DEEP DYSLEXIA

When deep dyslexia was first described in acquired form by Marshall and Newcombe in 1966, it generated a considerable reaction and through the 1970s and 1980s many research studies in the acquired neurological literature have focused upon the characteristics of this disorder, and the intriguing semantic errors that are generated on single word presentation. When for example, presented with a word such as *parrot*, the deep dyslexic may read it as "canary". There have now been descriptions of acquired deep dyslexia in a range of languages, but this syndrome has been harder to interpret in a simple way in relation to contemporary models of adult reading. It would be relatively easy to describe in relation to a developmental model of reading acquisition, since in some ways its characteristics represent reading, that could be described as reflecting the early stages of logographic reading. The cases, however, of developmental deep dyslexia in the literature are sparse.

Johnston (1983) described an 18-year-old girl with a reading age of 6;2 who could read no non-words. On testing with nearly 400 single words, CR made five semantic errors; one had a visual component (*office* →"occupation"). One so classified was a function word substitution and two involved the same word pair. The final example was a number substitution. Siegel (1985) described six children aged between 7;0 and 8;9 who had no phonological reading skills and made a few semantic substitutions and other errors characteristic of acquired deep dyslexia. Full individual data and precise error rates were not given. Neither of these papers demonstrated that the semantic error rate was above chance, when compared to performance of normal children. Thus, the degree of abnormality of the cases is unclear. Siegel (1985) suggested that her cases differed from normal. Although quantitative data was not reported, she looked at the reading performance of 64 children aged six to eight years and concluded that beginning readers tend to make visual errors involving the confusion of vowels. However, the involvement of chronological rather than reading age controls means that these children may already have developed some phonological reading skills.

A particularly convincing example of developmental deep dyslexia has been described by Stuart and Howard (1995). Their case KJ, a 13-year-old girl, had a 24% semantic error rate. She also made visual, morphological, visual and/or semantic errors, visual then semantic errors, and function word substitutions. She was unable to read any non-words. She showed no evidence of any attempted use of a phonological reading strategy; producing no neologisms, never sounding out a word, and producing no regularisations. Therapy experiments suggested that new words could only be learnt where there was extensive semantic representation suggesting that both a phonological and a direct lexical route were unavailable.

The case report given below provides an example of a case of developmental deep dyslexia.

Case Report: Developmental Deep Dyslexia KS

KS (Temple, 1988b) is a right-handed boy from a right-handed family. He is the eldest of three children and there is no family history of epilepsy, mental retardation or specific learning difficulties. Milestones were considered to be normal with first words appearing at 8–9 months, and a large vocabulary of single words established by 18–24 months. There is no record of head injury. Concern about hearing arose at four years and grommets were inserted following the detection of hearing impairment. Re-testing at age nine, indicated that KS was having difficulty with speech less than 40–45dbs. New grommets were inserted at this age. On examination at age nine, by a consultant in paediatric neurology, no neurological abnormality was found. No chromosome abnormality was found on genetic testing. However, total ridge count was low although mother's count was normal. Skull X-ray showed no abnormality. CT was normal. Sleep pattern and growth were satisfactory. On the Wechsler Intelligence Scale for Children, KS was found to have borderline intelligence with a Verbal IQ of 75 and a Performance IQ of 78. Subtest scores were as follows:

Verbal Scale		Performance Scale	
Information	5	Picture Completion	6
Similarities	8	Picture Arrangement	9
Arithmetic	4	Block Design	3
Vocabulary	6	Object Assembly	9
Comprehension	7	Coding	7
Verbal IQ	75	Performance IQ	78

(10 is an average subtest score, range 1–19, SD=3)

On Raven's Coloured Matrices, KS attained a score of 85 and on the Peabody Picture Vocabulary Test an IQ of 88. These suggested that there was not general depression of intellectual function that extended to all tasks. Reading age on the Schonell Single Word Reading Test at the age of nine years, was 5;2 with only two words identified: *tree* and *flower*. Presented with 300 words to read aloud, most were refused. 29 words were read correctly: 19 were highly imageable, high frequency nouns: *dog, window, door, roof, chimney, river, egg, friend, field, cat, queen, boy, nurse, caravan, frock, zebra, cake, doll, mother*; 3 were colour names: *blue, red,* and *green*; 1 was an adjective: *pretty*; 1 was a verb: *play*; 5 were function words: *of, by, get, we,* and *him.* Of the 77 overt errors all but two were paralexias and none were neologisms; 5% were semantic (e.g. *eye* → "blue"), 3% were visuo-semantic (e.g. *fresh* → "flowers"), and 3% were morphological (e.g. *tree* → "trees"). The largest error category was visual paralexias, with 39% of errors being of this type. In addition, 9% of errors were function word substitutions (e.g. *the* → "and") and 12% of errors were classified as visual plus semantic errors (e.g. *clue* → "red" [via blue]).

KS only produced a restricted repertoire of words as responses. Random pairings of the stimuli with which he was presented and the possible responses he might make enabled a series of random word pair items to be generated, which could then be subjected to an error classification and compared with the responses of KS. Such a comparison indicated that the incidence of errors with a semantic component was significantly above chance. The error pattern was also within that span of reported cases of acquired deep dyslexia.

In addition to the nature of the overt reading errors, other characteristics of deep dyslexia were also displayed. Non-words could not be read and letters could not be sounded. The data from KS were also compared with the data from normal children described by Seymour and Elder (1986). Seymour's and Elder's normal children were aged 4;6–5;6 and had been taught by a method emphasising sight vocabulary, with no explicit mention of letter sound associations. On average, 2% of the normal errors from these children had a semantic component. For KS the figure was 17%.

On text reading, the semantic error rate increased to 20% with an increase to 69% of function word substitutions. Visual errors declined to 4%. There is no comparable data for acquired deep dyslexics or beginning readers.

Theoretical Explanation. Developmental deep dyslexia can be explained in relatively simple terms in relation to the models of both Marsh and Frith by postulating an arrestment at the logographic stage of reading development. Alphabetic strategies have not been acquired. There is only a limited repertoire of words that can be identified. These are of high salience and may occasionally generate semantic errors. In this regard, the arrestment appears closer to stage two in the Marsh model than stage one. At this stage, there may be a meaning based relationship between the words that are substituted and visual cues are relevant in those words that are substituted. This was also seen in the data of KS. Such a distinction is not possible in Frith's models since stages one and two are combined into her logographic phase. As noted earlier, Wimmer and Hummer (1990) have argued that a logographic strategy for normal or poor readers is very limited and does not arise naturally when the writing system is phonologically transparent as in German and grapheme–phoneme correspondences are part of the instruction. Others also question the existence of a logographic reading stage within normal development (Stuart & Coltheart, 1988). The data from the developmental deep dyslexics indicate that it is a possible first stage in reading development even if it is relatively uncommon within normal readers for it to be to expressed in this way.

The theoretical interest in the disorder and the rare incidence of its report suggest that developmental deep dyslexia is indeed of low frequency of occurrence. Temple (1988b) has suggested that the combination of deficits which are required to generate it are unusual in combination and that when combined may be sufficiently intense to produce a non-reader rather than a dyslexic. KS appears to have hearing abnormalities which have required the insertion of grommets. Furthermore, there is also profound deficit in visual memory. Thus, he may have a combination of deficits which makes it very difficult for reading to become established in the first place. However, KJ (Stuart & Howard, 1995) had comparative strength in visual short-term memory and had no known hearing impairment, so this explanation cannot account for the performance of their convincing case of developmental deep dyslexia. Stuart and Howard (1995) also note that, unlike KS (Temple, 1988b), KJ's reading impairment was resistant to treatment aimed at improving phonological skills.

In attempting to explain developmental deep dyslexia in relation to an adult model of reading, one encounters the same difficulties that are encountered in explaining acquired deep dyslexia. Regardless of the model that is suggested, multiple deficits are necessary to account for the broad range of features, though all emphasise the absence of the phonological reading route.

In the case of developmental deep dyslexia, it is not clear that utilising an adult framework is particularly constructive in helping us to understand the nature of the disorder. However, although it has been argued in relation to acquired deep dyslexia that the complex of symptoms involved make it difficult for this disorder to provide information about normal function, with the use of a connectionist model Plaut and Shallice (1993) have argued that symptom patterns can arise from functionally distinct lesions because of the overall organisation of the system. They show that in deep dyslexia many of the characteristics of the syndrome can be explained with a connectionist model, given only one other major assumption concerning the number of features in the semantic representation of different classes of words. It is not yet clear whether such a model could be applied to a developmental system.

HYPERLEXIA

The term hyperlexia was first used by Silberberg and Silberberg (1967) to refer to children whose word recognition abilities are in advance of their abilities in comprehension. Aram and Healy (1988) reviewed cases of hyperlexia, noting that written words are recognised at a level beyond expectation on the basis of intellectual ability. Hyperlexia has most frequently been observed in children with autism, though the two conditions are also dissociable. Theoretical discussion has addressed the relationship of hyperlexia to generalised language disorder (e.g. Richman & Kitchell, 1981). Cossu and Marshall (1986, 1990) argue that the emergence of these precocious skills in children with otherwise severe cognitive and language difficulties supports the modular organisation of reading and writing and their independence from other cognitive abilities. Snowling (1987) has emphasised the contrast between dyslexia and hyperlexia, with dyslexia being associated with poor accuracy but good comprehension for the material read, but hyperlexia characterised by high accuracy but poor comprehension for the material read, a view confirmed by Aaron, Frantz, and Manges (1990). Healy, Aram, Horowitz, and Kessler (1982) found that hyperlexic children performed equally poorly on auditory and visual comprehension of language.

Aram, Rose and Horowitz (1984) have described a case of hyperlexia, in which reading has a similar character to that of surface dyslexia. Others have also explored this possibility (Goldberg & Rothermel, 1984; Welsh, Pennington, & Rogers, 1987). In contrast it has also been suggested that hyperlexia may form a parallel to the acquired reading disorder, direct dyslexia (Ellis, 1984; Marshall, 1984). In direct dyslexia, there is impairment of the semantic reading route, sometimes as a consequence of dementia, yet there is preserved ability to read irregular words suggesting preservation of a non-phonological reading route that bypasses semantics (Schwartz et al., 1980) (see Fig. 5.3 and 5.4). In hyperlexia, despite poor development of systems involved in extracting semantics from reading, pronunciation is of high accuracy.

Exploring these contrasting views of hyperlexia, Temple (1990a) reports a case of hyperlexia in a non-autistic child, for whom there was no significant regularity effect and no evidence of the over-reliance upon phonological reading mechanisms, characteristic of surface dyslexia. Words were read aloud correctly, which could not be understood from either auditory or written format. This was also true for irregular words. Significantly fewer irregular words could be defined correctly than could be read aloud correctly, despite a very loose criterion for the acceptance of a correct definition. This suggests direct reading route development. However, as Temple (1990a) points out the expanded phonological reading routes of Shallice et al. (1983) and Temple (1985c) could read the majority of the irregular words involved in the comprehension dissociation. These phonological reading routes (as discussed earlier) permit translation upon units above the level of the grapheme and the Temple (1985c) model posits a range of potential translations, which may be serially attempted in relation to frequency. Thus, an alternative explanation is that the hyperlexic had developed a sophisticated phonological reading route.

In Temple's case comprehension of single words is much better than comprehension of sentences. Temple (1990a) argues that semantic comprehension is relatively normal, but that it is syntactic comprehension which is deficient, arguing for the modularity of these components during acquisition.

Seymour and Evans (1992) have conducted a detailed study of a non-autistic child with hyperlexia and his school peers. They argued that the child progressed towards an orthographic phase of reading development more rapidly than his peers and appeared to omit aspects of an alphabetic phase. He showed significantly less evidence of overt sounding out than his peers, which had been taken as an index of alphabetic processing. His reaction time distributions were also more convergent than his peers, suggesting to Seymour and Evans the establishment of an orthographic framework rather than a dual (logographic + alphabetic) process. They found no evidence of semantic deficit in the processing of single words but greater difficulty with sentences. This was consistent with Snowling's (1987) proposal that the semantic deficit in hyperlexia is located at a sentence or text level, comprehension of single words being normal.

Seymour and Evans (1992) discuss their results in relation to several models of reading. They point out that the connectionist model of Seidenberg and McClelland (1989) is essentially a model of hyperlexic reading since the orthographic system operates without the support of a semantic or contextual level. However, the success of the normal peers, in the Seymour and Evans study, in non-word reading at a time when their word reading vocabularies were relatively low, could not be accounted for by the Seidenberg and McClelland model without the incorporation of an additional alphabetic principle, in effect reinstating a dual-route model. Seymour and Evans (1992) further argue that for their hyperlexic there is no evidence of interdependence of the semantic and orthographic systems supporting modularity within the overall system. They conclude that an orthographic system may develop normally in the absence of a semantic level but that the inclusion of an alphabetic process would be expected to convey an additional advantage.

Temple and Carney (1996) have documented hyperlexia in Turner's syndrome. Reading levels were significantly above those predicted by age and intelligence, and significantly above control levels. Reading accuracy was also significantly better than controls for both non-word reading and irregular words reading. Thus, hyperlexia in Turner's syndrome has neither the pattern of surface dyslexia nor of direct dyslexia but appears to reflect genuine hyperdevelopment of a skill. Further, reading comprehension was significantly better than controls indicating no necessary links between hyperlexia and a disorder of comprehension. The hyperdevelopment of reading and certain other linguistic skills in Turner's syndrome is counterbalanced by their selective spatial deficit (Temple & Carney, 1995).

IN CONCLUSION

Hinshelwood's (1917) historical analysis of the developmental dyslexias emphasised their relationship to the acquired dyslexias. Further, he described the components of a cognitive reading system within which there were separate subsystems for processing components and attempted to explain the patterns of reading impairment seen in the developmental dyslexias in relation to this model. He was thus an early user of cognitive neuropsychology applied to children even though he predated the cognitive revolution itself.

There continue to be debates regarding the diagnosis of the developmental dyslexias, with concern about the utility of an IQ-based classification system. However, despite the arguments about classification, an incidence of 6% is reported, with a male to female ratio of 2 or 3:1 (Lewis et al., 1994). Evidence for a biological basis for the disorder is now extensive, with support from genetic, electro-physiological, post-mortem, MRI, and PET studies.

Current models of normal reading differ in format. There continues to be reference to the traditional stage models (Frith, 1985; Marsh et al., 1981) of the development of reading, which argue for a single series of invariant stages through which every child must pass. In contrast dual and triple route models of reading recognise different ways in which words might be read aloud correctly, via either transformation of orthographic segments to phonological segments, or via semantic activation and thereby to a phonological representation, or directly from word detectors to phonological representations (Temple, 1985c). Connectionist models were derived from analogy theory and in the earlier formulations incorporated only one route for reading (Seidenberg & McClelland, 1989). However, these formulations had difficulties in generating good non-word reading and in accounting for the patterns of the acquired dyslexias. A revised connectionist model (Plaut et al., 1996) incorporates two routes to reading. Analogy theory and an earlier connectionist model have been partially integrated into models of reading development (Ehri, 1992; Perfetti, 1992), which as a consequence suffer from the weaknesses of these earlier formulations.

Three different forms of developmental dyslexia have been identified, which parallel those seen within the acquired dyslexias. In surface dyslexia, there is an impairment in irregular word reading, but no lexicality effect. Errors are dominated by regularisation/valid errors. There is confusion in the comprehension of homophones. Distortion of the global characteristics of words does not impair reading performance. In contrast, in phonological dyslexia, there is no regularity effect but an impairment in reading non-words. Errors include morphological errors. Distortion of the global characteristics of words can impair reading performance. Deep dyslexia is characterised by complete inability to read non-words and by the appearance of semantic errors in reading single words aloud.

In relation to standard developmental stage models, deep dyslexia could be interpreted as logographic reading and surface dyslexia could be interpreted as alphabetic reading but, in phonological dyslexia, orthographic reading has been attained without mastery of alphabetic principles. This pattern of performance violates such models.

In relation to the multiple route models, surface dyslexia is interpreted as reflecting impaired development of the lexical and semantic reading route with consequent over-reliance upon the phonological reading route. Phonological dyslexia is interpreted as reflecting impaired performance development of the phonological reading route, with over-reliance in lexical and semantic reading routes. Deep dyslexia reflects absence of both the phonological and the direct route and use of an isolated and intrinsically unstable semantic route, or an isolated and damaged semantic route. The double dissociations seen within these pattern of dyslexia could not be explained within the older connectionist models, but the new dual route connectionist model permits an explanation similar to a conventional dual route explanation, but without the flexibility of a triple route. The evidence for the developmental independence of the phonological and semantic reading routes is therefore strong, incorporating a modular organisation to the reading system within development.

In terms of underlying causative factors, it has been suggested that surface dyslexics might have poor visual memories and/or poor naming skills. However, neither of these suggestions is consistent with current data. It is, however, clear that in surface dyslexia there is not impairment of phonological skills and that these are therefore not the causal impairment in all cases of developmental dyslexia. In phonological dyslexia there is good evidence of impairment in phonological skills within both reading and purely oral tasks. This may impair the development of the phonological reading route, though despite this normal levels of word recognition may be attained.

CHAPTER SIX

Spelling Disorders

INTRODUCTION

There have been no reports of children with developmental dyslexia who have not also had a developmental dysgraphia. However, there have been reports of children with developmental dysgraphia who were thought to have good reading skills (Frith, 1980). Spelling difficulties are therefore more common than reading difficulties, but despite this they have received substantially less investigation than reading difficulties. This is as true for the developmental disorders of spelling as it is for acquired disorders of spelling amongst neurological patients. Even Hinshelwood, who in his 1917 book on congenital word-blindness, wrote in such detail about his interest in children with reading difficulties, made remarkably little comment about their spelling skills and abilities. He did note that his children were able to correctly form written letters and could copy pieces of writing placed in front of them. However, as a rule they failed when they were asked to write to dictation. His explanation for this also related to the deficit he believed the children had in the visual memory centre for words (Hinshelwood, 1917):

> Although this visual memory centre is not destroyed, it is functionally in abeyance, as it has not yet been furnished with the visual memory of words, and hence stimulation of the graphic centre is impossible. (p.61)

NORMAL DEVELOPMENT

Frith (1985) discussed a model of spelling acquisition which is similar to her model of reading acquisition. In spelling, it was proposed that the child learnt to spell some words as a continuous sequence without alphabetic mastery. For example, these might include the child's ability to write their own name. Alphabetic skills in writing then developed which involved the translation of phonemes to graphemes. Orthographic skills involve sophisticated spelling systems and would be necessary for the spelling of irregular words. Frith hypothesised that normal reading and writing development proceed out of step. To illustrate this, she divided each of her reading stages into substages. The logographic stage was divided into three and the orthographic stage into two. These divisions are illustrated in Table 6.1. In Frith's model prior to the development of the logographic stage in writing, at a time when the first substage of logographic reading has developed, occasional symbols may be used by the child in writing. Although the logographic phase in spelling is proposed to start after the logographic stage in reading, it also ends earlier. Integral to this, the alphabetic strategy is adopted first for writing and is only adopted in reading when it has reached a secondary level of development in relation to spelling. The alphabetic stage is seen as lasting longer in writing and the orthographic stage starts earlier in reading. These proposals have subsequently received criticism.

In the previous chapter, the proposal that reading does not necessarily start with a logographic phase was discussed, in relation to the studies of Stuart and Coltheart (1988) and Wimmer and Hummer (1990). They argue that for some children and for certain languages alphabetic skills are present in the initial phases of reading. However, since Frith considers that alphabetic skills are evident in spelling before they appear in reading, this also pushes back the onset of alphabetic skills in spelling to the earliest phase. Wimmer and Hummer (1990) argued

TABLE 6.1
Frith's Model of Reading and Spelling Substages (Frith, 1985)

Step	Reading	Writing
1A	logographic 1	(symbolic)
1B	logographic 2	logographic 2
2A	logographic 3	alphabetic 1
2B	alphabetic 2	alphabetic 2
3A	orthographic 1	alphabetic 3
3B	orthographic 2	orthographic 2

that, in German, alphabetic strategies were used for writing as well as reading in the first year at school. Most children had developed some competence in spelling unfamiliar pseudowords, though there were individual differences. Most spelling errors consisted of spellings that were at least partially phonologically correct. They concluded that a logographic strategy in spelling or reading is of limited value in a phonologically transparent language like German. One possible proviso to the Wimmer and Hummer (1990) study is the age of the children tested. Although they were in the first year of formal schooling and had attended only 8 months of schooling on average, they were aged 6;10–8;1, somewhat older than British or American children would tend to be in their first year at school. By this age, children in the UK would also have developed alphabetic strategies even if they had initially been taught by "look and say" methods (Seymour & Elder, 1986).

Stuart and Coltheart (1988) who have argued that alphabetic strategies may be employed from the earliest days of reading even with English, have made a similar case for spelling. Further, they have suggested that children with good phonemic segmentation skills and good knowledge of letter-sounds are able to construct an orthographic lexicon without necessarily having had experience of printed words. The children with good phonemic segmentation skills will not only be good readers but also good spellers. The acquisition of certain components of spelling will depend upon successful experience of print. For example, to successfully parse the word *went*, experience of print is required in order to learn that the nasal is represented by a consonant letter rather than as the property of the vowel. Prior to this realisation the word *went* would tend to be spelt as *wet*.

Ehri (1987) has delineated three phases in the acquisition of phonological spelling skills. The pre-reader, in stage 0, learns letter names and can use these to invent semi-phonetic spellings for words within which the first or last sounds of words are usually distinguished and represented by letters. As an example they suggest that "giraffe" may be spelt J-F. By stage 1, more conventional letter selections are employed, as the child has learnt more about letter-sound relations and phonemic segmentation and decoding. Now "giraffe" might be spelt as GERAF. Finally in stage 2, the child has learnt about the spelling patterns of English words and morphemic knowledge supersedes the need to depict one letter for every sound. For example, in depicting the past tense they are able to use *ed* consistently, even though the sound being represented is often a /t/, as in "stepped", rather than a /d/. Ehri (1987) also emphasises the central importance of reading and spelling acquisition by providing evidence of cases where knowledge of spelling influences pronunciation in speech. She argues that this supports the view that spellings are retained in memory by being analysed as sound symbols. The knowledge of printed word spellings also acts within the language to constrain phonological drift and maintains greater consistency in pronunciation from one generation to the next than for cultures without written language. Moreover the rigidity of spelling is evident in the observation that a culture will more rapidly accommodate a shift in the pronunciation of a written spelling than an alteration of the structure of the spelling itself.

Perfetti's (1992) model of reading was outlined in Chapter 5. Since Perfetti (1992) argues for a single representation which serves both reading and spelling, this model is also of relevance here. Speed of correct spelling is an index of the quality of a representation within the autonomous lexicon.

Treiman (1992, 1993) argues that children have difficulty in analysing intrasyllabic units into phonemes and that models of both reading and spelling must therefore accommodate orthographic–phonological translations based upon units intermediate between phonemes and words. She suggests that at the earliest stage of learning to spell some children do not have links between speech and print at the level of single phonemes. Other children may, from the beginning, use both correspondences — at the level of single phonemes and at the level of larger units, but the larger units remain important.

MODELS OF THE ADULT SPELLING SYSTEM

Models of adult spelling systems have been less well developed and discussed than models of reading systems. The traditional models of spelling emphasised aspects of phonic mediation, within which it was believed that the sound based aspects of a word must be derived prior to translation into letter forms. One of the contributions from adult cognitive neuropsychology, which encouraged a revision of this view, was the observation that spelling might proceed without such phonic mediation since patients were reported who lacked phonic skills yet remained able to spell certain types of stimuli. This led to the proposal of dual and triple routes models for spelling, in parallel to those for reading. A diagrammatic model of a simple two system spelling hypothesis was presented by Roeltgen and Heilman (1984) and is illustrated in Fig. 6.1. This simple proposal lacked semantic involvement and they also discussed an expansion of the system, in which semantic influence was added (see Fig. 6.2).

When Ellis and Young discussed spelling disorders (Ellis & Young, 1988a) they incorporated the speech production system into their

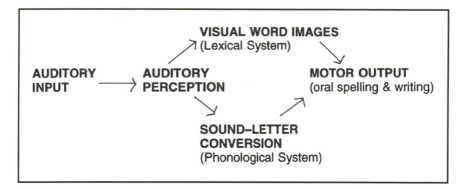

FIG. 6.1 Diagrammatic model of the two-system spelling hypothesis (Roeltgen & Heilman, 1984).

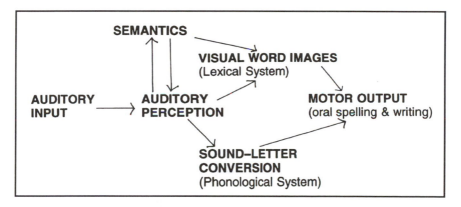

FIG. 6.2 Diagrammatic model of the two-system spelling hypothesis with the addition of semantic influence (Roeltgen & Heilman, 1984).

illustration of an underlying model. Their diagrammatic illustration of this is seen in Fig. 6.3. For the purposes of preliminary discussions here, the model that will be adopted is that which most closely parallels the models that were discussed in relation to reading. This model is illustrated in Fig. 6.4.

Margolin (1984) distinguished between non-lexical phonology and lexical phonology. Non-lexical phonology feeds into a system in which non-lexical phonological to orthographic recoding takes place (see Fig. 6.5). In the model, depicted in Fig. 6.4, following a process of auditory analysis, the auditory input may be parsed into phonological segments, which could be at the level of phoneme but could be a larger subdivision. These phonemes or phonological segments are then translated into orthographic segments in the translator. These are combined in the

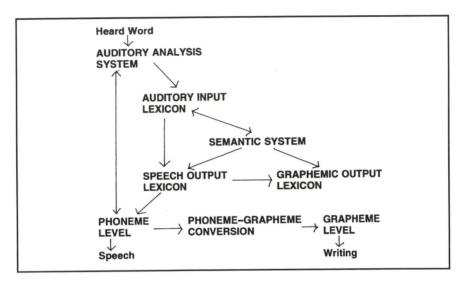

FIG. 6.3 Model of spelling (Ellis & Young, 1988a).

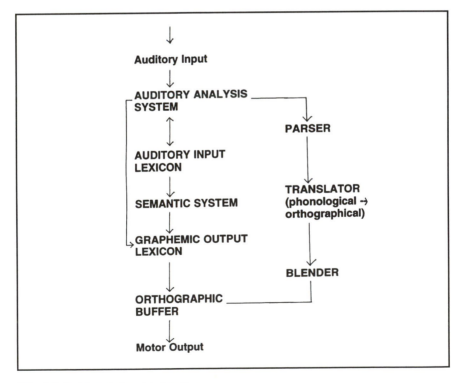

FIG. 6.4 An integrated model of spelling.

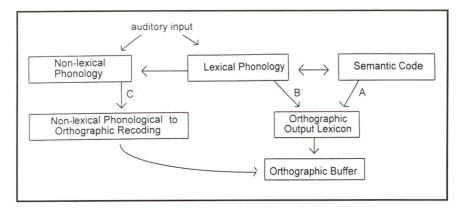

FIG. 6.5 Model of spelling (Margolin, 1984).

blender and held in an orthographic buffer from which motor output may be processed in the translation to the writing system. This is the system that would be used for the writing of non-words or unfamiliar words even in the accomplished adult speller.

In addition to this phonological decoding route, there are two other modes by which a word might be spelt. When processing takes place via a semantic route the auditory analysis system accesses an entry within the auditory input lexicon, this activates an entry in the semantic system. The entries between auditory input and semantics are bidirectional. This means that, following the identification of a word and its meaning, it is also possible from an output from the auditory input lexicon to feed into the system to be parsed for phonological processing. This may occur when we are trying to sound out a familiar word in order to work out how to spell it. Output from the semantic system may also feed directly into a graphemic output lexicon without the need for phonological decoding. This graphemic output lexicon contains stores of letter sequences, which make up words, and is comparable to the type of phonological output lexicon activated in reading. In addition to this, there is a direct route proceeding from auditory input lexicon to graphemic output lexicon which permits the spelling of words whose meanings are not well understood. The principal difference then between this model and the triple route reading models, presented in Fig. 5.3 and 5.4, is that the translation system between the auditory input lexicon and the semantic system is bidirectional. The objective of spelling is not to attain meaning but to record information. Semantic knowledge associated with particular auditory input may be activated prior to the production of its written spelling. The outputs of any of the three spelling routes may be held in the orthographic buffer. From here the information may be processed in order to produce oral spelling but most commonly is processed to produce a motor output and written spelling.

DEVELOPMENTAL DYSGRAPHIAS

Boder (1973) classified children with reading and spelling impairments on the assumption that their patterns of reading and spelling errors were similar. Those who made phonologically incorrect errors were termed dysphonetic and those who produced few phonologically correct errors were termed dyseidetic. The issue of the relationship between the pattern of spelling difficulties and the pattern of reading difficulties or reading style remains open. Certainly the patterns of errors within reading and spelling are not necessarily similar (e.g. Temple & Marshall, 1983). However, Boder (1973) did identify two broad classes of children who resemble those outlined later. She recognised that developmental dysgraphia is not homogeneous and that the informative distinctions to consider, in relation to variation within the sample, relate to the pattern of the literacy errors themselves.

Frith (1980) has also partitioned developmental dysgraphics on the basis of error pattern but also noted a related difference in reading skill. She described two groups of 11 to 13-year-old developmental dysgraphics. One group were good readers and spelt non-words well but in spelling made errors that were phonologically correct (Type B spellers). The other group were poor readers, and in spelling had difficulty with non-words and made errors that were not phonologically correct (Type A spellers).

Frith (1980) proposed that the type B speller reads on the basis of partial cues. In relation to her stage model, they experience developmental lag with late onset during the early orthographic stage and fail to become full cue readers (Frith, 1985). Alternatively, Bruck and Waters (1988) argue that type B spellers lack age-appropriate subword transcoding skills. They learn basic phoneme–grapheme rules, but not the slightly higher level constraints such as the "rule of e", which, in a terminal position, lengthens the preceding vowel, and the vowel influence to soften or harden "g".

Burden (1992) tested the reading and spelling of type A and type B spellers and confirmed that the type B, although good readers, were impaired in decoding skills. Further, their oral reading of text was marked by substitutions that preserved the meaning of the text. Their silent reading was slow.

In the cognitive neuropsychological analyses of the developmental dysgraphias detailed here, no assumptions about reading skills are made. Two contrasting disorders of spelling developmental surface dysgraphia and developmental phonological dysgraphia, seen in children of similar ages, who also have similar spelling ages will be discussed in relation to the model depicted in Fig. 6.4.

Case Report: Developmental Surface Dysgraphia, RB

At the age of ten, RB's spelling age was 7;6 on the Schonell Single Word Spelling Test (Temple, 1986b). The pattern of her reading development which is of a surface dyslexic nature was discussed in Chapter 5, where background details to her case report were also given.

The general characteristics of RB's spelling can be illustrated by the following passage of text which she wrote in response to a request to write a story. The story is about a little dog.

The Littl Dog

One apon a time there was a littl girl How had a pupy Every day as soon as she got home she wood take her pupy ot side One day she found her dog very ill in is baskit so here and here muthre went to the vets. the vat took a diyecnosis and the pupy had to have a very speshl oprashon wicht cost a lot of muny and so it had the oprashon and and it cost a lot of muny and the pupy grow up to de a very dig dog and diy of old age.

The correct spelling of this would have been as follows:

Once upon a time there was a little girl who had a puppy. Every day once she got home she would take her puppy outside. One day she found her dog very ill in his basket so her and her mother went to the vets. The vet took a diagnosis and the puppy had to have a very special operation, which cost a lot of money and so it had the operation and it cost a lot of money and the puppy grew up to be a very big dog and die of old age.

A further example is given by RB's description of how to use an old-fashioned type of telephone:

Mach the nudrs in the booke with those that are on the dyle and put your finger in the howl and push it arownd untill you rech the silve bare repet this with every nudr and wheil puting the reseve to your eare with the wier at the botom lisen for some one to anser the phone when they do there will be a nose and then you push in the coine any you may talk.

The correct spelling of what RB was trying to say is as follow:

Match the numbers in the book with those that are on the dial and put your finger in the hole and push it around until you reach the silver bar. Repeat this with every number and while putting the receiver to your ear with the wire at the bottom, listen for someone to answer the phone. When they do, there will be a noise and then you push in the coin and you may talk.

What is striking about these passages of text is that they convey coherent and logically structured ideas and messages. There is nothing inappropriate in the semantic content of what is conveyed. Moreover, the majority of spelling errors are logical. They preserve the majority of the sound characteristics associated with the word and so it is possible to work out what RB was attempting to write. Many of her errors were rule governed. This pattern of spelling impairment which closely preserves the phonological aspects of the words is referred to as surface dysgraphia and a more exact description of its major features follows.

Spelling Errors.   Following oral dictation of 160 words, RB made 97 errors. Of these 52% were phonologically plausible, e.g.:

"fire" → *fier*	"engine" → *engen*
"ought" → *orte*	"orchestra" → *orkestrer*
"whistle" → *wisle*	"clue" → *cloo*
"health" → *helth*	"choir" → *quier*

RB also had a tendency to confuse the letters "b" and "d". If "b" "d" confusions are ignored, a further 9% of errors are phonologically plausible, e.g. "design" → *bizine*; "doubt" → *bowt*; "ambition" → *amdision*; 8% of RB errors may be classified as phoneme–grapheme errors, in which the final "e" which contributes to the lengthening of vowels in English is either missing or added inappropriately; or following the letter "g", the terminal "e", which should produce a softening of the letter "g", is absent, e.g.:

missing final "e":	"sunshine" → *sunshin*;	"these" → *thes*
extra final "e":	"nip" → *nipe*;	"win" → *wine*
hard/soft "g":	"large" → *larg*;	"strange" → *strang*

Of RB's remaining errors, 11% involved the selection of an incorrect vowel and 20% involve consonant errors or combinations of the other error categories. Examples of incorrect vowels are as follows:

"peach" → *pech*	"join" → *jone*
"influence" → *inflowans*	"joyful" → *joyfell*

In summary, the majority of RB's errors were phonologically plausible. This is a dominant characteristic of developmental surface dysgraphia. In developmental surface dysgraphia, one sees the application of a logical rule system that may be appropriate and effective to write many regular words but is problematic for many irregular words in English. Moreover, in the spelling of regular words there can be ambiguities, since in the English language there are many different ways that one can spell certain vowel sounds and other phonemic sounds. Even in spelling words which we would consider to be regular for reading, word-specific information may be necessary to know how the particular word should be spelt. Thus, for example, there is no specific reason why the word "cheat" should be spelt *cheat*, whereas the word "feet" is spelt *feet*. The selection of one spelling over the other is dependent on word-specific information.

According to the rules of English, the word "meet" could be spelt in a phonologically valid form in any of the following ways: *meet, mete, meit, met, meete, meite, miete, meate*. In RB's case it was not simply ambiguity which accounted for the large number of phonologically valid misspellings, since RB's spelling was not only phonologically accurate but the rules used were restricted in number. Thus, although "meet" may be validly misspelt in a number of ways, if RB misspelt it she would do so as *met* since "e" is the preferred spelling for the vowel /i/, e.g. "peach" → *pech*; "these" → *thes*; "cheery" → *chery*; "cheat" → *chet*. Indeed, for all the words which were phonologically misspelt, those that contain the vowel /i/ are always transcribed with the grapheme "e". This could be an example of the use of letter names to represent sounds, similar to that discussed by Gentry (1982). The other consistent misspellings used by RB are indicated in Table 6.2. This lists specific vowel sounds, examples of the words that appeared in the spelling list, and the representations that were used for this vowel sound by RB. Thus, in RB's case, most of her spelling was rule governed but she used a restricted set of appropriate rules. She was insensitive to the context-specific and word-specific information that is necessary for correct spelling.

The suggestion that there is an absence of word-specific information predicts that there should be homophone confusion in spelling.

Homophone Spellings. RB was presented with the 40 stimuli on Temple's homophonic list (Temple, 1984c). This consists of 20 pairs of regular homophonic words. Each word has an attached phrase or sentence, which indicates the meaning which is associated with it. The child is requested not to start writing until the full sentence has been heard. For example, "sail, we went to sail the boat up the river, sail". Of the 40 stimuli, RB spelt 4 correctly and produced a further 5 with homophonic spellings. Thus, the incidence of correct spelling was no higher than the incidence of homophonic spelling. The selection between these two was random. Other spelling errors follow a similar pattern to those quoted previously. In particular the spelling of the vowel /i/ as "e" generated a number of errors.

TABLE 6.2
Letters Used Consistently by RB to Represent Vowels in Spelling Errors

Vowel	Example	Representation used by RB
/i/	peach	e
/ɪ/	hid	i, i-e
/eɪ/	weigh	a, terminal ay/ey
/ɛ/	chemist	e
/ae/	adjective	a
/ɑ/	large	a
/ɒ/	knob	o
/ɔ/	north	o
/oʊ/	motion	o, terminal ow
/u/	clue	oo
/ə/	anchor	e, a u
/ʌ/	brother	u
/ju/	jewel	u-e
/aɪ/	kite	y, itte, i
/aʊ/	doubt	ow
/aə/	fire	ie

Spelling of Non-words. RB was presented with 29 words and 29 non-words for written spelling. Each of the non-words differed from the words by only one letter. RB spelt correctly 19 words and 23 non-words. There was thus no significant difference between word and non-word spelling. Indeed the trend was in favour of a non-word superiority. Thus, RB displayed another major feature of surface dysgraphia, in that non-word spelling is as good as word spelling.

Rereading of Misspellings. Since RB's spelling errors largely preserved the sound of the word, it seemed probable that they would be easy to decode both by herself and by other adult readers. When RB was asked to read the 180 stimuli which had been presented for spelling she was able to read 69 of them when they were typewritten correctly. When on a different occasion she was asked to reread her own spelling of the same words, including a large number of erroneous stimuli, she was able to read 75 correctly. Thus, for RB her own spelling code was as effective as normal spelling. Normal adults also found RB's spelling relatively easy to reread. Three fluent adult readers were asked to read aloud the written spellings of RB, having been given no information about the target words that she was attempting to write. They were asked to make one guess at what the target was. On average, 80% of the words written by RB were identified correctly as the target word. This was a high hit rate given the number of errors in the corpus and the similarity of spelling of many English words.

Normal Spellers. RB's spelling performance was compared with spelling by children without dysgraphia. Ten children aged 7;6, with comparable accuracy levels to RB on the 160 word list, were selected for an analysis of spelling performance. The error classification applied was similar to that for RB, with a division into errors that were phonologically plausible, those that were phoneme–grapheme errors, those that were vowel errors, and other errors. RB's performance in comparison to the mean, standard deviation, and range of these seven-and-a-half-year-olds is given in Table 6.3. It can be seen that her performance was comparable to these spelling level controls. Thus, although RB is a developmental surface dysgraphic, the pattern of her spelling disorder did not appear to be grossly abnormal in comparison with younger children, who were developing spelling in a normal fashion.

An even larger proportion of phonologically valid spelling errors are found in the error corpus of NG (Temple, 1984c). This child also had surface dysgraphia and, of his errors, 88% were phonologically valid. The spelling of non-words of four, five, and six letters in length was also perfect. NG had a highly developed phonological spelling route.

Theoretical Interpretations. In relation to Frith's model of the acquisition of spelling, RB may be explained in a relatively straightforward fashion by suggesting that she had arrested development at the alphabetic stage of spelling acquisition and has failed to develop appropriate orthographic strategies. She had mastered some preliminary logographic skills and was able to spell a limited number of irregular words. She had also mastered good alphabetic skills which enabled her to spell non-words as competently as words, and which also enabled her, in many cases, to preserve the sound-based characteristics of words with which she was unfamiliar and generate

TABLE 6.3
RBs Spelling Errors Compared with Spelling Age Controls

	Control mean	*Control range*	*RB*
Correct	35	25–62	39
Phonologically plausible	3 (SD=12.5)	32–74	62
Phoneme–grapheme errors	5	0–13	8
Vowel errors	8 (SD=3)	4–15	10
Other errors	31 (SD=11.80)	15–52	20

phonologically appropriate errors. However, she had been unable to master the word-specific information and complexities of English that would enable normal adult orthographic skills. RB's performance may therefore be explained in terms of a delay in development of the reading system. Similarly, in relation to Ehri's (1987) model, RB appears to have reached stage 1 but has not fully mastered stage 2.

In relation to Perfetti's (1992) model, RB has established a functional lexicon for spelling (and reading) but only has a partial autonomous lexicon with fully specified and redundant representations. However, in Perfetti's model there is no difference in the representation for regular and irregular words, and RB's disproportionate difficulty with irregular words has to be explained as a normal emergent property of the acquisition algorithms. If the degree of RB's regularity effect was significantly greater than for normal children, it would be a problem for the Perfetti (1992) theory. Perfetti's model may also have difficulty in accounting for the degree of competency in non-word reading given the degree of impairment in reading non-words. For some other cases of surface dyslexia this distinction may be even more marked and thereby even more problematic for the theory.

This snapshot of RB's performance at one point in time does not provide information about whether performance was truly delayed and would develop normally later, or whether this pattern of performance would maintain the same characteristics and represent a stable character. In fact, re-analysis of RB's performance at the age of 14 indicated that, although her overall level of accuracy had increased somewhat, the pattern and characteristics of her spelling performance remain unchanged. She remained a surface dysgraphic at the age of 14 and there was no qualitative shift in the pattern of performance (Temple, 1990c).

Comparison with the model depicted in Fig. 6.5 also enables an interpretation of RB in relation to an adult model of spelling. RB had well-developed phonological translation systems within the phonological spelling route but had impaired development of the semantic-based graphemic spelling system. The locus of her disorder within this is unclear. She did not have any known auditory comprehension deficit, and so it seems probable that the difficulty was in accessing or generating output from the graphemic output lexicon itself. This store was either poorly developed for RB or was encoded in such a way that it was difficult to access or recover responses from within it.

The pattern of developmental surface dysgraphia described above can also be seen in children at a later age and with a higher spelling age. Temple (1985a) documents a case of developmental surface dysgraphia in a 17-year-old girl KM, with a spelling age of 8;6, which is a spelling age a year older than that documented for RB. Temple compared KM directly with the surface dysgraphic TP (Hatfield & Patterson, 1983), an acquired dysgraphic patient who has acquired surface dysgraphia (Hatfield and Patterson refer to this type of dysgraphia as phonological spelling but the dysgraphia that is being referred to is identical to surface dysgraphia). The direct comparison of KM and TP indicated not only that spelling of the same list of words was qualitatively and quantitatively similar but also that the relative difficulty of individual words on the list was also similar. Analysis of the particular words which were found to be easy and those that were found to be difficult indicated that the ease of spelling for KM and TP was influenced by word length, frequency, and with respect to exception words, by the presence or absence of similarly spelt words.

The notion that the phonological spelling route may operate upon segments larger than individual phonemes, and may be able to translate certain phonological to orthographic segments is supported by the ability of KM and TP to spell exception words when the exceptional feature occurs commonly in other words. For example, the ending "ign'" as in *sign*. Such a view is also supported by the presence of word subcomponents within their neologistic errors, and by the influence on exception word spelling, of the existence of a similarly spelt rhyme. Alternatively, some of the correct spelling of exception words in these subjects could be explained by the partial development of the semantic spelling route in addition to the phonological route. This partial system could permit correct spelling of some exception words that might have incomplete entries which could contribute to the spelling of other words. Word frequency might influence this system.

Finally, the spelling responses made by KM to non-words were compared to spelling responses made by normal children, in order to determine whether they were atypical selections. Frith (1980) has pointed out that children with unexpected spelling problems who were good readers tend to use unconventional correspondences between phonology and orthography when writing non-words and words to dictation. For these children, the phonological spelling route appears to have developed in an unusual way. However, the responses of KM were typical of normal children. There was thus no evidence that the phonological route she used to attempt to spell normal words was atypical in its development.

Hanley et al. (1992) have reported a case of surface dysgraphia still evident in a 22-year-old man, Allan. He performed well on tests of phonological awareness and he had established knowledge about the variable spelling for different phonemes, but had difficulty with uncommon phoneme-to-grapheme correspondences. Hanley et al. (1992)

argued that he had an orthographic processing deficit, and was reliant upon a sublexical phonology and a lexicon with only partial information about the spellings of words. They argued that such a deficit in generalised form would have greater impact upon spelling than reading because of the need for detailed letter-by-letter knowledge in spelling, whereas in reading partial cues may be sufficient for accurate identification.

For RB, reading and spelling performance mirrored each other, taking the form of surface dyslexia and surface dysgraphia. Patterns of her performance did not therefore provide any evidence for dissociability of reading and spelling systems. However, for KM the pattern of reading performance did not mirror the pattern of spelling development. Although KM was a surface dysgraphic, she was not a surface dyslexic. The lexical–semantic route to reading was well established in KM. This suggests that such a route is uni-directional as spelling does not proceed by a simple reversal of these processes. KM argues for the dissociability of reading and spelling mechanisms in development. Hanley et al.'s (1992) case, Allan, was also not a surface dyslexic. His reading of words was prompt and accurate. However, Hanley et al. argued that his lexical decision performance and his definitions of homophones suggested poorly specified lexical entries for reading as well as spelling. Thus, although the impact was different a similar type of deficit was postulated in both the reading and spelling systems. Coltheart and Funnell (1987) have also emphasised that the prediction of surface dyslexia in association with surface dysgraphia would only apply to certain forms of surface dysgraphia, even where there were unitary codes for reading and spelling.

The pattern of spelling development exhibited by RB, KM and Allan provides a double dissociation with an alternative pattern of spelling performance documented here, which is referred to as developmental phonological dysgraphia.

Case Report: Developmental Phonological Dysgraphia, AH

AH (Temple, 1985b, 1986b, 1990c) was a 10-year-old boy with developmental phonological dyslexia, whose reading performance was briefly commented upon in Chapter 5. He was from a professional family. At birth there was some concern about slowness to breathe but there was no other evidence of abnormality. Developmental milestones and speech development were within normal limits. Hearing and vision were normal. Gross and fine motor function was normal on history. Both handwriting and drawing were immature for age. However, on examination by a paediatric neurologist no apraxia was evident. No neurological abnormality was found although there was poor imitation of gesture. AH usually but not always writes with the left hand. Neither parent was left-handed but there was left-handedness in the family. There was no family history of reading or spelling difficulties but AH's mother, whose first language was Welsh, had early difficulties in translating between English and Welsh. AH was monolingual in English.

AH's scores on the Wechsler Intelligence Scale for Children — Revised were as follows:

Verbal Tests		Performance Tests	
Information	12	Picture Completion	15
Similarities	14	Picture Arrangement	14
Arithmetic	8	Block Design	12
Vocabulary	19	Object Assembly	12
Comprehension	16	Coding	9
Verbal IQ	123	Performance IQ	117
Full Scale IQ	123		

(10 is an average subtest score, range = 1–19, SD=3)

AH attained a score above the 95th percentile for his age on Raven's Coloured Progressive Matrices. He also had a large vocabulary, attaining the highest possible score for his age on both the WISC vocabulary subtest and the Peabody Picture Vocabulary Test. AH's single word spelling age on the Schonell Single Word Spelling Test was 7;8. His chronological age, and spelling age at the time of this case report are comparable to RB, who was discussed earlier.

Because AH had poorly formed handwriting, independent fluent adult readers were asked to interpret his spelling. Each adult was requested to identify the component letters and then, if possible, to suggest what the original stimulus word might have been. There was fairly high consistency across the adult readers. In most cases where there was disagreement about individual letter identification, at least two out of three adults agreed and this was the interpretation that was selected. Marking of spelling was then based on the responses of the adults. Of the 160 spelling responses of AH, there were 97 errors; an identical number to those produced by RB.

For AH, a minority of spelling errors were phonologically plausible: only 17%. Examples of these are as follows: "recent" → resent; "mattress" → matres; "motion" → moshon. 3% of errors resulted from phoneme–grapheme errors in relation to terminal "e"s. These largely consisted of the deletion of terminal "e"s. 16% of errors related to the use of an inappropriate vowel. Examples of these are as follows: "nation" → natoin; "throat" → throt; "cheery" → chery. The majority of AH's errors were consonant errors or combinations of other aspects. 60% of errors were of this form and, in combination with the dropping of vowels, or incorrect vowels, 80% of errors did not conform to phonological expectations. Examples of the unclassifiable errors are as follows:

"injure" → *infer*	"hid" → *hind*
"relation" → *rechon*	"mechanic" → *mician*
"press" → *perss*	"adjective" → *agiceft*
"jewel" → *jelly*	"child" → *childenre*
"possible" → *osbelle*	"either" → *arother*

It is clear that some of these unclassifiable errors in relation to alteration in spelling, are actually paragraphic responses. At least one was a function word substitution, and one may have been a function word substitution in which there may have been an incorrect judgement about an ambiguity in the second letter, i.e. "either" → *arother*.

In summary, AH displayed a pattern of spelling in which the majority of spelling errors did not preserve the sound-based characteristics of the word and there was also evidence of paragraphic responses. These patterns of performance are consistent with a diagnosis of developmental phonological dysgraphia.

When asked to spell balanced lists of regular and irregular words, AH was no better at spelling the regular than at spelling the irregular words. Thus regularity was not a psycholinguistic dimension that affects his spelling ability. Regularity for spelling is a different thing from regularity for reading, and the lists available to test such characteristics are less well developed for spelling than for reading. Nevertheless this aspect of AH's performance holds true across stimulus lists.

Non-word Spelling. AH was able to spell some non-words correctly. He was slightly poorer at spelling non-words than words. For a pure developmental phonological dysgraphic, one might wish that difference to be more marked. For AH, 19 words and 15 non-words were spelt on the balanced lists. However, the nature of the spelling errors produced suggest that AH was not using a phonological system to write these non-words. Examples of his spelling errors to non-words are as follows:

"ked" → *ged*	"trock" → *tok*
"faper" → *fape*	"plas" → *pllas*
"upple" → *upley*	"sutter" → *sater*

As noted, in comparison with RB, the developmental surface dysgraphic, AH made an identical number of errors to words. However, when comparing error rates to non-words, AH made significantly more errors to non-words than RB (RB, 23/29 correct vs AH, 15/29 correct, $X^2=3.6$, $P<0.05$).

AH's spelling errors were intuitively less logical, in that they did not preserve the sound-based aspects of the target. However, they were not entirely random and did bear a relationship to characteristics associated with the targets. It was of interest to determine how effective this non-phonological spelling code could be in triggering the original target words. For a spelling list of 160 items, AH was able to read 107 aloud correctly, when they were presented in written format and typescript. When he read instead his own written spellings of the same words, he was able to read only 72 correctly. Thus, for AH, the idiosyncratic code that he used for recording spelling was less effective than proper spelling. This meant that there was difficulty for him in deciphering the written code which he uses in his school books. When normal adults were presented with these written spellings to read aloud, they also had difficulty with them, being able to read only 40–60% correctly. The interpretation of this pattern of performance, as reflecting a less efficient code for recording information should be tempered by recognition that AH's handwriting is also of poor quality, which exacerbates the interpretive difficulties.

However, AH's spelling performance was not improved with oral spelling. It was not simply a graphemic output problem at a motor level. The Schonell Graded Spelling Test on which he attained the spelling age of 8;5 with written spelling produced an even lower spelling age with oral response. His oral spelling age in this test was 7;8. The pattern of his errors was such that they were phonologically inaccurate.

Theoretical Interpretations.   Just as phonological dyslexia is difficult to interpret in relation to a conventional stagewise model of reading development, so phonological dysgraphia is difficult to interpret in relation to a stagewise model of spelling development. The first logographic stage in spelling development, as proposed by Frith (1985), lasts for an even shorter time than the logographic stage in reading development. The logographic stage in spelling, where it appears at all, is only sufficient for the mastery of the spelling of a very small number of words, prior to the development of alphabetic knowledge. AH had mastered the ability to spell a substantial number of words despite his general dysgraphic difficulties. The number of words within his spelling repertoire far exceeded that which would normally be considered to be representative of a logographic stage of spelling development. Yet the nature of his difficulties and the pattern of his spelling errors indicated that he was not able to use an alphabetic strategy or system to attempt to spell familiar and unfamiliar words. He had not successfully proceeded through the alphabetic stage of spelling development. The presence amongst his spelling errors of responses which contain legal orthographic components suggest the use of an orthographic strategy.

For example, in misspelling the word "bright", AH spelt the irregular portion of the word correctly but produced an error: *bight*. Similarly, in attempting to spell the word "station", which includes the terminal section *tion*, AH produced a spelling error: *satation*. Once again some word specific orthographic knowledge was being employed. This was not a simple alphabetic translation. AH was utilising orthographic strategies, without having proceeded through alphabetic mastery. This creates a problem for the theories of Marsh, Frith, and Ehri. He did not appear to represent in any simple way a pattern of merely delayed spelling development.

This interpretation was confirmed by comparing the pattern of his spelling errors with those made by 10 normal children of comparable overall spelling accuracy. The error scores of these spelling age controls were classified in a similar way to those of AH. The comparison between AH's performance and the normal controls is given in Table 6.4. This indicates that the proportion of phonologically plausible errors made by AH lies outside the control range. AH produced significantly fewer phonologically plausible errors than spelling level controls. He produces a significantly larger number of errors which are unclassifiable or are multiple combinations of other categories. Thus, AH had not made the progress with the development of alphabetic spelling strategies that would normally be expected by his spelling age. His pattern of spelling development, although only at a 7;6 level, is already deviant in relation to the normal seven-year-old pattern. This was not the case for RB discussed previously, who although suffering from developmental dysgraphia had a pattern of performance that was consistent with delayed development at this stage.

AH's spelling performance is also a problem for the Perfetti (1992) model, since there is no obvious basis for a double dissociation between this pattern and that of surface dysgraphia. In both cases, the overall level of accuracy in word spelling is equivalent, yet within the same performance level there are two qualitatively different patterns of spelling. AH's absence of a regularity effect is not a problem for Perfetti, if the normal emergent property can be constrained in some way by a manipulation of the network. The relative absence of phonological spelling, given the overall degree of spelling access may be less easy to accommodate.

AH's pattern of spelling development is readily interpretable in relation to the model of the adult spelling system presented in Fig. 6.5. AH had impaired development of the phonological spelling route. It had become partially established since AH was able to spell some non-words correctly. However, the system had not developed sufficiently to permit the logical spelling of unfamiliar words.

TABLE 6.4
AH's Spelling Errors Compared with Spelling Age Controls

	Control mean	Control range	AH
Correct	35	25–62	41
Phonologically plausible	53 (SD=12.5)	32–74	17
Phoneme–grapheme errors	5	0–13	3
Vowel errors	8 (SD=3)	4–15	20
Other errors	31 (SD=11.80)	15–52	60

AH's neologistic responses should in principle arise from the phonological route since neologistic responses would not have entries in the graphemic output lexicon. The majority of AH's spelling errors are neologisms and they include illegal letter combinations, suggesting some abnormality in the development of the system of orthographic segments onto which phonological segments should map, within the phonological spelling route. They also include many inappropriate consonants, suggesting an abnormality in the translation system from phonological to orthographic segments. Many of the errors failed to preserve the length of the stimulus, indicating an abnormality either in parsing or the loss of information in blending orthographic segments.

In general, there is gross impairment in the establishment of the phonological spelling route in phonological dysgraphia. In contrast, the semantically based spelling system producing activation of the graphemic output lexicon is relatively well established. AH was able to spell many real words correctly. There were occasional paragraphic errors but although these were not as frequent as the paralexic errors of phonological dyslexia, AH may be interpreted as having a selected impairment in the establishment of a phonological spelling route with relative preservation in the development of the word specific spelling route.

It was shown that AH's spelling pattern was already deviant from spelling level controls aged 7;6. It may therefore be that, in normal spelling development, the demands placed upon the phonological spelling route are evident earlier with word-specific knowledge being of lesser import. This argument is illustrated in Fig. 6.6 taken from Temple (1986b). It is suggested that there are at least two independent spelling systems, one that requires phonological knowledge and one that requires word-specific knowledge. The phonological knowledge will be similar to that mastered in Frith's alphabetic stage of spelling development, and the word-specific knowledge will be similar to that mastered in Frith's orthographic spelling development. Critically, a distinction between a description here and Frith's description is that it is not necessary to proceed through phonological acquisition in order to acquire word-specific information. There is not an invariant series of stages, such that one must be mastered before the other.

This does not mean that in normal development it is not typical for a child to master one stage before the other. The two spelling routes may differ in strength. A quantitative scale can be arbitrarily assigned to these strengths by say that 0 represents a non-existent route and 15 represents a fully competent adult reader's route. It was established that RB had relatively good phonological skills and rather poor word-specific skills, typical of developmental surface dysgraphia. Let us say that RB has a phonological route of strength 9 and a word-specific route of strength 3. For the sake of symmetry and since they both ultimately

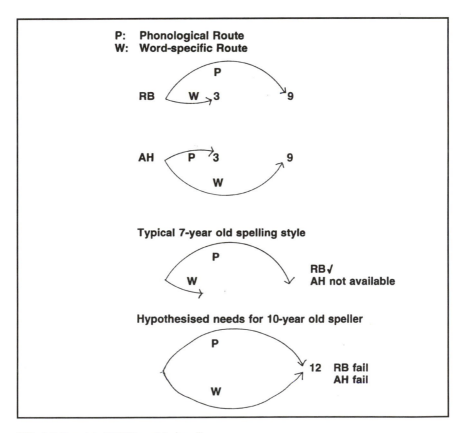

FIG. 6.6 Temple's (1986b) model of spelling.

perform at the same level, we may say that AH's phonological route has a strength of 3 and his word specific route a strength of 9. We know from the analysis of the spellers aged 7;6 that they have reasonably competent alphabetical skills since a good proportion of their errors are phonologically valid. In Frith's terms they would be at an alphabetic stage of spelling development though possibly with the beginnings of mastery of some orthographic information. Let us say that to display a typical seven-year-old pattern you need a phonological route strength of 8 and a word-specific route strength of 3 (see Fig. 6.6).

These seven-year-old demands would be within RB's capabilities, and she looked like a typical seven-year-old who was not deviant in her acquisition. AH did not have even this degree of phonological skill in spelling. However, he had better word-specific skills than both RB and the normal seven-year-olds and he could draw upon these to bring himself up to an overall seven-year performance level in terms of number of spellings produced correctly. By the age of 10, spelling demands could be defined as 12 for each route. Both AH and RB will fail to cope at this level and the spelling performance for both children was deviant by this age.

It should be noted that although in the sample described here the average seven-year-old resembled a surface dysgraphic rather than a phonological dysgraphic, nevertheless in principle seven-year-olds could acquire a pattern of spelling that was more similar to AH. There is a priori reason why phonological acquisition has to proceed word-specific acquisition. The data from AH and other developmental phonological dysgraphics illustrate this. Just as Baron and Strawson (1976) have discussed Phoenecian and Chinese readers, so there may be comparable variations in style in relation to spelling. Without a large-scale study of individual differences within the normal population, the relative proportion of children using different spelling strategies or the strength and consistency of the most typical pattern. In conclusion, the data for AH argue against sequential invariance in the establishment of components of an adult spelling system.

Studies of acquired dysgraphia by Roeltgen and Heilman (1984, 1985) have indicated distinct anatomical localisations underlying different types of dysgraphia. Patients with acquired phonological dysgraphia had lesions of the anterior supramarginal gyrus with sparing of the angular gyrus. In contrast, patients with acquired surface dysgraphia had lesions of the posterosuperior angular gyrus and the parieto-occipital lobule. It is possible that in the future PET studies or other scanning studies may be capable of revealing whether there are distinctions in the localised activations associated with developmental surface dysgraphia and developmental phonological dysgraphia.

Using accuracy results from a number of psycholinguistic measures of spelling (e.g. non-words, regular words), Roeltgen and Tucker (1988) used the statistical technique of multidimensional scaling to divide both acquired and developmental dysgraphics into phonological dysgraphics and surface dysgraphics. They found that the technique was equally effective for the acquired and the developmental cases and that the patterns of spelling error amongst the developmental dysgraphics confirmed their classification. They also suggest that if developmental phonological dysgraphia arises from congenital lesions of the perisylvian region, such children may have more pervasive language difficulties.

Long-term Follow-up

AH was re-tested at the age of 16, six years after the initial description of his impairments in phonological spelling (Temple, 1990c). Spelling age had increased substantively and had progressed from a 7;6 level to a 12;7 level. However, although the level of spelling had improved, the pattern of spelling errors remained unaltered. Less than one-fifth of spelling errors were phonologically plausible. The majority of errors remained consonant or combination errors. This is highly atypical of normal adult spelling errors. AH's spelling performance had improved somewhat with non-words and therefore a phonological spelling route had developed more than had been seen earlier. However, this system could not be used effectively in attempting to spell unfamiliar items. Examples of spelling errors on re-test include:

"join" → *journ*   "secretary" → *secerty*
"champion" → *champigon*   "throat" → *throught*

There were also paragraphic error responses:

"disgrace" → *disc*   "cheery" → *cherry*
"variation" → *various*

Six years after an assessment of spelling, which indicated that AH had an impaired phonological spelling route, the pattern of spelling had remained unaltered. There had been no progression to the mastery of an alphabetic strategy. However, there has been a substantial improvement in spelling ability and it is argued that this represents an expansion of orthographic spelling systems independent of the acquisition of phonological spelling rules.

A similar failure to acquire competent alphabetical skills was reported by Snowling and Hulme (1989; Hulme & Snowling, 1992) in a six-year follow-up of another case of phonological dysgraphia. Over this time they could find only a marginal increase in the proficiency of his phonological spelling strategies. The persistence of phonological dysgraphia into adulthood is reported by Temple (1988a). Here, despite good intelligence and successful career development, the dysgraphic difficulties persisted into middle age causing continual problems.

Stackhouse and Snowling (1992) also report the resistance of some cases of phonological dysgraphia to targeted remediation. Two of their cases, Michael and Caroline, who also had verbal dyspraxia, remained unable to use phonological strategies in spelling even after four years of remediation. Although word spelling skills improved over time, this was not matched by an improved ability to spell non-words. Michael persevered with attempts to spell by sound even though he was unable to use this strategy with any degree of accuracy. In contrast Caroline spelled words using word subcomponents, e.g. "adventure" → *andbackself*, "refreshment" → *withfirstmint*. A similar strategy was also reported by TW (Snowling et al. 1986).

Snowling et al. (1986) suggest that the format of the underlying phonological difficulties within phonological dysgraphia may vary from case to case. Case TW had difficulty within input phonology and had particular difficulty in representing the initial phonemes in words. Examples of her spelling errors were "lip" → *peryse*; "sack" → *canpe*; and "trap" → *mupter*. Case AS had segmentation problems but could spell initial phonemes correctly. Examples of errors included "sack" → *sed*; and "bump" → *bunt*. Case JM had difficulty with output phonology. Snowling et al. (1986) thought that the pattern of spelling errors reflected articulatory difficulties, for example the problems with voicing. His errors included "sack" → *sag*; "packet" → *pagit*; and "polish" → *bols*.

DEVELOPMENTAL AGRAPHIA

Hinshelwood (1917) documents children whose difficulties with written spelling are so severe as to persist into adulthood and in the face of extra instruction. In Chapter 5, it was noted that Hinshelwood argued that the severely impaired children were those who were truly congenitally word-blind whereas the more mildly impaired should be considered to have a congenital dyslexia. A parallel distinction could apply to the developmental dysgraphias. The children discussed earlier have all mastered some spelling knowledge and are able to spell some words correctly. However, KS, who was described as having developmental deep dyslexia in Chapter 5, also has profound difficulties in spelling (Temple, 1988b). Utilising 14 words he had been taught to read, spelling was tested over a three-and-a-half year period. At the age of nine years spelling was formally unscoreable on tests such as the Schonell. None of his spelling attempts at the age of nine were correct. None were phonologically accurate. Most violated the rules of English orthography. Nevertheless, the responses were not completely random and there were some letters in common with the stimulus and the response. Intensive remediation occurred between the ages of 9;0 and 11;0. Extensive targeted work aimed at teaching phonic and alphabetic skills. The degree of spelling development that resulted is illustrated in column two of the responses in Table 6.5. Formally, spelling was now scoreable at an age of 5;11. By the age of 11;0 most of the initial letters in the spelling responses were correct. After a further one-and-a-half years spelling remained six years below age level and only a few elementary words could be spelt correctly. It is argued that this child is effectively agraphic. He has neither developed alphabetic nor orthographic skills. He has some minimal logographic skills but despite intensive remedial efforts he was incapable of writing even a simple sentence to record information.

HYPERGRAPHIA

Whereas hyperlexia has been the focus of considerable interest and discussion, hypergraphia has received little attention. In principle, hypergraphia is a condition in which spelling performance exceeds what would be expected on the basis of intellectual development. In

TABLE 6.5

Target	Age 9	Age 11	Age 12;6
door	doo	door	door
roof	ʔoo	rood	foor
and	I	A	and
egg	goo	egg	eng
flower	forf	foole	fliwn
frock	foo	fow	frok
field	flier	fool	fnl
doll	dll	boll	doll
mummy	MooM	m	mm
my	gM	mi	miy
house	hoo	ha	hrse
tent	tot	tet	tent
pretty	fnrf	pit	pnt
he	no	(refusal)	he

relation to contemporary models, it would be interesting to know whether such well-developed skills proceed with or without understanding and whether they extend to both regularly spelt words and words that require word-specific orthographic information. Cossu and Marshall (1990), as discussed in Chapter 5, have investigated the reading and spelling difficulties in a group of Italian children of low intelligence. In relation to spelling, given the regular and consistent aspect to letter sound relationships in Italian, mastery of good phonological spelling skills should be sufficient to enable accurate and competent spelling of a large number of words. These children with low intelligence displayed high levels of competence in spelling in Italian despite absence of understanding for some of the material which was being produced. They therefore showed good establishment of a phonological spelling system in isolation from other systems. It is not clear whether hypergraphia always takes this form or whether in other cases word-specific information may also be mastered.

DEEP DYSGRAPHIA

As far as the author is aware there has been no reported case of developmental deep dysgraphia. This in itself is of considerable interest, since given the current theoretical interest in such a condition one could argue that the absence of any such description implies the absence of any such condition. If there are no cases of developmental deep dysgraphia, this would represent an acquired disorder of reading which does not have a developmental analogue. Even the convincing case of deep dyslexia documented by Stuart and Howard (1995), for whom 24% of reading errors were semantic, made only two errors that might be semantic when spelling. One was "mother" → *mum*, and the other was to write the letter *f* in response to "children", friends being a common semantic error to children in reading. Accounts of adult reading performance and the acquisition of reading must be capable of explaining why there are not more convincing examples of developmental deep dysgraphia.

IN CONCLUSION

The patterns of spelling disorder seen amongst the developmental dysgraphias argue for the separability of spelling mechanisms during acquisition. Such dissociations may currently be incorporated in a relatively straightforward fashion within multiple route models. In relation to traditional information processing ideas the depiction of these routes is clear. In relation to more recent distributed models, it remains to be determined whether the models can incorporate sufficient flexibility to account for the range of patterns of disordered performance as well as individual differences within normal skill. Traditional developmental stage models of spelling acquisition are not able to successfully account for the variable patterns of the developmental dysgraphias. Their requirement to explain disorder in terms of delay and to prohibit the passing to later stages without mastery of earlier stages constrains the possible putative patterns of disorder to a range which is too narrow. The ideas of Stuart and Coltheart (1988) within which there may be individual differences in the normal routes to acquisition have greater flexibility in accounting for the dysgraphic data.

The follow-up studies of phonological dysgraphia indicate its resistance to change of character over time. This is also problematic for explanations that account for disorder in terms of delays in the normal pathway of acquisition. In developmental phonological dysgraphia there is no obvious progression of stages over time yet spelling abilities do expand markedly.

In comparison to the normal patterns of spelling development, developmental phonological dysgraphia looks atypical in relation to peers, at an earlier age. However, the pattern of surface dysgraphia also emerges as atypical in relation to peers as normal skills progress to encompass greater degrees of word-specific knowledge.

Overall, the models of the adult spelling system are a helpful background against which to discuss spelling disorders in children. Although normal developmental models are also interesting for comparative discussion, they are perhaps as yet insufficiently explicit in relation to both component skills and individual differences to enable a full account of developmental disorders.

CHAPTER SEVEN

Arithmetical Disorders

DEFINITIONS

Developmental dyscalculia was defined by Kosc (1974) as:

> a structural disorder of mathematical ability, which has its origins
> in a genetic or congenital disorder of those parts of the brain, that
> are the direct anatomico-physiological substrates of the maturation
> of mathematical abilities adequate to age without simultaneous
> disorders of general mental functions.

In other words, developmental dyscalculia is a disorder of
mathematical ability, seen in children of normal intelligence. Further,
the disorder, according to Kosc, has a biological basis and possibly a
genetic aetiology, in which case there should be positive family histories
of developmental dyscalculia. From a cognitive neuropsychological
viewpoint, a further element of Kosc's definition is of interest, since he
proposes a direct biological relationship between the parts of the brain
implicated in developmental dyscalculia and the parts of the brain
employed for mature mathematical abilities. Within cognitive
neuropsychology, a functional analogue of this view would propose that
with developmental dyscalculia there is developmental impairment in
modules of the calculation system, which had they matured would have
formed modules of the adult calculation system. Such a view implies

hard-wiring of the biological substrates of calculation modules. This chapter will explore the developmental dyscalculias and discuss the behavioural data relevant to this debate. The following key questions are of relevance. Is it possible to explain the developmental dyscalculias in relation to a cognitive model of normal function? Is there evidence of independence or semi-independence in the establishment of components of the calculation system? Are there limitations to functional plasticity in relation to the developmental dyscalculias? Is there a single route to competence or alternative pathways?

Some of the interest in developmental dyscalculia has arisen because of the arithmetical problems sometimes seen in developmental dyslexia and the literature is skewed towards studies of children in whom the conditions co-occur. Each condition may occur independently of the other. It is known that developmental dyscalculia may occur in conjunction with developmental dyslexia but it is also dissociable from this condition.

Kosc (1981) estimated that 6% of school-age children have developmental dyscalculia. Lewis et al. (1994) report a slightly lower incidence, of 3.6%, in their epidemiological sample of 9- to 10-year-olds. Their sample comprised the complete population of 9- to 10-year-old children in a specified education authority district of England, which encompassed both rural and urban schools. Children with moderate learning difficulties or statements of special needs were included but children with severe learning difficulties were excluded. Complete data was gathered from 1056 children (497 girls and 559 boys). In this unselected sample, 1.3% of the children of normal ability had specific arithmetical difficulties but normal reading, and a further 2.3% of children of normal ability had both reading and arithmetical difficulties, yielding a combined incidence of 3.6% for arithmetical difficulties in children of otherwise good intelligence.

The potential dissociations of arithmetical skill from both intelligence and reading level were further emphasised by the existence of a proportion of children with specific reading difficulties for whom arithmetical skills were developing well. There was also a small percentage of children of low ability and poor reading skills, who were nevertheless at a normal level in their abilities with arithmetic. Although a sex difference, with a male preponderance, was found amongst the children in the sample with specific reading difficulties, there was no sex difference in the incidence of specific arithmetical difficulties, a finding confirmed recently amongst children from Israel (Gross-Tsur, Manor, & Shalev, 1996).

The incidence of 3.6–6%, across the Kosc (1981) and Lewis et al. (1994) studies is a surprisingly high percentage given the relative paucity of studies in the literature, in comparison to the thousands of studies of the developmental dyslexias. The educational implications of developmental dyslexia are severe and attention has focused upon them because of the disabling effect of impaired literacy skills upon subsequent career development and cultural adaptation. In contrast, although persistent developmental dyscalculia may create problems in entering or functioning effectively in certain occupations or professions, and in the not unimportant task of the management of money, their impact is nevertheless more focal. However, recognition of the developmental dyscalculias has increased. In both the clinical manuals of disorders *DSM-III* and *DSM-IV* (American Psychiatric Association, 1994) specific arithmetical disorder receives a distinct entry.

A LITTLE HISTORY

The idea that some of the skills involved in mathematics may be independent from other cognitive processes is seen in several historical discussions, in the second half of the 19th-century and the early 20th-century. Gall, the pioneer of phrenology in 19th-century Europe, divided the mind and personality into distinct faculties and many of his ideas were brought to England by his pupil Spurzheim, on a lecturing and demonstration tour in 1859. One of the phrenological faculties was called *calculation*, and another was called *size*. *Calculation* was an aptitude for the comprehension of numbers, figures, and dimensions. *Size* enabled judgements of proportion and space.

The phrenologists argued that there was an optimum level for each faculty, too much or too little leading to difficulties. Thus too much *size* led to overemphasis upon physical views and too little *size* led to inability to judge proportions. Too little *calculation* caused difficulty in assimilating and regulating facts and figures (Cooper & Cooper, 1983). Thus, a child who had difficulty in learning arithmetic might have been thought to have too little of the faculty of *calculation*. The faculties were thought to be reflected in the size of the skull lying over the critical brain area. The fashion for measuring these relative proportions was widespread in Victorian England, and Queen Victoria herself had her children's heads "read".

The phrenologists' belief in modular subsystems associated with arithmetical and numerical processes is comparable to the modular subsystems discussed by contemporary cognitive neuropsychologists. Of particular interest, in relation to developmental disorders, the phrenologists considered that the pattern of faculties was largely fixed from birth. Thus the child with too little *calculation* had not received a faulty education in *calculation*, rather he or she had had only a small area of the brain devoted to *calculation* from birth. Thus, the disorders were of constitutional origin and emerged when an inadequate biological system attempted to implement particular cognitive processes.

The phrenologists shared with current cognitive neuropsychologists the recognition that perception thought and intellectual processing are dissociable into different components and that poor endowment of these components leads to difficulties. They differ from the bulk of cognitive neuropsychology in their emphasis upon developmental disorders, rather than those acquired following neurological lesions. They also consider that excesses in component processes are as problematic as deficiencies. Since they discuss not only the areas of thought which constitute cognition but also the areas of personality, morality, motivation and interpersonal skills, they adopt a wider and a more integrated view of man's behaviour than most modern-day psychologists.

Hinshelwood, a surgeon at the eye infirmary in Glasgow, Scotland in the 1890s and early 20th-century, is well known for his discussions of developmental dyslexia, which he referred to as congenital word-blindness (see Chapter 5). The idea of distinctive processes involved with numbers also emerges in his work. Hinshelwood's (1900b) belief in separate centres for processing numbers is first recorded in relation to patients with brain damage when he noted that an alexic patient nevertheless:

> read at once the number standing at the top of each paragraph of the test type......On testing him with figures he could read them rapidly and fluently, not only the individual figures, but when combined into complicated groups of thousands, hundreds of thousands and millions, and even in the form of very complex fractions. (p. 12)

Hinshelwood noted that differential strength in this ability in subjects without brain damage was suggested by the studies of superior skills in mental arithmetic conducted by Binet (1894). The subject, Diamandi, had an extraordinary visual memory for figures, yet "his visual memory for words was by no means above normal". Hinshelwood (1917) also reported the reverse dissociation in which there is developmental disorder of arithmetical skill:

> We also see the converse condition, boys who excel in their studies on other departments, but are the greatest "duffers" in arithmetic. (p. 60)

He further cites a report by Stephenson from 1905:

> he once saw a boy, 10 years of age, who experienced extraordinary
> difficulty in reading figures, without any corresponding difficulty
> as to letters and words. (p. 60)

Despite these early references to developmental dyscalculia, Hinshelwood's principal interest was in the developmental dyslexias. In the twelve cases of congenital word-blindness, reported in his 1917 book, only three had difficulty which extended "to the recognition of figures". Indeed Hinshelwood emphasised that two of his subjects were markedly above average at arithmetic. He concludes:

> the visual memories of words and figures are deposited in distinct
> cerebral areas ... probably close together and possibly contiguous ...
> when the defective development was more extensive and thus
> involved the figure area, then the inability to read included both
> words and figures. (p. 58)

Further, Hinshelwood (1917) recognised the potential co-existence of these disorders with normal intelligence: "proficiency in figures or the reverse gives no indication as to the powers of the individual in other departments of study".

CLASSICAL BRAIN BASES FOR CALCULATION

The nature of the mechanisms that children must acquire for arithmetic computation and their representation in the brain has been discussed in relation to classical neuropsychological studies of acquired dyscalculia by Luria (1966, 1973). Luria was interested not simply in strict localisation of function in discrete areas of the cortex, but in the notion of functional systems. These functional systems were seen as having an anatomical basis in a number of cortical and subcortical areas which worked in coordination. Luria discussed the importance of the functional systems of the tertiary zones of the left hemisphere, in relationships which are logical or symbolic in character. In Luria's terms tertiary zones are supra-modal, being at a level where information from distinct sensory modalities has been integrated.

Disturbance in the tertiary zones of the left inferior-parietal area could cause inability to discern the "categorical structure of numbers". Luria's use of the term "quasi-spatial" for these problems, refers to the difference in significance of a particular digit in a number, in relation to its spatial position in that number. Thus, the figure 3 in the number 63 has a different significance from the digit 3 in the number 36. In

Luria's view, disintegration of visuo-spatial synthesis could directly lead to arithmetical malfunction and the development of number concept in children relates to how well the visuo-spatial system has developed. Some of these ideas recur in Rourke's work on developmental dyscalculia (see later), though he discusses a right hemispheric locus for the arithmetical problems, whereas Luria emphasised the left hemisphere in his discussions of the quasi-spatial disorders.

In a series of papers Rourke (1978; Rourke & Finlayson, 1978; Rourke & Strang, 1981) argues that right hemisphere based visuo-spatial skills are an essential precursor to the development of normal arithmetical skills. In particular, he suggests that early impairment of sensory-motor experience may lead to poor development of abstract conceptualisation, which affects the basic understanding of arithmetical operations. In support of this hypothesis, he reports that children with poor arithmetical skills, but with adequate reading skills, have defective visual perception, tactile perception, and psychomotor ability. He claims that the consequent absence of understanding of arithmetical operations leads them to have little understanding of arithmetical task requirements. In these ideas there is a clear echo of those of Luria, but with a less specific definition of abstract conceptualisation than Luria gives for his "quasi-spatial" symbolic disorders.

In principle, one could argue that the ability to develop abstract conceptualisation might help in the development of number concepts and consequently arithmetic itself. However, the development of abstract conceptualisation could also be argued to be important in the development of abstract verbal concepts, yet the children discussed by Rourke are good readers. The impact of their perceptual disturbance seems very specific. Abstract conceptualisation would also seem crucial for the establishment of the abstract reasoning skills, necessary for the attribution of beliefs, which is a fundamental component in the establishment of a "theory of mind" (e.g. Harris, Donnelly, Guz, & Pitt-Watson, 1986). Yet, developmental dyscalculics do not have impairment in theory of mind nor specific difficulties in social interaction. Presumably, Rourke is thinking of an abstract conceptualisation which has spatial dimensions. Yet, current research indicates that abstract conceptualisations such as spatial imagery may have a left rather than a right hemisphere basis (Farah, 1984). Further, Grafman, Passafiume, Faglioni, and Boller (1982), have confirmed Luria's view that the calculation disturbances of the acquired dyscalculias are most frequently associated with posterior left hemispheric lesions.

From a cognitive neuropsychological perspective, the difference in the localisation between left and right hemisphere proposed by Luria and Rourke is not critical. However, this localisation is a fundamental aspect of the Rourke model because he proposes a different type of arithmetical disorder associated with left hemisphere impairment.

Rourke divides his groups on the basis of their reading ability. He claims that the children with more linguistic difficulties have difficulty in mastering arithmetical tables. He argues that the basis of these difficulties lies in verbal memory, and left hemispheric impairment. Both of Rourke's groups missed out or failed to recall steps in the calculation procedures. Thus his subdivision is non-specific in its full impact upon calculation.

In contrast to Rourke, Luria has emphasised that linguistic difficulties within acquired disorders need not affect arithmetic. Although acoustic aphasia associated with left temporal lesions could impair verbal calculations, there need not be arithmetical difficulties if calculations were conducted on paper, since there could be preservation of the spatially oriented operations that give meaning to figures and the categorical structure of numbers. Thus, although he associates calculation disorders with the left hemisphere, he distinguishes between the functional systems of language and mathematics.

The potential association of developmental dyscalculia with the functional mechanisms involved in spelling and a parietal lobe localisation is implied by studies of the Developmental Gerstmann syndrome. Gerstmann's syndrome, in adulthood, is considered to reflect parietal lobe abnormality. It has four symptoms: dyscalculia; dysgraphia; difficulty telling left from right; and finger agnosia. Thus both calculation and spelling disorders are essential features of the syndrome.

Seven children with so-called Developmental Gerstmann syndrome were described by Kinsbourne and Warrington (1963). All had finger agnosia and at least two other elements of the "syndrome". None of the children had difficulty with number concepts themselves but they had difficulty in using place values in representing and manipulating numbers. Benson and Geschwind (1970) reported two children with all four Gerstmann symptoms. However, they noted that the calculation and spelling difficulties in these children were dissociated from reading skill which was normal.

Benton (1977) has argued that it is inaccurate to consider the constellation of the four parietal lobe signs of the Gerstmann syndrome as a syndrome. Other parietal lobe signs form similar groupings with some of the Gerstmann signs, with equal frequency. Thus, there is nothing special about the four symptoms selected by Gerstmann. Similarly, Spellacy and Peters (1978) have studied 14 children with developmental dyscalculia. None of the children showed deficits limited to the four elements of the Gerstmann syndrome and only five of the children had impairment on all four elements. These analyses based upon groupings of apparently unrelated cognitive processes have shed little light upon the underlying processes which are impaired in developmental dyscalculia.

Although developmental dyscalculia does frequently occur with dyslexia or dysgraphia, this may be, as Hinshelwood (1917) suggested, because the anatomical areas of the brain subserving these processes are contiguous rather than because of any fundamental cognitive association. Certainly developmental dyscalculia is dissociable from the other developmental disorders of literacy skills, as is evident from the epidemiological study of Lewis et al. (1994) discussed earlier.

CLASSIFICATION SYSTEMS

During the 1960s, 1970s and 1980s, there were several traditional attempts to classify the acquired dyscalculias into different types. These were based largely upon two factors: the functional factor causing the disorder and the lesions associated with the disorder (Boller & Grafman, 1983). Where functional factors were proposed, one might extrapolate that developmental disorder in these factors, could lead to developmental dyscalculia. However, the factors proposed were both varied and non-specific, including disorders of attention, memory, intelligence, spatial ability, language, abstraction, and body schema. Nor is it clear that any of these potential concomitant deficiencies are necessary and/or sufficient conditions for the emergence of a calculation disorder.

An attempt at a functionally based classification of the acquired dyscalculias, was proposed by Hecaen, Angelergues, and Houillier (1961) who studied large numbers of such patients. Patients were classified into three groups: alexia or agraphia for digits and numbers, in which the reading and writing impairments affect arithmetical operations; spatial dyscalculia where there is a disorder of spatial organisation for numbers leading to lack of respect of the rules used to place digits in their proper order; and anarithmetia in which neither of these deficits are apparent but there is difficulty in performing arithmetical operations. This tripartite classification assumes that normal number processing and calculation ability involves a number reading and writing ability, a spatial ability, and a calculation ability, but the quality of these is unspecified. It is not clear how each ability is involved in different tasks, nor the sorts of impairment which should result from their disruption. It is also a problem that the three types are insufficient to account for the great diversity of number processing and calculation impairments seen in brain-damaged patients. Thus, there is heterogeneity in each category.

Kosc (1970, 1974, 1979, 1981) attempts a more detailed functional classification system for the developmental dyscalculias. He distinguishes between six different types of developmental dyscalculia. In verbal dyscalculia there is difficulty with the verbal designation of mathematical terms. Practognostic dyscalculia results in difficulty manipulating objects in a mathematical way. Difficulty in reading the symbols of mathematics is called lexical dyscalculia, whereas difficulty in writing these symbols is called graphic dyscalculia. In ideognostic dyscalculia, there is difficulty in understanding mathematical ideas and in working out mental solutions to mathematical problems. Operational dyscalculia effects the execution of mathematical operations. Kosc (1974) argues that each of these forms of developmental dyscalculia can occur in isolation although they need not. Thus they are computationally distinct. Kosc (1974) did not integrate his classes of dyscalculia with any cognitive model of arithmetical processes, but his subdivisions are nevertheless theoretically rational and he stressed that developmental dyscalculia must be examined as an isolated deficit.

NORMAL ARITHMETICAL SKILL

Following the work of Piaget, classical models of the normal development of arithmetical abilities detailed a number of stages. The stages were invariant in sequence and none could be omitted. The child had to pass through each stage in order. The basis of arithmetical competence must begin before the child starts at school. In Ginsberg's (1977) model, system 1 addresses the pre-school child's ability to solve quantitative problems. This precedes the establishment of number processing skills. The skills are informal, since they develop outside school, and they are termed natural because they do not require specific information transmitted by culture. Starkey, Spelke and Gelman (1990) showed that 6- to 8-month-old infants were able to detect numerical correspondences between sets of entities presented in different sensory modalities and bearing no natural relationship to one another. This indicated that early numerical abilities do not depend upon the development of language or complex actions. Ability to make numerosity judgements appears at about the same time in children growing up in schooled and unschooled cultures (Saxe & Posner, 1983). In Piaget's (1952) schema the child is acquiring specific principles: one-to-one correspondence, equivalence, and seriation. These processes concern the mastery of basic concepts of quantity and quantitative comparison.

There has been little discussion of children who might have difficulty in mastering these fundamental concepts. Discussions of developmental dyscalculia predominantly address difficulties that arise in the later implementation and manipulation of symbols to represent these concepts.

In Ginsberg's (1977) conceptual framework, the second system involves counting skills. These are informal since most children acquire them before they begin school. However, they are cultural because they depend upon precise social transmission. A counting process has been found within the mathematical system of every culture that has been studied (Saxe & Posner, 1983). All involve establishing a one-to-one correspondence between the objects to be counted and a set of items in a fixed ordered list, the value of the set being given by the last number in the count sequence (Gelman & Gallistel, 1978). In Papua New Guinea the counting follows a fixed ordered set of body parts rather than number names.

Counting algorithms have been studied by Gelman and Gallistel (1978), who discuss their contribution to early performance on mental arithmetic. Later in development, the use of counting algorithms should be abandoned in favour of memory retrieval from an organised store of arithmetical facts, i.e. number tables (Ashcraft & Fierman, 1982). However, it is evident that some children with developmental dyscalculia do not make this transition successfully. Frequently, children with developmental dyscalculia can be seen to continue using finger counting strategies to circumvent their absence of automaticity in retrieving arithmetic facts or conducting simple computations. Often the finger counting strategies are implemented accurately and effectively if the numbers involved are small, but the system usually breaks down when larger numbers are involved. Older children are more subtle about the overt motor movements of the fingers which generally accompany the computations. On occasions where the strategy is successful, it at least indicates understanding of the basic concepts underlying the procedures of addition and subtraction.

Two of the four basic strategies for solving addition problems within the strategy choice model of Siegler involve overt counting (Siegler, 1986; Siegler & Robinson, 1982; Siegler & Shrager, 1984). The first involves finger counting, with the fingers physically representing the problem integers and counting on them being used to achieve the relevant sum. The second involved verbal counting with the child counting audibly or moving their lips. A further strategy also involves finger use, with the fingers representing the integers but visible counting is not seen. The final strategy involves retrieval of an addition answer from long-term memory. The specific strategy chosen, according to Seigler (1988), depends upon the peakedness of the distribution of associations between a problem and all the potential answers to that problem. The more peaked the distribution, the more easy it is to retrieve the answer from long-term memory and the more likely it is that the retrieval strategy will be used. The child's confidence in this strategy may also effect its selection or the reversion to finger or verbal counting.

A formal code taught by cultural instruction is learnt by the child at school. Normal children gradually develop the skill to use the retrieval strategy for addition, to solve the majority of simple addition problems by the age of eleven or twelve. Written symbolism, algorithms, and mathematical principles are also acquired. The development of these skills forms system 3 of Ginsberg's (1977) conceptual framework. Gelman and Gallistel (1978) argue that the subsequent use of algorithms is local. In one situation a child will display understanding of a particular algorithm, whereas in another he or she will not. This view contrasts with that of Piaget (1952) who believed that, at the stage of concrete operations, a diverse set of quantitative principles come to be understood simultaneously. The child is then able to carry out the formal manipulations of addition and subtraction. Riley, Greeno, and Heller (1982) point out that it is insufficient for the child to acquire rote memorisation of facts and problems. It is also necessary to develop both strategies and representational models of the arithmetical process.

Wolters, Beishuizen, Broers, and Knoppert (1990) have explored the procedures involved in normal children's calculations of arithmetical sums. They note that different procedures break down the original problem into different numbers of subproblems. They compare, in particular, two procedures. In the 10-10 or decomposition procedure (Beishuizen, 1985; Young & O'Shea, 1981) both addends are split into tens and units; these are added separately; they are then recombined (e.g. 24+13: 20+10=30, 4+3=7, 30+7=37). In the N-10 procedure, only the second addend is split and the components are added onto the unsplit first addend (e.g. 24+13: 24+10=34, 34+3=37). The N-10 procedure involves fewer subproblems than the 10-10 procedure. Children who made greater use of the N-10 strategy had quicker solution times, suggesting that analysis into a smaller number of subproblems leads to better performance.

The third system in Ginsberg's model, which involves formal schooling covers acquisition of many differing arithmetical and computational skills, whose interrelationship is not specified. Most developmental dyscalculics have difficulties which could be functionally localised within system 3 of Ginsberg's model, but in itself, this has little explanatory power. It reveals little about the nature of the difficulties.

The only mechanism to account for developmental disorders in relation to stage models of normal development, is to argue that the child has arrested development and has failed to attain a particular stage. This makes it impossible to account for double dissociations in performance. Double dissociations occur when given two tasks, A and B, one child can do A but not B, whereas a second child can do B but not A. For example, suppose within level 3 of Ginsberg's system, A is the substage of mastering multiplication tables and B is the substage of mastering the procedures for division. Further, let us suppose that in the normal developmental path, substage A precedes substage B. Then the child who knows their tables (substage A) but cannot do division (substage B), may be accounted for in terms of arrested development. They have developed so far along the normal pathway and then stopped. However, suppose there is a double dissociation and there are also children who show the reverse pattern — understanding the procedures of division (substage B) but without mastery of tables (substage A) — then interpretation of arrested development cannot be invoked. The latter children have apparently progressed to a later stage without passing through the earlier stage. A resolution of this problem cannot be found by reordering the stages, only by permitting alternative progressions of stages, and thereby individual differences in the sequence of stages. Alternatively, it could be proposed that developmental dyscalculics do not proceed through the stages in an invariant sequence. Neither solution fits with standard practice in developmental theory. The critical issue is whether there is one uniform series of stages in the acquisition of formal codes of arithmetic or whether there are individual differences in the nature of their development.

COGNITIVE NEUROPSYCHOLOGY
OF THE ACQUIRED DYSCALCULIAS

Recent cognitive neuropsychological analyses of the acquired dyscalculias have distinguished between disorders of number processing, number facts, and procedural knowledge. The number processing system comprises the mechanisms for perceiving, comprehending, and producing numbers. The calculation system consists of both the facts and the procedures which are specifically required for carrying out calculations.

McCloskey and colleagues (McCloskey, 1992; McCloskey, Caramazza, & Basili, 1985; McCloskey, Sokol, & Goodman, 1986; Sokol & McCloskey, 1988, 1992) have proposed a general cognitive architecture for both number processing and calculation, with particular emphasis upon the number processing elements. Their schema is depicted in Fig. 7.1.

The model posits functionally independent numeral comprehension and numeral production mechanisms. The former converts numerical inputs into internal semantic representations, which are then available for subsequent cognitive processing such as conducting a calculation. The production mechanisms translate the internal representations of numbers into a verbal or arabic form for output. The internal semantic representations specify the basic quantities in a number and their associated power of 10. McCloskey adopts a specific format to represent this. Thus, for example, the number 246, which consists of 6 units — 4 tens to the power one, and 2 tens to the power two — is depicted as {2}10EXP2,{4}10EXP1,{6}10EXP0.

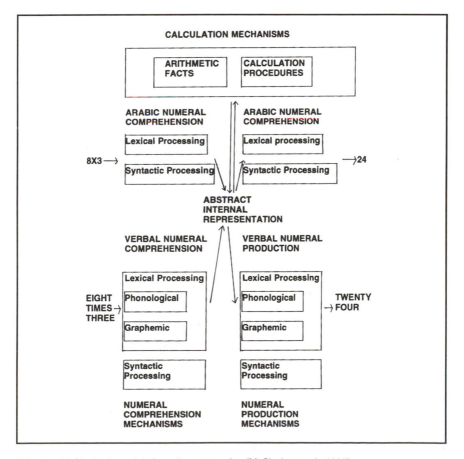

FIG. 7.1 McCloskey's model of number processing (McCloskey et al., 1985).

In addition to distinguishing between comprehension and production mechanisms, McCloskey et al. (1985) also distinguish between the mechanisms for processing arabic numerals and those for processing verbal numerals. Within these processes, they further distinguish between lexical and syntactic mechanisms. The syntax of the number involves the relations between its elements, whereas the lexical aspects of the number involve the individual elements or digit words.

The modularity of this model allows a given task (e.g. reading numbers, writing numbers, repeating numbers) to be decomposed into all the subcomponents involved in doing that task. Number processing disorders, incorporating selective deficits of the system and demonstrating fractionation of its modular constituents, have now been described by several authors, supporting many of the proposed distinctions between the processing components (McCloskey et al., 1985, 1986; Noel & Seron, 1993).

In the McCloskey model, semantic activation is involved in transcoding tasks. A contrasting view, within which transcoding takes place without semantic involvement has also been proposed (Cohen & Dehaene, 1991; Seron & Deloche, 1984). The issue of whether this may be an additional or alternative system remains open.

A further alterative view, is proposed by Campbell and Clark (1988; Clark & Campbell, 1991). They propose a non-modular architecture, within which multiple numerical codes (e.g. phonological, semantic, visual, etc.) are interconnected in an associative network. Individual codes may activate one another producing a multi-component encoding complex. Although, Sokol, Goodman-Schulman, and McCloskey (1989) argue that the model is insufficiently specified to generate testable predictions, and the model has also, as yet, had less explanatory power in accounting for focal dissociations, the extent of its utility continues to be explored.

We know that normal children make errors in number processing as they are developing arithmetical skill. One-third of six-year-olds reverse single integers and, in writing three digit numbers, seven-year-olds often introduce extra placed zeros. However by eight-years-old, children can correctly write three digit numbers (Cohn, 1968).

In addition to number processing, calculation skills depend upon recognition of operational symbols (e.g. +), retrieval of arithmetical table facts and execution of calculation procedures. Selective difficulties in these components amongst acquired dyscalculics have also been documented: confusion in signs (Ferro & Botelho, 1980); impairment of arithmetical facts (McCloskey, Aliminosa, & Sokol, 1991; Warrington,1982); disorders of arithmetical procedures (Caramazza & McCloskey, 1987; McCloskey et al., 1985).

Thus the core components of the adult arithmetical system as proposed by McCloskey are:

Number Processing
(i)   with comprehension distinct from production
(ii) with lexical and syntactic elements
(iii) with distinct arabic and numeral processes

Knowledge of Number Facts
(i) including knowledge of the meaning of signs
(ii) including knowledge of tables

Procedural Knowledge
(i) including the precise algorithms to do arithmetic: addition, subtraction, multiplication and division.

DEVELOPMENTAL DISORDERS

The cognitive neuropsychological perspective discussed above has been applied to a series of children with developmental dyscalculia, with the aim of delineating potential modular fractionation within the development of component subsystems of arithmetic, and also to provide more theoretically relevant descriptions of the disorders for remedial purposes.

DEVELOPMENTAL DISORDERS OF NUMBER PROCESSING

Temple (1989, 1992a) describes a developmental disorder of number processing in an 11-year-old boy with developmental dyscalculia.

Case Report: Number Processing Disorder, Digit Dyslexia, Paul
Paul (Temple, 1989, 1992b) came to the attention of the School Psychological Service, following referral over his teacher's concern that he was unable to manage even the easiest of mathematical activities. There had been no other significant concerns at school but a history was given of persistent difficulties with mathematics. There was no evidence of any deterioration in his skills. Rather, he was reported to always have had difficulties with arithmetic.

Paul was of low average intelligence and had a reading age for both single words and text that was appropriate for chronological age. Paul did not have developmental dyslexia. He had a well-established phonological reading route, being able to sound out long unfamiliar words, e.g. *hectographic* and *intertergal*. He also had a well-established lexical reading route, being able to recognise irregular words, e.g. *orchestra* and *antique*. Thus, the reading of verbal material was normal.

Reading Arabic Numbers. However, when reading arabic numbers aloud Paul made errors with a consistent pattern. He would correctly identify the numerical relationship between the elements by generating a response with the appropriate number "syntax". Thus, numbers in their thousand were read with correct placement of thousand and hundred words and correct linkage between digits. However the precise lexical value attached to the individual digits was frequently incorrect, e.g. 9172 → "six thousand, six hundred and seventy-two"; 34 → "seventy-six"; 153 → "one hundred and twenty-three". Further examples are given in Table 7.1.

This pattern of errors suggests that syntactic frames for number production are set up independently from lexical retrieval of number values. It implies two distinct and semi-independent modules in the acquisition of number reading skills: one that addresses syntax and one that addresses lexical content. A prediction from this hypothesis is that children should exist who have selective difficulty with the syntax of numbers, even though they are correct in their lexical identification of the component digits.

A more fine-grain analysis of Paul's number reading errors revealed further consistent patterns. The probability of reading an individual digit correctly was independent of the ·size of the number in which it was contained. Thus, there was an equal probability of error in reading a digit in isolation, e.g. 1 → "nine", and in reading it within a four digit number. Although longer numbers were more often read incorrectly than short numbers, this resulted from the greater cumulative probability of an error with more digits to read. Thus, the length of syntax surrounding the digit did not effect its retrieval.

TABLE 7.1
Arabic Number Reading Errors Made by Paul

1	→	"nine"
85	→	"eighty-two"
34	→	"seventy-six"
711	→	"seven hundred and eighteen"
153	→	"one hundred and twenty-three"
592	→	"two hundred and ninety-two"
9172	→	"six thousand, six hundred and eighty-two"
7621	→	"seven thousand, six hundred and eighty two"
8483	→	"eight thousand, four hundred and eighty-four"

The probability of an error was however affected by the *position* of a digit in a number. Errors were more likely to be made to digits at the end of a number than to digits at the beginning of the number. This effect was independent of stimulus length. The fourth digit of a four digit number was no more likely to provoke error than the second digit of a two digit number. Thus, it was the terminal position that was crucial rather than the distance of the final digit from the start of the number. Temple (1989) interpreted these results by suggesting that there were separate mechanisms in accessing lexical representations from the different positions in the syntactic frame. For Paul, there was an increased impairment in the terminal position, which either affected slotting the lexical item in the terminal position into its frame or affected retrieving its phonological representation for pronunciation. Although number syntax had developed normally, lexical number processing mechanisms were impaired, and there was a differential effect of the severity of the impairment in relation to the syntactic position of the lexical item.

Writing Arabic Numbers. The selective impairment in the lexical processing of numbers was mirrored in writing arabic numbers to dictation, [e.g. "eight thousand one hundred and forty-seven" → 8897; "twenty-one" → 28; "two" → 3]. This argues for distinct lexical and syntactic number processing skills in graphic arabic production as well as oral verbal production. The impairment in lexical processing was also evident in repeating numbers. Thus, the deficit is a feature of the verbal production of numbers, independent of whether task input was visual or auditory, and the output arabic or verbal.

There was concern that writing long numbers was complicated by the need to remember the details of the long stimulus. Perhaps the difficulties with writing arabic numbers was really one of short-term memory. To investigate this further, two sets of shorter stimuli were generated by the removal of the syntax from the numbers. Thus three thousand, four hundred and seventy-six was transformed into the sequence three-four-seven-six, which makes the same demands upon lexical retrieval of digit entries but which is much shorter to remember. In addition, each number was assigned to a letter between A and I so that the number sequence three-four-seven-six became C-D-G-F, and a further set of letter sequences was constructed in this way. All the items were dictated aloud for Paul to write down: 47% of the number strings were written correctly, a performance level which is the same as that attained when the full numeral stimuli were dictated including all their syntax. In contrast, 78% of the letter stimuli were written correctly, a significantly better performance. It was evident that errors were being made to four item stimuli in all sets. When the four item elements were removed, the comparison became clearer: 53% of the full numbers including syntax were correct; 53% of the derived digit strings were correct; and 93% of the derived letter strings were correct. Short-term memory difficulties cannot account for this pattern of results.

Temple (1989) also reports a specific effect with "teens" numbers. There was a significant difference between the processing of ones in the teens position and ones in the units position such that ones in the teens position tend to be translated accurately, producing the substitution of one teens number for another, e.g. 711 → "seven hundred and eighteen", whereas ones in other positions would invoke errors. Thus, whereas error rate to ones in the teens position was 0%, the error rate to ones in the terminal position was 45%. For other digits a discrepancy of this sort did not appear. Thus, for example the error rate to the digit 3 in the teens position was 25% and to the digit 3 in the terminal position was 33%, a difference of only 8%. For other digits, the differences ranged form 0–19%, never reaching the 45% level seen with the digit 1.

Using data from the acquired dyscalculias, McCloskey et al. (1986) have suggested that teens constitute a distinct lexical class. Paul's data support this idea and suggest that it is a distinction which is also delineated during the maturation of arithmetical systems. These ideas would also be consistent with the ideas of Deloche and Seron (1982a, 1982b). They have looked at transcoding of numbers from one modality to another, in studies of adults, and have introduced the idea of stack structure. Stacks are one-dimensional arrays. Items belong to a particular stack and have a specified position within the stack. When a stack error is made the information relating to stack membership is incorrect but position information is correct, e.g. 30 → 3. Position within stack errors indicate that the information relating to stack membership is correct but position information is incorrect, e.g. 30 → 40 or 60. The teen numbers may form a special type of stack, with a marker that tends to preserve stack membership, so that errors occur as position errors within the stack.

Reading Numeral Words.   It was expected that because Paul was good at reading words, he would also be good at reading numeral words. However, Paul displayed a category-specific impairment in reading, which affected the reading of numeral words. That is, despite good phonological and lexical word reading mechanisms for other material, he had difficulty in reading aloud numbers written in numeral words. As with reading arabic numbers, syntax was correctly preserved but there were many lexical errors, e.g. *nine hundred and twenty-one* → "two hundred and twenty-two"; *seventeen* → "eighteen"; *nine* → "three". Further examples are given in Table 7.2. The incidence of reading errors to numeral words was even higher than the incidence to arabic numbers. The deficit in reading numeral words suggests that reading mechanisms for this category of words are distinct from reading

TABLE 7.2
Numeral Word Reading Errors Made by Paul

five	→	"six"
three	→	"eight"
four	→	"two"
nine	→	"three"
seventy-eight	→	"seventy-two"
seventeen	→	"eighteen"
three hundred and seventy-one	→	"three hundred and eighty-eight"
nine hundred and twenty-one	→	"two hundred and twenty-two"
four hundred and ninety-eight	→	"four hundred and eighty-eight"
nine thousand, four hundred and thirty-eight	→	"one thousand, four hundred and thirty-eight"
seven thousand, two hundred and seventy-one	→	"seven thousand, two hundred and thirty-two"

mechanisms for other categories of input, since his other reading skills were excellent. Such a conclusion is not readily compatible with contemporary models of reading unless a categorical organisation is introduced into some of the reading mechanisms.

Could the difficulty in reading numeral words relate to their membership of a closed set of conceptually related items? Another set of stimuli that form a closed class are colours. A set of stimuli were therefore constructed by substituting each of the numeral lexical items from 1 to 10, in the stimulus set, with a colour name. This generated some odd-looking reading material, examples of which were: "white thousand, red hundred and grey-green"; "red hundred and orange-red". The 40 resultant stimuli were given to read aloud; 95% of them were read correctly. This contrasts with only 41% read correctly when the stimuli were entirely comprised of numeral words. The problem does therefore seem specific to numeral words and not simply to the closed class nature of numerals.

It was possible that there had been a central impairment in the development of the lexical representation for numbers, even though the processing of numeral words and arabic numbers were differentially affected. However, since counting was accurate and the dyscalculic number processing difficulties did not affect every trial, a lexical store for numbers did exist. Further, since Paul could count from 1 to 12 and could position the numbers 1 to 12 on a clock face, number sequence information could be produced both orally and graphically. Yet, retrieval of individual digits from the lexical store was faulty. The error pattern in relation to specific digits varied from task to task and Temple (1989) therefore argued for distinct input and output paths specific to distinct number processing tasks. Such a model would also permit task-specific impairments in number processing, though such cases are as yet undocumented.

Discussion.   The study of this case of digit dyslexia indicated that word reading and number reading may occupy distinct centres in development, since they are differentially affected in Paul's development. This confirms Hinshelwood's (1917) proposal of a centre for processing numbers which is distinct from centres for processing words. Within number reading, the distinction between syntactic and lexical processes proposed by McCloskey is also applicable in relation to the acquisition of the number processing system. The case of Paul indicates that syntactic processes are distinct from lexical processes and one may develop normally despite selective disorder of the other.

The analysis of errors in relation to position within the syntactic frame indicated that lexical access is affected by position and that position must therefore be marked in some way prior to lexical access. The error pattern for teen numbers was found to be distinct, supporting the view of teens as a distinct class.

Within word reading, it also appeared that numeral words involved a distinct centre from other words since there was selective impairment of reading of these words despite excellent word reading skills. It was also noted in Chapter 3 that this excellent word reading developed despite a poor short-term memory, countering suggestions of a causal association between STM and reading problems.

DEVELOPMENTAL NUMBER FACT DYSCALCULIA

Number processing disorders appear to be relatively rare. In contrast, developmental dyscalculias which affect the establishment of arithmetical facts and tables are relatively common. In order to carry out arithmetical operations, it is necessary to learn a range of facts about numbers which are used within the operations.

Even normal children find some arithmetical table facts easier to learn than others. Facts which involve small numbers, e.g. 2x4, 3x1, are easier than those which involve large numbers, e.g. 9x7, 6x8. Ultimately, most children master even the latter. Where mastery of facts is not achieved, there can be a relatively selective form of developmental dyscalculia with other elements of the arithmetical system established normally.

HM, a teenage girl, was first described in a study of her phonological dyslexia (Temple & Marshall, 1983). She had selective difficulty in the acquisition of a phonological reading route, which was detected in her impaired performance reading non-words and in the characteristic pattern of her errors. Subsequently, HM's developmental dyscalculia was documented (Temple, 1991). She had difficulty in the mastery of arithmetical tables. Despite her difficulty with tables, HM had normal number processing skills. She read and wrote numbers accurately and rapidly, making no errors. Thus, there was no generalised difficulty with oral number production. Given two different written numbers, she was able to make correct magnitude judgements about their relative values. This indicated intact comprehension of arabic numbers. Further, HM also understood the procedures that are involved in actually conducting arithmetical operations. She was able to describe the processes of addition and division, and illustrate the stages that should be conducted to work out solutions to such problems. Thus, she had learnt calculation procedures. However, her ability to produce accurate answers to calculations was affected by her failure to master facts. Her disorder in mastering arithmetical facts was not even across all tasks. Her knowledge of addition and subtraction facts was normal. However, her knowledge of multiplication tables was significantly poorer than that of her peers.

HM's errors to tables were not random. An analysis of the errors categorised them into groups. One group was labelled *bond errors*. Here, HM produced an answer which was in the correct table for one of the numbers in the computation but was an incorrect selection (e.g. 7 x 6 = 49, which would be the correct response to the question 7 x 7). In these errors, she appeared to access the correct table but located the incorrect position within that table for the response. Thus the storage of table facts had an interlinking. Facts involving common numbers, or in the same table set, were more closely connected than those from differing table sets. Since bond errors do not have any correct surface characteristics, i.e. digits, but do have semantic features in common with the correct answer, i.e. belong to the same table, they could be considered to represent semantic errors.

A second group of errors was labelled *shift errors*. Here, the error response was not an alternative table value but contained only one digit that was incorrect (e.g. 3 x 7 = 25, which has the correct first digit and is not present in either the three times or seven times table). Part of the table value had been activated correctly but the other part had been selected incorrectly. In addition to making significantly more errors than controls, HM also made a larger proportion of shift errors.

Thus, although the type of errors she made were also seen in the normal population, her system made the errors in different relative proportions. It is not clear whether there is an association between HM's difficulties in mastering phonic rules and her difficulty in mastering table rules. Both are abstracted sets of coded pairings.

Case Reports: Number Fact Disorder, AW and RW
AW and RW (Temple, 1994) are 12-year-old boys, who are twins. Although genetic typing is not available, it is thought that the twins are identical. At

the age of nine years, AW and RW were referred by their parents for an investigation of "persistent written language difficulties". Intellectual ability was assessed on the Wechsler Intelligence Scale for Children—Revised (Wechsler, 1974). Both twins were found to be of high intelligence with the following scores obtained:

Verbal Scale	RW	AW	Performance Scale	RW	AW
Information	17	16	Picture Completion	15	15
Similarities	19	17	Picture Arrangement	10	12
Arithmetic	8	9	Block Design	16	14
Vocabulary	18	14	Object Assembly	15	14
Comprehension	14	17	Coding	8	9

(10 is an average subtest score; range 1–19; SD=3)

Verbal IQ	145	136	Performance IQ	129	129
(Pro-rated for Arithmetic)			(Pro-rated for Coding)		

AW had fluent speech and good verbal and non-verbal memory. He was above age level in both reading and naming. His auditory discrimination was also good. However, spelling was 20 months below his reading age, and took the form of a mild phonological dysgraphia, though with some additional impairment of lexical mechanisms. Over time AW's dysgraphic difficulties reduced and were only detectable on rigorous testing.

RW also had fluent and articulate speech with excellent verbal and non-verbal memory. At the age of 10;0, RW was assessed as having a reading performance at or above age level but with a tendency to misread short grammatical words in text. Reading was in general not as rapid and decisive as observed in his twin brother. Spelling was over 18 months below the level expected from his chronological age, and relied upon mechanisms related to whole words with poorer ability to use phonological rules. The developmental dysgraphic difficulties persisted with age and continued to present problems in the classroom. RW was also found to have difficulties with arithmetic and it was decided to investigate these in detail. It was initially considered that the problems were more extensive in RW than in AW.

Number Processing. A set of 40 numerical stimuli were presented to both AW and RW, within four different tasks: reading arabic numbers; writing arabic numbers; reading numeral words; and writing numeral words. All of the number processing tasks were performed with 95–100% accuracy. The only errors were of spelling in the writing of numeral words, and did not relate to the production of the syntax of lexical items of numbers. Examples of AW's spelling errors were as follows: thousand → *thousnd*; hundred → *hundered*; ninety → *ninty*; fifty → *fity*; forty → *fourty*. Examples of spelling errors for RW included: thousand → *thouseand*; thousand → *thousan*; thousand → *thosand*; ninety → *ninty*; forty → *fourty*; thirty → *therty*; eleven → *elleven*.

Magnitude Judgement. AW and RW were asked to circle the larger of two stimuli presented as a pair. There were fifty trials of two digit stimuli. In similar fashion, sixty pairs of randomised two and three digit stimuli were presented again for the selection of the larger item in each pair. The twins performed with greater than 97% accuracy on both tasks.

AW and RW were therefore shown to have no specific difficulty with either number processing in relation to the reading and writing of numbers or in the number comprehension required to make magnitude judgements.

Definition of Operations. Both AW and RW could recognise the symbols used for arithmetical operations and could also describe the operations themselves. Multiplication was defined as, "Making something larger by adding itself to the other. Add the number by itself a certain number of times" [RW]. Addition was defined as, "Adding two numbers together. One number with another equals putting them together" [RW]. Division was defined as, "Sharing it out between a certain number" [RW]. Subtraction was defined as, "Taking something away" [RW]. AW provided similar definitions to his twin. Neither twin had any difficulty in defining operations.

Procedural Knowledge. Procedural knowledge was investigated by asking the twins to talk through the steps they were conducting, when carrying out multiplication, addition, division, and subtraction problems. Each twin was able to articulate, easily and accurately, the steps involved in carrying out these computations, according to the algorithms which they had been taught in school. There was no conceptual difficulty in understanding these items and their explanations were sufficiently clear that it was quite straightforward to follow the set of steps that was being proposed. There was thus no evidence of any impairment in the acquisition of knowledge of the procedures of arithmetic.

Number Facts. The twins' ability to retrieve number facts was compared with a sample of 10 control children. At the time of assessment the twins were aged 12;1, and the controls also had a mean age of 12;1 with a range from 11;6 to 12;6. Addition, subtraction, and multiplication were all tested following the procedure of Warrington (1982) in her investigation of a case of acquired number fact dyscalculia.

Addition. Each child attempted to add all combinations of numbers between one and nine. This matrix (45 cells) was given in random order;

each addition being spoken by the experimenter at a one word per second rate, the larger of the two numbers being given first (e.g. *6 + 2*). Accuracy, the nature of the response, and time to respond were all recorded. The timing score assigned was the response time recorded on a stop watch rounded up to the nearest second. In this way, all times were assigned integral values, with rapid responses of less than 1s assigned an integral value of 1s. The analysis of the resultant response times (RT) was conducted on four different measures: (1) overall average RT; (2) average RT for correct responses; (3) average RT time for incorrect responses; (4) the number of items for which the response was correct but the RT had been 3s or above. The latter measure was designed to assess the accuracy of slow responding. The results from this analysis of addition are illustrated in Table 7.3.

AW and RW were both significantly poorer than controls at accuracy in knowledge of arithmetical facts. The difference, although statistically significant, was not substantive in quantitative terms in relation to accuracy. However, the analysis of reaction times shows that the twins were not only less accurate but were significantly slower than controls in producing their responses. This elongation of reaction times was true both for responses that were correct and for responses that were incorrect. The slow but accurate responses appeared to reflect complicated strategies that the twins were invoking, in order to work out the responses that they were unable to retrieve automatically. These are discussed later.

Subtraction. Each subject attempted to subtract number combinations of 1–9 from 1–9 (calculations with zero as a remainder were excluded as were negative remainders). The problems were spoken aloud in random order in a similar fashion to the addition problems.

TABLE 7.3
Addition Results from the Twins

	Controls	*AW*	*RW*
Number	43.5 (0.97)	40*	38*
RT	1.66 (0.44)	3.4*	2.78*
RT Correct	1.54 (0.47)	3.2*	2.32*
RT Errors	2.53 (1.29)	5.0*	5.29*
Correct but RT *3 or above*	6.4 (4.84)	21*	14

RT response time; * p<0.01; Standard deviations are given in brackets.

The results again indicated that the twins were significantly less accurate than controls in the retrieval of subtraction facts. Response times indicated that both twins were also significantly slower at producing their responses, and that this significant slowing was true, both for responses that were correct, and for responses that were incorrect. The comparison of the number of items which were correct as a result of non-automatic retrieval, reflected by the response times of 3s or more, was also significantly larger for both AW and RW. Whereas controls, on average, produced only 3.6 responses (8%) which took 3s or more to activate accurately, AW produced 27 (60%) responses of this sort and RW produced 20 (44%).

Multiplication. Each child was asked to multiply all combinations of numbers between 2 and 9. This matrix consisted of 64 cells, which were dictated in random order. Each pair of multiplication items was dictated in both formats, (e.g. *6 x 7* and *7 x 6*). The results of the analysis of the multiplication responses is given in Table 7.4.

Overall response time (RT), RT to correct responses, and RT to incorrect responses, were all significantly longer for the twins than for controls. The order of magnitude of the effect was such that RW took three times as long as the controls to produce a response. A further analysis was conducted of the number of items correct, despite an RT of 6s or above. Table 7.4 illustrates that both AW and RW produced significantly more responses that are correct but that resulted from long non-automatic responses. For each twin, at least 73% of responses were non-automatic and yet were correct. Further, for both AW and RW, over 60% of these correct slow responses took 6s or more to be produced. This further indicated that the overall accuracy score might mask unusual strategies.

TABLE 7.4
Multiplication Results from the Twins

	Controls	AW	RW
Number Correct	56.2 (4.78)	61	48*
RT	3.29 (1.52)	8.0*	10.19*
RT Correct	2.94 (1.58)	7.38*	7.81*
RT Errors	6.74 (4.14)	20.7*	20.55*
Correct but RT 3 or above	21.6 (10.9)	48*	47*
Correct but RT 6 or above	7.9 (7.13)	34*	29*

RT reaction time; * $p < 0.01$; Standard deviations are given in brackets.

Strategies. For a series of the multiplication problems, a detailed verbal protocol was requested from the twins. The protocols that the twins described indicated their use of a variety of strategies during the response delay. In many cases, a process of serial multiplication by simpler numbers was being invoked. So, for example, in working out the answer to the problem *6 x 6*, AW had a 24s RT, to respond with the correct answer, *36*.

He described what he had been doing as follows: "2 x 6 = 12; x 2 = 24, + 12 again". In this example, he had used knowledge of his two times table, to elicit the response *12*. Since, *2 x 12* also falls into his two times table, he was able to produce the response *24*. With good conceptual understanding he then added *12* to the *24*, arriving at the correct solution. The response was not only accurate, but reflected a detailed understanding of what *6 x 6* meant conceptually and numerically. However, although this strategy was competent and accurate and AW was not considered to have particular difficulties in the classroom, it was evident that the strategy was highly inefficient. In any timed or examination situation, he would be impaired by his inability to retrieve facts.

Although the two times table seemed to be relatively well mastered, there were other very simple bonds which AW did not know. Thus, for example, in order to elicit the response *16* to the question *4 x 4*, AW took 11s to respond. His protocol was as follows "2 x 4 is 8 and times this by 2 is 16".

Sometimes, however, the strategy did not work. In responding to the question *6 x 7*, AW took 6 seconds to produce the incorrect answer, *32*. He gave the following protocol: "2 x 7 = 14; x 2 = 28; + 14 (2 x 7) is 32". Here the error occurred as a result of the final addition in the procedure. When adding *14* to *28* he lost *10*, which resulted in the response *32* rather than *42*.

This was not the only type of strategy that was involved. Thus, for example, in producing the response *4 x 9 = 36*, which took 6s, AW indicated that he subtracted 4 from 40. This strategy in relation to the nine times table, again showed good conceptual understanding.

A number of other items were correctly executed by conducting a process of serial addition. For example, in calculating that *3 x 7 = 21*, a response which took 8s to produce, AW produced the following protocol: "3, 6, 9, 12, 15, 18". Similarly, in order to calculate that *3 x 4 = 12*, which took 8s, AW produced the protocol: "3, 6, 9, 12". These are interpreted as serial addition but they could also reflect the learning of tables in a rote fashion, where the automatic sequence could be produced in order, but it was not possible to activate individual entries from the sequence without previously activating the earlier entries. Similar examples appeared in the five times table, where *5 x 4 = 20* took 5s to produce. The following protocol was given: "5, 10, 15, 20".

On certain occasions a combination of strategies was employed. This can be illustrated by the calculation *8 x 6 = 48*, which took 28s. The following protocol was produced: "3 x ..., 3, 6, 9, to 24, so 8 x 3 = 24, then I doubled it".

It is clear from these examples for AW that the elongated RTs that produced accurate responses did not reflect the automatic retrieval of arithmetical facts. Comparable examples are available from RW. The twins have established a small number of arithmetical facts, but a good understanding of concepts and procedures, which enables them to work out the appropriate solutions. This shows good mastery of the procedural aspects associated with calculation but poor mastery of the use of number facts. For both twins protocols of addition and subtraction similarly indicated that they could not retrieve table facts but frequently they could reconstruct them.

Discussion. Several conclusions were drawn from this study of the twins' arithmetical skills. Firstly, number fact knowledge was distinct from procedural knowledge and number processing skills, since number fact knowledge had failed to become established, despite excellent mastery of both number processing skills and procedural knowledge. Thus, it is possible for there to be a selective impairment of number fact knowledge, despite intact development of other components of arithmetical skill, including procedural knowledge. If arithmetic develops in a series of invariant stages, then the acquisition of procedures precedes the acquisition of arithmetical facts. The reverse ordering should therefore not occur (but see the case of SW later). The errors made by the twins were not random. They were often rule governed and logical. In the case of the twins, accuracy of response was not equivalent to normal performance, since it often reflected reconstruction of facts rather than retrieval of facts, evident from the substantially increased reaction times to respond.

There remain some unanswered questions about the relationship of the number fact disorder to processes outside arithmetical skill. One interpretation of the results for HM, SW, and RW, who have arithmetical difficulties which selectively affect the mastery of arithmetical facts, is that there is a module dedicated to storing and processing arithmetical facts. Another interpretation is that there is an impairment in central processes which leads to difficulties with the acquisition of arbitrary associations or abstracted sets of coded pairings across domains, in several underlying systems. In the latter case, the difficulties in the acquisition of arithmetical facts might relate to difficulties in the acquisition of other facts in other areas of cognitive skill. Rather than a module dedicated to the storage and retrieval of arithmetical facts, there would be a domain general disorder in the storage and recall of facts or arbitrary associations.

We know that in the case of the twins the disorder does not extend to generalised difficulty in the storage and retrieval of facts. They have well-established factual and semantic knowledge in relation to language with excellent vocabularies, general knowledge, and knowledge of language concepts, as assessed by the vocabulary, information and similarities subtests on the WISC-R (see previously). In each case, their scores are 2 standard deviations above the normal level. They are also able to produce excellent definitions of mathematical operations, showing detailed understanding of mathematical concepts. Thus knowledge of arithmetical facts is distinct from knowledge about the meanings of words; knowledge about concepts linked to words; general factual knowledge; and knowledge about mathematical concepts.

However, all three of the cases of number fact disorder mentioned above have some weakness, albeit mild, in the development of phonological reading and spelling skills (Temple, 1991, 1992a, 1994), which in many models is dependent upon the acquisition of a set of arbitrary grapheme–phoneme rules (Coltheart, 1978) or arbitrary rules based upon a variable size of letter clusters (e.g. Temple, 1985c). Thus, although children with number fact disorder have no generalised difficulty with the acquisition of factual and semantic knowledge, it remains possible that they have a generalised difficulty in learning arbitrary associations, a hypothesis testable on the basis of their skills in learning paired associates of low association value, but for which there is currently no pertinent data.

If there were to be a link between impairments in the acquisition of arithmetical facts and impairments in the acquisition of phonological skills, it would integrate with the ideas of Rourke (1978; Rourke & Finlayson, 1978; Rourke & Strang, 1981). Rourke has claimed that the children with arithmetical difficulties who have linguistic difficulties have a left hemisphere impairment and that the basis for both disorders lies within verbal memory. The evidence from the twins suggests that if there is such an association it must relate to very specific aspects of memory since their general verbal memory is excellent. Further, since procedural difficulties in arithmetic (see later) may also have a left hemisphere basis (Ashcraft, Yamashita, & Aram, 1992), Rourke's theory may as yet be insufficiently differentiated to account for the differing patterns of developmental dyscalculia.

Any intrinsic link in the cause of number fact disorders in arithmetic and phonological difficulties in reading or spelling, also leads to specific prediction about those who have developmental dyscalculia but do not have developmental difficulties with reading or spelling. For if the basis for the disorder is the same, absence of phonological difficulties in reading and spelling should mean that there is also absence of number fact difficulty. Developmental dyscalculia in the absence of developmental dyslexia or dysgraphia should not therefore take the form of a number fact disorder. This is a further testable hypothesis for the central processing deficit theory.

Geary (1993) views the deficit as reflecting a difficulty in the representation and retrieval of arithmetical facts from long-term semantic memory (e.g. Geary 1990; Geary & Brown, 1991) and also discussed the possible association of arithmetical fact-retrieval deficits and poor phonological awareness. However, he also suggests that the impairment is related to a relatively fast rate of information decay in working memory, a slow speed in carrying out computational strategies or a high frequency of computational errors. This view is based on the idea that it is the execution of a computational strategies which leads to the development of the association between the problem integers and the generated answers (Siegler & Jenkins, 1989). According to Geary, in order for the computational strategy to lead to the establishment of a representation between the problem and the answer, the numbers involved in the problem and the number which constitutes the answer must be simultaneously active in working memory (Geary, Brown, & Samaranayake, 1991). Rapid decay in working memory might prohibit this. Moreover, a short working memory span might lead to more frequent computational errors and thereby the association of an incorrect answer with a problem. Geary (1993) argues that working memory resources can be measured by counting speed. Those with number fact disorders should therefore have poorer counting speeds. Geary claims that this type of arithmetical impairment is fundamental and does not disappear with development (Geary, 1993). Despite the link to working memory, and the hypothesis of a link to poor phonological awareness, he claims that the divergence in the developmental trajectories for fact retrieval and procedural skills suggests that these skills are functionally distinct and largely modular.

DEVELOPMENTAL PROCEDURAL DYSCALCULIA

Even with the ability to read and write arabic numbers and numeral words, and with full knowledge of arithmetical facts and the ability to recite tables, the number of arithmetical problems which could be solved would be limited. For most arithmetic calculations, a problem must be abstracted and then a procedure or plan must be constructed, as to how the calculation should proceed. At the simplest level, a series of planned steps must be executed, in conducting any addition involving numbers greater than 10. The decimal code requires that when tallies in one column exceed 10, they should be carried to the next column at one-tenth of their original value. Thus, 10 units in a terminal position, carry a value of one in a tens position. This requires the appropriate manipulation of numbers in relation to their positions. Similarly, in subtraction, if a value is carried from one column to the other, it must be balanced by the subtraction of an integer. For example, if 10 is carried from the tens column to the units column, the tens column must simultaneously be reduced by one. When these procedures are highly automated they may appear easy or even obvious. Yet, they are not always simple to explain verbally. Long division also requires full mastery of the decimal code. It has to be clear why 0.1 is the same as .10 but 1.0 and .01 are completely different.

Case Report: Procedural Disorder, SW

Traditional neuropsychological analyses of neurological patients indicate that the frontal lobes of the brain have an important role in the construction and execution of plans and procedures (see Chapter 8). SW (Temple, 1991, 1992a) was a 17-year-old boy with frontal lobe abnormalities associated with tuberous sclerosis, a developmental pathology whose phenotype is variable in its severity. SW's difficulties were documented throughout childhood and persisted despite focused remedial efforts. There was no evidence that he ever had a superior level of ability which had been lost. He was attempting to master cognitive skills with an impaired biological substrate. A more detailed case history is given in Chapter 8, when SW's difficulties in other areas of executive skill are discussed.

On standardised testing, SW had an IQ on the Wechsler Intelligence Scales of 89. Thus, there was no generalised intellectual impairment. SW's number processing skills were normal. He could both read and write numbers accurately. He could also count and arrange the numbers on the face of a clock.

Further, unlike HM, RW, and AW, he had mastered arithmetical tables and could respond to questions about specific arithmetic facts, including multiplication tables, rapidly and accurately. Given the addition, subtraction, and multiplication problems that created problems for HM and for which the twins were so slow, SW was quick and accurate with over 98% correct.

SW understood the concepts of arithmetical operations. He gave the following definition of division "Division is when the number is divided by another number ... Seeing how many times a number will go into another number". Addition is "trying to find out what the total is of the two numbers". "If you multiply a number by 2 it's twice as big". Nevertheless, he had persistent difficulties with arithmetic which affected the use of arithmetical procedures (Temple, 1991).

With some problems, the initial implementation of a procedure was correct but the procedure was then switched off before the calculation was completed. For example, in attempting on paper to carry out the calculation 168 divided by 2, with the problem already written for him, SW wrote a zero above the number one and then an eight above the number 6. This was correct. However, instead of continuing, SW then stopped. He did not realise that the execution of the procedure was incomplete.

In other errors, a procedure was apparently conducted to the end but the sequence of substeps chosen to carry out the calculation was incorrect. For example, the problem of subtracting 25 from 169 is illustrated in Fig. 7.2

SW invoked a carrying procedure at the start of each subtraction involving the subtraction of a number greater than a single digit. His error was therefore greater in the sums when carrying was inappropriate, than when it was appropriate. All of SW's errors in calculations arose from procedural errors. None resulted from errors with number facts themselves. In this case, the procedural difficulties seen in arithmetic may have related to procedural and planning difficulties which were also observed in other areas of cognitive skill (see Chapter 8). Thus, there may be an impairment in the supervisory system which has had an impact upon several underlying systems.

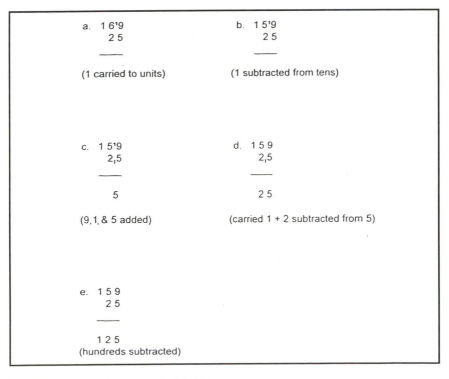

FIG. 7.2 Illustration of the error 169–25=125.

Discussion.   The study of SW provides a double dissociation with the study of the number fact dyscalculias. For SW, procedural knowledge is seen as distinct from number processing and number fact knowledge, since the former was impaired but the latter both are intact. This indicated that it is possible for there to be selective impairment in the acquisition of procedural knowledge in development, despite the normal acquisition of other components of arithmetical skill. If arithmetic proceeds by the mastery of a series of invariant stages of acquisition, the data from SW argue for mastery of number fact knowledge prior to mastery of procedures, but the data from the number fact dyscalculias discussed earlier reached the opposite conclusion in relation to the sequencing of stages. The two disorders are not compatible with the same model of invariant stages if the dyscalculias are to be seen as delay or arrestment at a particular developmental stage. They argue for different routes to acquisition.

The relationship of the deficits observed in this case of developmental dyscalculia, to more central processes merits further discussion. For the child, SW, with arithmetical difficulties that selectively affect the mastery of procedures, one interpretation of the data is that there is a module dedicated to processing arithmetical procedures. Another is that there is an executive disorder in the supervisory system which leads to difficulties with the implementation of knowledge across domains, in several underlying systems. In the latter case, the procedural difficulties in arithmetic might relate to procedural or planning difficulties in other areas of cognitive skill and the procedural component of the McCloskey et al. (1985) model (Fig. 7.1) would require interconnections to other procedural and executive skills, when applied to children.

The development of executive disorders and disorders of these systems are discussed in Chapter 8. SW's performance on a variety of measures of executive skill is discussed further there. It is seen that SW's difficulties in implementing plans do extend to other domains. For example, he is abnormally slow in solving problems on the Tower of London task (Shallice, 1982). However, his performance level on the Tower of London is normal. He is as accurate as controls, but is simply slower. This is in marked contrast to implementing plans and procedures in arithmetic, where his level of accuracy is significantly impaired. Thus, any central difficulty with supervisory control is having a markedly different degree of impact in these different tasks.

Another measure of executive skill discussed in Chapter 8 is the Stroop task, within which the subject has to name the colours of ink, which has been used to write contrasting colour names. The weaker the executive skills, the greater the degree of distraction produced by the irrelevant colour word names, and the slower the subject's performance.

Yet, SW has a normal performance on this task. This means that any executive disorder is not pervasive across all domains requiring supervisory control.

The response time results from the Tower of London suggest that procedural difficulties extend beyond an isolated module dedicated to arithmetical procedures. However, the intact level of accuracy on the Tower of London and normal Stroop indicate that any interlinking from the control of arithmetical procedures to other elements of central processes must be selective and not generalised. The results do not support a generalised impairment of central executive processes, nor do they indicate that executive impairments in mathematics will necessarily extend to executive impairments on other language tasks (such as the Stroop).

IN CONCLUSION

The three different forms of selective impairment within the developmental dyscalculias suggest a modular organisation to the developing arithmetical system. The double dissociation evident between the mastery of facts and procedures, discussed earlier, shows that neither is an essential precursor of the other, prohibiting any straightforward post-Piagetian stage account of the development of the components of arithmetical skill. An alternative explanation of double dissociations within development is that there are individual differences in the acquisition of some cognitive skills and that different children with disorders may reflect arrested development of different developmental pathways. This need not mean that their final adult state of acquisition is also different since there could be different pathways to attaining a similar adult state. However, it does rule out a single developmental series of invariant stages of acquisition. As discussed in Chapter 1, there would be an evolutionary advantage, in permitting individual differences in the pathways of acquisition, since if there is a series of invariant stages in the acquisition of component skills then a problem encountered at a particular stage will have repercussions for all consequent development. This would introduce a developmental interdependence of modules which may be absent in adulthood and render the system more vulnerable to widespread failure to develop.

The cases of developmental dyscalculia provide further support for the model of McCloskey and colleagues. Their model is consistent with the patterns of deficit we observe if selective impairment of specific subcomponents is permissible not only as a consequence of injury or disease but also as a consequence of congenital anomaly. The developmental cases illustrate that the potential functional fractionation of the modules in development is comparable to the functional fractionation seen in cases of neurological injury in adulthood which result in acquired dyscalculia.

The possibility of links between the developmental dyscalculias and disorders of central processes were discussed. In relation to procedural dyscalculia, it was noted that the discussion of SW's executive skills, which will be detailed in Chapter 8, does not support a generalised impairment in central executive processes, nor that any executive impairments in mathematics will necessarily extend to executive impairments on other language tasks. In relation to number fact dyscalculia, the possibility of a more broadly based memory impairment was discussed but it was noted that for the twins, despite poor knowledge of arithmetical facts, they have excellent knowledge of mathematical concepts, knowledge of the meanings of words, knowledge of concepts linked to words, and general factual knowledge, so any link to other aspects of memory would have to be very specific. The co-occurrence of number fact disorder and weakness (albeit mild) in the development of phonological skills for reading and spelling was noted, with the possibility of an intrinsic connection between these two skills remaining open.

The cases of developmental dyscalculia also provide further evidence for the limitations of functional plasticity in development. Reorganisation to compensate for the deficits does not appear to have occurred and the character of the disorders remains clearly delineated.

We know little about the long-term prognosis for developmental dyscalculia. These disorders tend to receive less systematic remediation than the other developmental disorders of literacy. It is certain that long-term impairments can persist, whose impact will depend upon the occupation or employment of the dyscalculic. With widespread use of calculators, number processing disorders may be more problematic than disorders of facts and procedures.

CHAPTER EIGHT

Executive Disorders

EXECUTIVE SKILLS AND THE FRONTAL LOBES

In adults, the frontal lobes are believed to subserve specific types of cognitive behaviour. These generally relate to higher order control processes and have been termed executive functions (e.g. Luria, 1973; Shallice, 1982). Executive skills include the ability to plan ahead and organise behaviour across time and space in order to fulfil goals and intentions. They enable shifting of strategies and adaptation to changing circumstances. Thus, they involve planning, decision making, directed goal selection, and monitoring of on-going behaviour. They also involve self-awareness, empathy, and social sensitivity. Stuss (1987) articulates a number of components which are necessary for the purposeful, goal-directed behaviours associated with the executive functions of the frontal lobes. These include the ability to shift from one concept to another; the ability to modify behaviour, particularly in response to new or modified information about task demands; the ability to synthesise and integrate isolated details into a coherent whole; the ability to manage multiple sources of information; and the ability to make use of relevant acquired knowledge.

Impairment of the frontal lobes may affect these skills and may also produce changes in personality and behaviour, though the direction of these is unpredictable (e.g. Harlow, 1868). Disruption of cognitive skills may include irrelevant distraction by extraneous stimuli and therefore inability to maintain attention on task; perseveration; failure to initiate appropriate activity; failure to maintain effort over time; failure to use feedback; and failure to plan and organise activity (Stuss & Benson, 1986).

In relation to behaviour, medial lesions may be linked to akinetic mutism with reduced spontaneous behaviour and difficulties in the initiation of speech. Medial lesions or lesions to the anterior convexity or frontal poles are also linked to a pseudodepressed syndrome with reduced awareness and emotional blunting. Orbital lesions are linked to euphoric behaviour, with hypomania, disinhibition, and disregard for ethical principles and the feelings of others (Fuster, 1989; Pennington & Ozonoff, 1996; Stuss & Benson, 1986).

Duncan (1995; Duncan, Burgess, & Emslie, 1995) argues that the frontal lobes are involved in skills which reflect "fluid" intelligence rather than for sustaining and using the established knowledge of "crystallised" intelligence. Duncan et al. (1995) showed that there was a significant difference between the IQs attained by frontal lobe patients on the traditional Wechsler scale, largely measuring crystallised intelligence and knowledge (e.g. vocabulary, general information) and Culture Fair IQ tests which incorporate more fluid measures such as novel problem solving, with difference of 22–38 points in the IQs derived. They argue that this accounts for the paradox of preserved "intelligence" in frontal lobe patients despite deficient planning and problem-solving.

In the neuropsychological literature, several tests have classically been used to examine frontal lobe functioning (see Table 8.1). These include the Wisconsin Card Sorting Test (WCST) (Grant & Berg, 1948; Heaton, 1981), the Stroop task (Stroop, 1935), verbal fluency tasks (e.g. Milner, 1964; Newcombe, 1969; Thurstone, 1938), and the copy of the figure of Rey (Osterrieth, 1944; Taylor, 1989). Two frontal lobe tasks, which have been devised more recently, following the expansion of cognitive psychology, are the Tower of London (Shallice, 1982) and the Self Ordered Pointing tasks of Petrides and Milner (1982). Since these tasks are referred to in many of the subsequent papers to be discussed,

TABLE 8.1
Executive Tasks

Wisconsin Task Sorting Task (Grant & Berg, 1948; Heaton, 1981)
Stroop (Perret, 1974; Stroop, 1935)
Oral Fluency (Milner, 1964; Newcombe, 1969; Thurstone, 1938)
Copy of the figure of Rey (Osterrieth, 1944; Taylor, 1989)
Tower of Hanoi/London (Anzai & Simon, 1979; Shallice, 1982)
Self-ordering Pointing (Petrides & Milner, 1982)

a few more details about them will be given at the outset. Other tasks that are less commonly employed include organised visual searching and maze learning.

The WCST (Grant & Berg, 1948; Heaton, 1981) assesses problem solving and the ability to change strategy in response to altered feedback about performance. Deficits are marked by perseveration, in which the subject continues to produce a formerly appropriate response that is no longer appropriate. There are a variety of reasons for which failure on the WCST could occur but some consider it to reflect rigidity of processing and the incapacity to adapt an ongoing schema of action. Such perseverative and inflexible responding has been reported following prefrontal damage in adults (Milner, 1963). PET study indicates relatively selective activation of prefrontal cortex by the WCST (Weinberger, Behrman, Gold, & Goldberg, 1994) and maintenance of this activation even when the task has been mastered.

The *Stroop task* (Stroop, 1935) was developed to study verbal processes. The test consists of a comparison of the ability to name the colours of patches and the ability to name coloured ink when it is used to produce words of non-congruent colours. When asked to name the colour in which each word is printed, most people find it difficult to attend to the ink colour alone, if the written word is not congruent with that colour. The resulting interference effect and slowing of response speed is called the Stroop effect. The Stroop effect therefore results from an inability to suppress irrelevant extraneous information. Cognitive psychologists have recently regarded the Stroop as a language independent task, that allows the experimenter to pit automatic and intentional processes against each other and thereby explore executive aspects of attentional systems. The Stroop effect is greater in some cases of frontal lobe impairment, and this is thought to reflect the increased inability to sustain intentional focused attention and suppress irrelevant aspects of the task which are automatically processed (Perret, 1974). The Stroop task also requires rapid automatised colour naming.

Verbal fluency tasks (e.g. Milner, 1964; Newcombe, 1969; Thurstone, 1938) require the subject to use a self-generated strategy. The subject is required to produce as many words as possible that either begin with a specific letter or belong to a specific semantic category. A time limit is imposed, and within this constraint the subject has to search within their vocabulary to find relevant items. This organised searching is believed to be dependent upon executive skills and deficits are seen following frontal damage in adults (Milner, 1964).

The *figure of Rey* (Osterrieth, 1944; Taylor, 1989) is a complex non-verbal design, which is presented initially to the subject for copying and then after a delay, recall is requested. Task instructions vary slightly dependent upon the version used. However, in the copy condition, some examiners request a change at regular intervals in the colour of pencil being used, to enable subsequent analysis of the strategy employed, in addition to the accuracy of the depiction. The complexity of the design means that a piecemeal copy will be less successful than one in which a systematic plan of action is constructed at the start. Although visuo-spatial disorders may disrupt performance, task performance is also disrupted following frontal lobe pathology, when the ability to construct and implement a sensible plan of action is deficient.

The *Tower of London task* (Shallice, 1982) was adapted from the earlier Tower of Hanoi (Anzai & Simon, 1979). It tests the ability to organise a coherent series of steps and subgoals so that an overall goal may be achieved. Subjects have to rearrange coloured balls to form a target display whilst being restrained by set rules. It is necessary for the subject to anticipate and plan ahead in order to accomplish the task correctly. Some researchers consider that the Tower of London is a complex procedural learning task which is difficult to verbalise and may be sensitive to basal ganglia disorders.

Petrides and Milner (1982) devised a task which maximises strategic aspects of memory processes. In their *Self Ordered Pointing task*, subjects were presented with a series of arrays in which the same items were presented in different locations. The subject's task was to point to one item on each array, until all the items had been selected. The task requires the use of both storage and executive systems within working memory. Patients with frontal lobe lesions are significantly impaired in their ability to plan effectively within this task and to keep track of their progress. Petrides and Milner (1982) also employed a task which pitted recency judgements against frequency of occurrence. Subjects were asked which of two items had occurred in a series most recently, but judgements were complicated by distracter stimuli which had appeared frequently, though not recently. They reported frontal impairments reflecting a deficit in making temporal judgements of recency. However, this task has seldom been employed elsewhere.

THE NORMAL DEVELOPMENT OF EXECUTIVE SKILLS

The development of executive skills in children, as a possible window to the development of prefrontal function, has been studied by Welsh, Pennington, and Groissier (1991). They utilised a combination of tasks derived from the neuropsychological literature. As Welsh et al. (1991) point out, their results are concordant with the studies of Passler, Isaac, and Hynd (1985) and Becker, Isaac, and Hynd (1987), which utilised different measures and argue for at least three stages of skill integration and maturation at the ages of six years, ten years, and in adolescence. By the age of six years, adult levels of performance were reached on simple planning and organised visual searching. By the age of 10 years, adult levels were attained on set maintenance, hypothesis testing, and impulse control, reflected by performance on tasks such as the WCST. This confirms the findings of Chelune and Baer (1986), who report normative performance for 10-year-olds on the WCST which is equivalent to adult levels. In contrast, Welsh et al. (1991) found that verbal fluency had not reached adult level by the age of 12 years. Adult levels of complex planning, motor sequencing, and verbal fluency were not reached until adolescence.

Utilising factor analysis, Welsh et al. (1991) found three emergent components of executive skill. The first factor they tentatively labelled as reflecting fluid and speeded response. This factor included verbal fluency. They argued that the tasks loading on this factor require a less complex representation or response set to guide behaviour than for other tasks. They also argue that the set has to be sustained for less time and is subject to fewer competing response alternatives, than for other tasks. Their second factor involved hypothesis testing and impulse control and included the WCST. The tasks within this factor include salient but incorrect response alternatives. Inhibition of relevant but incorrect responding is therefore an important component of them. Verbal mediation of the analysis of visual details may also be involved. The third factor that emerged in this study of normal children involved planning and included the Tower of Hanoi task (e.g. Simon, 1975), the developmental predecessor of the Tower of London (Shallice, 1982).

The latter two of these factors tie in with Fuster's (1989) view of prefrontal function. The second factor of hypothesis testing and impulse control overlaps with Fuster's interference control. The third factor, planning, is comparable to Fuster's future-oriented planning. However, Welsh et al.'s (1991) first factor of fluid and speeded responding differs somewhat from Fuster's other factor, that of retrospective working memory.

Of further interest, the Welsh et al. (1991) study found that executive function was relatively independent of IQ, with test performance either inversely or not related to intelligence. This confirms that the measures that are generally used to appraise intelligence within standardised intelligence scales of "crystallised" intelligence, such as the Wechsler, place little emphasis upon executive skills (Duncan et al., 1995).

Motor impersistence, that is the inability to sustain motor acts, has been suggested to reflect right frontal pathology, in many cases (Kertesz, Nicholson, Cancelliere, Kassa, & Black, 1985). During development,

Chadwick and Rutter (1983) report marked improvement in such sustained performance between the ages of five and seven. Executive skills have also been considered to be involved in some of the more complex motor skills, such as inhibition of motor reactions. Becker et al. (1987) found marked development in the control of motor skills between the ages of six and eight, but incomplete mastery of complex skills before adolescence. Motor sequencing may not reach maturity until late adolescence (Levin et al., 1991; Welsh et al., 1991).

The executive skills controlling temporal ordering, processes which are disrupted by frontal pathology, have been studied by Milner, Petrides, and Smith (1985). Becker et al. (1987) report marked improvements in temporal ordering skills, between the ages of 6 and 12. However, Kates and Moscovitch (1989) found that in temporal ordering tasks requiring a recency judgement, adult levels of performance were attained relatively early, by the age of seven years.

Finally, it has been suggested that the frontal lobes are involved in the development of self-consciousness and self-reflectiveness (Stuss, 1991a,1991b; Stuss & Benson, 1986; Welsh and Pennington, 1988), in a discussion of frontal lobe functioning in children, suggest that the acquisition of self-regulation is extended throughout childhood. Gallup and Suarez (1986) also emphasise the slow development of self-awareness in children. Frith and Frith (1991) propose that the frontal lobes are the substrate for the thought processes which form the core of "theory of mind" which will be discussed further in the section on autism below.

As Smith, Kates, and Vriezen (1992) discuss some behaviours that emerge at a young age in children, that may subsequently become redundant and disappear. Executive skills may therefore be involved in certain behaviours in childhood that are no longer evident as the child becomes older. Therefore, investigating only those executive skills considered to be of interest within the adult literature may lead to exclusion from study of certain executive functions of particular importance in childhood. Smith et al. (1992) discuss functions which may be mediated by the prefrontal cortex, rather than executive skills per se but, in either case, they provide no possible candidates for the potentially overlooked skills.

Russell (1948) considered that the frontal lobes were of critical importance during the childhood years, by serving to condition patterns of behaviour for the rest of the brain. It was suggested that the frontal systems may be important in skill acquisition and in learning functions that subsequently become automated elsewhere (see also Stuss, 1992). The relatively intact development of language, perception, and spatial skill in those who have sustained early frontal pathology (discussed later) may limit the extent of the applicability of this hypothesis.

THE EFFECTS OF FRONTAL LOBE LESIONS IN CHILDHOOD

An early report and 30-year follow-up of the effects of a frontal lobe abnormality with early onset is provided by Ackerly and Benton (1947; Ackerly, 1964). There was cystic degeneration of the left frontal areas and atrophy of the right prefrontal area. JP had normal intelligence but was grossly impaired in "tests of the puzzle type that required keeping a goal in mind and inhibiting overt action in favour of deliberation and analysis" (Benton, 1991, p. 277). JP lacked anxiety and concern, was impulsive, displayed inappropriate sexual conduct and was boastful, yet polite. This study of JP suggests both cognitive and behavioural alterations, though there has been some discussion about the subsequent interpretation, as the child had an atypical upbringing both prior to and subsequent to the injury sustained.

Williams and Mateer (1992) describe two cases of children who have sustained frontal lobe injuries in middle childhood and the consequent effect upon both cognition and behaviour. The first case, DR, sustained a closed head injury from a falling beam at the age of 8;11. Six years later, EEG indicated bilateral frontal slowing, and the subsequent year, MRI showed an abnormal left frontal lobe and a small area of atrophy in the left temporal tip.

Unusually, DR had an intellectual assessment 17 days before he was injured. On the WISC-R, Verbal IQ was 141, Performance IQ was 129, and Full Scale IQ was 139, indicating high intelligence. One month after injury, Verbal IQ was 125 and Performance IQ was 120. Assessment after one year suggested recovery of intellectual skills with a Verbal IQ of 134, Performance IQ of 130, and Full Scale IQ returned to the premorbid level of 139. After a further seven years, Full Scale IQ was measured at 125, suggesting some failure to sustain the same level of intellectual height.

A variety of cognitive difficulties were documented. There was difficulty with social and metaphorical language and over-literalness in the interpretation of communications. Although sustained attention and vigilance were generally within normal limits, there was impairment when attentional tasks required linguistic input, e.g. oral reading, fluency, letter scanning. Verbal and non-verbal memory were grossly intact but there was significant proactive interference which disrupted the acquisition of new information. On spontaneous open-ended drawing tasks, inordinate amounts of time were spent in erasing, redrawing, and superfluous embellishment. There was little spontaneous activity and difficulty with the initiation and maintenance of motivational efforts.

On the behavioural side, there were temper tantrums, unpredictable emotional and aggressive outbursts, and periodic impulsivity. Between these, DR appeared emotionally passive with a limited range of emotions. He was expelled from school at the age of 15. He had difficulty with social interactions and was without friends.

The second case, described by Williams and Mateer (1992), was also a case of closed head injury, sustained in this case at the age of 11 years, as a result of falling from a tree. CT scan showed bilateral frontal lobe contusions which were greater on the left than on the right. Prior to injury, the boy, SN, was reported to have had a superior IQ of approximately 126. Eight weeks after injury, Verbal IQ was 119 but Performance IQ was only 60. However, two months later the Performance IQ had risen to 95. Deficits were noted in sustained attention, visuo-spatial planning, and motor control. Following discharge there were behavioural problems, including tantrums, aggressive behaviour, inappropriate laughter, eating disturbance, argumentativeness, and stubbornness.

Follow-up indicated a series of specific cognitive difficulties. There was a tendency to overestimate abilities and to employ inappropriate problem solving strategies. Excessive distractibility meant that there was a need for continued reorientation to the task in hand. There was impaired performance on the WCST, with inflexible problem solving and poor ability to respond to feedback. Although verbal reasoning and expressive vocabulary were superior, verbal inductive reasoning was out of line, at just an average level. Written expression had excellent use of vocabulary and mature construction of sentences but was limited in quantity.

One year after injury, SN continued to have problems with mental flexibility, sustaining attention and response set, verbal fluency, and perceptual organisation. Two years after injury, bifrontal abnormalities were evident on EEG. Although still showing superior verbal abilities on standardised tests, academic performance at school was only average or below average. When the special educational help he had been receiving was stopped, non-compliant behaviour increased and he started running away.

Four years after injury, a series of selective cognitive effects remained evident. There was difficulty in inhibiting verbal responses, with the quality of conversation disrupted by tangential verbalisations. There was extreme literalness in his own expressions and in the interpretation of rules. A compulsive attention to detail often resulted in failure to extract the key features of the task demands. Problems occurred in organising and completing assignments. There were also difficulties with the direction of attention, with a need for frequent repetition of directions, and high distractibility.

A case report of similar effects, following injury at a much earlier age, is provided by Marlowe (1992). PL was a right-handed boy who sustained a penetrating prefrontal lesion at the age of 3;11, from a lawn dart. There was no loss of consciousness. He had a depressed skull fracture in the right frontal region and bony fragments, hair and grass were embedded in the brain parenchyma. Following surgery, there were no seizures and no EEG abnormalities. MRI indicated a right prefrontal lesion.

Fourteen days after the accident, marked behavioural changes were noted with mood swings, emotional lability, agitation, and destructiveness. He was aggressive and impulsive with increased activity levels.

The first neuropsychological evaluation took place at the age of 5;1. Tested on the WPPSI, Verbal IQ was 122, Performance IQ was 123, and Full Scale IQ was 125, indicating good intellectual levels. However, on Kaufman's Assessment Battery, although simultaneous processing was good, sequential processing was at a significantly lower level. Although verbal abilities were excellent on test scores, extensive repetition of instructions was required before compliance.

Tactile performance was within normal limits for the left hand but was twice as fast with the right hand, being significantly elevated for age with this hand. In bimanual task performance, the left hand repeatedly sabotaged the right by removing blocks which had been correctly placed by the right. This suggested callosal disconnection, and a separation of the purposeful intent associated with the control mechanisms for each hand.

A final evaluation took place one year later, at the age of 6;1. Intellectual level was similar, except for a decline in the age scaled score on the Information subtest of the Wechsler, suggesting reduced efficiency in the acquisition or retrieval of new facts. A series of other selective cognitive deficits were evident. PL took longer to extract task expectations and had poor anticipatory behaviour. He processed verbal information slowly, requiring verbatim verbalisation of the task instructions before beginning a task. There were difficulties with visuospatial organisation and production. He was unable to organise the basic aspects of the figure of Rey. He had difficulty in maintaining a mental set, being easily distracted by irrelevant extraneous factors. There had been difficulty in inhibiting impulsive actions long enough to execute strategic thinking. Although he could verbally describe a plan, he was then unable to implement it to direct his behaviour purposefully. With novel tasks, he would generate a set of expectations on the basis of experience and then perseverated and was unable to shift strategy if his analysis was incorrect. Tantrums were often precipitated when his assessments of cognitive or social situations was inaccurate.

There were major school problems, with suspension in the first grade. PL responded violently to the unexpected and showed no remorse for bad behaviour. There was difficulty in convincing the educational services that the problems had a physical basis, since IQ measured as normal, and the family were initially blamed for the problems. However, following transfer to a lower class at school, classroom behaviour improved. PL reported that the teacher spoke at a slower speed and that he had more time to think before he had to act. He enjoyed school, once he was able to follow the activities. At home, rapid mood swings and catastrophic reactions reduced with the class shift but irritability and hypersensitivity remained problematic.

The Marlowe (1992) study indicated that classical frontal lobe symptoms are displayed following focal frontal lobe injury in a child as young as three years, and are sustained into the school years. Childhood frontal lesions may also have long-term effect into adulthood. A follow-up study of a child who had sustained an intraparenchymal haemorrhage of the left frontal region at the age of seven years was carried out at the age of 33 years (Eslinger, Gratton, Damasio, & Damasio, 1992; Grattan & Eslinger, 1992). At this age, low blood flow was found in both left and right frontal cortices. Long-term problems included a disorganised approach to problem solving, with difficulty in establishing a plan and in executing multiple steps towards a relatively remote goal. There was an impulsive response style and inflexibility in adapting behaviour. Verbal associative fluency was impaired although semantic fluency was intact. Copy of the figure of Rey was spatially disorganised, perseverative and sloppy. There was poor ability in making cognitive estimates. For example, "she reported that 90% of the US population was male; proposed that one could drive from New York to Los Angeles in 6 hours; and decided that race horses galloped at a rate of 5 miles per hour" (Eslinger et al., 1992, p. 765). She also had difficulty in integrating individual skills to achieve an objective. Although she could "wipe a table, wash a dish, measure a quantity, and open a can, she could not plan or execute the steps necessary for meal preparation or even cleaning a room".

On the behavioural side, there were difficulties in managing and expressing strong emotions. She had a low score on standardised measures of empathy and had an unusual degree of difficulty in understanding the viewpoints and situations of other people. Her moral reasoning skills were limited, with concrete and stereotyped analyses of complex situations. Friendships and relationships were spoilt by overstepping of interpersonal boundaries and poor interpersonal skills. A first marriage ended in divorce and she lost custody of her child because of impulsive and immature behaviour. A second marriage to a religious man led to increased church involvement, which may have helped to provide structure in her daily life. However, her MMPI profile continued to indicate a highly deviant pattern of responses, associated with a chronic history of social maladjustment.

DEVELOPMENTAL DISORDERS OF EXECUTIVE SKILLS

Case Report: Developmental Executive Disorder, SW
SW was reported in Chapter 7, in relation to his difficulties with arithmetic. A disorder of procedural arithmetical skills was documented, despite good number processing and number fact knowledge. Details of SW's abilities in other areas will be documented here, as he illustrates the effects of childhood disorder of frontal lobe systems.

As noted in Chapter 7, SW has tuberous sclerosis. Birth was normal, and there were no early concerns until infantile spasms started at six–seven months. Regression in the ability to sit alone and roll over were reported. Development then progressed: sitting by 10 months, walking alone by 18 months, and single words at 18 months. There were seizures until the age of six but then no overt seizures for the next eight years. EEG at the age of eight years suggested a possible right frontal focus. He had no epileptic fits at that time and was on no medication. At the age of 14, startle episodes were reported, with several seconds of repetitive movements or eye-blinking, but no loss of consciousness. EEG at this time indicated some left parieto-occipital sharp waves at rest and a predominantly right frontal slow wave abnormality during over-breathing. A right frontal tuber was evident on CT. A repeat CT, six months later, indicated no change in appearances and no evidence of the tuber enlarging. Myoclonic epilepsy was diagnosed.

Assessment of executive skills took place when SW was 17 years old. There had been no behavioural difficulties. Throughout his education, SW had attended a normal mainstream school. At the time of the reported assessment he had a place on a Youth Training Scheme at a printing works.

On the Wechsler Adult Intelligence Scale, SW had a Verbal IQ of 85 and a Performance IQ of 95, producing a Full Scale IQ of 89, which is within the normal range. Comprehension of vocabulary on the Peabody Picture Vocabulary Scale was at a high average level for age. Word finding skills on the Boston Naming Test were average. Schonell single word reading age and Schonell single word spelling age were at a normal level for a school leaver. Conversational speech was clear and fluent.

Executive Tasks Employed
The tasks employed were the WCST (Grant & Berg, 1948; Heaton, 1981), the Stroop task (Stroop, 1935), fluency tasks (Milner, 1964; Newcombe,

1969; Thurstone, 1938), copy of the figure of Rey (Osterrieth, 1944), the Tower of London (Shallice, 1982), the Self-ordered pointing task (Petrides & Milner, 1982) and recency discrimination (Milner et al., 1985; Petrides & Milner, 1982).

The Wisconsin Card Sorting Task WCST. The WCST consists of 64 response cards which subjects must match to 4 key cards differing in colour, form and number. The examiner informs the subject whether the choice is correct or not. Colour is the first correct sorting dimension, but a change in sorting principle to form and then number is made after 10 correct placements by the subject. Subjects are not informed of the change but must modify their responses taking into consideration the new feedback. Scores were derived by calculating the number of categories correctly sorted, the percentage of responses which were correct, the percentage of perseverative responses given and also the percentage of perseverative errors made. A perseverative response is a response that would have been correct for the previous category, but is not necessarily correct now. Perseverative errors are a subset of perseverative responses which are incorrect matches for the current category.

The Stroop Task. The version of the Stroop employed, consisted of three cards each containing 10 rows of 5 items. On card A, there were 50 randomised colour names (red, green, orange, and blue) printed in black ink. On card B were similar randomised colour names but each was printed in an ink colour other than the one it named. On card C there was an array of coloured crosses. There was one reading trial and two naming trials. SW was instructed to read the colour names printed on card A, then to name the colour of the crosses on card C, and finally to name the colour of the ink in which each word is written on card B. Each section of the task is timed. The Stroop effect is the time increment between the two naming trials.

Verbal Fluency. In the verbal fluency task, subjects were asked to generate as many words as possible in one minute, beginning with each of the letters F, A, and S and for the categories, animals, objects, and occupations.

The Figure of Rey. The figure of Rey was presented for copying. A sequence of coloured pencils was laid out beside the figure, and every 30s, the child was asked to change pencil. Approximately three minutes after the copying was completed, the subjects was asked to draw the design from memory. No warning of this forthcoming task was given at the time of the original copy.

The Tower of London.   The Tower of London has a board with three vertical pegs, graded in size, which can accommodate 1, 2, or 3 coloured balls. The hands-on version of this task required the subject to move the balls from an initial position, which remains constant, to an end position, illustrated on a card, using a specified number of moves, between two and five. The rules are that only one ball may be moved at a time, and that once a ball is picked up it must be placed on a peg, and not on the table or held in the hand while another move is being made. Scores were the number of problems solved correctly, and the time taken per problem. In a hands-off version of the task the subject had to solve a similar set of problems but described his solution to the experimenter, rather than moving the balls himself.

Self-ordered Pointing.   Since it was not possible to obtain copies of the identical test stimuli to that used by Petrides and Milner (1982), two new versions of these tasks were constructed by Sean Mullarkey, a research assistant in our group. One employed abstract designs and the other representational (or concrete) drawings of everyday objects (taken from Snodgrass & Vanderwart, 1980). Each task is divided into four sections. The first section consists of six pages, each with an array of six different stimuli. The set of stimuli are the same on each page, but appear in different spatial positions. The subject is asked to point to one stimulus per page and to point to each stimulus only once. Subjects are left to determine their own order of responding. The other sections of the task are the same except that they contain eight, ten, and twelve stimuli respectively, with the corresponding number of pages.

The abstract version is administered in exactly the same manner, with each page having an array of abstract stimuli which are black and white patterns designed to be verbally non-descriptive but easily discriminated. Scores were derived from the percentage of pages completed correctly before each error, the number of errors in the series, the number of points made to the same item (item perseveration), and the number of repeated points made to the same spatial position (position perseveration).

Recency Discrimination.   The recency discrimination task was also modelled on the task of Petrides and Milner (1982). There were two versions: one employed representational drawings and the other employed abstract modern pictures. The stimuli in each set were presented one at a time in sequence. At preset intervals, a pair of previously shown stimuli were presented and the subject had to decide which of the two had been displayed most recently.

Controls

SW's performance was compared to that of 10 young adult controls, who were male domestic staff, assisting in the University kitchens. They had a mean age of 22;5. On one task, the Tower of London, and on one section of the self-ordered pointing task, control data from the kitchen staff could not be obtained because of time constraints and the length of the test battery. On these two sections, SW's performance was compared to that of ten 13-year-old boys, who were an unselected sample from a mainstream school.

Results

WCST. SW did not differ from controls on the number of categories achieved but made significantly more perseverative errors than the controls (see Table 8.2).

Stroop. On the Stroop task, there were no significant differences between SW and the controls (see Table 8.2).

Verbal Fluency. SW's performance was below the control average on five of the six categories employed, but was only significantly impaired on

TABLE 8.2
WCST, Stroop and Fluency Results for SW

	SW	Controls
WCST		
Number of categories	2	2.20(SD=1.32)
% Perseverative responses	46.87	28.43(SD=11.56)
% Perseverative errors	37.5*	20.15(SD=9.54)
Stroop		
Read black ink	27.0	20.5(SD=3.98)
Name coloured dots	37.0	33.3(SD=6.00)
Name coloured ink	56.5	53.5(SD=11.01)
Increment between naming trials	19.5	20.2(SD=10.44)
Verbal fluency		
F	3*	12.0(SD=5.31)
A	12	10.4(SD=6.13)
S	13	14.8(SD=3.65)
Animals	15	20.9(SD=5.3)
Household items	9	21.5(SD=7.78)
Occupations	11	15.4(SD=6.78)

* Z>1.64; P<0.05.

one category (see Table 8.2). Overall performance averaged one standard deviation below that of controls.

The Figure of Rey. SW scored at the 25th percentile on the Laughlin–Taylor norms, compared to adults, for his copy of the figure of Rey. This indicated a somewhat weak capacity to organise the structure of his drawing. His recall of the design, after a three minute delay, fell below the 25th centile for the Laughlin–Taylor norms, which are based on a 30 minute delay. There is thus relatively rapid loss of the structure of the design.

The strategy which was adopted in the copy of the figure of Rey was highly unusual, and fell into category V, as described by Osterrieth (1944). Strategy V is described as one in which the subject copies parts of the drawing without any semblance of organisation. Of Osterrieth's adult controls, no subjects adopted strategy V and of the traumatically brain-injured subjects only one followed strategy V. In this sense SW is highly unusual in his perceptual organisation abilities. A further striking aspect to his production of the Rey was the presence of embellishments in the form of parts of the drawing being filled in with solid colour. No behaviour of this kind was seen amongst Osterrieth's brain-damaged subjects but seven patients diagnosed as having a "syndrome d'automatisme mental" and "syndrome catatonique" did produce such embellishments.

Tower of London. In both the hands on and hands off versions of the Tower of London task, the number of problems solved correctly did not differ between SW and controls. However, the length of time taken by SW to plan the solutions and implement them was significantly longer than for controls. In the hands-on version, this was evident for two- and three-move problems (see Table 8.3). In the hands-off version, the difference was significant for all problem lengths. It should also be noted that the controls employed for this task were significantly younger than SW, and deficits in comparison to age-matched controls might have been even more marked.

Self-ordered Pointing. On both the concrete and abstract versions of the self-ordered pointing task, SW performed at a level comparable to controls. For the abstract version, the mean percentage of the set performed correctly before error was 60.5 (SD=10.5) for controls and 64.2 for SW. For the representational version, the mean percentage was 87.6 (SD=8.4) for controls and 88.3 for SW. For both SW and the controls, item, and position perseverations were rare.

Recency Discrimination. The abstract version of this task proved difficult for both SW and the controls. Both performed at chance level (control mean correct 50%, SW 57%). For the representational version, control performance was above chance, at 82% (SD=14%) correct. SW's performance remained very poor at 24% correct.

Discussion. In summary, SW made significantly more perseverative errors than controls on the WCST, indicating rigidity in shifting from a pre-established response. There were deficits in organising a structurally adequate course of action in copying and recall of the figure of Rey, with additional insertion of irrelevant actions in the drawing. On the Tower of London, performance was significantly slower than controls on both the hands-on and hands-off versions, indicating increased difficulty in planning ahead and effective implementation of plans of action. SW did not show any ability in making judgements of recency of events even when the items involved could be easily labelled verbally. In addition, verbal fluency was at the lower end of the control range and suggestive of weaker skills in strategic word retrieval. Performance on the Stroop did not indicate any excessive distractibility by irrelevant aspect of the task. Self-ordered pointing was also unimpaired indicating intact ability in storage and executive components of short-term memory.

Thus, in this individual case of developmental frontal lobe abnormality, there are a number of deficits in the development of executive skills, particularly those involved in planning and implementing plans, adapting to novel task demands, and making judgements of temporal recency. In relation to Welsh et al.'s (1991) three components of executive skill, there were impairments in all three: fluid and speeded responding (verbal fluency); hypothesis testing and impulse control (perseverations on the WCST); and planning (the Tower of London). However, the impairment in executive skill is not comprehensive. There is neither excessive distractibility (the Stroop)

TABLE 8.3
Response Times (Secs) on the Tower of London for SW

	SW	*Controls*
Hands-on version		
2 Moves	7.0*	5.18(SD=1.05)
3 Moves	11.6*	7.25(SD=1.71)
4 Moves	12.3	11.01(SD=3.43)
5 Moves	14.5	14.40(SD=4.46)
Hands- off version		
2 Moves	15.0*	4.08(SD=1.15)
3 Moves	25.0*	5.29(SD=1.97)
4 Moves	52.5*	11.38(SD=6.58)
5 Moves	32.0*	14.86(SD=5.67)

* $Z > 1.64$; $P < 0.05$.

nor impaired executive short-term memory (self-ordered pointing). Both could require the impulse control described in Welsh et al.'s (1991) second factor. The Stroop might also involve fluid and speeded responding. Thus, there is either fractionation within Welsh et al.'s factors, or they are insufficiently comprehensive to encompass the components of executive skills. SW has normal intelligence, vocabulary, and literacy attainments. Yet, he has significant impairment in a number of elements of executive skill consistent with his right frontal tuber. The absence of a generalised impairment in executive skill supports the potential fractionation of executive skills (Ellis & Young, 1988a; Shallice, 1988).

Case studies of developmental frontal lobe abnormality are sparse, but descriptions of syndromes within which executive skills are implicated are more prevalent and several such syndromes will now be addressed.

PHENYLKETONURIA

Phenylketonuria (PKU; Folling, 1994) is an autosomal recessive genetic disorder of metabolism, in which there is inability to metabolise phenylalanine, which is found within many protein foods. This leads to a build-up of phenylalanine and its derivative phenylpyruvic acid, instead of the normal metabolite tyrosine. This in turn affects dopamine levels. The disorder affects the process of myelination, with later myelinating areas such as the frontal lobes thought to be particularly vulnerable. The incidence of PKU is 1 per 10,000 to 15,000 live births (Harris, 1995). Untreated PKU leads to learning disabilities, often severe in level (Bickel, Gerrad, & Hickmans, 1953, 1954). A characteristic personality is also documented, with temper tantrums, irritability, hyperactivity, inattentiveness, impulsiveness, and poor cooperation.

Widespread newborn screening was introduced in the 1960s (Guthrie, 1961; Guthrie & Susi, 1963), and dietary treatment with a restriction of protein intake is now applied. In most cases, PKU treated in this way leads to intellectual levels in the normal range, if the diet is maintained throughout childhood. Prognosis is best, with early detection, good dietary adherence, and in cases with higher maternal IQ (Williamson, et al, 1981). Pennington, van Doorninck, McCabe, and McCabe (1985) argue that even treated PKU may involve deficient dopaminergic activity related to elevated phenylalanine (Guttler & Lou, 1986; Krause et al., 1985) and that in Parkinson's disease similar neurochemical disruption is associated with disorders of executive function.

Children with treated PKU, although of normal intelligence, have lower IQs than their parents and siblings (Netley, Hanley, & Rudner, 1984; Smith, Beasley, & Ades, 1990) and a higher incidence of abnormal behaviour than controls (Smith, Beasley, Wolff, & Ades, 1988). Selective disorders in the development of cognitive function have also been reported in children with treated PKU. Welsh, Pennington, Ozonoff, Rouse, and McCabe (1990) in a study of treated preschoolers, employed four of the executive tasks which they had previously used in their study of normal children (Welsh et al., 1991). Three of the tasks, visual search, verbal fluency, and motor planning, loaded on the factor they described as reflecting fluid and speeded responding. The fourth task, the Tower of Hanoi, loaded on a separate planning factor. Significant impairments were found on both factors. The disorder of planning on the Tower of Hanoi is consistent with other studies, which have also reported difficulties with problem solving and concept formation (Brunner, Berch, & Berry, 1987; Brunner, Jordan, & Berry, 1983; Crowie, 1971). Failure on the WCST, with perseverative and inflexible responding, has also been reported by Pennington et al. (1985). Attentional difficulties have been reported in treated PKU children across the age span (Berry, O'Grady, Perlmutter, & Bofinger, 1979; Cabalska et al., 1977; Griffen, Clark, & d'Entremont, 1980; Holtzman, Kronmall, Van Doorninck, Azen, & Koch, 1986; Smith et al., 1988).

Welsh et al. (1990) also confirmed a negative correlation between phenylalanine levels and executive function skills, supporting the proposed underlying biochemical mechanism for prefrontal dysfunction. Diamond (1994) found impairment in executive skill in cases of PKU with phenylalanine levels of 6–10mg/dl, once thought to be a benign level, though 3–5 times the normal level. Tasks required keeping information in mind whilst simultaneously inhibiting the desire to respond. In this study arguments for a dopaminergic involvement were also bolstered by findings of reduced contrast sensitivity believed to be a measure of dopamine function.

AUTISM

Autism is classified as a pervasive developmental disorder (American Psychiatric Association, 1994), in which there is reduced social interaction, impaired verbal and non-verbal communication, an absence of imaginative play, and a restricted repertoire of interest. The pragmatic language difficulties associated with autism were discussed in Chapter 2.

Current developmental theories have discussed autism in relation to a deficit in "theory of mind" (Premack & Woodruff, 1978). This is believed to underlie the ability to attribute a mental state or belief to another person, and, at a higher level, predict what a person thinks about another person's beliefs or thoughts. The ability to attribute a mental state is referred to as a first order attribution and in normally developing children is mastered by the age of four. The second order attributions which require recursive thinking about mental states, and what one person thinks about another's thoughts, are mastered later at about the age of six or seven (Perner & Wimmer, 1985).

The classic experiment, which formed a basis for much subsequent work, was Wimmer and Perner's (1983) paradigm using two dolls, Sally and Anne. Whilst Sally is absent from the room, Anne moves Sally's marble, out of the basket where Sally had put it, and hides it instead in Anne's own box. The examiner checks that the child remembers where the marble was in the beginning and where the marble is now. The child is then asked, "Where will Sally look for the marble?" This task requires a first order attribution of theory of mind, and normal three- to four-year-olds understand that Sally's belief about the position of the marble differs from the reality of its new hiding place. Autistic children at a comparable intellectual level have a high error rate, making reality-based judgements (Baron-Cohen et al., 1985). Further experiments support the proposal of difficulty in reasoning about beliefs, desires, and mental states. Leslie (1987) calls the failure in the development of theory of mind, a problem with metarepresentations which link the child's difficulties with pretence, social interaction, and communication. He argues that the autistic child does not have difficulty in all social situations but has difficulties in social situations where it is necessary to take into account what someone else knows or expects.

It has further been suggested that the construction and manipulation of these cognitive metarepresentations may be dependent upon the activities of the frontal lobes (Frith & Frith, 1991; Ozonoff, Pennington, & Rogers, 1991). Disorder of the mesolimbic cortex of the mesial frontal lobes was hypothesised as dysfunctional in autism by Damasio and Maurer (1978), who argued that the pattern of deficits in motor skill, language, and goal-directed activity were thereby explicable in comparison to human and animal studies of lesions to the mesolimbic cortex. Deficits in interpersonal role-taking have also been reported in two subjects after extensive prefrontal damage early in development (Price, Daffner, Stowe, & Mesulam, 1990). Both SPECT and PET blood flow studies show reduced flow to frontal areas in young adults with autism (George, Costa, Kouris, Ring, & Ell, 1992), children and adolescents with high functioning autism and Asperger's syndrome

(Pennington & Ozonoff, 1996), and preschool subjects with autism (Zilbovicius et al., 1995).

Even in high functioning autistic individuals, deficits in executive functions are reported and the relationship of these to theory of mind has been investigated (Ozonoff et al., 1991) and discussed (Bishop, 1993).

The first report of executive functions deficits in a case of residual state autism reported inflexible problem-solving strategies and perseveration (Steel, Gorman, & Flexman, 1984). In a series of studies, Rumsey (1985; Rumsey & Hamburger, 1988, 1990) confirmed executive functions deficits in adults with autism. She found deficiencies in the number of categories achieved in the WCST and an increased degree of perseveration. The autistic subjects also scored more poorly than controls on word fluency. In contrast performance on copying the figure of Rey was comparable to controls, although as Bishop (1993) highlights delayed recall was not assessed. Prior and Hoffman (1990) compared autistic children of low normal intelligence, with matched controls on a task of maze learning, the WCST (incorporating Nelson's 1976 modification, within which the subject is informed when the rule changes), and the figure of Rey. Deficits were found for the autistic children on maze learning, on the WCST, and on recall of the figure of Rey. On both the maze learning task and the WCST, the autistic children made three times as many errors as controls.

Ozonoff et al. (1991) hypothesised that the theory of mind deficit was primary to autism and that the executive function impairment was a correlated deficit on the basis of neuroanatomical proximity. They predicted that theory of mind deficits, on first and second order tasks, would be relatively universal among autistics but that executive function deficits would be present in only a subset of the group, those with more severe brain damage. Their subjects ranged in age from 8 to 20 years, with a mean of 12 years. Controls were matched pairwise for age, sex, and verbal IQ.

Ozonoff et al. (1991) employed a series of theory of mind tasks and executive function tasks within the same subject groups. First order theory of mind tasks included mental–physical distinctions, for which the child had to make behavioural and sensory judgements about mental and physical events (Baron-Cohen, 1989); appearance-reality judgements, in which the children had to use their own mental states to judge aspects of the environment (Baron-Cohen, 1989); and the M and Ms false belief task (Perner, Frith, Leslie, & Leekam, 1989). Second order attributions were assessed with the Perner and Wimmer task (1985), employing a toy town and a story about two children playing in a park. Second order belief attributions were assessed on the basis of questions given about the story. The executive tasks employed were the WCST and the Tower of Hanoi. Memory and perceptual tasks were also included.

The autistic group performed significantly less well than controls on executive functions, first order beliefs, and second order beliefs. They were significantly less efficient on the Tower of Hanoi task and made more perseverative responses on the WCST.

Ozonoff et al. (1991) calculated the proportions of autistic children performing more poorly than the control group mean and found proportions of 96% for executive tasks, 52% for first order theory of mind tasks, and 87% for second order theory of mind tasks. Further, second order theory of mind deficits were less specific to the autistic group than the executive function deficits. In relation to second order theory of mind tasks, 56% of autistics failed all tasks but so did 15% of the control group. On the executive function tasks, nearly 2 standard deviations separated the lowest scoring autistic subject from the lowest scoring control. The Tower of Hanoi alone enabled the correct classification of 80% of subjects. The authors argued that their results did not fit with their own original predictions since deficits in executive function and second order theory of mind tasks were significantly more widespread than other deficits. Impairment on first order theory of mind tasks was present for only a subset of the group. They suggested that the universality of the executive function deficits suggest that these may be a primary deficit in autism. They proceeded to discuss how a prefrontal abnormality may cause both the executive function and theory of mind deficits.

In a companion paper, Ozonoff et al. (1991) contrast the neuropsychological profiles of high functioning autistic subjects and those with Asperger's syndrome (Asperger, 1944/1991). Only the high functioning autistic subjects were found to be impaired on the theory of mind tasks but both groups were impaired on executive function tasks. The lack of theory of mind impairments in Asperger's syndrome suggests that this deficit may not be primary to all of the autistic continuum, but may be a correlated deficit present in more severely affected individuals. In contrast deficits in emotion perception and executive function may be pervasive (Ozonoff et al., 1991).

The persistence of both executive function deficits and theory of mind impairment has been explored by Ozonoff and McEvoy (1994) in adolescents with autism. The group showed no evidence of improvement in executive functions, over a three-year period, as measured by performance on the WCST and the Tower of Hanoi. This was in marked contrast to matched controls. There was also little evidence of improvement on theory of mind tasks. Although four subjects did manifest some development, this was counterbalanced by three who seemed to regress. The proportion passing the second order tasks did not improve over the three-year period. Ozonoff and McEvoy (1994) suggest that in autism there may be a developmental ceiling for both the development of executive skills and the development of theory of mind.

Ozonoff et al. (1991) argue that the common feature between executive tasks and theory of mind tasks is in the use of stored information to govern behaviour but Bishop (1993) notes that such an explanation is so general that it could explain almost any behaviour.

Shallice (1988; Shallice & Burgess, 1991) has argued that the frontal lobes are the substrate for a supervisory attentional system (SAS). He argues that we have available a finite set of actions and schema which are triggered when specific triggers are activated. The selection of the schema involves contention scheduling, which is under SAS control. Where there is frontal lobe impairment, behaviour appropriate to the species may be triggered but it is not planned. Problems are particularly encountered when there is an environmental stimulus which normally triggers habitual response but that response must be inhibited and another function performed instead. Bishop (1993) discusses how these ideas integrate with those of Russell (e.g. Hughes & Russell, 1993; Russell, Mauthner, Sharpe, & Tidswell, 1991) who argues that executive skills are involved when there is a prepotent response which must be inhibited and behaviour must be governed by an arbitrary rule held in memory. Russell et al. (1991) argue that children with autism may have a theory of mind but are unable to inhibit a dominant prepotent response in order to act on their theory of mind. Children with autism therefore have difficulty on tasks requiring subjects to disengage from objects and use internal rules to govern behaviour.

Perner (1993) suggests that it is not that autistic children lack a genetically specified theory of mind but that they have a genetically based lack of the personal database necessary to build a theory of mind. They are able to develop a certain level of competence in understanding their own and other's minds but their skill in this area lags behind their other abilities, with particular difficulty in managing conflicting desires and in personal insight.

A primary impairment in executive functions is thus one of several current theories about the fundamental basis of autism. Lack of a theory of mind is a second widespread theory, which continues to enjoy considerable support. A third theory suggests that the fundamental disorder is in interpersonal relatedness (e.g. Hobson, 1986a, 1986b, 1989, 1993) and emphasises the affective and emotional disorder within the syndrome. The theories need not be mutually exclusive but the primacy of one or the other continues to be debated.

GILLES DE LA TOURETTE SYNDROME

Gilles de la Tourette syndrome (GTS) was first described by Itard in 1825, with further descriptions of eight more cases, in 1885, by Gilles de la Tourette. The syndrome is characterised by both motor and vocal tics. Motor tics frequently include eye-blinking and grimacing, but may also include licking, spitting, hitting, jumping, smelling, squatting, and forced touching (Robertson, 1994). Vocal tics may be non-verbal, including throat-clearing, barking, hissing, and clicking, or verbal, including explosive utterances, echolalia, and coprolalia (the inappropriate and involuntary uttering of obscenities) (Robertson, 1994). Copropraxia (involuntary and inappropriate obscene gestures) and echopraxia (imitation of the actions of others) are also relatively common. Twin studies suggest a genetic element in GTS (Hyde, Aaronson, Randolph, Rickler, & Weinberger, 1992; Price, Kidd, Cohen, Pauls, & Leckman, 1985). Obsessive-compulsive disorder may be genetically related to GTS (Eapen, Pauls, & Robertson, 1993; Pauls, Towbin, Leckman, Zahner, & Cohen, 1986) and some consider obsessive thinking to be a cardinal feature of GTS itself (Baron-Cohen, Cross, Crowson, & Robertson, 1994). It is suggested that obsessive-compulsive behaviours are a phenotype of a putative gene, involved in the genetic determination of GTS (Eapen et al., 1993; Robertson, 1989).

The incidence of GTS is 5 per 10,000, and it is three times as common in males as in females (Robertson, 1989). It is found across cultures and social classes, though cultural and modification may contribute to the lower incidence of coprolalia reported in Japan (Nomura & Segawa, 1982).

There is evidence of reduced glucose uptake and reduced blood flow in both frontal areas and basal ganglia (Chase, Geoffrey, Gillespie, & Burrows, 1986; Hall et al., 1990; Riddle, Rasmussen, Woods, & Hoffer, 1992; Stoetter et al., 1992). Brain imaging reveals abnormalities in the frontal cingulate cortex and inferior corpus striatum (Chase et al., 1984, 1986) as well as basal ganglia (Leckman, Knorr, Rasmussen, & Cohen, 1991). The amygdaloid complex has also been implicated (Jadrisec, 1992). Focal disruptions in the neurochemical systems, involving dopamine, 5-hydroxytryptamine, glutamate, and cyclic AMP, have all been proposed. In obsessive-compulsive disorder, which as discussed earlier may have a genetic link to GTS, it has been proposed that dysfunction of basal ganglia-thalamic frontal cortical loops are instrumental in producing the positive symptoms of excessive grooming, checking, and doubt (Rapoport, 1991) and that in children, hard-wired complex behaviours subsumed by basal ganglia frontal cortical pathways are released in the disorder (Rapoport, Swedo, & Leonard, 1992). According to

Comings (1987), anomalies of the mesostriatal dopamine neurons result in the motor and vocal tics of GTS, and defects of the mesocortical prefrontal system contribute to other frontal effects.

Baron-Cohen et al. (1994) have proposed that a primary cognitive deficit in GTS results from disorder in an Intention Editor. They see the Intention Editor as being a subcomponent of the Supervisory Attentional System (SAS), proposed by Shallice (1988; Shallice & Burgess, 1991), which serves inhibition in general. A primary function of the SAS is to inhibit schemata of action in response to novelty. The Intention Editor is triggered when there are several intentions competing in parallel and will interrupt and prohibit one or some of these from occurring. Baron-Cohen et al. (1994) describe intentions as "representations of future action, speech or thought" which drive actions, speech, and thought (p. 31). Intentions specify not only the goal state but how to achieve that state. Even after access and activation, the intentions can be edited at both a conscious and preconscious level. Intentions are thus separate from the actions they drive. Intentions which are dangerous or may elicit social disapproval are more likely to trigger the Editor. In normal children, the mechanism will develop in the first five to six years of life, but in GTS development is impaired.

Baron-Cohen et al. (1994) demonstrate the effects of the dysfunctional Intention Editor in two experiments. In the first experiment, children with GTS were found to have particular difficulty with Luria's (1966) Hand Alternation Task, in which the hands are required to make two simultaneous but different movements, which are then alternated across the hands. Each hand must therefore inhibit its previous action, whilst the other hand is simultaneously making it. The second experiment involved vocal inhibition. The subjects were told that they must not say "yes" or "no" in response to anything the experimenter asked. So, for example, if asked if their name was John and it was, they should say "it is" or "that's right", rather than "yes". In this task, as for the hand alternation task, two intentions are activated simultaneously, one of which is edited and the other of which is translated into action. GTS children were also impaired on the vocal inhibition task. On both tasks, the performance of the GTS children at the age of 12 years was poorer than that of control children aged 6 years.

Baron-Cohen et al. (1994) contrast the role of the Intention Editor with that of the Intention Monitor, discussed by Frith and Done (1989). Whereas the Intention Monitor's role is to track the source of an intention and its effects, the Intention Editor's role is to select among competing willed intentions.

Impairments in other executive skills have also been reported in GTS. These include deficits in verbal fluency, attention, and concentration

(Bornstein 1991; Brookshire, Butler, Ewing-Cobbs, & Fletcher, 1994; Sutherland, Kolb, Schoel, Whishaw, & Davies, 1982). Channon, Flynn, and Robertson (1992) also report deficits in attention, particularly on more complex tasks, including serial addition, block sequence span, and letter cancellation vigilance tasks. However, no impairment has been found on the WCST (Bornstein 1990, 1991; Bornstein & Yang, 1991; Randolph, Hyde, Gold, Goldberg, & Weinberger, 1993; Sutherland et al., 1982). Other tasks have as yet, either not been given or have been given in only one or two studies, with contradictory or unconfirmed results.

ATTENTION DEFICIT DISORDER

Studies of adult patients with focal frontal lobe lesions have demonstrated deficits in the direction of extrapersonal attention, selective attention, orienting responses, habituation, and sustained attention (Foster, Eskes, & Stuss, 1994). Behaviourally these deficits may be manifest as both distractibility and impulsivity. In child neuropsychology, attention deficit hyperactivity disorder (ADHD) has been a pervasive clinical classification, particularly in the United States, though with clear variation in the classification criteria deployed and within the clinical entity itself. The incidence is approximately 1%, with a sex ratio of 3:1 (Spreen, Tupper, Risser, Tuckko, & Edgell, 1984; Szatmari, Offord & Boyle, 1989). A genetic underpinning has been proposed with twin studies supporting heritability (e.g. Eaves et al., 1993; Stevenson, 1992; Willerman, 1973). A frontal lobe underpinning has been proposed for the syndrome (Dykman, Ackerman, Clements, & Peters, 1971; Mattes, 1980; Satterfield, & Dawson, 1971). MRI suggests absence of the usual right greater than left frontal asymmetry (Hynd et al., 1990). Reduced frontal blood flow is also reported in ADHD (Lou, Henriksen, & Bruhn, 1984).

The hypothesis that there are structural brain abnormalities, relevant to frontal lobe circuitry, in children with ADHD has been explored by Giedd et al. (1994). Using magnetic resonance images, they measured seven regions of the mid-sagittal cross-sectional area of the corpus callosum, in 18 children with ADHD and 18 controls. Two anterior regions, the rostrum and the rostral body were found to have significantly smaller areas in the ADHD group, supporting theories of abnormal frontal lobe development. The areas correlated with teacher and parent ratings of hyperactivity.

McBurnett, Harris, Swanson, Pfiffner, Tamm, and Freeland (1993) examined the association of frontal lobe functioning, as reflected by performance on the WCST, and teachers ratings of inattention/overactivity in both normal and clinic-referred children. Electrodermal activity was also recorded. Poor WCST performance was associated with higher ratings of inattention/overactivity, but was unrelated to electrodermal activity. Other studies have also found impaired performance on the WCST in ADHD children (Boucugnani & Jones, 1989; Chelune, Ferguson, Koon, & Dickey, 1986; Gorenstein, Mammato, & Sandy, 1989; Reader, Harris, Schuerholz, & Denckla, 1994), but an absence of impairment has also been reported (e.g. Fischer, Barkley, Edelbrock, & Smallish, 1990; Loge, Stanton, & Beatty, 1990; McGee, Williams, Moffitt, & Anderson, 1989). Similarly although verbal fluency deficits have been reported in ADHD (Felton, Wood, Campbell, & Harter, 1987), the result has not been consistent (e.g. Fischer et al, 1990; Loge et al., 1990; McGee et al., 1989). Small sample sizes and variation in diagnostic criteria may have contributed to those results which are contradictory.

Consistent impairments have been reported in ADHD on continuous performance tasks (Barkley, 1988; Douglas, 1983; Loge et al., 1990; Pennington, Groissier, & Welsh, 1993) and in problem solving (Hamlett, Pelligrini, & Conners, 1987; Pennington et al., 1993; Tant & Douglas, 1982; Weyandt & Willis, 1994). Impairments on the Stroop are also fairly consistent (Boucugani & Jones, 1989; Gorenstein et al., 1989; Hopkins, Perlman, Hechtman, & Weiss, 1979). A summary of the studies of executive function in ADHD is given by Pennington and Ozonoff (1996), who suggest that the most consistently impaired measures include the Tower of Hanoi, the Stroop, trail-making (e.g. sequential connection of randomly placed numbers), and a measure of motor inhibition.

Grodzinsky and Diamond (1992) studied a relatively large sample, consisting of 66 ADHD boys and 64 controls, and attempted to employ strict diagnostic criteria, in particular by utilising extensive exclusion criteria. The children were administered a battery of executive function tasks. The ADHD boys were impaired on a vigilance task, the Stroop, oral fluency, copy of the figure of Rey, and a mazes task. They were unimpaired on the WCST. Performance on vocabulary and block design did not differ between subjects and controls. Although performance for both ADHD boys and controls improved with age, the relative impairment for the ADHD boys was stable.

Shue and Douglas (1992) compared the performance of children with ADHD and controls on both tasks of frontal lobe function (executive tasks) and tasks of temporal lobe function. The executive tasks included the WCST, a trail-making task (sequential connection of randomly placed numbers), a task of conflicting motor responses (If I show you my finger, you show me your fist. If I show you my fist, you show me your finger), a go–no go task, and a self-ordered pointing task. The temporal lobe tasks involved a series of memory tasks. The ADHD children were unimpaired on the memory tasks but differed significantly from controls on the executive tasks. The differential sensitivity of the frontal and temporal tasks confirmed that the ADHD children do not have generalised cognitive impairment. The authors argued that interpretations based only upon inhibitory or attentional mechanisms, address only partial aspects of a wider mechanism, and that the integrative aspects of linking prior learning and motivation with current conditions, and the modulation of responses are important.

EXECUTIVE DISORDERS IN OTHER SYNDROMES

Turner's Syndrome

The features of Turner's syndrome (TS) and the characteristics of the spatial disorder with which it is associated were discussed in Chapter 3. In 1979, Waber reported impairment on the WCST, verbal fluency, and slow performance on all items of the Stroop, in Turner's syndrome, which would be consistent with a deficit in frontal lobe functioning, but this has received little subsequent exploration.

Brun and Skold (1968) found a right frontal abnormality in an autopsy of a single case of TS but no such consistent abnormality has been reported subsequently. The frontal lobes were not specifically implicated in the study of glucose metabolism by Clark et al. (1990) nor in the study of MRI volumes of Murphy et al. (1993). However, Reiss et al. (1993) in a study of monozygotic twins discordant for TS, found a marked discrepancy between the twins in right frontal areas, in addition to parieto-occipital differences.

McGlone (1985) found no impairment on either verbal fluency or a modified card sorting tasks amongst 11 girls with TS, who had a mean age of 15 years. Pennington, Heaton et al. (1985) also failed to find consistent deficits in 10 girls with TS on either the WCST or verbal fluency. However, Clark et al. (1990) administered a word fluency task as part of their regional blood flow study and found significantly lower performance in the subjects with TS. However, it is relevant in the interpretation of their results that the control group had a significantly higher verbal IQ than the subject group. In their study of monozygotic twins discordant for TS, Reiss et al. (1993) found impairment in the twin with TS on both verbal fluency and copy and recall of the figure of Rey. They further suggested that the deployment of executive skills affected performance on a memory task.

Temple et al. (1996) report results from a study of sixteen girls with TS, with a mean age of 10 years on, a battery of executive tasks comprising the WCST, the Stroop, verbal fluency, the Tower of London, and self-ordered pointing. The children with TS were significantly impaired in comparison to controls but the effects were task specific. They were impaired on the Stroop, verbal fluency and the abstract Self Ordered Pointing task. Their performance was entirely normal on the WCST, the Tower of London (both in relation to accuracy and response time), and the concrete version of the self-ordered pointing task.

The results for the WCST are in agreement with those of McGlone (1985) and Pennington et al. (1985), suggesting that subjects with TS can rapidly shift concepts and extract organisational principles from information. The results from the Tower of London also suggest that basic planning ability is intact. However, the impairment in verbal fluency suggests poor ability to hunt in vocabulary to retrieve information in an organised way. This is despite the good vocabulary levels of the children and their good verbal reasoning skills (Temple & Carney, 1993). On the Stroop tasks, there was a significantly exaggerated Stroop effect indicating heightened distractibility to the irrelevant sources of information in the stimuli.

In terms of Welsh et al.'s (1991) three executive factors in development, the results are only partially integrable. The poor fluency scores suggest impaired development of "speeded responding". In contrast, normal performance on the WCST argues for normal development of factor 2, "set maintenance". However, the description of this factor, which includes inhibition of salient but incorrect response alternatives, seems a close description of the characteristics of the Stroop, for which the subjects with TS have difficulty. Since the Stroop was not included in the Welsh et al. (1991) study, its assignment to a factor is speculative. As it does require speeded responding of a relatively automated and less complex response set, it might load like verbal fluency on factor 1. In this case the subjects with TS have impaired development of factor 1 but normal development of factor 2. The normal performance on the Tower of London also argues for normal development of factor 3 "planning".

Survivors of Acute Lymphoblastic Leukaemia

Executive memory impairment has been suggested in studies of long-term survivors of acute lymphoblastic leukaemia (ALL). Such effects may be a consequence of the toxic effects of their treatments. Poor recall of word lists has been suggested as reflecting restricted strategic planning, and organisational problems are reported in memory for prose, with incomplete and ambiguous recall (Kleinman & Waber, 1994; Rodgers, Britton, Morris, Kernahan, & Craft, 1992).

Visuo-spatial reasoning has been implicated in a number of studies (Copeland et al., 1988; Cousens, Ungerer, & Crawford, 1991; Moore,

Kramer, Wara, Halberg, & Ablin, 1991), and Waber, Isquith, & Kahn (1994) explored whether such impairment in recall of the figure of Rey could be attributable to an impairment in metacognition strategies, rather than having a visuo-perceptual/visuo-spatial basis. They noted that in free recall their ALL subjects recalled elements connected with the organisational structure of the figure less well than controls but recalled incidental features more well. They then manipulated the encoding phase of the task, by either dividing the stimulus item into three left to right sections (the control condition) or into an organisational scheme and incidental additional features (the metacognitive condition). The metacognitive condition significantly improved recall, whereas the other subdivision did not affect performance. Waber et al. (1994) concluded that the visuo-spatial reasoning problems in the children had an executive basis.

IN CONCLUSION

There have been several attempts to summarise the common features of the executive skills subserved by the frontal lobes. For example, Russell (e.g. Hughes & Russell, 1993; Russell et al., 1991) argues that executive skills are involved when there is a prepotent response which must be inhibited and behaviour must be governed by an arbitrary rule. Shallice (1988; Shallice & Burgess, 1991) proposed that executive skills are tasks that a Supervisory Attentional System controls, selecting the appropriate actions and schema from a repertoire of possibilities, some of which have specific triggers. Others emphasise the apparent contradictions in behaviours generated by frontal lobe pathology: apathy and overactivity; anxiety and lack of concern; depression and euphoria; rigidity and distractibility (Benton, 1991). In the cognitive domain, executive impairments generate difficulties in sustained attention and effort, perseveration, impaired initiation of action, poor use of feedback, failure in planning and organisation (Stuss & Benson, 1986), and difficulties in sustaining and manipulating the mental representations that may underlie theory of mind (Frith & Frith, 1991; Ozonoff et al., 1991). In relation to normal child development, Welsh et al., 1991) have proposed three distinct factors: fluid and speeded responding; hypothesis testing and impulse control; and planning.

There are only a limited number of case studies of acquired or developmental pathology of the frontal lobes but those described are sufficient to show the validity of using assessment measures derived from adult measures. Both the cognitive and behavioural parallels between some of the adult and child cases are also striking (Ackerly,

1964; Ackerly & Benton, 1947; Grattan & Eslinger, 1992; Marlowe, 1992; Williams & Mateer, 1992).

There are a number of syndromes within which disorders of executive function have now been described. These include autism, for which the impairments in executive skill appear to be pervasive both across tasks and across subjects, severe and sustained over time. More task-specific impairments in executive skill are reported for other syndromes: phenylketonuria; Gilles de la Tourette syndrome; attention deficit hyperactivity disorder; Turner's syndrome; and acute lymphoblastic leukaemia. The patterns of performance within some of these syndromes are noted to vary in consistency, severity and profile by Pennington and Ozonoff (1996). The additional syndromes discussed here confirm that view. The difference in profiles suggests different fractionations of executive skills linked to distinct syndromes. However, the range of potential component skills within executive function has not been explored across all syndromes. Further, the status of current models of the core components of executive skills are insufficiently specified to integrate the results in any straightforward fashion or to enable theoretical predictions about likely behaviour on as yet untested tasks.

Despite the limitations, there remain some patterns within the executive skills results for the childhood syndromes and more detailed investigation of the character of these across syndromes may enable better specification of double dissociation allowing a more elaborated model of executive skills to be constructed.

The variation in performance across studies also suggests that for those with developmental syndromes affecting the frontal lobes, just as for adults with frontal lobe lesions, the specification of a task as a frontal task is not necessarily a predictor of consistent failure by all frontal lobe subjects. It may be that within adult acquired disorders of executive skill reliable delineation of their variation may also be constructive in model building.

The dissociations in performance, seen in both the case report presented in this chapter and within the syndromes discussed, and the variation in the impact of the impairment upon subsequent cognitive ability and behaviour, argue strongly against Fodor's (1983) original premise that executive skills do not fractionate and are common across cognitive systems and in favour of the views articulated by Shallice (1988) and Ellis and Young (1988) suggesting modularity within the executive system.

Indeed the dominating influence of the idea that executive skills do not fractionate may have contributed to the very limited attempts to construct models of executive skills in comparison to the model building within the other domains of cognitive neuropsychology.

CHAPTER NINE

Concluding Comments

In Chapter 1, a series of questions and issues were outlined, which were relevant to developmental cognitive neuropsychology. Having discussed all the disorders in the preceding chapters, are we any further ahead in attempting to answer any of the questions, and in determining the significance of some of the issues raised?

MODULARITY

A fundamental assumption of adult cognitive neuropsychology is that there is modularity in the organisation of cognitive systems, in that there are discrete and relatively independent subcomponents within cognitive systems that function in a semi-autonomous way. A basic assumption of this book is that a cognitive neuropsychological approach can be applied to developmental disorders, and this raises the question, is the modularity seen in studies of adult neuropsychological disorders, mirrored by modularity in development?

It was noted that the strict tenets of modularity argued by Fodor (1983) have largely given way now to a more flexible use of the concept with recognition that the operation of all modules is not necessarily outside voluntary control (violating Fodor's mandatory status); there may be some degree of intercommunication between modules (violating Fodor's principle of information encapsulation); and executive processes may also be amenable to fractionation (violating Fodor's principles of domain specificity). It is this more flexible concept of modularity that is being applied to the developmental disorders.

The cognitive neuropsychological approach has been so successful in the study of adult patients, that it is not necessary to establish for the developmental disorders that the approach is as successful as in adulthood, but that at least it is successful within some domains and perhaps that it may have potential for further application within other domains.

Within a developmental field, the question of modularity relates to the question, how independent are different components of cognitive skills during development? As evidence of independence, we take the same evidence used in other areas of cognitive neuropsychology: double dissociation. In children, this takes the form: child A has learnt skill 1 but not skill 2. Child B has learnt skill 2 but not skill 1. The first child tells us that the acquisition of skill 1 is not intrinsically dependent upon skill 2. The second child tells us that the acquisition of skill 2 is not intrinsically dependent upon skill 1. This is taken as evidence that the acquisition of these two skills is relatively independent during development.

In relation to the cognitive areas which have been discussed here, the most successful examples of double dissociations are probably found within the application of cognitive neuropsychology to the literacy skills: reading, spelling, and arithmetic. In reading, there are marked double dissociations between developmental surface dyslexia and develop-mental phonological dyslexia, in relation to all the cardinal features which also differentiate them in acquired form.

In surface dyslexia, there is impaired irregular word reading but intact reading of non-words. In phonological dyslexia there is intact irregular word reading but impaired reading of non-words. Other double dissociations relate to the degree of occurrence of particular features. In surface dyslexia, there are high levels of regularisation or valid errors and low levels of morphological errors. In phonological dyslexia, there are high levels of morphological errors but low levels of regularisation or valid errors. Also highlighted in the analyses here, were the difficulties that phonological dyslexics encounter if the global characteristics of words are changed to render them unfamiliar — by writing letters typed in reverse order. The surface dyslexic was completely unaffected by this manipulation. The double dissociations between surface and phonological dyslexia and their straightforward interpretation in relation to multiple route models of reading (e.g. Fig. 5.4) argue strongly for the mutual independence of the phonological and semantic reading route during development. In similar fashion in spelling, there are sharp double dissociations between developmental surface dysgraphia and developmental phonological dysgraphia, arguing again for the relative independence of two distinct components of spelling within development.

Within the arithmetical system, there are double dissociations between number fact knowledge and procedural skill. In number fact disorder, knowledge of procedures is intact but knowledge of arithmetical facts, typically tables, is significantly impaired. In contrast, within procedural dyscalculia, knowledge of number facts is intact but knowledge of arithmetical procedures is significantly impaired. These argue for the relative independence within development of the establishment of the arithmetical subsystem devoted to facts and the arithmetical subsystem devoted to procedures.

Within the spatial and perceptual disorders, there appear to be double dissociations in relation to the putative three channels of visual perception dedicated to form, movement, and position. McCloskey et al.'s (1995) case shows a very specific impairment in the analysis of position, but had intact skills in recognition. Similarly, the adults who had congenital strabismus (Tychsen et al., 1996) and the case description of Ahmed and Dutton (1996), have impairment in the perception of motion but intact skill in the perception of identity. The case of childhood prosopagnosia following illness in infancy (Young & Ellis, 1989) also had difficulty with object identification when the objects were foreshortened, in ways similar to those that affect adults with parietal lesions (Warrington & Taylor, 1973). This child was not, however, reported to have impairments in the perception of either location or movement.

Within the object and face recognition systems, evidence for double dissociations is not as extensive but is nevertheless evident. Although there is no convincing case of developmental object agnosia and its status therefore remains unclear, within the face processing system there is evidence that the parallel channels depicted in the standard model (Bruce & Young, 1986) may develop independently. The Mancini et al. (1994) study reported a double dissociation between lip-reading and tasks involving directed visual processing. The de Gelder et al. (1991) study also finds intact lip-reading despite impairments in face recognition. Within the face recognition system, there are distinct forms of developmental prosopagnosia, which can also be explained in relation to the standard model (Bruce & Young, 1986). These indicate that different components of the face processing system may be separately and independently affected during development.

There are further double dissociations within spatial and perceptual disorders, in relation to the ability to process complex visual information from different domains. Dr S, one of the developmental prosopagnosics

(Temple, 1992b), had difficulty with face recognition, with a possible basis in visual memory but yet had excellent reading skill. In surface dyslexia there is a specific impairment in establishing or using a store of representations to enable recognition of irregular words, yet there may be intact face recognition and visual memory for other complex patterns (Castles & Coltheart, 1996).

There were also double dissociations in the processing of local and global forms between Williams syndrome and Down's syndrome (Bihrle et al., 1989).

In the language sphere, a range of different types of developmental language impairments may occur. A number reflect selective impairment of components of the language system. There can be impairments in auditory reception of language, in naming, in grammatical function, in praxis, and in the pragmatics of language.

In cases of grammatical disorder, there is little evidence of pragmatic disturbance. In cases of semantic–pragmatic disorder, grammatical function is relatively intact. However, there may also be limitations to the application of modularity within the linguistic domain. Tallal and Leonard and colleagues (e.g. Leonard, 1989; Tallal et al., 1996) argue that difficulties with the discrimination and sequencing of speech sounds characterised by rapid transitional information, or perceptual limitations affecting specific grammatical markers in speech, have downstream effects upon other stages of language development, specifically an impact upon grammatical development. This view contrasts with that of Clahsen (1989,1991), Gopnik (1990a, 1992), and Van der Lely (1994), all of whom propose more specific theories of grammatical impairment, which could be accounted for by a deficit in a grammatical module rather than as a knock-on effect of a receptive phonological difficulty.

In relation to executive disorders, a surprising degree of double dissociation was evident given the original premise of Fodor (1983) that as such systems are not domain specific they are not modular and will not therefore fractionate. There are hints of specific patterns of executive impairment linked to specific syndromes. There is the possibility that a more detailed model of executive skill would enable a more comprehensive explanation for the differing executive impairments linked to a series of disorders: phenylketonuria, Gilles de la Tourette syndrome, autism, ADHD, Turner's syndrome, and acute lymphoblastic leukaemia. For example, in Turner's syndrome, performance on the Tower of London is intact but performance on verbal fluency is impaired (Temple et al., 1996). In ADHD, performance on the Tower of London is impaired but performance in the majority of studies of verbal fluency in intact (Pennington & Ozonoff, 1996). Welsh et al. (1991) propose three distinct factors is the normal acquisition of executive skills. In Turner's syndrome there appears to be impaired fluid and speeded responding but intact planning. In ADHD, there appears to be impaired planning but intact fluid and speeded responding, at least as reflected by fluency scores. It would be interesting to determine whether any modular organisation to the executive system reflects the distinct emergent factors of executive skill proposed for normal development.

The application of a cognitive neuropsychological approach to memory is only just beginning. The double dissociation in relation to memory for complex visual material (faces/patterns vs words) was noted above in relation to surface dyslexia (Castles & Coltheart, 1996) and developmental prosopagnosia (Temple, 1992b). In relation to temporal lobectomies for seizure control, left temporal lobectomy impairs verbal memory but not non-verbal memory (Cavazutti et al., 1980), whereas right temporal lobectomy is associated with memory impairment for faces but leaves intact memory for verbal material (Beardsworth & Zaidel, 1994). There is also evidence, as for adult amnesia, of preserved procedural memory in a case of developmental amnesia (Julia). In Julia's case, vocabulary stores were also impaired but procedural learning was intact. In contrast, a further developmental amnesic, MS (de Renzi & Lucchelli, 1990), had impaired procedural memory but intact vocabulary. Both had severe impairment in long-term semantic memory. Our own studies (Temple, in preparation), suggest that episodic impairment might be a feature of Turner's syndrome, though there is no general amnesia or reported deficit in skill acquisition.

Thus, within each of the key areas which have been addressed there is evidence supporting double dissociations within patterns of acquisition. This has implications for the internal structure of developmental models.

DEVELOPMENTAL AND COGNITIVE MODELS

Several questions relating to models of explanation were raised in Chapter 1: Are developmental neuropsychological disorders explicable against cognitive models? How many routes are there to competence? Is there a single developmental pathway?

In the three areas of literacy acquisition — reading, spelling, and arithmetic — the double dissociations make the standard developmental stage models untenable. Descriptive stage models do not permit double dissociations. In a stage model, one set of skills always precedes another, or if they both form part of the same stage of acquisition they should both be at a similar performance level. Any single dissociation may be explained within a stage model by proposing that the skill which is intact must precede the skill that is impaired in acquisition. Thus, any single dissociation could in principle reflect delayed development, although the data from normal child development would also have to be accommodated and compatible. In this regard, surface dyslexia and surface dysgraphia are more easily explained in relation to models of normal reading and spelling development, than phonological dyslexia with its excellent orthographic skills but poor alphabetic competence. However, whenever the model is fixed and capable of explaining the single dissociation, the double dissociation, where the reverse pattern is manifest, becomes untenable. Here, the child has failed to acquire the preceding skill, yet has acquired the later skill. If surface dyslexia is explicable then phonological dyslexia is not. Similarly, if phonological dyslexia is explicable, surface dyslexia is not.

The same arguments apply to double dissociations in the developmental dysgraphias and also within the calculation system. Neither knowledge of number facts nor knowledge of number procedures can be seen as a precursor of the other. They are relatively independent in acquisition and must therefore be acquired via distinct channels.

Within memory, the dissociations within the developmental disorders argue both for independent types of memory mechanism: procedural memory vs. general semantic knowledge vs. the semantics of vocabulary, and also independent content-specific memories: faces vs. words. The temporal lobectomy data suggests that the anatomical substrates for different content specific memories may have linked lateralisations similar to those seen in adulthood.

Within vision, developmental psychologists have not argued for any stage progression of perception for form, motion, and identity. The concept of parallel routes in the acquisition of these channels as supported by the double dissociations is therefore relatively uncontroversial. There is also some evidence from the double dissociations discussed earlier that the parallel routes within the standard model of face recognition can develop independently.

In relation to language, it is possible to interpret the general model of the language system, depicted in Fig. 2.1, in two quite different ways. Each component of this model could be conceived of as an independent module capable of selective impairment and data from the different types of language disorder could be gathered to support this view, though in the absence of many double rather than single dissociations, the case would have to remain open. Alternatively, some of the components could be interpreted as intrinsically interlinked during development, with deficits in the initial processing stages prohibiting the normal development of later systems such as grammar. This would accommodate those theories arguing for downstream effects. At present, there is insufficient evidence to decide between these two alternatives, although the Tallal et al. (1996) data strengthens the arguments for the latter interpretation.

Within the executive skills, there is neither a very detailed specification of a normal adult model nor a detailed specification of a developmental model with which to discuss the data. The adult Supervisory Attentional System model of Shallice (1988; Shallice & Burgess, 1991) applies across executive tasks and does not really address the issue of fractionation within the executive processes. The developmental descriptions of Pennington et al. (1991) indicate the ages at which children plateau or fail to reach adult level of competence on differing executive tasks, which could enable a standard stage description of acquisition but as discussed previously such models are quite ineffective in accounting for double dissociations. There is a need to develop more fine-grain models that accommodate the different types of executive skill and enable an explanation of the possible double dissociation between differing developmental disorders.

In summary, in relation to the questions raised at the outset of this section, developmental neuropsychological disorders are explicable against cognitive models, although in the case of the executive disorders more fine-grain models are required. However, developmental neuropsychological disorders are not explicable in relation to traditional stage models that permit only one route to competence. There may be multiple routes to competence within several of the main cognitive systems. There is not a single developmental pathway. Variations in the development of differing pathways may also contribute to individual differences within the normal population.

ADULT/CHILD PARALLELS

How similar to the patterns of disorder in adulthood are these patterns within the developmental disorders? It is sometimes implied that the data from children is difficult to analyse as they may have partial acquisition of a skill. The double dissociations are not usually based on the total failure of one skill and the perfect development of the other. However, exactly the same is true for the analyses of the acquired neuropsychological disorders. Cases of absolute impairment in one skill and perfect retention of the other occur only within restricted domains. Generally, double dissociations relate to high and low levels of component skills. For example, although the terms high and low are imprecise, both the qualitative and quantitative analyses of the component skills in the analyses of disorders of literacy development are performed in the same way and with similar data to that employed in the analyses of disorders of literacy skill within adult cognitive neuropsychology. Indeed, Roeltgen and Tucker (1988), have highlighted in relation to surface dysgraphia and phonological dysgraphia, the statistically and qualitatively based similarity in the data from the developmental and acquired dysgraphias. Having worked with both data sets, were one to give the data from adult and child cases to a cognitive neuropsychologist and ask the question, which are the adults and which the children, there are no apparent criteria by which to distinguish them. The same is true for the developmental dyslexias and the developmental dyscalculias.

There are of course some areas where there are absolute dissociations. No non-words are read in acquired deep dyslexia but then no non-words are read in developmental deep dyslexia either. Some of the acquired dyscalculics retain perfect mastery of arithmetical facts, but so can cases of procedural dyscalculia.

Amongst the memory disorders, both Julia and the case MS (de Renzi & Lucchelli, 1990) had patterns of performance which were strikingly similar to adult amnesic disorders. In particular, Julia appeared to have preserved procedural memory. However, Julia also had impaired vocabulary, suggesting that in developmental form amnesia may result in specific impairment in the developing language system. In adults with amnesia the language system remains unimpaired. However, the case of MS indicates that developmental amnesia need not always have this impact and that language development may occur relatively independently and successfully in the face of severe memory deficit. For Julia, there was also a content-specific impairment of short-term memory, whereas in acquired amnesia short-term memory is usually intact. The relationship between short- and long-term memory in development, if such a distinction retains any theoretical validity, remains open.

Within language, there are parallels between the Landau–Kleffner syndrome and acquired auditory agnosia. The paper of van Hout (1993) demonstrated clearly the similarities between the developmental semantic access anomia and acquired semantic access anomia of childhood. There are also parallels between the developmental cases of semantic level anomias and adult acquired cases of semantic level anomia (e.g. Ellis & Young, 1988a). Parallels between developmental and acquired category-specific anomic disorders are also striking (e.g. McCarthy & Warrington, 1990). The parallels between grammatical disorders in childhood and agrammatic or paragrammatic aphasias of adulthood are less obvious, though dominant impairments in morphology or aspects of morphology are a major focus in both arenas. There are superficial similarities between developmental apraxia and some cases of acquired verbal apraxia but the range of the cases of developmental apraxia has not yet been delineated. Parallels can again be drawn between developmental pragmatic disorders and some descriptions of frontal language impairments, in terms of the over-literalness, abnormalities of topic focus, and failure to maintain conversational rules. However, as noted earlier and later, there is the possibility that downstream effects may also generate specific linked components of developmental language disorder whereas such components remain independent in the acquired disorders.

Within the spatial and perceptual disorders, there is no convincing case of developmental object agnosia and an adult–child parallel is thereby absent. It would be of significance if such an impairment never occurred in developmental form but it is probably too early to reach such a conclusion. The cases of developmental prosopagnosia, limited though they are in number do parallel cases of acquired prosopagnosia. Impairments in structural encoding have been described within both groups, as have difficulties in accessing person identity information from faces (e.g Young, 1992).

In relation to impairments in the visual channels of location and movement, the impaired movement perception of those who had congenital strabithmus is quite unlike the impaired movement perception of Zihl, Von Cramon, and Mai (1983), who saw the world in "snapshots". However, the case report of Ahmed and Dutton (1996) appears to be a direct parallel. Although the specificity of the impairment in the McCloskey et al. (1995) case, in which specific parameters of location are distorted, is certainly compatible with a system organised like adult systems, there is not the severity of impairment of Holmes, case of Private M, discussed by Ellis and Young (1988a). The adult and child cases of blindsight appear more directly analagous.

DOWNSTREAM EFFECTS

The issue of possible downstream effects was addressed above in relation to the development of grammar. To recap, those who believe in a specific grammatical module would argue that the data from Clahsen (1989, 1991), Gopnik (1990a, 1992), and van der Lely (1994) are compatible with a system containing a specific dedicated and independent grammatical processor. However, Tallal et al. (1996) and Leonard (1989) argue that such impairment arises as a downstream effect resulting from earlier problems in the discrimination of speech sounds. Downstream effects have also been discussed in relation to phonological awareness and reading, though with increasing evidence that the degree of phonological skill which is required as a prerequisite to reading is considerably below the level previously considered necessary. Indeed the cases of developmental deep dyslexia indicated that some degree of reading, albeit limited, can be established with no phonological awareness at all (Stuart & Howard, 1995). Explicit phonemic awareness and phonological awareness may develop as a consequence of exposure to written text, rather than as an essential precursor of development (Goswami, 1991; Perfetti, 1992).

Within the face processing system, the possibilities for sharp double dissociations may be restricted by downstream effects. In particular, impairments in structural encoding may have knock-on effects within the rest of the face processing system so that any structural encoding deficit affects the development of a number of subsequent components within the normal system. The same is true, in functional terms, in relation to acquired prosopagnosic patients with structural encoding deficits, in that all the subsequent components of face processing are inaccessible or the disrupted quality of input to them affects their output.

Although the issue of downstream effects might seem to be a weakness for developmental cognitive neuropsychology, in practice it creates a range of other potential applications of theoretical significance. The cognitive neuropsychological approach may be useful where modularity does not apply, since the case study analysis enables the identification of subjects who have a supposed precursor deficit but do not have the supposed resultant disorder. This enables the rejection of causally based theories structured in a precursor-causal consequence mode. Some of these theories are articulated in a unitary cause mode, where the cause of a group of disorders is specified to be X. However, if a cognitive neuropsychological analysis reveals that a child has X but does not have the supposed resultant disorder, the theory can be rejected. Cognitive neuropsychology also enables such universal theories to be rejected if child Y has the supposed causal consequence deficit but does not have the precursor impairment. Where the theory is specified in such a way that the precursor is a cause of some cases of the disorder but it is not a universal cause, the identification of a child with the resultant disorder but without the supposed precursor, would not enable the theory to be rejected but would confirm that its application can only be to a subsection of the relevant population.

There are a number of examples of such theory rejection. Within reading, the cases of surface dyslexia provide evidence that deficits in phonological processing are not the universal cause of the developmental dyslexias. Some developmental dyslexics do not have impairments in phonological processing (e.g. Castles & Coltheart, 1996). Similarly the relatively intact visual memory in surface dyslexia (Castles & Coltheart, 1996) indicates that visual memory impairments are not the basis of surface dyslexia. The impaired rapid automatised naming within Turner's syndrome (Temple et al., 1996) indicates general deficits in rapid automatised naming are not the causal basis of dyslexic disorders (Denckla et al., 1981) since children with Turner's syndrome are hyperlexic rather than dyslexic (Temple & Carney, 1996). Number processing disorders in development are not the result of generalised reading difficulties nor of phonological difficulties, since Paul (Temple, 1989) had normal lexical and phonological reading for all words except numeral words for which he was profoundly dyslexic and dysgraphic. Further, short-term memory impairments cannot be the generalised cause of lexical or phonological reading impairments since Paul had very poor short-term memory skills. Thus, cognitive neuropsychology applied to the developmental disorders can play an important role in constraining the viable theories of normal developmental and cognitive psychology.

Some theory rejections themselves raise interesting theoretical questions. For example, it has been shown that intellectual deficits are not the cause of memory or executive disorders. Normal intellect can develop in children with executive impairments or severe memory disorder. This raises issues about the mechanisms of learning involved in developing, acquiring, and expressing intelligent behaviour.

DIFFERENT DISORDERS IN THE SAME CHILD

The cognitive areas of language, memory, perception, reading, spelling, arithmetic, and executive disorder have largely been discussed within this book as distinct entities. However, some children had disorders which were described in more than one domain and this raises questions about the possible interlinking of different disorders.

Since all children with developmental dyslexia have developmental dysgraphia, it seems probable that the two groups of disorders are interlinked. For cases like RB (Chapters 5 and 6), the pattern of the disorder in spelling also appears to mirror that of spelling, with the co-occurrence of surface dyslexia and surface dysgraphia. However, phonological dyslexia can also co-occur with surface dysgraphia, suggesting that the two systems are quite independent. Coltheart and Funnell (1987) have argued that such a conclusion is unwarranted since spelling is not the exactly reciprocal process to reading and, although certain forms of surface dyslexia should have surface dysgraphia, for other forms there could be a dissociation in the features of reading and spelling despite unitary codes for reading and spelling. This could occur where the surface dyslexia arose from difficulties in accessing lexical representations but the lexical representations were themselves normal, and accessible to the spelling system. Indeed Coltheart and Funnell (1987) argue that there is evidence for unitary codes underlying the acquired disorders. Many developmental models also imply unitary codes of reading and spelling, but the issue had not been systematically explored within the cognitive neuropsychological domain in relation to analyses of literacy.

Another possible, though not necessarily intuitive, interlinking is between phonological disorders in literacy and disorders of number facts within the developmental dyscalculias. A co-occurrence of at least a mild phonological literacy difficulty and number fact disorder was seen for each of the three cases described in Chapter 7. One possibility would be that both disorders have their routes in a memory impairment (Geary, 1993). However, the intact development of semantic memory, vocabulary, and general knowledge in the twins RW and AW (Temple, 1994) argues against such a generalised impairment. Another possibility is an impairment in forming arbitrary associations or abstracted sets of coded pairs across domains, which would predict parallel deficits in paired associates tasks. A still further possibility is a common impairment in rate of information decay within working memory, or slow speed in carrying out computational strategies (Geary, 1993). All of these theoretical possibilities are testable empirically.

In relation to visual recognition, impairments in visual memory or in aspects of object identification raise the issue of the distinction of face processing mechanisms from the remainder of the perceptual system, a debate with an extensive history within the acquired disorders. In relation to memory the co-occurrence of developmental amnesia and anomia, despite their dissociation in one case, raises questions about the role of the semantic memory system in the development of language and the relationship of semantic system(s) to the rest of the cognitive architecture. Again this issue has an extensive history within adult neuropsychology.

Interlinked disorders within differing systems weaken claims of strict modularity (by violating the principle of information encapsulation), though they do not negate the value of discussing such disorders in relation to models of individual systems. They do, however, highlight the ultimate need for a specification of how the models derived within the differing cognitive domains interrelate, in a broader superstructure. The endeavour of modelling such interaction has not yet been attempted within either acquired or developmental neuropsychology.

DEVELOPMENTAL PLASTICITY/GENETIC CONSTRAINTS

We turn finally to the issue of the existence of all the varied developmental disorders described in this volume. In Chapter 1, the question was raised as to what restrictions there are to developmental plasticity. The simple answer to this question on the basis of all the data discussed here is that there are many restrictions to developmental plasticity evident within each of the major cognitive domains: language, memory, perception, reading, spelling, arithmetic, and executive skill. The brain is not capable of functional reorganisation to eliminate focal and selective deficits in each of these areas.

Given that we know functional plasticity can operate in some circumstances, why has it not eliminated the range of disorders discussed here? The issue of limitations in general mechanisms of plasticity was raised in Chapter 1. However, the possibility of a more specific limitation can also be raised. My belief is that compensatory mechanisms of plasticity are not activated when the basis of a disorder is under genetic control, but are instead responses to injury or disease. There is increasing evidence for genetic influences across a range of the developmental disorders. Within language, Landau–Kleffner syndrome, grammatical impairments, apraxias, and autism which encompasses pragmatic disorder all have possible genetic underpinnings (Bailey et al., 1995; Bishop et al., 1995; Landau, 1992; Lewis et al., 1989). Reading and spelling disorders may have a major gene or polygenetic transmission (Pennington et al., 1991). Perhaps arithmetical disorders may have a similar basis. The executive disorders in autism, phenylketonuria, and Turner's syndrome are all linked to genetically based disorders. In relation to memory and perception, the available data are limited, although Dr S reports other members of her family with face recognition difficulties. The objective here is not to argue that all developmental disorders have a genetic basis but rather that a genetic underpinning is evident for many of the disorders for which mechanisms of plasticity have failed to compensate.

There may also be other antenatal, congenital, or perinatal influences, which do not trigger plasticity. Hormonal or biochemical influences could distort the normal development of the brain in such a way that specific circuits are more implicated than others. This is also an alternative explanation for the effects of phenylketonuria and Turner's syndrome.

The two accounts are of course not mutually exclusive since a gene or multiple genes could dictate a specific hormonal or biochemical impact.

Atypical early environmental feedback or input could distort the consolidation of circuits during critical periods beyond which there is no further flexibility. This might underlie the abnormalities of perception in congenital strabismus.

More speculatively, events constraining the flow of oxygen to the foetus might specifically impact upon the oxygen-hungry cells of the hippocampus with large mitochondria, thereby inducing specific impacts upon memory circuitry, for which there is no viable alternative substrate.

Even more speculatively, in cases where the basis of the disorder is genetic, there is interest in considering why/how the gene(s) are sustained in the population. One possibility is that not all genetic influences are negative. For example, in Turner's syndrome there is evidence of superior verbal skills (e.g. Temple & Carney, 1996). In other developmental disorders, there may be no such evident compensating talent, but there are other possibilities. Genes linked to a disorder might also be linked to something beneficial that is unrelated to brain development (cp. resistance to malaria in sickle cell disease). Genes linked to a disorder might have some phenotypical expressions which are positive (cp. the fine dividing line between highly creative thought and disordered thought). There might also be interactional mechanisms, such that a particular cognitive weakness or vulnerability runs through a family creating only minor effects, but for some reason in a particular child the weakness is given much stronger expression and a disorder with significant impact emerges.

References

Aaron, P.G., Frantz, S.S., & Manges, A.R. (1990). Dissociation between comprehension and pronunciation in dyslexic and hyperlexic children. *Reading and Writing: An Interdisciplinary Journal, 2,* 243–264.

Ackerly, S. (1964). A case of paranatal bilateral frontal lobe defect observed for thirty years. In J. M. Warren & K. Albert (Eds.), *The frontal granular cortex and behaviour.*(pp.192–218). New York: McGraw-Hill.

Ackerly, S.S., & Benton, A.L. (1947). Report of a case of bilateral frontal lobe defect. *Association for Research in Nervous and Mental Diseases, 27,* 479–504.

Ahmed, M., & Dutton, G. N. (1996). Cognitive visual dysfunction in a child with cerebral damage. *Developmental Medicine & Child Neurology,* 38, 736–743.

Albert, M.L., & Bear, D. (1974). Time to understand: A case study of word deafness with reference to the role of time in auditory comprehension. *Brain,* 97, 373–384.

Albright, T.D., Desimone, R., & Gross, C.G. (1984). Columnar organisation of directionally selective cells in visual area MT of the macaque. *Journal of Neurophysiology, 51,* 16–31.

Alexander, D., Erhardt, A.A., and Money, J. (1966) Defective figure drawing, geometric and human, in Turner's Syndrome. *The Journal of Nervous and Mental Diseases, 142,* 161–167.

Alexander, D., & Money, J. (1966). Turner's syndrome and Gerstmann's syndrome: Neuropsychologic comparisons. *Neuropsychologia, 4,* 165–273.

American Psychiatric Association (1994). *Diagnostic statistical manual of mental disorders 4th ed. (DSM IV).* Washington, DC: American Psychiatric Association.

Andrews, G., Craig, A., Feyer, A., Hoddinott, S., Howie, P. , & Neilson, M. (1983). Stuttering: A review of research findings and theories circa 1982. *Journal of Speech and Hearing Disorders, 48,* 226–245.

Anzai, Y, & Simon, H.A. (1979). The theory of learning by doing. *Psychological Review*, *86*, 124–140.

Aram, D.M. (1988) Language sequelae of unilateral lesions in children. In F. Plum (Ed.) *Language, communication and the brain.* (pp. 171–197). New York: Raven Press.

Aram, D.M., & Eisele, J.A. (1992). Plasticity and recovery of higher cognitive function following brain injury. In I. Rapin & S. Segalowitz (Eds.), *Handbook of neuropsychology, Vol. 10.* (pp. 73–92). Amsterdam/London. Elsevier.

Aram, D.M., & Ekelman, B.L. (1986). Cognitive profiles of children with early onset of unilateral lesions. *Developmental Neuropsychology*, *2*, 155–172.

Aram, D.M., Ekelman, B.L., Rose, D.F, & Whitaker, H.A. (1985). Verbal and cognitive sequelae following unilateral lesions acquired in early childhood. *Journal of Clinical and Experimental Neuropsychology*, *7*, 55–78.

Aram, D.M., Ekelman, B.L., & Whitaker, H.A. (1986) Spoken syntax in children with acquired unilateral hemisphere lesions. *Brain and Language*, *27*, 75–100.

Aram, D.M., & Healy, J.M. (1988) Hyperlexia: A review of extraordinary word recognition. In L.K. Obler & D. Fein (Eds.), *The exceptional brain*. New York: Guilford.

Aram, D.M., Myers, S., & Ekelman, B. (1990) Fluency of conversational speech in children with unilateral brain lesions. *Brain and Language*, *38*, 105–121.

Aram, D.M., Rose, D.F., & Horowitz, S.J. (1984). Hyperlexia: Developmental reading without meaning. In R.N. Malatesha & H.A. Whitaker (Eds.), *Dyslexia: A global issue*. The Hague, The Netherlands: Martinus, Nijhoff.

Arnold, R., Yule, W., & Martin, N. (1985). The psychological characteristics of infant hypercalcaemia: A preliminary investigation. *Developmental Medicine and Child Neurology*, *27*, 49–59.

Ashby, H., & Stephenson, S. (1903). Acute amaurosis following infantile convulsions. *Lancet*, *1*, 1294–1296.

Ashcraft, M., & Fierman, B. (1982) Mental addition in third, fourth and sixth graders. *Journal of Experimental Child Psychology*, *33*, 216–234.

Ashcraft, M.H., Yamashita, T.S., & Aram, D.M. (1992). Mathematics performance in left and right brain-lesioned children. *Brain and Cognition 19*, 208–252.

Asperger, H. (1979) Problems of infantile autism. *Communication 13*, 45–52.

Asperger, H. (1991) Autistic psychopathies in childhood. In U. Frith (Ed. and trans.) *Autism and Asperger's Syndrome*. Cambridge, UK: Cambridge University Press. (Original work published 1944).

Auerbach, S.H., Allard, T., Naeser, M., Alexander, M.P., & Albert, M.L. (1982) Pure word deafness: An analysis of a case with bilateral lesions and a defect at the pre-phonemic level. *Brain*, *104*, 271–300

Ayala, G. (1929) Status epilepticus amauroticus. *Bolletino dell'Academia di Medicina di Roma*, *55*, 288–290.

Baddeley, A., & Hitch, G. (1974). Working Memory. In G.A. Bower (Ed.), *The psychology of learning and motivation*, (Vol. 8). New York. Academic Press.

Bailey, A., Le Couteur, A., Gottesman, I., Bolton, P., Simonoff, E., Yudzda, E., & Rutter, M. (1995). Autism as a strongly genetic disorder: Evidence from a British twin study. *Psychological Medicine*, *25*, 63–77.

Ballantyne, J., & Martin, J.A.M. (Eds.) (1984). *Deafness,* (4th ed). Edinburgh, UK: Churchill Livingstone.

Ballantyne, A.O., Scarvie, K.M., & Trauner, D.A. (1994). Verbal and performance IQ patterns in children after perinatal stroke. *Developmental Neuropsychology, 10*, 39–50.

Barkley, R.A. (1988). Attention. In M.G. Tramontana & S.R. Hooper (Eds.) , *Assessment issues in child neuropsychology.* (pp. 145–176). New York: Plenum.

Baron, J., & Strawson, C. (1976). Use of orthographic and word-specific knowledge in reading words aloud. *Journal of Experimental Psychology: Human Perception and Performance, 2*, 386–393.

Baron-Cohen, S. (1989). Are autistic children behaviourists? An examination of their mental–physical and appearance–reality distinctions. *Journal of Autism and Developmental Disorders, 19*, 579–600.

Baron-Cohen, S. (1992). Debate and argument: On modularity and development in autism: A reply to Burack. *Journal of Child Psychology and Psychiatry, 33*, 623–629.

Baron-Cohen, S., Cross, P., Crowson, M., & Robertson, M. (1994). Can children with Gilles de la Tourette syndrome edit their intentions? *Psychological Medicine, 24*, 29–40.

Baron-Cohen, S., Leslie, A.M., & Frith, U. (1985). Does the autistic child have a "theory of mind"? *Cognition, 21*, 37–46.

Barraga, N.C., & Morris, J.E. (1980). *Program to develop efficiency in visual functioning: Source book on low vision.* Louisville, KY: American Printing House for the Blind.

Bartak, L., Rutter, M., & Cox, A. (1975). A comparative study of infantile autism and specific developmental language disorder. *British Journal of Psychiatry, 126*, 127–145.

Bartlett, F.C. (1932). *Remembering: A study in experimental and social psychology.* Cambridge, UK: Cambridge University Press.

Bartolucci, G., Pierce, S. Streiner, D., & Epel, P. (1976). Phonological investigation of verbal autistic and mentally retarded subjects. *British Journal of Disorders of Communication, 12*, 137–147.

Bauer, R.M. (1984). Autonomic recognition of names and faces in prosopagnosia: A neuropsychological application of the guilty knowledge test. *Neuropsychologia, 22*, 457–469.

Beardsworth, E.D., & Zaidel. D.W. (1994). Memory for faces in epileptic children before and after brain surgery. *Journal of Clinical and Experimental Neuropsychology, 16*, 589–596.

Beauvois, M.F., Derouesne, J., & Bastard, V. (1980, June) *Auditory parallel to phonological alexia.* Paper presented at the third European conference of the International Neuropsychological Society, Chianciano, Italy.

Becker, M.G., Isaac, W., & Hynd, G. (1987). Neuropsychological development of non-verbal behaviours attributed to "frontal lobe" functioning. *Developmental Neuropsychology, 3*, 275–298.

Beishuizen, M. (1985). Evaluation of the use of structured materials in the teaching of primary mathematics. In B.S. Alloway & G.M. Mills (Eds.), *New directions in education and training technology: Aspects of educational technology.* (Vol 18). (pp. 246–258). London: Kogan Page.

Bellugi, U., Birle, A., Jernigan, T., Trauner, D., & Doherty, S. (1990). Neuropsychological, neurological and neuroanatomical profile of Williams Syndrome. *American Journal of Medical Genetics, 6*, 115–125.

Bellugi, U., Marks, S., Bihrle, A., & Sabo, H. (1988). Dissociation between language and cognitive functions in Williams syndrome. In D. Bishop & K. Mogford (Eds.), *Language development in exceptional circumstances*. Edinburgh, UK: Churchill Livingstone.

Bellugi, U., Sabo, H., & Vaid, J. (1988). Spatial deficits in children with Williams syndrome. In J. Stiles-Davis, M. Kritchevsky, & U. Bellugi (Eds.), *Spatial cognition: Brain bases and development*. Hillsdale, NJ: Lawrence Erlbaum Associates Inc.

Bender, B., Puck, M., Salbenblatt, J., & Robinson, A. (1984). Cognitive development of unselected girls with complete and partial X monosomy. *Paediatrics, 73*, 175–182.

Benson, D.F., & Geschwind, N. (1970). Developmental Gerstmann syndrome. *Neurology, 20*, 293.

Bentler, P.M. (1989). *EQS structural equations program manual*. Los Angeles: BMDP Statistical Software.

Benton, A.L. (1974). *Revised visual retention test*. New York: The Psychological Corporation.

Benton, A.L. (1977). Reflections on the Gerstmann syndrome. *Brain and Language, 4*, 45–62.

Benton, A.L. (1991). Prefrontal injury and behaviour in children. *Developmental Neuropsychology, 7*, 275–281.

Benton, A.L., Hamsher, K. des, Varney, N.R., & Spreen, O. (1983). *Contributions to neuropsychological assessment*. New York: Oxford University Press.

Benton, A.I., Varney, N.R., & Hamsher, K. des (1978). Visuospatial judgement: A clinical test. *Archives of Neurology, 35*, 364–367.

Berger, M., Yule, W,. & Rutter, M. (1975). Attainment and adjustment in two geographical areas: II The prevalence of specific reading retardation. *British Journal of Psychiatry, 126*, 510.

Berry, H.K., O'Grady, D.J., Perlmutter, L.J., & Bofinger, M.K. (1979). Intellectual development and academic achievement of children treated early for phenylketonuria. *Developmental Medicine and Child Neurology, 21*, 311–320.

Besner, D. (in press). Basic processes in reading: Multiple routines in localist and connectionist models. In P.A. McMullen & R.M. Klein (Eds.), *Converging methods for understanding reading and dyslexia*. Cambridge, MA: MIT Press.

Besner, D.E., Twilley, I., McCann, R.S., & Seergobin, K. (1990). On the connection between connectionism and data: Are a few words necessary? *Psychological Review, 97*, 432–446.

Bickel, H., Gerrad, J., & Hickmans, E.M. (1953). Influence of phenylalanine intake on phenlyketonuria. *Lancet, ii*, 812.

Bickel, H., Gerrad, J., & Hickmans, E.M. (1954). The influence of phenylalanine intake on the chemistry and behaviour of a phenylketonuric. *Acta Paediatrica Scandinavica, 43*, 64–77.

Biederman, I. (1985). Human image understanding. *Computer Vision, Graphics and Image Processing, 32*, 29–73.

Biegler, R., & Morris, R.G.M. (1993) Landmark stability is a prerequisite for spatial but not discrimination learning. *Nature, 361*, 631–633.

Bihrle, A.M., Bellugi, U., Delis, D., & Marks, S. (1989). Seeing either the forest or the trees: Dissociation in visuospatial processing. *Brain and Cognition, 11*, 37–49.

Binet, A. (1894). *Psychologie des Grands Calculateurs*. Paris: Alcan.

Bird, J., & Bishop, D.V.M. (1992). Perception and awareness of phonemes in phonologically impaired children. *European Journal of Disorders of Communication, 27*, 289–311.

Bisgaard, M.L., Eiberg, H., Moller, N., Niebuhr, E., & Mohr, J. (1987). Dyslexia and chromosome 15 heteromorphisms: Negative lod score in a Danish material. *Clinical Genetics, 32*, 118–119.

Bishop, D.V.M. (1982) Comprehension of spoken, written and signed sentences in childhood language disorders. *Journal of Child Psychology and Psychiatry, 23*, 1–20.

Bishop, D.V.M. (1983). Linguistic impairment after left hemidecortication for infantile hemiplegia? A reappraisal. *Quarterly Journal of Experimental Psychology, 35A*, 199–207.

Bishop, D.V.M. (1985). Age of onset and outcome in acquired aphasia with convulsive disorder (Landau–Kleffner Syndrome). *Developmental Medicine and Child Neurology, 27*, 705–712.

Bishop, D.V.M. (1988). Can the right hemisphere mediate language as well as the left? A critical review of recent research. *Cognitive Neuropsychology, 5*, 353–367.

Bishop, D.V.M. (1989). Autism, Asperger's syndrome and semantic-pragmatic disorder: Where are the boundaries? *British Journal of Disorders of Communication, 24*, 107–121.

Bishop, D.V.M. (1990). *Handedness and developmental disorder. Clinics in developmental medicine 110*. Oxford, UK: Blackwells.

Bishop, D.V.M. (1992). The underlying nature of specific language impairment. *Journal of Child Psychology and Psychiatry, 33*, 3–66.

Bishop, D.V.M. (1993). Annotation: Autism, executive functions and theory of mind: A neuropsychological perspective. *Journal of Child Psychology and Psychiatry, 3*, 279–293.

Bishop, D.V.M. (1994a). Developmental disorders of speech and language. In M. Rutter, E. Taylor, & L. Hersov (Eds.) *Child and adolescent psychiatry,* (3rd ed., pp. 546–568).Oxford, UK: Blackwell Scientific Publications.

Bishop, D.V.M. (1994b). Grammatical errors in specific language impairment: Competence of performance limitations? *Applied Psycholinguistics, 15*, 507–550.

Bishop, D.V.M., & Adams, C. (1989). Conversational characteristics of children with semantic-pragmatic disorder: II. What features lead to a judgement of inappropriacies? *British Journal of Disorders of Communication, 24*, 241–263.

Bishop, D.V.M., & Adams, C. (1990). A prospective study of the relationship between specific language impairment, phonological disorders and reading retardation. *Journal of Child Psychology and Psychiatry, 31*, 1027–1050.

Bishop, D.V.M., & Edmundson, A. (1986). Is otitis media a major cause of specific developmental language disorders? *British Journal of Disorders of Communication, 21*, 321–338.

Bishop, D.V.M., North, T. and Donlan, C. (1995) Genetic basis of specific language impairment: Evidence from a twin study. *Developmental Medicine and Child Neurology, 37*, 56–71.

Bishop, D.V.M., & Rosenbloom, L. (1987). Classification of childhood language disorders. In W. Yule & M. Rutter (Eds.) *Language development and disorders. Clinics in Developmental Medicine, 101/102.* London: MacKeith Press.

Bjorklund, D.F., & Muir, J.E. (1988). Children's development of free recall memory: Remembering on their own. In R. Vasta (Ed.), *Annals of child development.* (pp 79–123). New York: JAI Press.

Blank, M., Gessner, M., & Eposito, A. (1978). Language without communication: A case study. *Journal of Child Language, 6,* 329–352.

Bloodstein, O., & Gantwek, B. (1967). Grammatical function in relation to stuttering in young children. *Journal of Speech and Hearing Research, 10,* 786–789.

Bodamer, J. (1947) Die Prosopagnosie. *Archiv fur Psychiatrie und Nervenkrankheiten, 179,* 6–53.

Boder, E. (1973). Developmental dyslexia: A diagnostic approach based on three atypical reading–spelling patterns. *Developmental Medicine and Child Neurology, 15,* 663–687.

Boller, F., & Grafman, J. (1983). Acalculia: Historical developments and current significance. *Brain and Cognition, 2,* 205–223.

Bonnet, C. (1769). *Essai Analytique sur les Facultes de l'Ame* (Vol. 2). Copenhagen, Denmark/Geneva, Switzerland. Philibert.

Bookheimer, S.Y., Zeffiro, T.A., Blaxton, T., Gaillard, W., & Theodore, W. (1995). Regional cerebral blood flow during object naming and word reading. *Human Brain Mapping, 3,* 93–106.

Bornstein, R.A. (1990). Neuropsychological performance in children with Tourette syndrome. *Psychiatry Research, 33,* 73–81.

Bornstein, R.A. (1991). Neuropsychological performance in adults with Tourette syndrome. *Psychiatry Research, 37,* 229–236.

Bornstein, R.A., & Yang, V. (1991). Neuropsychological performance in medicated and unmedicated patients with Tourette disorder. *American Journal of Psychiatry, 148,* 468–471.

Boucher, J., & Lewis, V. (1992). Unfamiliar face recognition in relatively able autistic children. *Journal of Child Psychology and Psychiatry, 33,* 843–859.

Boucugnani, L.L., & Jones, R.W. (1989). Behaviours analogous to frontal lobe dysfunction in children with attention deficit hyperactivity disorder. *Archives of Clinical Neuropsychology, 4,* 161–173.

Bowers, P.G., & Wolf, M. (1993) Theoretical links among naming speed, precise timing mechanisms and orthographic skill in dyslexia. *Reading and Writing: An Interdisciplinary Journal, 5,* 69–85.

Braddick, O., Atkinson, J., Hood, B., Harkness, W., Jackson, G., & Vargha-Khadem, F. (1992). Possible blindsight in infants lacking one hemisphere. *Nature, 360,* 461–463.

Bradley, L. (1980). *Assessing reading difficulties: A diagnostic and remedial approach.* Basingstoke/London, UK: Macmillan Education.

Bradley, L. and Bryant, P. (1983). Categorising sounds and learning to read: A causal connection. *Nature, 301,* 419–421.

Brady, S., Mann, V., & Schmidt, R. (1987). Errors in short-term memory for good and poor readers. *Memory and Cognition, 15,* 444–453.

Brady, S., Shankweiler, D., & Mann, M. (1983). Speech perception and memory coding in relation to reading ability. *Journal of Experimental Child Psychology, 35,* 345–367.

Brainerd, C.J., & Reyna, V.F. (1992). Explaining "memory free" reasoning. *Psychological Science, 3*, 332–339.

Bramwell, B. (1984). Illustrative cases of aphasia. *Cognitive Neuropsychology, 1*, 245–258. Reprinted from *Lancet*, 1897 *1*, 1256–1259.

Brandes, P.J., & Ehinger, D.M. (1971). The effects of early middle ear pathology on auditory perception and academic achievement. *Journal of Speech and Hearing Disorders, 46*, 301–307.

Brennen, T., David, D., Fluchaire, I., & Pellat, J. (1996). Naming faces without comprehension: A case study. *Cognitive Neuropsychology, 13*, 93–110.

Broca, P. (1861). Remarques sur la siege de la faculte du langage articule suivies d'une observation d'aphemie (peste de la parole). *Bulletin Societe d'Anatomie, 6*, 330–337.

Brooks, N., & Baddeley, A. (1976). What can amnesic patients learn. *Neuropsychologia 14*, 111–122.

Brookshire, B., Butler, I.J., Ewing-Cobbs, L., & Fletcher, J.M. (1994). Neuropsychological characteristics of children with Tourette syndrome: Evidence for a nonverbal learning disability? *Journal of Clinical and Experimental Neuropsychology, 16*, 289–302.

Brown, I.S., & Felton, R.H. (1990) Effects of instruction on beginning reading skills in children at risk for reading disability. *Reading and Writing: An Interdisciplinary Journal, 2*, 223–241.

Brown, R. (1973). *A First Language*. Cambridge, MA: Harvard University Press.

Bruce, V., Cowey, A., Ellis, A. W., & Perrett, D. I., (Eds.) (1992). *Processing the Facial Image*. Oxford: Clarendon Press.

Bruce, V., & Young, A. (1986) Understanding face recognition. *British Journal of Psychology, 77*, 305–327.

Bruck, M. (1992). Persistence of dyslexics' phonological awareness deficits. *Developmental Psychology, 28*, 874–886.

Bruck, M., & Waters, G.S. (1988). An analysis of the spelling errors of children who differ in their reading and spelling skills. *Applied Psycholinguistics, 9*, 77–92.

Brun, A., & Skold, G. (1968). CNS malformation in Turner's syndrome. *Acta Neuropathologica, 10*, 159–161.

Brunner, R.L., Berch, D.B., & Berry, H. (1987). Phenylketonuria and complex spatial visualisation: An analysis of information processing. *Developmental Medicine and Child Neurology, 29*, 460–468.

Brunner, R.L., Jordan, M.K., & Berry, H.K. (1983). Early-treated phenylketonuria: Neuropsychologic consequences. *Journal of Paediatrics, 102*, 831–835.

Bryant, P., & Goswami, U. (1987). Development of phonemic awareness. In J. Beech & A. Colley (Eds.), *Cognitive approaches to reading*. Chichester, UK: Wiley.

Bryant, P., MacLean, M., Bradley, L., & Crossland, J. (1990). Rhyme, alliteration, phoneme detection and learning to read. *Developmental Psychology, 26*, 429–438.

Bub, D.N., Cancelliere, A., & Kertesz, A. (1985). Whole-word and analytic translation of spelling to sound in a non-semantic reader. In K.E. Patterson, J.C. Marshall, & M. Coltheart (Eds.), *Surface dyslexia.* (pp. 15–34). Hillsdale, NJ: Lawrence Erlbaum Associates Inc.

Buckley, F. (1971). Preliminary report on intelligence quotient scores of patients with Turner's Syndrome: A replication study. *British Journal of Psychiatry, 119,* 513–514.

Burden, V. (1992). Why are some "normal" readers such poor spellers? In C. Stirling & C. Robson (Eds.), *Psychology, spelling and education.* (pp. 200–213). Bristol, UK: Longdunn Press.

Burkhalter, A., Bernardo, K.L., & Charles, V. (1993). Development of local circuits in human visual cortex. *Journal of Neuroscience, 13,* 1916–1931.

Cabalska, B., Durzynska, N., Borzymonwska, J., Zorska, K., Kaslacz-Folga, A., & Bozkowa, K. (1977). Termination of dietary treatment in phenylketonuria. *European Journal of Pediatrics, 126,* 253–262.

Campbell, J., & Clark, J.M. (1988). An encoding complex view of cognitive 50 number processing: Comment on McCloskey, Sokol and Goodman (1986). *Journal of Experimental Psychology: General, 117,* 204–214.

Campbell, R. (1992). Face to face: Interpreting a case of developmental prosopagnosia. In R. Campbell (Ed.), *Mental lives: Case studies in cognition.* Oxford, UK: Basil Blackwell

Campbell, R., & Butterworth, B. (1985). Phonological dyslexia and dysgraphia and a highly literate subject: A developmental case with associated deficits of phonemic processing. *Quarterly Journal of Experimental Psychology, 37A,* 435–477.

Cantwell, D., Baker, I., & Rutter, M. (1978). A comparative study of infantile autism and specific developmental receptive language disorder: IV. Analysis of syntax and language function. *Journal of Child Psychology and Psychiatry, 19,* 351–362.

Caramazza, A. (1984). The logic of neuropsychological research and the problem of patient classification in aphasia. *Brain and Language, 21,* 9–20.

Caramazza, A., Berndt, R. & Basili, A. (1983) The selective impairment of phonological processing: A case study. *Brain and Language, 18,* 128–174.

Caramazza, A., & McCloskey, M. (1987). Dissociations of calculation processes. In G. Deloche & X. Seron (Eds.), *Mathematical disabilities: A cognitive neuropsychological perspective.* (pp. 221–234). Hillsdale, NJ: Lawrence Erlbaum Associates Inc.

Caramazza, A., Miceli, G., & Villa, G. (1986). The role of the (output) phonological buffer in reading, writing and repetition. *Cognitive Neuropsychology, 3,* 37–76.

Carey, S. (1978) A case study: Face recognition. In E. Walker (Ed.) *Explorations in the Biology of Language.* Montgomery, VT. Bradford Books.

Carey, S., & Diamond, R. (1977). From piecemeal to configurational representation of faces. *Science, 195,* 312–314.

Carey, S., Diamond, R., & Woods, B. (1980). Development of face recognition-maturational component? *Developmental Psychology, 16,* 257–269.

Carey, S., & Gelman, R.(Eds.) (1991). *The epigenesis of mind.* Hillsdale, NJ/Hove, UK: Lawrence Erlbaum Associates.

Carlson, J., Netley, C., Hendrick, E., & Pritchard, J. (1968). A reexamination of intellectual disabilities in hemispherectomized patients. *Transactions of the American Neurological Association, 93,* 198–201.

Carpentieri, S.C., & Mulhern, R.K. (1993). Patterns of memory dysfunction among children surviving temporal lobe tumours. *Archives of Clinical Neuropsychology, 8,* 345–357.

Castles, A., & Coltheart, M. (1993). Varieties of developmental dyslexia. *Cognition, 47*, 149–180.

Castles, A., & Coltheart, M. (1996). Cognitive correlates of developmental surface dyslexia: A single case study. *Cognitive Neuropsychology, 13*, 25–50.

Cavazzutti, V., Winston, K., Baker, R., & Welch, K. (1980). Psychological changes following surgery for tumours in the temporal lobes. *Journal of Neurosurgery, 53*, 618–626.

Chadwick, O., & Rutter, M. (1983). Neuropsychological assessment. In M. Rutter (Ed.), *Developmental neuropsychiatry.* (pp. 181–212). New York: Guildford Press.

Channon, S., Flynn, D., & Robertson, M.M. (1992). Attentional deficits in Gilles de la Tourette syndrome. *Neuropsychiatry, Neuropsychology and Behavioural Neurology, 5*, 170–177.

Chase, T.N., Foster, N.L., Fedio, P., Brooks, R., Mansi, L., Kessler, L., & Chiro, G.D. (1984) Gilles de la Tourette's Syndrome: Studies with the fluorine-18-labelled fluorodeoxyglucose positron emission tomographic method. *Annals of Neurology, 15*, 175.

Chase, T.N., Geoffrey, V., Gillespie, M., & Burrows, G. (1986). Structural and functional studies of Gilles de la Tourette syndrome. *Revue Neurologique (Paris) 142*, 851–855.

Chelune, G.T., & Baer, R.A. (1986). Developmental norms for the Wisconsin card sorting task. *Journal of Clinical and Experimental Neuropsychology, 8*, 219–228.

Chelune, G.L., Ferguson, W., Koon, R., & Dickey, T.O. (1986). Frontal lobe disinhibition in attention deficit disorder. *Child Psychiatry and Human Development, 16*, 221–234.

Chomsky, N. (1957). *Syntactic structures.* The Hague, The Netherlands: Mouton.

Chomsky, N. (1965). *Aspects of the theory of syntax.* Cambridge, MA: MIT Press.

Christensen, A.L., & Nielsen, J. (1981). A neuropsychological investigation of 17 women with Turner's syndrome. In W. Schmid & J. Nielsen (Eds.), *Human behaviour and genetics.* Amsterdam: North Holland/Elsevier.

Clahsen, H. (1989). The grammatical characterisation of developmental dysphasia. *Linguistics, 27*, 897–920.

Clahsen, H. (1991). *Child language and developmental dysphasia. Linguistic studies of the acquisition of German.* Amsterdam: Benjamins.

Clahsen, H. (1992). Linguistic perspectives on specific language impairment. *Arbeiten des SFB282 (Theorie des Lexikons), 37.*

Clahsen, H. (in press). Linguistic perspectives on specific language impairment. In W. Ritchie & T. Bahtie (eds.) *Handbook of Language Acquisition.* New York: Academic Press.

Clahsen, H., & Hansen, D. (1993). The missing agreement account of specific language impairment: Evidence from therapy experiments. *Essex Research Reports in Linguistics, 2*, 1–37.

Clahsen, H., & Hansen, D. (1996). The grammatical agreement deficit in specific language impairment: Evidence from therapy experiments. In M. Gopnik (ed.) *The biological foundations of language.* Oxford, UK: Oxford University Press

Clahsen, H., & Mohnhaus, B. (1987). Die profilanalyse — Einsatz moglichkeiten und erste Ergebnisse. In I. Fussenich & B. Glab (Eds.), *Dysgrammatismus*. (pp. 76–97). Heidelberg, Germany: Schindler.

Clahsen, H., Rothweiler, M., Woest, A., & Marcus, G. (1992). Regular and irregular inflection in the acquisition of German noun plurals. *Cognition, 45*, 225–255.

Claparede, E. (1911). Recognition et moite. *Archives de Psychologie, (Geneve), 11*, 79–90.

Clark, C., Klonoff, H., & Hayden, M. (1990). Regional cerebral glucose metabolism in Turner's syndrome. *Canadian Journal of Neurological Sciences, 17*, 140–144.

Clark, J., & Campbell, J. (1991). Integrated versus modular theories of number skills and acalculia. *Brain and Cognition, 17*, 204–239.

Clarke, A.M., & Clarke, A.D. (1974). Experimental studies: An overview. In A.M. Clarke & A.D. Clarke (Eds.), *Mental deficiency: The changing outlook*, (3rd ed.). New York: The Free Press.

Cohen, H. (1962). Psychological test findings in adolescents having ovarian dysgenesis. *Psychosomatic Medicine, 24*, 249–256.

Cohen, L., & Dehaene, S. (1991). Neglect dyslexia for numbers? A case report. *Cognitive Neuropsychology, 8*, 39–58.

Cohn, R. (1968). Developmental dyscalculia. *Paediatric Clinics of North America*, 15, 651–668.

Cole, A.J., Andermann, F., Taylor, L., Olivier, A., Rasmussen, T., Robitialle, Y., & Spire, J.P. (1988). The Landau–Kleffner syndrome of acquired epileptic aphasia: Unusual clinical outcome, surgical experience and absence of encephalitis. *Neurology, 38*, 31–38.

Cole, C.B., & Loftus, E.F. (1987). The memory of children. In S.J. Ceci, M.P. Toglia, & D.F. Ross (Eds.), *Children's eyewitness memory*. (pp. 178–208). New York: Springer Verlag.

Coltheart, M. (1978). Lexical access in simple reading tasks. In G. Underwood (Ed.) *Strategies of information processing*. London: Academic Press.

Coltheart, M., Besner, D., Jonasson, J.T., & Davelaar, E. (1979). Phonological recoding in the lexical decision task. *Quarterly Journal of Experimental Psychology, 31*, 489–508.

Coltheart, M., Curtis, B., Atkins, P., & Haller, M. (1993). Models of reading aloud: Dual-route and parallel-distributed processing approaches. *Psychological Review, 100*, 589–608.

Coltheart, M., & Funnell, E. (1987). Reading and writing: One lexicon or two? In D.A. Allport, D.G. MacKay, W. Prinz & E. Scheerer (eds.) *Language perception and production*. (pp. 313–339). London: Academic Press.

Coltheart, M., Masterson, J., Byng, S., Prior, M., & Riddoch, J. (1983). Surface dyslexia. *Quarterly Journal of Experimental Psychology, 35*, 469–496.

Coltheart, V., & Leahy, J. (1992). Children's and adults' reading of nonwords: Effects of regularity and consistency. *Journal of Experimental Psychology: Learning, Memory and Cognition, 18*, 718–729.

Comings, D.E. (1987). A controlled study of Tourette syndrome: VII Summary: A common genetic disorder causing disinhibition of the limbic system. *American Journal of Human Genetics, 41*, 839–866.

Cooper, H., & Cooper, P. (1983). *Heads or the art of phrenology*. London: Phrenology Company.

Copeland, D.R., Dowell, R.E., Fletcher, J.M., Sullivan, M.P., Jaffe, N., Cangir, A., Frankel, L.S., & Judd, B.W. (1988). Neuropsychological test performance of pediatric cancer patients at diagnosis and one year later. *Journal of Pediatric Psychology*, *16*, 475–470.

Cossu, G., & Marshall, J.C. (1986). Theoretical implications of the hyperlexic syndrome: Two new Italian cases. *Cortex*, *22*, 579–589.

Cossu, G. and Marshall, J.C. (1990). Are cognitive skills a prerequisite for learning to read and write? *Cognitive Neuropsychology*, *7*, 21–40.

Cossu, G., Rossini, F., & Marshall, J.C. (1993). When reading is acquired but phonemic awareness is not: A study of literacy in Down's syndrome. *Cognition*, *46*, 129–138.

Cousens, P., Ungerer, J.A, & Crawford, J.A. (1991). Cognitive effects of childhood leukemia therapy: A case for four specific deficits. *Journal of Pediatric Psychology*, *16*, 475–488.

Craft, S., White, D.A., Park, T.S., & Figiel, G. (1994). Visual attention in children with perinatal brain injury: Asymmetric effects of bilateral lesions. *Journal of Cognitive Neuroscience*, *6*, 165–173.

Craik, F.I.M., Morris, L.W., Morris, R.G., & Loewen, E.R. (1990). Relations between source amnesia and frontal lobe functioning in older adults. *Psychology and Aging*, *5*, 148–151.

Crary, M.A. (1984). A neurolinguistic perspective on developmental verbal dyspraxia. *Communicative Disorders*, *9*, 33–49.

Critchley, M. (1970). *The Dyslexic Child*. Springfield, Illinois, Thomas.

Cromer, R. (1981). Reconceptualising language acquisition and cognitive development. In R. Schiefelbusch & D. Brichner (Eds.) *Early language acquisition and intervention*. (pp. 51–138). Baltimore: University Park Press.

Crowie, V.A. (1971). Neurological and psychiatric aspects of phenylketonuria. In H. Bickel, F. Hudson, & L. Woolf (Eds.), *Phenylketonuria and some other inborn errors of amino acid metabolism*. (pp. 29–39). Stuttgaart, Germany: Verlag.

Curcio, F. and Paccia, J. (1987). Conversations with autistic children: Contingent relationships between features of adult input in children's response adequacy. *Journal of Autism and Developmental Disorders*, *17*, 81–93.

Damasio, A.R., & Damasio, H. (1986). The anatomical substrate of prosopagnosia. In R. Bruyer (Ed.), *The neuropsychology of face perception and facial expression*. Hillsdale, NJ: Lawrence Erlbaum Associates Inc.

Damasio, A.R., & Maurer, R.G. (1978). A neurological model for childhood autism. *Archives of Neurology*, *35*, 777–786.

Davies-Eysenck, M. (1952). Cognitive factors in epilepsy. *Journal of Neurology, Neurosurgery and Psychiatry*, *15*, 39–44.

De Gelder, B., Vroomen, J., & van der Heide, L. (1991). Face recognition and lip-reading in autism. *European Journal of Cognitive Psychology*, *3*, 69–86.

De Haan, E., & Campbell, R. (1991). A fifteen year follow-up of a case of developmental prosopagnosia. *Cortex*, *27*, 489–509.

De Haan, E., Young, A., & Newcombe, F. (1987). Faces interfere with name classification in a prosopagnosic patient. *Cortex*, *23*, 309–316.

De Haan, E., Young, A., & Newcombe, F. (1991). A dissociation between sense of familiarity and access to semantic information concerning familiar people. *European Journal of Cognitive Psychology*, *3*, 51–67.

Dejerine, J. (1892). Contribution a l'etude anatomopathologique et clinique des differentes varieties de decite verbale. *Compte Rendues des Seances de la Society de Bilogie, 4*, 61–90.

Dekker, R., Drenth, P.R.D., & Zaal, J.N. (1991). Results of the intelligence test for visually impaired children (ITVIC) *Journal of Visual Impairment and Blindness, 85*, 261–268.

Dekker, R., & Koole, F.D. (1992). Visually impaired children's visual characteristics and intelligence. *Developmental Medicine and Child Neurology, 34*, 123–133.

Delaney, R.C., Rosen, A.J., Mattson, R.H., & Novelly, R.A. (1980). Memory function in focal epilepsy: A comparison of non-surgical, unilateral temporal lobe and frontal lobe samples. *Cortex, 16*, 103–117.

Delis, D., Robertson, I., & Efron, R. (1986). Hemispheric specialisation of memory for visual hierarchical stimuli. *Neuropsychologia, 24*, 205–214.

Delis, D.C., Kiefner, J., & Fridlund, A. (1988). Visuo-spatial dysfunction following unilateral brain damage: Dissociations in hierarchical and hemispatial analysis. *Journal of Clinical and Experimental Neuropsychology, 10*, 421–431.

Deloche, G., & Seron, X. (1982a). From one to 1: An analysis of a transcoding process by means of neuropsychological data. *Cognition, 12*, 119–149.

Deloche, G., & Seron, X. (1982b). From three to 3: A differential analysis in transcoding quantities between patients with Broca's and Wernicke's aphasia. *Brain, 105*, 719–733.

Denckla, M., & Rudel, R.G. (1976). Rapid "automatized," naming (RAN): Dyslexia differentiated from other learning disabilities. *Neuropsychologia, 14*, 471–479.

Denckla, M.B. (1979). Childhood learning disabilities. In K.M. Heilman & E. Valenstein (Eds.), *Clinical Neuropsychology*. (pp. 535–573). New York/Oxford: Oxford University Press

Denckla, M.B., Rudel, R.G., & Broman, M. (1981). Tests that discriminate between dyslexic and other learning disabled boys. *Brain and Language, 13*, 118–129.

Denes, G., Balliello, S., Volterra, V., & Pellegrini, A. (1986). Oral and written language in a case of childhood phonemic deafness. *Brain and Language, 29*, 252–267.

Dennis, M. (1980). Capacity and strategy for syntactic comprehension after left or right hemidecortication. *Brain and Language, 10*, 287–317.

Dennis, M., Farrell, K., Hoffman, H., Hendrick, B., Becker, L., & Murphy, E. (1988). Recognition memory of item, associative and serial order information after temporal lobectomy for seizure disorder. *Neuropsychologia, 25*, 53–65.

Dennis, M., & Kohn, B. (1975). Comprehension of syntax in infantile hemiplegia after cerebral decortication: Left hemisphere superiority. *Brain and Language, 2*, 472–482.

Dennis, M., Lovett, M., & Weigel-Crump, C.A. (1981). Written language acquisition after left or right hemidecortication in infancy. *Brain and Language, 12*, 54–91.

Dennis, M., & Whitaker, H.A. (1976). Language acquisition following hemidecortication: Linguistic superiority of the left over the right hemisphere. *Brain and Language, 3*, 404–433.

Deonna, T., Peter, C., & Ziegler, A. (1989). Adult follow-up of the acquired aphasia epilepsy syndrome in childhood: Report of seven cases. *Neuropaediatrics, 20,* 132–138.

De Renzi, E. (1986). Current issues on prosopagnosia. In H.D. Ellis, M.A. Jeeves, F. Newcombe, & A.W. Young (Eds.), *Aspects of face processing.* (pp. 243–252). Dordrecht, The Netherlands: Martinus Nijhoff.

De Renzi, E., & Lucchelli, F. (1990). Developmental dysmnesia in a poor reader. *Brain, 113,* 1337–1345.

De Schonen, S., de Diaz, G., & Mathivet, E. (1986). Hemispheric asymmetry in face processing in infancy. In H.D. Ellis, M.A. Jeeves, F. Newcombe, & A. Young (Eds.), *Aspects of face processing.* (pp. 199–209). Dordrecht, The Netherlands: Nijhoff

De Schonen, S., & Mathivet, E. (1990). Hemispheric specialisation in face recognition in human infants. *Child Development, 61,* 112–158.

Diamond, A. (1994). Phenylalanine levels of 6–10mg/dl may not be a benign as once thought. *Acta Pediatrica, 407 (Supple.),* 89–91.

Diamond, R., & Carey, S. (1986). Why faces are and are not special. *Journal of Experimental Psychology: General, 115,* 107–117.

Dilts, C.V., Morris, C.A., & Leonard, C. (1990). Hypothesis for development of a behavioural phenotype in Williams syndrome. *American Journal of Medical Genetics Supplement, 6,* 126–131.

Dobie, R.A., & Berlin, C.I. (1979). Influence of otitis media on hearing and development. *Annals of Otology, Rhinology and Laryngology, 88,* 48–53.

Douglas, V.I. (1983). Attentional and cognitive problems. In M. Rutter (Ed.) *Developmental neuropsychiatry.* (pp. 280–329). New York: Guildford.

Downey, J., Elkin, E., Ehrhardt, A., Meyer-Bahlburg, H., Bell, J., & Morishima, A. (1991). Cognitive ability and everyday functioning in women with Turner syndrome. *Journal of Learning Disabilities, 24,* 32–39.

Downs, M.T. (1985). Effective mild hearing loss on auditory processing. *Otolaryngologic Clinics of North America, 18,* 337–344.

Duara, R., Kushch, A., Gross-Glenn, K., Barker, W.W., Jallad, B., Pascal, S., Lowenstein, D., Sheldon, J., Rabin, M., Levin, B., & Lubs, H. (1991). Neuroanatomic differences between dyslexic and normal readers on magnetic resonance imaging scans. *Archives of Neurology, 48,* 410–416.

Duffy, F.H., Denckla, M. Bartels, P., & Sandini, G. (1980). Dyslexia: Regional differences in brain electrical activity by topographical mapping. *Annals of Neurology, 7,* 412–420.

Duffy, F.H., & McAnulty, G.B. (1985). Brain electrical activity mapping (BEAM): The search for a physiological signature of dyslexia. In F.H. Duffy & N. Geschwind (Eds.), *Dyslexia: A neuroscientific approach to clinical evaluation.* Boston: Little, Brown and Co.

Dugas, M., Masson, M., Le Heuzey, M.F., & Regnier, N. (1982). Aphasie "acquise" de l'enfant avec epilepsie (syndrome de Landau et Kleffner): douze observations personelles. *Revue Neurologique, 138,* 755–780.

Duncan, J. (1995). Attention, intelligence and the frontal lobes. In M.S. Gazzaniga (Ed.), *the cognitive neurosciences.* (pp. 721–733). Cambridge, MA: The MIT Press.

Duncan, J., Burgess, P., & Emslie, H. (1995). Fluid intelligence after frontal lobe lesions. *Neuropsychologia, 33,* 261–268.

Dykman, R.A., Ackerman, P.T., Clements, S.D., & Peters, J.E. (1971). Specific learning disabilities: An attentional deficit syndrome. In H. Myklebust (Ed.), *Progress in learning disabilities*. (Vol II, pp. 56–93). New York: Grune & Stratton.

Eapen, V., Pauls, D.L., & Robertson, M.M. (1993). Evidence for autosomal dominant transmission in Gilles de la Tourette syndrome — United Kingdom cohort. *British Journal of Psychiatry, 162*, 593–596.

Eaves, L., Silberg, J., Hewitt, J.K., Meyer, J., Rutter, M., Sononoff, S., Neale, M., & Pickles, A. (1993). Genes, personality and psychopathology: A latent class analysis of heredity to symptoms of attention-deficit hyperactivity disorder in twins. In R. Plomin & G.E. McClearn (Eds.), *Nature, nurture and psychology*. Washington, DC: APA Books.

Edelman, G.M. (1987). *Neural Darwinism*. New York: Basic Books.

Ehri, L.C. (1980). The development of orthographic images. In U. Frith (Ed.), *Cognitive processes in spelling*. (pp. 311–338). San Diego, CA: Academic Press.

Ehri, L.C. (1984). How orthography alters spoken language competencies in children learning to read and spell. In J. Downing & R. Valtin (eds.) *Language awareness and learning to read* (pp. 119–147). New York: Springer-Verlad.

Ehri, L.C. (1987). Learning to read and spell words. *Journal of Reading Behaviour, 19*, 5–31.

Ehri, L.C. (1991). Development of the ability to read words. In R. Barr, M.L. Kamil, P.B. Mosenthal, & P.D. Pearson (Eds.), *Handbook of reading research*. (Vol. 2, pp. 383–417). New York: Longman

Ehri, L.C. (1992). Reconceptualizing the development of sight word reading and its relationship to recoding. In P.B. Gough, L.C. Ehri, & R. Trieman (Eds.), *Reading acquisition*. Hillsdale, New Jersey: Lawrence Erlbaum Associates Inc.

Eimas, P.D., & Clarkson, R.L. (1986). Speech perception in children: Are there effects of otitis media. In, J.F. Kavanagh (Eds.), *Otitis media and child development*. Parkton, Maryland: York Press,

Ekelman, B., & Aram, D. (1983). Syntactic findings in developmental verbal apraxia. *Journal of Communication Disorders, 16*, 237–250.

Ellis, A.W. (1984). *Reading, writing and dyslexia*. London: Lawrence Erlbaum Associates Ltd.

Ellis, A.W. (1985). The cognitive neuropsychology of developmental (and acquired) dyslexia: A critical survey. *Cognitive Neuropsychology, 2*, 169–206.

Ellis, A.W. (1987). On problems in developing culturally transmitted cognitive modules. *Mind and Language, 2*, 242–251.

Ellis, A.W., & Young, A.W. (1988a). *Human cognitive neuropsychology*. London: Lawrence Erlbaum Associates Ltd.

Ellis, H.D., (1986). Processes underlying face recognition. In R. Bruyer (Ed.), *The neuropsychology of face perception and facial expression*. Hillsdale, NJ: Lawrence Erlbaum Associates Inc.

Ellis, H.D. & Flynn, R.H. (1990). Encoding and storeage effects in 7-year-olds' and 10-year-olds' memory for faces. *British Journal of Developmental Psychology, 8*, 77–92.

Ellis, H.D., & Young. A.W. (1988b). Training in face-processing skills for a child with acquired prosopagnosia. *Developmental Prosopagnosia, 4*, 283–294.

Ellis, N.C. (1989). Reading development, dyslexia and phonological skills. *Irish Journal of Psychology, 10*, 551–567.

Ellis, N.C., & Large, B. (1988). The early stages of reading: A longitudinal study. *Applied Cognitive Psychology, 2*, 47–76.

Ellis, N.C., & Miles, T.R. (1981). A lexical encoding deficiency: I, Experimental evidence. In, G.T. Pavlidis & T.R. Miles (Eds.), *Dyslexia research and its applications.* (pp. 177–215). London: Wiley and Sons.

Enright, M.K., Rovee-Collier, C.K., Fagen, J.W. & Caniglia, K. (1983). The effects of distributed training on retention of operant conditioning in human infants. *Journal of Experimental Child Psychology, 36*, 209–225.

Epir, S., Renda, Y., & Baser, N. (1984). Cognitive and behavioural characteristics of children with idiopathic epilepsy in a low-income area of Ankara, Turkey. *Developmental Medicine and Child Neurology, 26*, 200–207.

Eslinger, P.J., Grattan, L.M., Damasio, H., & Damasio, A.R. (1992). Developmental consequences of childhood frontal lobe damage. *Archives of Neurology, 49*, 764–769.

Estes, W.K. (1988). Human learning and memory. In R.C. Atkinson, R.J. Hernstein, G. Lindzey, & R.D. Luce (Eds.), *Stevens handbook of experimental psychology: Vol. 2: Learning and cognition (2nd ed.).* New York: John Wiley and Sons.

Faglioni, P., Spinnler, H., & Vignolo, L.A. (1969). Contrasting behaviour of right and left hemisphere damaged patients on a discriminative and semantic test of auditory recognition. *Cortex, 5*, 366–389.

Fanconi, G., Girardet, P., Schlesinger, B., Butler, H., & Black, J. (1952), Chronische Hypercalcamie kombiniert mit Osteosklerose, Hyperazotamie, Minderwuchs und kongenital Missbildungen. *Helvetica Paediatrica Acta, 7*, 314–339.

Farah, M.J. (1984). The neurological basis of mental imagery: A componential analysis. *Cognition, 18*, 245–272.

Fedio, P., & Mirsky, A. (1969). Selective intellectual deficits in children with temporal lobe or centrencephalic epilepsy. *Neuropsychologia, 3*, 287–300.

Felton, R.H., Wood, F.B., Campbell, S.K., & Harter, M.R. (1987). Separate verbal memory and naming deficits in attention deficit disorder and reading disability. *Brain and Language, 31*, 171–184.

Ferro, J.M., Martins, I.P., & Tavora, L. (1984). Neglect in children. *Annals of Neurology, 15*, 281–284.

Ferro, J., & Botelho, M.A.S. (1980) Alexia for arithmetical signs: A cause of disturbed calculation. *Cortex, 16*, 175–180.

Ferry, P.C., Hall, S.M., & Hicks, J. (1975). "Dilapidated" speech: Developmental verbal dyspraxia. *Developmental Medicine and Child Neurology, 17*, 749.

Fischer, M., Barkley, R.A., Edelbrock, C.S., & Smallish, L. (1990). The adolescent outcome of hyperactive children diagnosed by research criteria: II. Academic, attentional and neuropsychological status. *Journal of Consulting and Clinical Psychology, 58*, 580–588.

Fisher, J.H. (1910). A case of congenital word blindness (inability to learn to read). *Transactions of the Ophthalmological Society, 30*, 216–225.

Flowers, D.L., Wood, F.B., & Naylor, C.E. (1991). Regional cerebral blood flow correlates of language processes in reading disability. *Archives of Neurology, 48*, 637–643.

Flynn, R.H. (1980). Age differences in children's memory for unfamiliar faces. *Developmental Psychology, 16*, 373–374.

Flynn, R.H. (1985). Development of face recognition: An encoding switch? *British Journal of Psychology, 76*, 123–134.

Fodor, J.A. (1983). *The modularity of mind*. Cambridge, MA: Bradford/MIT Press.

Folling, I. (1994). The discovery of phenlyketonuria. *Acta Pediatrica, 407* (Suppl., 4–10).

Folstein, S., & Rutter, M. (1977b). Infantile autism: A genetic study of twenty-one twin pairs. *Journal of Child Psychology and Psychiatry, 18,* 297–321.

Folstein, S., & Rutter, M. (1977b). Genetic influences and infantile autism. *Nature, 265,* 726–728.

Ford, C.E., Jones, K.W., Polani, P.E., De Almeida, J.C., & Briggs, J.H. (1959). A sex chromosomal anomaly in a case of gonadal dysgenesis (Turner's syndrome). *Lancet 2,* 711–713.

Foster, J.K., Eskes, G.A., & Stuss, D.T. (1994). The cognitive neuropsychology of attention: A frontal lobe perspective. *Cognitive Neuropsychology, 11,* 133–147.

Foster, K.I. (1979). Levels of processing and the structure of the language processor. In W.E. Cooper & E.C.T. Walker (Eds.), *Sentence processing: psycholinguistic studies presented to Merrill Garrett.* (pp. 27–85). Hillsdale, New Jersey: Lawrence Erlbaum Association Inc.

Fox, E. (1994). Grapheme–phoneme correspondence in dyslexic and matched control readers. *British Journal of Psychology, 85,* 41–53.

Frith, C., & Done, J. (1989). Experiences of alien hand control in schizophrenia reflect a disorder in the central monitoring of action. *Psychological Medicine, 19,* 359–363.

Frith, C.D., & Frith, U. (1991). Elective affinities in schizophrenia and childhood autism. In P. Bebbington (Ed.) *Social psychiatry: Theory, methodology and practice.* New Brunswick, NJ: Transactions.

Frith, U. (1985). Beneath the surface of developmental dyslexia. In K.E. Patterson, J.C. Marshall, & M. Coltheart (Eds.), *Surface Dyslexia.* (pp. 301–330). Hillsdale, New Jersey: Lawrence Erlbaum Associates Inc.

Frith, U. (1980). Unexpected spelling problems. In U. Frith (Ed.), *Cognitive processes in spelling.* (pp. 495–515). London: Academic Press.

Frith, U. (1991). *Autism and Asperger's syndrome.* Cambridge, UK: Cambridge University Press.

Fuster, J.M. (1989). *The prefrontal cortex: Anatomy, physiology and neuropsychology of the frontal lobe.* New York: Ravens Press.

Gainotti, G., Misserlie, P., & Tissot, T. (1972). Qualitative analysis of unilateral spatial neglect in relation to laterality of lesion. *Journal of Neurology, Neurosurgery and Psychiatry, 35,* 545–550.

Galaburda, A.M. (1985). Developmental dyslexia: A review of biological interactions. *Annals of Dyslexia, 35,* 21–33.

Galaburda, A.M. (1994). Developmental dyslexia and animal studies: At the interface between cognition and neurology. *Cognition, 50,* 133–149.

Galaburda, A.M., & Livingstone, M.S. (1993). Evidence for a magnocellular defect in developmental dyslexia. *Annals of the New York Academy of Sciences, 682,* 70–82.

Galaburda, A.M., Sherman, G.F., Rosen, G.D., Aboitiz, F., & Geschwind, N. (1985). Developmental dyslexia: Four consecutive cases with cortical anomalies. *Annals of Neurology, 18,* 222–233.

Gallup, G.G., & Suarez, S.D. (1986). Self-awareness and the emergence of mind in humans and other primates. In J.M. Suls & A. Greenwald (Eds.) *Psychological perspectives on the self.* (pp. 3–26). Hillsdale, NJ: Lawrence Erlbaum Associates Inc.

Garron, D.C. (1977). Intelligence among persons with Turner's syndrome. *Behavioural Genetics, 7*, 105–127.

Gathercole, S.E., & Baddeley, A.D. (1993). *Working memory and language.* Hillsdale, NJ/Hove, UK: Lawrence Erlbaum Associates.

Geary, D.C. (1990). A componential analysis of an early learning deficit in mathematics. *Journal of Experimental Child Psychology, 4*, 363–383.

Geary, D.C. (1993). Mathematical disabilities: Cognitive, neuropsychological and genetic components. *Psychological Bulletin, 114*, 345–362.

Geary, D.C., & Brown, S.C. (1991). Cognitive addition: Strategy choice and speed-of-processing differences in gifted, normal and mathematically disabled children. *Developmental Psychology, 27*, 398–406.

Geary, D.C., Brown, S.C., & Samaranayake, V.A. (1991). Cognitive addition: A short longitudinal study of strategy choice and speed-of-processing differences in normal and mathematically disabled children. *Developmental Psychology, 27*, 787–797.

Gelman, R. (1990). First principles organise attention to and learning about relevant data: Number and the animate–inanimate distinction as examples. *Cognitive Science, 14*, 79–106.

Gelman, R., & Gallistel, C.R. (1978). *The child's understanding of numbers.* Cambridge, Mass.: Harvard University Press.

Gelman, S.A., & Kremner, K.E. (1991). Understanding natural cause: Children's explanations of how objects and their properties originate. *Child Development, 62*, 396–414.

Gentry, J.R. (1982). An analysis of developmental spelling in GNYS AT WRK. *The Reading Teacher, 36*, 192–200.

George, M.S., Costa, D.C., Kouris, K., Ring, H.A., & Ell, P.J. (1992). Cerebral blood flow abnormalities in adults with infantile autism. *Journal of Nervous and Mental Disease, 180*, 413–417.

Gerard, C., Dugas, M., Valdois, S., Franc, S., & Lecendreux, M. (1993). Landau–Kleffner syndrome diagnosed after 9 years of age: Another Landau-Kleffner syndrome? *Aphasiology, 7*, 463–473.

Geschwind, N. (1974). Disorders of higher cortical function in children. In N. Geschwind (Ed.). *Selected Papers on Language and the Brain. Boston studies in the philosophy of science; (Vol. XVI).* Boston: Reidel.

Geschwind, N. (1975). The apraxias: Neural mechanisms of disorders of learned movement. *American Scientist, 63*, 188–195.

Geschwind, N., & Galaburda, A.M. (1985). Cerebral lateralisation: Biological mechanisms, associations and pathology. *Archives of Neurology, 42*, 428–521, 521–552, 634–654.

Giedd, J.N., Castellanos, F.X., Casey, B.J., Kozuch, P., King, A.C., Hamburger, S.D., & Rapoport, J.L (1994). Quantitative morphology of the corpus callosum in attention deficit hyperactivity disorder. *American Journal of Psychiatry, 151*, 665–669.

Gillberg, C., & Gillberg, C. (1989). Research note: Asperger syndrome: Some epidemiological considerations. *Journal of Child Psychology and Psychiatry, 30*, 631–638.

Gilles de la Tourette, G. (1885). Etude sur une affection nerveuse caracterisee par de l'incoordination motrice accompagnee d'echolalie et de copralalie. *Archives of Neurology, 9,* 19–42, 158–200.

Ginsberg, H. (1977). *Children's arithmetic: The learning process.* New York: D. Van Nostrand.

Glowinski, H. (1973). Cognitive deficits in temporal lobe epilepsy: An investigation of memory functioning. *Journal of Nervous and Mental Diseases, 157,* 129–137.

Glushko, R.J. (1979). The organisation and activation of orthographic knowledge in reading aloud. *Journal of Experimental Psychology: Human Perception and Performance, 5,* 674–691.

Goldberg, E. (1995). Rise and fall of modular orthodoxy. *Journal of Clinical and Experimental Neuropsychology, 17,* 193–208.

Goldberg, T.E., & Rothermel, R. (1984). Hyperlexic children reading. *Brain, 107,* 759–785.

Goodglass, H., & Kaplan, E. (1983). *The assessment of aphasia and related disorders,* (2nd ed.). Philadelphia: Lea & Febiger.

Gopnik, M. (1990a). Feature blindness: A case study. *Language Acquisition, 1,* 139–164.

Gopnik, M. (1990b). Feature-blind grammar and dysphasia. *Nature, 344,* 715.

Gopnik, M. (1992). When language is a problem. In R. Campbell (Ed.), *Mental lives: Case studies in cognition.* Oxford: Basil Blackwell

Gopnik, M., & Cragow, M. (1991). Familial aggregation of developmental language disorder. *Cognition, 39,* 1–50.

Gordon, N. (1968). Visual agnosia in childhood: VI. Preliminary communication. *Developmental Medicine and Child Neurology, 10,* 377–379.

Gordon, P., Luper, H., & Peterson, H. (1986). The effects of syntactic complexity on the occurrence of dysfluencies in 5 year old non-stutterers. *Journal of Fluency Disorders, 11,* 151.

Gorenstein, E.E., Mammato, C.A., & Sandy, J.M. (1989). Performance of inattentive-overactive children on selected measures of prefrontal-type function. *Journal of Clinical Psychology, 45,* 619–632.

Goswami, U. (1986). Children's use of analogy in learning to read: A developmental study. *Journal of Experimental Child Psychology, 42,* 73–83.

Goswami, U. (1991). Learning about spelling sequences: The role of onsets and rimes in analogies in reading. *Child Development, 62,* 1110–1123.

Goswami, U., & Bryant, P. (1990). *Phonological skills and learning to read.* London: Lawrence Erlbaum Associates Ltd.

Goulandris, N.K., & Snowling, M. (1991). Visual memory deficits: A plausible cause of developmental dyslexia? Evidence from a single case study. *Cognitive Neuropsychology, 8,* 127–154.

Goy, R.W., & McEwan, B.S. (1980). *Sexual differentiation of the brain.* Cambridge, MA: MIT Press.

Grafman, J., Passafiume, D., Faglioni, P., & Boller, F. (1982). Calculation disturbances in adults with focal hemispheric damage. *Cortex, 18,* 37–50.

Grant, D.A., & Berg, E.A. (1948). A behavioural analysis of degree of reinforcement and ease of shifting to new responses in Weigl-type card sorting problems. *Journal of Experimental Psychology, 38,* 404–411.

Grattan, L.M., & Eslinger, P.J. (1992). Long-term psychological consequences of childhood frontal lobe lesion in patient DT. *Brain and Cognition, 20,* 185–195.

Greco, C., Hayne, H., & Rovee-Collier, C. (1986). *Category acquisition by 3-month-old infants*. Paper presented at the meeting of the Eastern Psychological Association, New York. (Cited by Rovee-Collier, 1989).

Greco, C., Rovee-Collier, C., Hayne, H., Griesler, P., & Earley, L. (1986). Ontogeny of early event memory: 1. Forgetting and retrieval by 2- and 3-month olds. *Infant Behaviour and Development, 9,* 441–460.

Griffin, F.D., Clarke, J.T.R., & d'Entremont, D.M. (1980). Effect of dietary phenylalanine restriction on visual attention span in mentally retarded subjects with phenylketonuria. *Journal Canadien des Sciences Neurologiques, 128,* 127–131.

Griffiths, P. (1991). Word finding ability and design fluency in developmental dyslexia. *British Journal of Clinical Psychology, 30,* 47–60.

Griffiths, P., & Hunt, S. (1984). Specific spatial defect in a child with septo-optic dysplasia. *Developmental Medicine and Child Neurology, 26,* 395–400.

Grimm, H., & Weinert, S. (1990). Is the syntax development of dysphasic children deviant and why? New findings to an old question. *Journal of Speech and Hearing Research, 33,* 220–228.

Grodzinsky, G.M., & Diamond, R. (1992). Frontal lobe functioning in boys with attention-deficit hyperactivity disorder. *Developmental Neuropsychology, 8,* 427–445.

Groenveld, M., Pohl, K., Espezel, H., & Jan, J. (1994). The septum pellucidum and spatial ability of children with optic nerve hypoplasia. *Developmental Medicine and Child Neurology, 36,* 191–197.

Gross-Tsur, V., Manor, O., & Shalev, R.S. (1996). Developmental dyscalculia: Prevalence and demographic features. *Developmental Medicine and Child Neurology, 38,* 25–33.

Gupta, P.D., & Richardson, K. (1995). Theories of cognitive development. In V.L. Lee and P.D. Gupta (Eds.), *Children's cognitive and language development*. Milton Keynes, UK: Open University Press.

Guthrie, R. (1961). Blood screening for phenylketonuria. *Journal of the American Medical Association, 178,* 863.

Guthrie, R., & Susi, A. (1963). A simple phenylalanine method for detecting phenylketonuria in large populations of newborn infants. *Paediatrics, 32,* 338–343.

Guttler, F., & Lou, H. (1986). Dietary problems of phenylketonuria: Effect on CNS transmitters and their possible role in neuropsychological function. *Journal of Inherited Metabolic Disease, 9,* 169–177.

Hagram, J.O., Wood, F., Buchsbaum, M.S., Tallal, P., Flowers, L., & Katz, W. (1992). Cerebral brain metabolism in adult dyslexic subjects assessed with positron emission tomography during performance of an auditory task. *Archives of Neurology, 49,* 734–739.

Hall, J., Wilson, K., Humphreys, M., Tinzman, M., & Bowyer, P. (1983). Phonemic similarity effects in good vs. poor readers. *Memory and Cognition, 11,* 520–527.

Hall, M., Costa, D.C., Shields, J., Heavens, J., Robertson, M., & Ell, P.J. (1990). Brain perfusion patterns with Te99HMPAO/SPECT in patients with Gilles de la Tourette syndrome. *European Journal of Nuclear Medicine, 16,* 56.

Hallgren, B. (1950). Specific Dyslexia ("congenital word blindness"): A clinical and genetic study. *Acta Psychiatrica et Neurologica Scandinavica, 65 (Supp.).*

Halligan, P.W., & Marshall, J.C. (1994). Toward a principled explanation of unilateral neglect. *Cognitive Neuropsychology, 11,* 167–206.

Hamlett, K.W., Pellegrini, D.S., & Conners, C.K. (1987). An investigation of executive processes in the problem-solving of attention deficit disorder-hyperactive children. *Journal of Pediatric Psychology, 12,* 227–240.

Hanley, J.R., Hastie, K., & Kay, J. (1992). Developmental surface dyslexia and dysgraphia: An orthographic processing impairment. *Quarterly Journal of Experimental Psychology, 44,* 285–319.

Harlow, J.M. (1868). Recovery after severe injury to the head. *Publications of the Massachusetts Medical Society, 2,* 327–346.

Harris, D.B. (1963). *Children's drawings as measures of intellectual maturity: A revision and extension of the Goodenough draw-a-man-test.* New York: Harcourt, Brace and World.

Harris, J.C. (1995). *Developmental Neuropsychiatry.* Oxford, UK: Oxford University Press.

Harris, P., Donnelly, K., Guz, G., & Pitt-Watson, R. (1986). Children's understanding of the distinction between real and apparent emotion. *Child Development, 57,* 895–909.

Harris, W. (1897). Hemianopsia with special reference to its transient varieties. *Brain, 20,* 308–364.

Hatcher, P.J., Hulme, C., & Ellis, A.W. (1994). Ameliorating early reading failure by integrating the teaching of reading and phonological skills: The phonological linkage hypothesis. *Child Development, 65,* 41–57.

Hatfield, F.M., & Patterson, K.E. (1983). Phonological spelling. *Quarterly Journal of Experimental Psychology, 35,* 451–468.

Hayne, H., & Rovee-Collier. C. (1985). *Contextual determinants of reactivated memories in infants.* Paper presented at the meeting of the Society for Research in Child Development, Toronto. (Cited by Rovee-Collier, 1989).

Haynes, C., & Naidoo, S. (1991). *Children with specific speech and language impairment. Clinics in Developmental Medicine, 119.* Oxford: Blackwell Scientific Publications.

Healy, J.M., Aram, D.M., Horowitz, S.J., & Kessler, J.W. (1982). A study of hyperlexia. *Brain and Language, 17,* 1–23.

Heaton, R.K. (1981). *Wisconsin card sorting test manual.* Odyssa, FL: Psychological Assessment Resources Inc.

Hecaen, H., Angelergues, R., & Houillier, S. (1961). Les varieties cliniques des acalculies au cours lesions retrolandiques: Approche statistique du probleme. *Revue Neurologique, 105,* 85–103.

Heller, W., & Levine, S.C. (1989). Unilateral neglect after early brain damage. *Journal of Clinical and Experimental Neuropsychology, 11,* 79.

Hermann, B., Seidenberg, M., Haltiner, A., & Wyler, A.R. (1992). Adequacy of language function and verbal memory performance in unilateral temporal lobe epilepsy. *Cortex, 28,* 423–433.

Heron, W., Doane, B.K., & Scott, T.H. (1956). Visual disturbances after prolonged perceptual isolation. *Canadian Journal of Psychology, 10,* 13–18.

Herskowitz, J., & Rosman, N.P. (1982). *Pediatrics, neurology and psychiatry — common ground: Behavioural, cognitive, affective and physical disorders in childhood and adolescence.* New York: Macmillan.

Hess, R.F., & Anderson, S.J. (1993). Motion sensitivity and spatial undersampling in amblyopia. *Vision Research, 33,* 3541–3548.

Hinshelwood, J. (1900b). Congenital word-blindness. *Lancet, 1,* 1506–1508.

Hinshelwood, J. (1900a). *Letter, word and mind-blindness*. London: H.K. Lewis.

Hinshelwood, J. (1902). Congenital word blindness, with reports of two cases. *Opthalmology Review, 21,* 91–97.

Hinshelwood, J. (1917). *Congenital word-blindness*. London: H.K. Lewis.

Hobson, R., Ouston, J., & Lee, A. (1988). Emotion recognition in autism: Coordinating faces and voices. *Psychological Medicine, 18,* 911–923.

Hobson, R.P. (1986a). The autistic child's appraisal of emotion. *Journal of Child Psychology and Psychiatry, 27,* 321–342.

Hobson, R.P. (1986b). The autistic child's appraisal of expressions of emotion: A further study. *Journal of Child Psychology and Psychiatry, 27,* 671–680.

Hobson, R.P. (1989). Beyond cognition: Theory of autism. In G. Dawson (Ed.), *Autism: New perspectives on diagnosis, nature and treatment.* (pp. 22–48). New York: Guildford.

Hobson, R.P. (1993). *Autism and the development of mind.* Hillsdale, NJ: Lawrence Erlbaum Associates Inc.

Hodges, J.R., Patterson, K.E., Oxbury, S., & Funnell, E. (1992). Semantic dementia: Progressive fluent aphasia with temporal lobe atrophy. *Brain, 115,* 1783–1806.

Hodges, J.R., & Ward, C.D. (1989). Observations during transient global amnesia: A behavioural and neuropsychological study of five cases. *Brain, 112,* 595–620.

Holligan, C., & Johnston, R.S. (1988). The use of phonological information by good and poor readers in memory and reading tasks. *Memory and Cognition, 16,* 522–542.

Holmes, G.L., McKeever, M., & Saunders, Z. (1981). Epileptiform activity in aphasia of childhood: An epiphenomenon? *Epilepsia, 22,* 631–639.

Holmes, J. (1973). *Dyslexia: A neurolinguistic study of traumatic and developmental disorders of reading.* Unpublished PhD thesis, University of Edinburgh, UK.

Holtzman, N.A., Kronmall, R.A., Van Doorninck, W., Azen, C., & Koch, R. (1986). Effect of age at loss of dietary control on intellectual performance and behaviour of children with phenylketonuria. *New England Journal of Medicine, 314,* 593–598.

Hopkins, J., Perlman, T., Hechtman, L., & Weiss, G. (1979). Cognitive style in adults originally diagnosed as hyperactive. *Journal of Child Psychology and Psychiatry, 20,* 209–216.

Howe, M.L., & Brainerd, C. (1989). Development of children's long-term retention. *Developmental Review, 9,* 301–340.

Hudson, J., & Nelson, K. (1986). Repeated encounters of a similar kind: Effects of familiarity on children's autobiographic memory. *Cognitive Development, 1,* 253–271.

Hughes, C., & Russell, J. (1993). Autistic children's difficulty with mental disengagement from an object: Its implications for theories of autism. *Developmental Psychology, 29,* 498–510.

Hulme, C. (1981). *Reading retardation and multi-sensory teaching.* London: Routledge & Kegan Paul.

Hulme, C. (1987). Reading retardation. In J. Beech & A. Colley (Eds.), *Cognitive approaches to reading.* Chichester: Wiley.

Hulme, C. (1988). The implausibility of low-level visual deficits as a cause of children's reading difficulties. *Cognitive Neuropsychology, 5,* 369–374.

Hulme, C., Maughan, S., & Brown, G.D.A. (1991). Memory for familiar and unfamiliar words: Evidence for a long-term contribution to short-term memory span. *Journal of Memory and Language, 30,* 685–701.

Hulme, C., & Snowling, M. (1992). Deficits in output phonology: An explanation of reading failure. *Cognitive Neuropsychology, 9,* 47–72.

Humphreys, G.W., & Riddoch, M.J. (Eds.) (1987). *Visual object processing: A cognitive neuropsychological approach.* Hillsdale, NJ/Hove, UK: Lawrence Erlbaum Associates.

Hunkin, N.M., Parkin, A.J., & Longmore, B.E. (1994). Aetiological variation in the amnesic syndrome: Comparisons using the list discrimination task. *Neuropsychologia, 32,* 819–825.

Hurst, J.A., Baraitser, M., Auger, E., Graham, F., & Norell, S. (1990). An extended family with a dominantly inherited speech disorder. *Developmental Medicine and Child Neurology, 32,* 352–355.

Hyde, T.M., Aaronson, B.A., Randolph, C., Rickler, K.C., & Weinberger, D.R. (1992). Relationship of birthweight to the phenotypic expression of Gilles de la Tourette syndrome in monozygotic twins. *Neurology, 42,* 652–658.

Hynd, G., Hall, J., Novey, E., Eliopulos, D., Black, K., Gonzalez, J.J., Edmonds, J.E., Riccio, C., & Cohen, M. (1995). Dyslexia and corpus callosum morphology. *Archives of Neurology, 52,* 32–38.

Hynd, G., Semrud-Clikeman, M., Lorys, A., Novey, E., & Epiopulos, R. (1990). Brain morphology in developmental dyslexia and attention deficit disorder/hyperactivity. *Archives of Neurology, 47,* 919–926.

Itard, J.M.G. (1825). Memoire sur quelques fonctions involontaires des appareils de la locomotion de la prehension et de la voix. *Archives of General Medicine, 8,* 385–407.

Jacobs, P.A., Betts, P.R., Cockwell, A.E., Crolla, J.A., Mackenzie, M.J., Robinson, D.O., & Youings, S.A. (1990). A cytogenetic and molecular reappraisal of a series of patients with Turner's syndrome. *Annals of Human Genetics, 54,* 209–223.

Jacobs, R.A., & Jordan, M.I. (1992). Computational consequences of a bias toward short connections. *Journal of Cognitive Neuroscience, 4,* 323–336.

Jadrisec, D. (1992). The role of the amygdaloid complex in Gilles de la Tourette's Syndrome. *British Journal of Psychiatry, 161,* 532–534.

Jeeves, M.A., & Temple, C.M. (1987). A further study of language function in callosal agenesis — A reply to Dennis. *Brain and Language, 32,* 325–335.

Jenkins, W.M., Merzenich, M.M., & Recanzone, G. (1990). Neocortical representational dynamics in adult primates: Implications for neuropsychology. *Neuropsychologia, 28,* 573–584.

Jerger, F., Jerger, J., Alford, B.R., & Abrams, S. (1983). Development of speech intelligibility in children with recurrent otitis media. *Ear and Hearing, 4,* 138–145.

Jernigan, T., & Bellugi, U. (1990). Anomalous brain morphology on magnetic resonance images in Williams syndrome and Down syndrome. *Archives of Neurology, 47,* 529–533.

Johnson, M., & Morton, J. (1991). *Biology and cognitive development.* Oxford, UK: Blackwells.

Johnston, C.W., & Shapiro, E. (1986). Hemi-inattention resulting from left hemisphere brain damage during infancy. *Cortex, 22,* 279–287.

Johnston, R.S. (1982). Phonological coding in dyslexic readers. *British Journal of Psychology, 73,* 455-460.

Johnston, R.S. (1983). Developmental deep dyslexia? *Cortex, 19,* 133–140.

Kanner, L. (1943). Autistic disturbance of affective contact. *The Nervous Child, 2,* 217–250.

Karmiloff-Smith, A. (1992). *Beyond modularity: A developmental perspective on cognitive science.* Cambridge, MA: MIT/Bradford.

Karmiloff-Smith, A., Klima. E., Bellugi, U., Grant, J., & Baron-Cohen, S. (1995). Is there a social module? Language, face processing and theory of mind in individuals with Williams syndrome. *Journal of Cognitive Neuroscience, 7,* 196–208.

Kataria, S., Goldstein, D., & Kushnick, T. (1984). Developmental delays in Williams ("elfin faces") syndrome. *Applied Research in Mental Retardation, 5,* 419–423.

Kates, M., & Moscovitch, M. (1989). *Development of frontal-lobe functioning in children.* Unpublished manuscript (cited by Smith et al., 1992).

Katz, R.B., & Shankweiler, D. (1985). Repetitive naming and the detection of word retrieval deficits in the beginning reader. *Cortex, 21,* 617–625.

Kaushall, P.J., Zetin, M., & Squire, L.R. (1981). Amnesia: Detailed report of a noted case. *Journal of Nervous and Mental Diseases 169,* 383–389.

Kerr, J. (1887). School hygiene, its mental, moral and physical aspects. *Journal of the Royal Statistical Society, 10,* 613–680.

Kertesz, A., Nicholson, I., Cancelliere, A., Kassa, K., & Black, S.E. (1985). Motor impersistence: A right hemisphere syndrome. *Neurology, 34,* 662–666.

Kidd, K. (1980). Genetic models of stuttering. *Journal of Fluency Disorders, 5,* 187–201.

Kimura, D., & McGlone, J. (1979). Children's stories for testing LTM. In D. Kimura & J. McGlone (Eds.), *Neuropsychological test manual.* London/Ontario, Canada: D.K. Consultants.

Kinsbourne, M., & Warrington, E.K. (1963). The developmental Gerstmann syndrome. *Archives of Neurology, 8,* 490.

Klein, R., & Harper, J. (1956). The problem of agnosia in the light of a case of pure word deafness. *Journal of Mental Science, 102,* 112–120.

Klein, S.K., & Rapin, I. (1988). Intermittent conductive hearing loss and language development. In D. Bishop & K. Mogford (Eds.), *Language development in exceptional circumstances.* Edinburgh, UK: Churchill Livingstone.

Kleinman, S.N., & Waber, D.P. (1994). Prose memory strategies of children treated for leukemia: A story grammar analysis of the Anna Thompson passage. *Neuropsychology, 10,* 464–470.

Kolb, J.E., & Heaton, R.K. (1975). Lateralised neurologic deficits and psychopathology in a Turner's syndrome patient. *Archives of General Psychiatry, 32,* 1198–2000.

Korsakoff, S.S. (1887). Disturbance of psychic function in alcoholic paralysis and its relation to the disturbance of the psychic sphere of multiple neuritis of non-alcoholic origin. *Vestnik Psichiatrii, 4,* 2.

Kosc, L. (1970). Psychology and psychopathology of mathematical abilities. *Studies of Psychology, 12,* 159–162.

Kosc, L. (1974). Developmental dyscalculia. *Journal of Learning Disabilities, 7,* 164–177.

Kosc, L. (1979). To the problems of diagnosing disorders of mathematical functions in children. *Studies in Psychology, 21,* 62–67.

Kosc, L. (1981). Neuropsychological implications of diagnosis and treatment of mathematical learning disabilities. 19–30.

Kosnik, E., Paulson, G.W., & Laguna, J.F. (1976). Postictal blindness. *Neurology*, *26*, 248–250.

Kracke, I. (1994). Developmental prosopagnosia in Asperger syndrome: Presentation and discussion of an individual case. *Developmental Medicine and Child Neurology*, *36*, 873–886.

Krause, W., Halminski, M., McDonald, L., Debmure, P., Salvo, R., Freides, D., & Elsas, L. (1985). Biochemical and neuropsychological effects of elevated plasma phenylalanine in patients with treated phenylketonuria. *Journal of Clinical Investigations*, *75*, 40–48.

Kucera, H., & Francis, W.N. (1967). *Computational analysis of present-day American English*. Providence RI: Brown University Press.

Kushch, A., Gross-Glenn, K., Jallad, B., Lubs, H., Rabin, M., Feldman, E., & Duara, R. (1993). Temporal lobe surface area measurements on MRI in normal and dyslexic readers. *Neuropsychologia*, *31*, 811–821.

Kussmaul, D. (1877). Disturbances of speech. *Zeimssen's Cyclopaedia*, *14*.

Lahood, B. (1981). Cognitive functioning and spatial ability in adolescent Turner's syndrome patients. Unpublished dissertation. Ann Arbor, MI: University Microfilm International.

Lahood, B.J., & Bacon, G.E. (1985). Cognitive abilities of adolescent Turner's syndrome patients. *Journal of Adolescent Health Care*, *6*, 358–364.

Lamb, M.R., & Robertson, L.C. (1989). Do response time advantage and interference reflect the order of processing of global and local information? *Perception and Psychophysics*, *46*, 254–258.

Landau, B. (1991). Spatial representation of objects in the young blind child. *Cognition*, *38*, 145–178.

Landau, B., & Gleitman, L.R. (1985). *Language and experience: Evidence from the blind child*. Cambridge, MA: Harvard University Press.

Landau, B., Spelke, E., & Gleitman, H. (1984). Spatial knowledge in a young blind child. *Cognition*, *16*, 225–260.

Landau, W. (1992). Landau–Kleffner syndrome: An eponymic badge of ignorance. *Archives of Neurology*, *49*, 353.

Landau, W., & Kleffner, F. (1957). Syndrome of acquired aphasia with convulsive disorder in children. *Neurology*, *7*, 523–530.

Langdell, T. (1978). Recognition of faces: An approach to the study of autism. *Journal of Child Psychology and Psychiatry*, *19*, 255–268.

Lansdell, H. (1968). Effect and extent of temporal lobe ablation on two lateralised deficits. *Physiology and Behaviour*, *3*, 271–273.

Larsen, J.P., Hien, T., Lundberg, I., & Odegaard, H. (1990). MRI evaluation of the size and symmetry of the planum temporale in adolescents with developmental dyslexia. *Brain and Language*, *39*, 289–301.

Larsen, J.P., Hoein, T., & Odegaard, H. (1992). Magnetic resonance imaging of the corpus callosum in developmental dyslexia. *Cognitive Neuropsychology*, *9*, 123–134

Lassonde, M., Sauerwein, H.C., & Lepore, F. (1995). Extent and limits of callosal plasticity: Presence of disconnection symptoms in callosal agenesis. *Neuropsychologia*, *33*, 989–1008.

Leckman, J., Knorr, A., Rassmusson, A., & Cohen, D. (1991). Basal ganglia research and Tourette's syndrome. *Trends in Neuroscience*, *14*, 94.

Leng, N.R.C., & Parkin, A.J. (1989). Aetiological variation in the amnesic syndrome: Comparisons using the Brown–Peterson task. *Cortex, 25,* 251–259.

Lenneberg, E.H. (1967). *Biological foundations of language.* New York: John Wiley.

Leonard, C.M., Voeller, K., Lombardino, L.J., Morris, M.K., Hynd, G.W., Alexander, A.W., Andersen, H.G., Garofalakis, M., Honeyman, J.C., Mao, J., Agee, F., & Staab, E.V. (1993). Anomalous cerebral structure in dyslexia revealed with magnetic resonance imaging. *Archives of Neurology, 50,* 461–469.

Leonard, L.B. (1989). Language learnability and specific language impairment in children. *Applied Psycholinguistics, 10,* 179–202.

Leonard, L., Bertolini, U., Caselli, M., McGregor, K., & Sabbadini, L. (1992). Two accounts of morphological deficits in children with specific language impairment. *Language Acquisition, 2,* 151–179.

Leonard, L.B., Sabbadini, I., Leonard, J.S., & Volterra, V (1987). Specific language impairment in children: A cross-linguistic study. *Brain and Language, 32,* 233–252.

Lepore, F.E. (1990). Spontaneous visual phenomena with visual loss: 104 patients with lesions of the retinal and neural afferent pathways. *Neurology, 40,* 444–447.

Leslie, A.M. (1987). Pretence and representation: The origins of "theory of mind." *Psychological Review, 94,* 412–426.

Leslie, A.M., & Frith, U. (1988). Autistic children's understanding of seeing, knowing and believing. *British Journal of Developmental Psychology, 6,* 315–324.

Levin, H.S., Culhane, K.A., Hartmann, J., Evankovich, K., Mattson, A.J., Harward, H., Ringholz, G., Ewing-Cobbs, L., & Fletcher, J.M. (1991). Developmental changes in performance on tests of purported frontal lobe functioning. *Developmental Neuropsychology, 7,* 377–395.

Levinson, E., & Sekuler, R. (1975). The independence of channels in human vision selective for direction of motion. *Journal of Physiology, 150,* 347–366.

Lewandowski, L., Costenbader, V., & Richman, R. (1985). Neuropsychological aspects of Turner's syndrome. *International Journal of Clinical Neuropsychology, 7,* 144–147.

Lewis, B.A., Ekelman, B.L., & Aram, D.M. (1989). A family study of severe phonological disorders. *Journal of Speech and Hearing Research, 32,* 713–724.

Lewis, C., Hitch, G., & Walker, P. (1994). The prevalence of specific arithmetic difficulties and specific reading difficulties in 9- to 10-year-old boys and girls. *Journal of Child Psychology and Psychiatry, 35,* 283–292.

Lewis, S.W. (1989). Congenital risk factors for schizophrenia. *Psychological Medicine, 19,* 5–13.

Liben, I.S. (1981). Copying and reproducing pictures in relation to subject's operative levels. *Developmental Psychology, 17,* 357–365.

Liberman, I.Y., Mann, V., Shankweiler, D., & Werfelman, M. (1982). Children's memory for recurring linguistic and nonlinguistic material in relation to reading ability. *Cortex, 18,* 367–375.

Liberman, I.Y., Shankweiler, D., Liberman, A.M., Fowler, C., & Fischer, F.W. (1977). Phonetic segmentation and recoding in the beginning reader. In A.S. Reber & D.L. Scarborough (Eds.), *Towards a psychology of reading: The proceedings of the CUNY conference*. Hillsdale, NJ: Lawrence Erlbaum Associates Inc.

Lindner, K., & Johnston, J.R. (1992). Grammatical morphology in language-impaired children acquiring English or German as their first language — A function perspective. *Applied Psycholinguistics, 13*, 115–129.

Loge, D.V., Stanton, D., & Beatty, W.W. (1990). Performance of children with ADHD on tests sensitive to frontal lobe dysfunction. *Journal of the American Academy of Child and Adolescent Psychiatry, 29*, 540–545.

Loiseau, P., Strube, E., & Signoret, J-L. (1988). Memory and epilepsy. In M.R. Trimble & E.H. Reynolds (Eds.), *Epilepsy, behaviour and cognitive function*. Wiley: Stratford-upon-Avon.

Lopez-Rangel, E., Maurice, B., McGillivray, B., & Friedman, J. (1992). Williams syndrome in adults. *American Journal of Medical Genetics, 44*, 720–729.

Lou, H.C., Brandt, S., & Bruhn, P. (1977). Aphasia and epilepsy in childhood. *Acta Neurologica Scandinavica, 56*, 46–54.

Lou, H.C., Henriksen, L., & Bruhn, P. (1984). Focal cerebral hypoperfusion in children with dysphasia and/or attention deficit disorder. *Archives of Neurology, 41*, 825–829.

Lovegrove, W., Martin, F., & Slaghuis, W. (1986). A theoretical and experimental case for a visual deficit in specific reading disability. *Cognitive Neuropsychology, 2*, 225–267.

Lovett, M.W., Dennis, M., & Newman, J.E. (1986). Making reference: The cohesive use of pronouns in the narrative discourse of hemidecorticate adolescents. *Brain and Language, 29*, 224–251.

Low, A.A. (1931). A case of agrammatism in the English language. *Archive of Neurology and Psychiatry, 25*, 556–597.

Ludwig, B.I., & Marsan, C.A. (1975). Clinical ictal patterns in epileptic patients with occipital electroencephalographic foci. *Neurology, 25*, 463–471.

Luria, A. (1966). *The higher cortical functions of man*. New York: Basic Books.

Luria, A.R. (1973). *The working brain*. London: Allen Lane, Penguin.

Macaluso-Haynes, S. (1985). Developmental apraxia of speech: Symptoms and treatment. In D.F. Johns (Ed.) *Clinical management of neurogenic communicative disorders*. Boston: Little Brown & Co.

Mackintosh, N.J. (1983). *Conditioning and associative learning. Oxford Psychology Series, No 3*. Oxford, UK: Clarendon Press.

Mancini, J., de Schonen, S., Deruelle, C., & Massoulier, A. (1994). Face recognition in children with early right or left brain damage. *Developmental Medicine and Child Neurology, 36*, 156–166.

Mandler, J.M., & Bauer, P.J. (1988). The cradle of categorisation: Is the basic level basic? *Cognitive Development, 3*, 247–264.

Mann, V.A. (1986). Phonological awareness: The role of reading experience. *Cognition, 24*, 65–92.

Mann, V.A., Liberman, I.Y., & Shankweiler, D. (1980). Reading disability: Methodological problems in information processing analysis. *Science, 200*, 801–802.

Marcel, T. (1980). Surface dyslexia and beginning reading: A revised hypothesis of the pronunciation of print and its impairments. In M. Coltheart, K.E. Patterson, & J.C. Marshall (Eds.), *Deep Dyslexia*. (pp. 227–258). London: Routledge & Kegan Paul.

Marchman, V.A., Miller, R., & Bates, E. (1991). Babble and first words in children with focal brain injury. *Applied Psycholinguistics, 12,* 1–22.

Margolin, D., Marcel, A., & Carlson, N. (1985). Dysnomia and post-semantic surface dyslexia: Processing deficits and selective attention. In K. Patterson, J.C. Marshall, & M. Coltheart (Eds.), *Surface dyslexia*. (pp. 139–169). London: Lawrence Erlbaum Associates Ltd.

Margolin, D.I. (1984). The neuropsychology of writing and spelling: Semantic, phonological, motor and perceptual processes. *Quarterly Journal of Experimental Psychology, 34,* 459–489.

Marlowe, W.B. (1992). The impact of a right prefrontal lesion on the developing brain. *Brain and Cognition,* 20, 205–213.

Marr, D. (1976). Early processing of visual information. *Philosophical Transactions of the Royal Society (London), 275B,* 483–524.

Marr, D. (1980). Visual information processing: The structure and creation of visual representations. *Philosophical Transactions of the Royal Society (London), 290B,* 199–218.

Marr, D. (1982). *Vision*. San Francisco: W.H. Freeman.

Marsh, G., Friedman, M., Welch, V., & Desberg, P. (1981). A cognitive-developmental theory of reading acquisition. In G.E. MacKinnon & T.G. Walker (Eds.), *Reading research: Advances in theory and practice,* (Vol. 3). New York: Academic Press.

Marshall, J.C. (1984). Toward a rational taxonomy of the developmental dyslexias. In R.N. Malatesha & H.A. Whitaker (Eds.), *Dyslexia: A global issue*. (pp. 45–58). The Hague, The Netherlands: Nijhoff.

Marshall, J.C. (1987). The cultural and biological context of written languages: Their acquisition, deployment and breakdown. In J.R. Beech & A.M. Colley (Eds.), *Cognitive approaches to reading*. Chichester, UK: John Wiley.

Marshall, J.C., & Newcombe, F. (1966). Syntactic and semantic errors in paralexia. *Neuropsychologia, 4,* 169–176.

Marshall, J.C., & Newcombe, F. (1973). Patterns of paralexia: A psycholinguistic approach. *Journal of Psycholinguistic Research, 2,* 175–199.

Martins, I.P., Antunes, N.L., Castro-Caldas, A., & Antunes, J.L. (1995). Atypical language dominance in developmental aphasia. *Developmental Medicine and Child Neurology, 37,* 85–90.

Mattes, J.A. (1980). The role of frontal lobe dysfunction in childhood hyperkinesis. *Comprehensive Psychiatry, 21,* 358–369.

Maunsell, J.H.R., & van Essen, D.C. (1983). Functional properties of neurons in the middle temporal visual area of the macaque monkey: I. Selectivity for stimulus direction, speed and orientation. *Journal of Neurophysiology, 49,* 1127–1147.

Maurer, R.G. (1992). Disorders of memory and learning. In S.J. Segalowitz & I. Rapin (Eds.), *Handbook of neuropsychology: Vol. 7. Child neuropsychology*. (pp. 241–259). Amsterdam: Elsevier Science Publishers.

McBurnett, K., Harris, S.M., Swanson, J.M., Pfiffner, L.J., Tamm, L., & Freeland, (1993). Neuropsychological and psychophysiological differentiation of inattention/overactivity and aggression/defiance symptom groups. *Journal of Clinical Child Psychology, 22,* 165–171.

McCarthy, R., & Warrington, E.K. (1990). *Cognitive neuropsychology: A clinical introduction*. London/New York: Academic Press.

McClelland, J.L., & Rumelhart, D.E. (1981). An interactive activation model of context effects in letter perception: Pt. 1. An account of basic findings. *Psychological Review, 88*, 375–407.

McCloskey, M. (1992). Cognitive mechanisms in numerical processing: Evidence from acquired dyscalculia. *Cognition, 44*, 107–157.

McCloskey, M., Aliminosa, D., & Sokol, S.M. (1991). Cognitive mechanisms in normal and impaired number processing. In G. Deloche & X. Seron (Eds.), *Mathematical disabilities: A cognitive neuropsychological perspective* (pp. 201–220). Hillsdale, NJ: Lawrence Erlbaum Associates Inc.

McCloskey, M., Caramazza, A., & Basili, A. (1985). Cognitive mechanisms in number processing and calculation: Evidence from dyscalculia. *Brain and Cognition, 4*, 171–196.

McCloskey, M., Rapp, B., Yantis, S., Rubin, G., Bacon, W.F., Dagnelie, G., Gordon, B., Aliminosa, D., Boatman, D.F., Badecker, W., Johnson, D.N., Tusa, R.J., & Palmer, E. (1995). A developmental deficit in localising objects from vision. *Psychological Science, 6*, 112–117.

McCloskey, M., Sokol, S.M., & Goodman, R.A. (1986). Cognitive processes in verbal-number production: Inferences from the performance of brain-damaged patients. *Journal of Experimental Psychology: General, 115*, 307–330.

McConachie, H.R. (1976). Developmental prosopagnosia: A single case report. *Cortex, 12*, 76–82.

McConachie, H.R. (1995). Relation between Asperger syndrome and prosopagnosia. *Developmental Medicine and Child Neurology, 37*, 563–564.

McDougall, S., Hulme, A., Ellis, A., & Monk, A. (1994). Learning to read: The role of short-term memory and phonological skills. *Journal of Experimental Child Psychology, 58*, 112–133.

McGee, R., Williams, S., Moffitt, T., & Anderson, J. (1989). A comparison of 13-year-old boys with attention deficit and/reading disorder on neuropsychological measures. *Journal of Abnormal Child Psychology, 17*, 37–53.

McGlone, J. (1985). Can spatial deficits in Turner's syndrome be explained by focal CNS dysfunction or atypical speech lateralisation? *Journal of Clinical and Experimental Neuropsychology, 7*, 375–394.

Mehta, Z., & Newcombe, F. (1991). A role for the left hemisphere in spatial processing. *Cortex, 27*, 153–167.

Mellet, E., Tzourio, N., Denis, M., & Mazoyer, B. (1995). A positron emission tomography study of visual and mental spatial exploration. *Journal of Cognitive Neuroscience, 7*, 433–445.

Menyuk, P. (1986). Predicting speech and language problems with persistent otitis media. In, J.F. Kavanagh (Ed.), *Otitis media and child development*. Parkton, Maryland: York Press.

Meyer, F., Marsh, R., Laws, E., & Sharborough, F. (1986). Temporal lobectomy in children with epilepsy. *Journal of Neurosurgery, 64*, 371–376.

Miller, M.A., Innes, W.C., & Enloe, I.J. (1977). Performance on a four-choice search task following septal lesions in rats. *Physiological Psychology, 5*, 433–439.

Milner, B. (1963). Effects of different brain lesions on card sorting: The role of the frontal lobes. *Archives of Neurology, 9*, 90–100.

Milner, B. (1964). Some effects of frontal lobectomy in man. In, J.M. Warren & K. Akert (Eds.), *The frontal granular cortex and behaviour*. New York: McGraw-Hill.

Milner, B. (1966). Amnesia following operation on the temporal lobes. In C.W. M. Whitty & O.L. Zangwill (Eds.), *Amnesia*. London: Butterworths.

Milner, B. (1970). Memory and the medial temporal regions of the brain. In K.H. Pribram & D.E. Broadbent (Eds.), *Biology of memory*. New York: Academic Press.

Milner, B. (1971). Interhemispheric differences in the localisation of psychological processes in man. *British Medical Bulletin*, *27*, 272–277.

Milner, B. (1975). Psychological aspects of focal epilepsy and its neurosurgical management. In, Pupera, D.O., Penny, J.K., & Walter, R.D. (Eds.), *Advances in neurology*. New York: Raven Press.

Milner, B., Petrides, M., & Smith, M.L. (1985). Frontal lobes and the temporal organisation of memory. *Human Neurobiology*, *4*, 137–142.

Mishkin, M., & Appenzeller, T. (1987). The anatomy of memory. *Scientific American*, *256*, 80–89.

Mohindra, I., Zwaan, J., Held, R., Brill, S., & Zwaan, F. (1985). Development of acuity and stereopsis in infants with esotropia. *Opthalmology*, *92*, 691–697.

Money, J., & Alexander, D. (1966). Turner's syndrome: Further demonstration of the presence of specific cognitional deficiencies. *Journal of Medical Genetics*, 3, 47–48.

Moore, I.M., Kramer, J.H., Wara, W., Halberg, F., & Ablin, A.R. (1991). Cognitive function in children with leukemia: Effect of radiation dose and time since irradiation. *Cancer*, *68*, 1913–1917.

Morais, J., Bertelson, P., Cary, L., & Alegria, J. (1986). Literacy training and speech segmentation. *Cognition*, *24*, 45–53.

Morais, J., Cary, L., Alegria, J., & Bertelson, P. (1979). Does awareness of speech as a sequence of phones arise spontaneously? *Cognition*, *7*, 323–331.

Morgan, W.P. (1896). A case of congenital word-blindness. *British Medical Journal*, *2*, 1378.

Morley, M. (1965). *The development and disorders of speech in childhood*. London: Churchill Livingstone.

Morris, C., Thomas, I., & Greenberg, F. (1993). Williams syndrome: Autosomal dominant inheritance. *American Journal of Medical Genetics*, *47*, 478–481.

Morris, R.G.M., Garrud, P., Rawlins, J.N.P., & O'Keefe, J. (1982). Place navigation impaired in rats with hippocampal lesions. *Nature*, *297*, 681–683.

Morton, J. (1969). Interaction of information in word recognition. *Psychological Review*, *76*, 165–178.

Morton, J. (1979). Word recognition. In J. Morton & J.C. Marshall (Eds.), *Psycholinguistic series*. (pp. 107–155). Cambridge, Mass: MIT Press.

Morton, J. (1989). An information-processing account of reading acquisition. In A. Galaburda (Ed.), *From reading to neurons*. (pp. 43–66). Cambridge, MA: MIT Press.

Morton, J., & Patterson, K.E. (1980). A new attempt at an interpretation or an attempt at a new interpretation. In M. Coltheart, K.E. Patterson & J.C. Marshall (Eds.), *Deep dyslexia*. London: Routledge and Kegan Paul.

Mouridsen, S.E., Videboek, C., Sogaard, H., & Andersen, A.R. (1992). Regional cerebral blood flow measured by HMPAO and SPECT in a 5-year-old boy with Landau–Kleffner Syndrome. *Neuropaediatrics*, *24*, 47–50.

Murphy, D., De Carli, C., Daly, E., Haxby, J., Allen, G., White, B., McIntosh, A., Powell, C., Horwitz, B., Rapoport, S., & Schapiro, M. (1993). X-chromosome effects on female brain: a magnetic resonance imaging study of Turner's syndrome. *The Lancet, 342*, 1197–200.

Murphy, L.A., Pollatsek, A., & Well, A.D. (1988). Developmental dyslexia and word retrieval deficits. *Brain and Language, 35*, 11–23.

Nakano, S., Okuno, T., & Mikawa, H. (1989). Landau–Kleffner syndrome EEG topographic studies. *Brain and Development, 11*, 43–50.

Navron, D. (1977). Forest before tree: The precedence of global features in visual perception. *Cognitive Psychology, 9*, 353–383.

Navron, D., & Norman, J. (1983). Does global precedence really depend upon visual angle? *Journal of Experimental Psychology: Human Perception and Performance, 9*, 955–965.

Neale, M.D. (1966). *The Neale analysis of reading ability* (2nd edit.). London: Macmillan Education Ltd.

Nelson, H.E. (1976). A modified card sorting test sensitive to frontal lobe defects. *Cortex, 12*, 313–324.

Nelson, K. (1973). Structure and strategy in learning to talk. *Monographs of the Society for Research in Child Development, 38* (149), 1–138.

Nelson, K. (1989). Remembering: A functional developmental perspective. In P.R. Soloman, G.R. Goethals, C.M. Kelley, & B.R. Stephens (Eds.), *Memory: Interdisciplinary approaches*. New York: Springer-Verlag.

Nelson, K. (1993). The psychological and social origins of autobiographical memory. *Psychological Science, 4*, 7–14.

Netley, C., Hanley, W.B., & Rudner, H.L. (1984). Phenylketonuria and its variants: Observations on intellectual functioning. *Canadian Medical Association Journal, 131*, 751–755.

Netley, C. and Rovet, J. (1982). Atypical hemispheric lateralisation in Turner's syndrome subjects. *Cortex, 18*, 377–384.

Nettleship, E. (1901). Cases of congenital word blindness (inability to learn to read). *Opthalmic Review, 20*, 61–67.

Neville, H.J., Coffey, S.A., Holcomb, P.J., & Tallal, P. (1993). The neurobiology of sensory and language processing in language-impaired children. *Journal of Cognitive Neuroscience, 5*, 235–253.

Newcombe, F. (1969). *Missile wounds of the brain: A study of psychological deficits*. Oxford, UK: Oxford University Press.

Newcombe, F., & Marshall, J.C. (1981). On psycholinguistic classification of the acquired dyslexias. *Bulletin of the Orton Society, 31*, 29–44.

Newcombe, N., & Fox, N.A. (1994). Infantile amnesia: Through a glass darkly. *Child Development, 65*, 31–40.

Nielsen, J., Nyborg, H., & Dahl, G. (1977). Turner's syndrome: A psychiatric-psychological study of 45 women with Turner's Syndrome compared with their sisters and women with normal karyotype, growth retardation and primary amenorrhoea. *Acta Jutlandica, 45*, 21.

Noel, M., & Seron, X. (1993). Arabic number reading deficit: A single case study of when 236 is read (2306) and judged superior to 1258. *Cognitive Neuropsychology, 10*, 317–340.

Nomura, Y., & Segawa, M. (1982). Tourette syndrome in Oriental children: Clinical and pathophysiological considerations. In A.J. Friedhoff & T.N. Chase (Eds.), *Gilles de la Tourette syndrome* (Vol 35). *Advances in Neurology*. (pp. 277–280). New York: Raven Press.

O'Keefe, J., & Nadel, L. (1978). *The hippocampus as a cognitive map.* Oxford, UK: Oxford University Press.

Olson, R., Wise, B., Conners, F., & Rack, J. (1989). Specific deficits in component reading and language skills: Genetic and environmental influences. *Journal of Learning Disabilities, 22,* 339–348.

Olson, R., Wise, B., Conners, F., & Rack, J. (1990). Organisation, heritability, and remediation of component word recognition and language skills. In, T.H. Carr & B.A. Levy (Eds.), *Reading and its development: Component skills approaches.* (pp. 261–322). New York: Academic Press. pp 261–322.

Olurin, O. (1970). Cortical blindness following convulsions and fever in Nigerian children. *Pediatrics, 46,* 102–107.

Orton, S.T. (1928). Specific reading disability strephosymbolia. *Journal of the American Medical Association, 90,* 1095–1099.

Orton, S.T. (1937). *Reading, writing and speech problems in children.* New York: Norton.

Ostergaard, A.L. (1987). Episodic, semantic and procedural memory in a case of amnesia at an early age. *Neuropsychologia, 25,* 341–357.

Ostergaard, A.L., & Squire, L. (1990). Childhood amnesia and distinctions between forms of memory: A comment on Wood, Brown and Felton. *Brain and Cognition, 14,* 127–133.

Osterrieth, P.A. (1944). Le test de copie d'une figure complexe. *Archives de Psychologie, 30,* 206–256.

Otero, E., Cordova, S., Diaz, F., Garcia-Teruel, I., & Del Brutto, O. (1989). Acquired epileptic aphasia (the Landau–Kleffner syndrome) due to neurocysticercosis. *Epilepsia, 30,* 569–572.

Ozonoff, S., & McEvoy, R.E. (1994). A longitudinal study of executive function and theory of mind development in autism. *Development and Psychopathology, 6,* 415–431.

Ozonoff, S., Pennington, B.F., & Rogers, S.J. (1991). Executive function deficits in high-functioning autistic individuals: Relationship to theory of mind. *Journal of Child Psychology and Psychiatry, 32,* 1081–1105.

Ozonoff, S., Rogers, S.J., & Pennington, B.F. (1991). Asperger's syndrome: Evidence of an empirical distinction from high-functioning autism. *Journal of Child Psychology and Psychiatry, 32,* 1107–1122.

Papagno, C., & Basso, A. (1993). Impairment of written language and mathematical skills in a case of Landau–Kleffner syndrome. *Aphasiology, 7,* 451–461.

Papanicolaou, A.C., DiScenna, A., Gillespie, L., & Aram, D. (1990). Probe-evoked potential findings following unilateral left-hemisphere lesions in children. *Archives of Neurology, 47,* 562–566.

Paquier, P.F., van Dongen, H., & Loonen, C. (1992). The Landau–Kleffner syndrome or "Acquired aphasia with convulsive disorder". *Archives of Neurology, 49,* 354–359.

Parkin, A.J. (1992). Functional significance of aetiological factors in human amnesia. In L.R. Squire & L. Butters (Eds.), *Neuropsychology of memory,* (2nd edn.). New York: Guildford Press.

Parkin, A.J. (1996). *Memory and amnesia: An introduction,* (2nd edn.). Oxford, UK: Basil Blackwell.

Parkin, A.J., Dunn, J.C., Lee, C., O'Hara, P.F., & Nussbaum, L. (1993). Neuropsychological sequelae of Wernicke's encephalopathy in a 20-year-old woman: Selective impairment of a frontal memory system. *Brain and Cognition, 21,* 1–19.

Parkin, A.J., & Leng, N.R. (1988). Comparative studies of the amnesic syndrome. In H. Markowitsch (Ed.), *Information processing by the brain: Views and hypotheses from a physiological-cognitive perspective.* Toronto, Canada: Hans Huber.

Parkin, A.J., & Leng, N.R. (1993). *Neuropsychology of the amnesic syndrome.* Hillsdale, NJ: Lawrence Erlbaum Associates Inc.

Passler, M.A., Isaac, W., & Hynd, G.W. (1985). Neuropsychological development of behaviour attributed to frontal lobe functioning in children. *Developmental Neuropsychology, 1,* 349–370.

Pathak, K., & Pring, L. (1989). Tactual picture recognition in blind and sighted children. *Applied Cognitive Psychology, 3,* 337–350.

Patterson, K.E. (1982). The relation between reading and phonological coding: Further neuropsychological observations. In A. Ellis (Ed.), *Normality and pathology in cognitive functions.* (pp. 77–111). London: Academic Press.

Patterson, K.E., Marshall, J.C., & Coltheart, M. (Eds.). (1985), *Surface dyslexia: neuropsychological and cognitive studies of phonological reading.* London: Lawrence Erlbaum Associates Ltd.

Paul, R. (1987). Communication. In D.J. Cohen & A.M. Donellan (Eds.), *Handbook of autism and pervasive developmental disorders.* New York: Wiley.

Pauls, D.L., Towbin, K.E., Leckman, J.F., Zahner, G., & Cohen, D.J. (1986). Gilles de la Tourette syndrome and obsessive compulsive disorder: Evidence supporting a genetic relationship. *Archives of General Psychiatry, 43,* 1180–1182.

Penfield, W., & Kristiansen, K. (1951). *Epileptic seizure patterns.* Springfield, IL: Charles C. Thomas.

Pennington, B.F. (1990). Annotation: The genetics of dyslexia. *Journal of Child Psychology and Psychiatry, 31,* 193–201.

Pennington, B.F., Gilger, J.W., Pauls, D., Smith, S.A., Smith, S.D., & DeFries, J.C. (1991). Evidence for major gene transmission of developmental dyslexia. *Journal of the American Medical Association, 266,* 1527–1534.

Pennington, B.F., Groissier, D., & Welsh, M.C. (1993). Contrasting deficits in attention deficit hyperactivity disorder versus reading disability. *Developmental Psychology, 29,* 511–523.

Pennington, B.F., Heaton, R.K., Karzmark, P., Pendleton, M.G., Lehman, R., & Shucard, D.W. (1985). The neuropsychological phenotype in Turner's syndrome. *Cortex, 21,* 391–404.

Pennington, B.F., & Ozonoff, S. (1996). Executive functions and developmental psychopathology. *Journal of Child Psychology and Psychiatry, 37,* 51–88.

Pennington, B.F., Van Doorninck, W.J., McCabe, L.L., McCabe, E.R.B. (1985). Neuropsychologic deficits in early treated phenylketonuric children. *American Journal of Mental Deficiency, 89,* 467–474.

Perfetti, C.A. (1992). The representation problem in reading acquisition. In P.B. Gough, L.C. Ehri, & R. Trieman (Eds.), *Reading acquisition.* Hillsdale, NJ: Lawrence Erlbaum Associates Inc.

Perin, D. (1983). Phonemic segmentation in spelling. *British Journal of Psychology, 74,* 129–144.

Perner, J. (1993). The theory of mind deficit in autism: Rethinking the metarepresentation theory. In, S. Baron-Cohen, H. Tager-Flusberg, & D.J. Cohen (Eds.), *Understanding other minds: Perspectives from autism*. Oxford, UK: University Press

Perner, J., Frith, U., Leslie, A.M., & Leekam, S.R. (1989). Exploration of the autistic child's theory of mind: Knowledge, belief and communication. *Child Development*, *60*, 689–700.

Perner, J., & Wimmer, H. (1985). "John thinks that Mary thinks that..." Attribution of second-order beliefs by 5–10 year old children. *Journal of Experimental Child Psychology*, *39*, 437–471.

Perret, E. (1974). The left frontal lobe in man and suppression of habitual responses in verbal categorical behaviour. *Neuropsychologia*, *12*, 323–330.

Petrides, M., & Milner, B. (1982). Deficits on subject-ordered tasks after frontal- and temporal-lobe lesions in man. *Neuropsychologia*, *20*, 249–262.

Piaget, J. (1952). *The child's conception of number*. New York: Humanities Press.

Piaget, J, & Inhelder, B. (1958). *The growth of logical thinking from childhood to adolescence*. New York: Basic Books.

Piaget, J. and Inhelder, B. (1973). *Memory and intelligence*. New York: Basic Books.

Pierce, S., & Bartolucci, G. (1977). A syntactic investigation of verbal autistic, mentally retarded and normal children. *Journal of Autism and Childhood Schizophrenia*, *7*, 121–134.

Pinker, S., & Prince, A. (1992). Regular and irregular morphology and the psychological status of rules of grammar. *Proceedings of the 17th annual meeting of the Berkeley Linguistics Society*. Berkeley, CA: Berkeley Linguistic Society.

Plaut, D.C., & McClelland, J.L. (1993). Generalisation with componential attractors: Word and nonword reading in an attractor network. *Proceedings of the 15th annual conference of the Cognitive Science Society*. Hillsdale, NJ: Lawrence Erlbaum Associates Inc.

Plaut, D.C., McClelland, J.L., Seidenberg, M.S., & Patterson, K.E. (1996). Understanding normal and impaired word reading: Computational principles in quasi-regular domains. *Psychological Review*, *103*, 56–115.

Plaut, D., & Shallice, T. (1993). Deep dyslexia: A case study of connectionist neuropsychology. *Cognitive Neuropsychology*, *10*, 377–500.

Plumet, M-H., Goldblum, M-C., & Leboyer, M. (1995). Verbal skills in relatives of autistic females. *Cortex*, *31*, 723–733.

Plunkett, K., & Marchman, V. (1993). From rote learning to system building: Acquiring verb morphology in children and connectionist nets. *Cognition*, *48*, 21–69.

Poppel. E., Held, R., & Frost, D. (1973). Residual visual function after brain wounds involving the central visual pathways in man. *Nature*, *243*, 295–296.

Posner, M.I. (1980). Orienting of attention: The Seventh Sir F.C. Bartlett Lecture. *Quarterly Journal of Experimental Psychology*, *32*, 3–25.

Premack, D., & Woodruff, G. (1978). Does the chimpanzee have a theory of mind? *Behavioural and Brain Sciences*, *1*, 515–526.

Price, B.H., Daffner, K.R., Stowe, R.M., & Mesulam, M.M. (1990). The compartmental learning disabilities of early frontal lobe damage. *Brain*, *113*, 1383–1393.

Price, R.A., Kidd, K.K., Cohen, D.J., Pauls, D.L., & Leckman, J.F. (1985). A twin study of Tourette Syndrome. *Archives of General Psychiatry, 147,* 734–739.

Pring, L. (1987). Picture processing by the blind. *British Journal of Educational Psychology, 57,* 38–44.

Pring, L. (1992). More than meets the eye. In R. Campbell (ed.), *Mental lives: Case studies in cognition.* Oxford, UK: Basil Blackwell.

Pring, L., & Rusted, J. (1985). Picture for the blind: The influence of pictures on the recall of text by blind children. *British Journal of Developmental Psychology, 3,* 41–45.

Prior, M.R., & Hoffman, W. (1990). Brief report: Neuropsychological testing of autistic children through an exploration with frontal lobe tests. *Journal of Autism and Developmental Disorders, 20,* 581–590.

Pritchard, E. (1918). Case of amaurosis following violent convulsions. *Proceedings of the Royal Society of Medicine, 11,* 1–2.

Randolph, C., Hyde, T.M., Gold, J.M.. Goldberg, T.E., & Weinberger, D.R. (1993). Tourette syndrome in monozygotic twins: Relationship of tic severity to neuropsychological function. *Archives of Neurology, 50,* 725–728.

Rapin, I. (1987). Developmental dysphasia and autism in pre-school children: Characteristics and sub-types. *Proceedings of the First International Symposium in Specific Speech and Language Disorders in Children.* London: AFASIC.

Rapin, I., & Allen, D. (1983). Developmental language disorders: nosologic considerations. In U. Kirk (Ed.), *Neuropsychology of language, reading and spelling.* New York: Academic Press.

Rapin, I., Allen, D.A., & Dunn, M. (1992). Developmental language disorders. In, S.J. Segalowitz & I. Rapin (Eds.), *Handbook of neuropsychology: Vol. 7. Child neuropsychology.* Amsterdam: Elsevier Science Publishers.

Rapin, I., Mattis, S., Rowan, A.J., & Golden, G.S. (1977). Verbal auditory agnosia in children. *Developmental Medicine and Child Neurology, 19,* 192–207.

Rapoport, J. (1991). Recent advances in obsessive-compulsive disorder. *Neuropharmacology, 5,* 1–10.

Rapoport, J.L., Swedo, S.E., & Leonard, H.L. (1992). Childhood obsessive compulsive disorder. *Journal of Clinical Psychiatry, 53,* 11–16.

Rasmussen, T., & Milner, B. (1977). The role of early left-brain injury in determining lateralisation. *Annals of the New York Academy of Sciences, 299,* 355–369.

Rausch, R., Boone, K., & Ary, C. (1991). Right hemisphere language dominance in temporal lobe epilepsy. *Journal of Clinical and Experimental Neuropsychology, 13,* 217–231.

Read, C., Yun-Fei, Z., Hong-Yin, N., & Bao-Qing, D. (1986). The ability to manipulate speech sounds depends on knowing alphabetic writing. *Cognition, 24,* 31–45.

Reader, M., Harris, E.L., Schuerholz, L.J., & Denckla, M.B. (1994). Attention deficit hyperactivity disorder and executive dysfunction. *Developmental Neuropsychology, 10,* 493–512.

Reeves, D.L. (1941). Congenital absence of septum pellucidum. *Bulletin of the John Hopkins Hospital, 26,* 61–71.

Reiss, A.L., Freund, L., Plotnick, L., Baumgardner, T., Green, K., Sozer, A.C., Reader, M., Boehm, C., & Denckla, M. (1993). The effects of X monosomy on brain development: Monozygotic twins discordant for Turner's syndrome. *Annals of Neurology, 34,* 95–107.

Reynolds, E.H., Elwes, R.D.C., & Shorvon, S.D. (1983). Why does epilepsy become intractable? Prevention of chronic epilepsy. *Lancet, 2,* 952–954.

Rhodes, G., & McLean, I.G. (1990). Distinctiveness and expertise effects with homogeneous stimuli: Towards a model of configurational coding. *Perception, 19,* 773–794.

Rhodes, G., & Tremewan, T. (1993). The Simon then Garfunkel effect: Semantic priming, sensitivity and the modularity of face recognition. *Cognitive Psychology, 25,* 147–187.

Richman, L.C., & Kitchell, M.M (1981). Hyperlexia as a variant of developmental language disorder. *Brain and Language, 12,* 203–212.

Ricks, D.M., & Wing, L. (1976). Language, communication and the use of symbols. In L. Wing (Ed.), *Early childhood autism.* (2nd edn., pp. 93–134). Oxford, UK: Pergamon Press.

Riddle, M.A., Rasmussen, A.M., Woods, S.W., & Hoffer, P.B. (1992). SPECT imaging of cerebral blood flow in Tourette syndrome. *Archives of Neurology, 58,* 207–212.

Riley, M.S., Greeno, J.G., & Heller, J.I. (1982). Development of children's problem solving ability in arithmetic. In H.P. Ginsberg (Ed.), *The development of mathematical thinking.* New York: Academic Press.

Riva, D., & Cazzaniga, L. (1986). Late effects of unilateral brain lesions before and after the first year of life. *Neuropsychologia, 24,* 423–428.

Robertson, M.M. (1989). The Gilles de la Tourette syndrome: The current status. *British Journal of Psychiatry, 154,* 147–169.

Robertson, M.M. (1994). Annotation: Gilles de la Tourette Syndrome — An update. *Journal of Child Psychology and Psychiatry, 35,* 597–611.

Rodgers, J., Britton, P.G., Morris, R.G., Kernahan, J., & Craft, W.W. (1992). Memory for treatment for acute lymphoblastic leukemia. *Archives of Disease in Childhood, 67,* 266–268.

Roeltgen, D.P., & Heilman, K.M. (1984). Lexical agraphia: Further support for the two-system hypothesis of linguistic agraphia. *Brain, 107,* 811–827.

Roeltgen, D.P., & Heilman, K.M. (1985). Review of agraphia and a proposal for an anatomically-based neuropsychological model of writing. *Applied Psycholinguistics, 6,* 205–230.

Roeltgen, D.P., & Tucker, D.M. (1988). Developmental phonological and lexical agraphia in adults. *Brain and Language, 35,* 287–300.

Rom, A., & Leonard, L.B. (1990). Interpreting deficits in grammatical morphology in specifically language-impaired children: Preliminary evidence from Hebrew. *Clinical Linguistics and Phonetics, 4,* 93–105.

Rondal, J.A. (1994). Exceptional language development in mental retardation: Natural experiments in language modularity. *Cahiers de Psychologie Cognitive, Current Psychology of Cognition, 13,* 427–467.

Rourke, B. (1978). Reading, spelling and arithmetic disabilities: A neuropsychological analysis. In H. Myklebust (Ed.), *Progress in learning disabilities,* (Vol. 4). New York: Grune & Stratton.

Rourke, B., & Finlayson, M. (1978). Neuropsychological significance of variations in patterns of academic performance: Verbal and visuo-spatial abilities. *Journal of Abnormal Child Psychology, 6,* 121.

Rourke, B., & Strang, J. (1981). Subtypes of reading and arithmetic disabilities: A neuropsychological analysis. In M. Rutter (Ed.), *Behavioral syndromes of brain dysfunction in children.* New York: Guildford.

Rovee-Collier, C. (1989). The joy of kicking: Memories, motives and mobiles. In P.R. Soloman, G.R. Goethals, C.M. Kelley, & B.R. Stephens (Eds.), *Memory: Interdisciplinary approaches.* New York: Springer-Verlag.

Rovet, J. (1990). The cognitive and neuropsychological characteristics of females with Turner syndrome. In D. Berch & B. Bender (Eds.), *Sex chromosome abnormalities and human behaviour: Psychological studies.* (pp. 38–77). Boulder, CO: Western Press & the American Association for the Advancement of Science.

Rovet, J., & Netley, C. (1982). Processing deficits in Turner's syndrome. *Developmental Psychology, 18,* 77–94.

Rudel, R.G. (1985). Definition of dyslexia: Language and motor deficits. In F. Duffy & N. Geschwind (Eds.), *Dyslexia, current status and future directions.* Boston, MA: Little, Brown.

Rumelhart, D.E., Hinton, G.E., & Williams, R.J. (1986). Learning internal representations by error propagation. In D.E. Rumelhart & J.I. McClelland (Eds.), *Parallel distributed processing,* (Vol. 1). Cambridge, MA: MIT Press.

Rumsey, J.M. (1985). Conceptual problem-solving in highly verbal, nonretarded autistic men. *Journal of Autism and Developmental Disorders, 15,* 23–36.

Rumsey, J.M., Andreason, P., Zametkin, A., Aquino, T., King, C., Hamburger, S., Pikus, A., Rapoport, J., & Cohen, R. (1992). Failure to activate the left temporoparietal cortex in dyslexia. *Archives of Neurology, 49,* 527–534.

Rumsey, J.M., & Hamburger, S.D. (1988). Neuropsychological findings in high-functioning men with infantile autism, residual state. *Journal of Clinical and Experimental Neuropsychology, 10,* 201–221.

Rumsey, J.M., & Hamburger, S.D. (1990). Neuropsychological divergence of high-level autism and severe dyslexia. *Journal of Autism and Developmental Disorders, 20,* 155–168.

Rumsey, J.M., Zametkin, A.J., Andreason, P., Hanahan, A.P., Hamburger, S.D., Aquino, T., King, C., Pikus, A., & Cohen, R.M. (1994). Normal activation of frontotemporal language cortex in dyslexia, as measured with oxygen 15 positron emission tomography. *Archives of Neurology, 51,* 27–38.

Russell, J., Mauthner, N., Sharpe, S., & Tidswell, T. (1991). The "windows task" as a measure of strategic deception in preschoolers and autistic subjects. *British Journal of Developmental Psychology, 9,* 331–349.

Russell, W.R. (1948). Function of frontal lobes. *Lancet, 254,* 356–360.

Rutter, M. (1967). Psychotic disorders in early childhood. In A.J. Coppen & A. Walk (Eds.), *Recent developments in schizophrenia.* Ashford, UK: Headley Brother.

Rutter, M., Tizard, J., Yule, W., Graham, P., & Whitmore, K. (1976). Research Report: Isle of Wight Studies 1964-1974. *Psychological Medicine, 6,* 313–332.

Rybash, J.M., & Colilla, J.L. (1994). Source memory deficits and frontal lobe functioning in children. *Developmental Neuropsychology, 10,* 67–73.

Sadeh, M., Goldhammer, Y., & Kuritzky, A. (1983). Postictal blindness in adults. *Journal of Neurology, Neurosurgery and Psychiatry, 46,* 566–569.

Saffran, E.M. (1982). Neuropsychological approaches to the study of language. *British Journal of Psychology, 73,* 317–337.

Satterfield, J.H., & Dawson, M.E. (1971). Electrodermal correlates of hyperactivity in children. *Psychophysiology*, *8*, 191–197.

Saxe, G.B., & Posner, J. (1983). The development of numerical cognition: Cross-cultural perspectives. In H.P. Ginsberg (Ed.), *The development of mathematical thinking*. New York: Academic Press.

Schor, C., & Levi, D.M. (1980). Direction selectivity for perceived motion in strabismus and anisometropic amblyopia. *Investigative Ophthalmology and Visual Sciences*, *19*, 1094–1104.

Schwartz, M.F., Saffran, E.M., & Marin, O.S.M. (1980). Fractionating the reading process in dementia: Evidence for word-specific print-to-sound associations. In M. Coltheart, K. Patterson & J.C. Marshall (Eds.), *Deep dyslexia*. London: Routledge & Kegan Paul.

Scoville, W. B., & Milner, B. (1957). Loss of recent memory after bilateral hippocampal lesions. *Journal of Neurology, Neurosurgery and Psychiatry*, *20*, 11–21.

Segal, M., Greenberger, V., & Pearl, E. (1989). Septal transplants ameliorate spatial deficits and restore cholinergic functions in rats with damaged septo-hippocampal connection. *Brain Research*, *500*, 139–148.

Seidenberg, M., & McClelland, J. (1989). A distributed, developmental model of word recognition and naming. *Psychological Review*, *96*, 523–568.

Seidenberg, M., Plaut, D.C., Peterson, A.S., McClelland, J.L., & McCrae, K. (1994). Nonword pronunciation and models of word recognition. *Journal of Experimental Psychology: Human Perception and Performance*, *20*, 1177–1196.

Sergent, J. (1984). An investigation into component and configurational processes underlying face perception. *British Journal of Psychology*, *75*, 221–242.

Seron, X., & Deloche, G. (1984). From 2 to two: An analysis of a transcoding process by means of neuropsychological evidence. *Journal of Psycholinguistic Research*, *13*, 215–236.

Seymour, P.H.K. (1986). *Cognitive analysis of dyslexia*. London: Routledge & Kegan Paul.

Seymour, P.H.K., & Elder, L. (1986). Beginning reading without phonology. *Cognitive Neuropsychology*, *3*, 1–37.

Seymour, P.H.K., & Evans, H.M. (1992). Beginning reading without semantics: A cognitive study of hyperlexia. *Cognitive Neuropsychology*, *9*, 89–122.

Seymour, P.H.K., & MacGregor, C.J. (1984). Developmental dyslexia: A cognitive experimental analysis of phonological, morphemic and visual impairments. *Cognitive Neuropsychology*, *1*, 43–83.

Shaffer, J. (1962). A specific cognitive deficit observed in gonadal aplasia (Turner's syndrome). *Journal of Clinical Psychology*, *18*, 403–406.

Shallice, T. (1982). Specific impairments of planning. *Philosophical Transactions of the Royal Society of London*, *B298*, 199–209.

Shallice, T. (1988). *From neuropsychology to mental structure*. Cambridge, UK: University Press.

Shallice, T., & Burgess, P. (1991). Higher-order cognitive impairments and frontal lobe lesions in man. In H.S. Levin, H.M. Eisenberg, & A.L. Benton (Eds.) *Frontal lobe function and dysfunction*. Oxford, UK/New York: Oxford University Press.

Shallice, T, & McCarthy, R. (1985). Phonological reading: From patterns of impairment to possible procedures. In K.E. Patterson, J.C. Marshall, & M. Coltheart (Eds.), *Surface dyslexia.* (pp. 361–397). London: Lawrence Erlbaum Associates Ltd.

Shallice, T. and Warrington, E.K. (1970) Independent functioning of the verbal memory stores: A neuropsychological case study. *Quarterly Journal of Experimental Psychology, 22*, 261-273.

Shallice, T., & Warrington, E.K. (1980). Single and multiple component central dyslexic syndromes. In M. Coltheart, K.S. Patterson, & J.C. Marshall (Eds.), *Deep dyslexia.* (pp. 119–145). London: Routledge & Kegan Paul.

Shallice, T., Warrington, E.K. and McCarthy, R. (1983) Reading without semantics. *Quarterly Journal of Experimental Psychology, 35A*, 111–138.

Shankweiler, D., Liberman, I.Y., Mark, L.S., Fowler, C.A., & Fuscher, F.W. (1979). The speech code and learning to read. *Journal of Experimental Psychology:Human Learning and Memory, 5*, 531–545.

Shaywitz, S., Escobar, M., Shaywitz, B., Fletcher, J., & Makuch, R. (1992). Evidence that dyslexia may represent the lower tail of a normal distribution of reading ability. *New England Journal of Medicine, 326*, 145–150.

Shucard, D., Shucard, J., Clopper, R., & Schachter, M. (1992). Electro-physiological and neuropsychological indices of cognitive processing deficits in Turner syndrome. *Developmental Neuropsychology, 8*, 299–323.

Shue, K.L., & Douglas, V.I. (1992). Attention deficit disorder and the frontal lobe syndrome. *Brain and Cognition, 20*, 104–124.

Siegel, L.S. (1985). Deep dyslexia in childhood? *Brain and Language, 216*, 16–17.

Siegel, L.S. (1988). Evidence that IQ scores are irrelevant to the definition and analysis of reading disability. *Canadian Journal of Psychology, 42*, 201–215.

Siegel, L.S. (1989). IQ is irrelevant to the definition of learning disabilities. *Journal of Learning Disabilities, 22*, 469–478.

Siegler, R.S. (1986). Unities across domains in children's strategy choices. In M. Perlmutter (Ed.), Perspectives for intellectual development. *Minnesota Symposium on child development.* (Vol. 19, pp. 1–48). Hillsdale, NJ: Lawrence Erlbaum and Associates Inc.

Siegler, R.S. (1988). Individual differences in strategy choice: Good students, not-so-good students and perfectionists. *Child Development, 59*, 833–851.

Siegler, R.S., & Jenkins, E. (1989). *How children discover new strategies.* Hillsdale, NJ: Lawrence Erlbaum Associates Inc.

Siegler, R.S., & Robinson, M. (1982). The development of numerical understandings. In H. Reese & L.P. Lipsitt (Eds.), *Advances in child development and behaviour.* (Vol. 16, pp. 229–293). Hillsdale, NJ: Lawrence Erlbaum Associates Inc.

Siegler, R.S., & Shrager, J. (1984). A model of strategy choice. In C. Sophian (Ed.), *Origins of cognitive skills.* (pp. 229-293). Hillsdale, NJ: Lawrence Erlbaum Associates Inc.

Silberberg, N.E., & Silberberg, M.C. (1967). Hyperlexia: Specific word recognition skills in young children. *Exceptional Children, 34*, 41–42.

Silberberg, N.E., & Silberberg, M.C. (1968). Case histories in hyperlexia. *Journal of School Psychology, 7*, 3–7.

Silbert, A., Wolff, P.H., & Lilienthal, J. (1977). Spatial and temporal processing in patients with Turner's syndrome. *Behaviour Genetics, 7*, 11–21.

Simon, H.A. (1975). The functional equivalence of problem solving skills. *Cognitive Psychology, 7*, 268–288.

Sitdis, J.S. and Volpe, B.T. (1988) Selective loss of complex pitch or speech discrimination after unilateral lesion. *Brain and Language, 34*, 235–245.

Skolik, S.A., Mizen, T.R., & Burde, R.M. (1987). Transient postictal cortical blindness. *Journal of Clinical Neuro-ophthalmology, 7*, 151–154.

Skysgaard, H.B. (1942) *Den knostitutionelle dyslexia*. Kobenhavn.

Small, S.L., Hart, J., Nguyen T., & Gordon, B. (1995). Distributed representations of semantic knowledge in the brain. *Brain, 118*, 441–453.

Smith, I., Beasley, M.G., & Ades, A.E. (1990). Intelligence and quality of dietary treatment in phenylketonuria. *Archives of Diseases of Childhood, 472–478*.

Smith, I., Beasley, M.G., Wolff, O.H., & Ades, A.E. (1988). Behavioural disturbance in eight-year old children with early treated phenylketonuria (PKU). *Journal of Paediatrics, 112*, 403–408.

Smith, J., & Kellaway, P. (1963). Occipital foci in children: An analysis of 452 cases. *Electroencephalography and Clinical Neurophysiology, 15*, 1047.

Smith, M.L., Kates, M.H., & Vriezen, E.R. (1992). The development of frontal lobe functions. In S.J. Segalowitz & I. Rapin (Eds.), *Handbook of neuropsychology: Vol. 7. Child neuropsychology*. Amsterdam: Elsevier.

Smith, S.D., Kimberling, W.J., Pennington, B.F., & Lubs, H.A. (1983). Specific reading disability: Identification of an inherited form through linkage and analysis. *Science, 219*, 1345–1347.

Snodgrass, J.G., & Vanderwart, M. (1980). A standardised set of 260 pictures: Norms for name agreement, image agreement, familiarity, and visual complexity. *Journal of Experimental Psychology: Human Learning and Memory, 6*, 174–215.

Snowling, M. (1980). Development of grapheme–phoneme correspondence in normal and dyslexic readers. *Journal of Experimental Child Psychology, 29*, 294–305.

Snowling, M.J. (1981). Phonemic deficits in developmental dyslexia. *Psychological Research, 43*, 219–234.

Snowling, M. (1987). *Dyslexia: A cognitive developmental perspective*. Oxford, UK: Blackwells.

Snowling, M., Goulandris, N., Bowlby, M., & Howell, P. (1986). Segmentation and speech perception in relation to reading skill: A developmental analysis. *Journal of Experimental Child Psychology, 41*, 489–507.

Snowling, M., & Hulme, C. (1989). A longitudinal case study of developmental phonological dyslexia. *Cognitive Neuropsychology, 6*, 379–403.

Snowling, M., Hulme, C., & Goulandris, N. (1994). Word recognition in developmental dyslexia: A connectionist interpretation. *Quarterly Journal of Experimental Psychology, 47*, 895–916.

Snowling, M., & Stackhouse, J. (1983). Spelling performance of children with developmental verbal dyspraxia. *Developmental Medicine and Child Neurology, 25*, 430–437.

Snowling, M., Stackhouse, J., & Rack, J. (1986). Phonological dyslexia and dysgraphia: A developmental analysis. *Cognitive Neuropsychology, 3*, 309–339.

Sokol, S.M., Goodman-Schulman, R., & McCloskey, M. (1989). In defence of a modular architecture for the number processing system: Reply to Campbell and Clark. *Journal of Experimental Psychology: General, 118*, 105–110.

Sokol, S.M.,& McCloskey, M. (1988). Levels of representation in verbal number production. *Applied Psycholinguistics, 9,* 267–281.

Spellacy, F., & Peters, B. (1978). Dyscalculia and elements of the developmental Gerstmann syndrome in school children. *Cortex, 14,* 197.

Spencer, S.S., Spencer, D.D., Williamson, P.D., & Mattson, R. (1990). Combined depth and subdural electrode investigation in uncontrolled epilepsy. *Neurology, 40,* 74–79.

Spreen, O., Tupper,D., Risser, A., Tuckko, H., & Edgell, D. (1984). *Human developmental neuropsychology.* New York: Oxford University Press.

Squire, L. (1982a). Comparisons between forms of amnesia: Some deficits are unique to Korsakoff's syndrome. *Journal of Experimental Psychology: Learning, Memory and Cognition, 8,* 560–571.

Squire, L.R. (1982b). The neuropsychology of human memory. *Annual Review of Neuroscience, 5,* 241–273.

Squire, L.R., Amaral, D.G., Zola-Morgan, S., Kritchevsky, M., & Press, G. (1989). Description of brain injury in the amnesic patient N.A. based on magnetic resonance imaging. *Experimental Neurology, 105,* 23–35.

Squire, L.R., & Moore, R.Y. (1979). Dorsal thalamic lesions in a noted case of human memory dysfunction. *Annals of Neurology, 6,* 603–606.

Stackhouse, J. (1982). An investigation of reading and spelling performance in speech disordered children. *British Journal of Communication, 17,* 52–59.

Stackhouse, J. (1992a). Developmental verbal dyspraxia: I. A Review and critique. *European Journal of Disorders of Communication, 27,* 19–34.

Stackhouse, J. (1992b). Developmental verbal dyspraxia: A longitudinal case study. In, R. Campbell (Ed.), *Mental lives: Case studies in cognition.* Oxford, UK: Basil Blackwell.

Stackhouse, J., & Snowling, M. (1992). Barriers to literacy development in two cases of developmental verbal dyspraxia. *Cognitive Neuropsychology, 9,* 273–299.

Stanovich, K.E. (1988). Explaining the differences between the dyslexic and the garden-variety poor reader: The phonological-core variable-difference model. *Journal of Learning Disabilities, 21,* 590–604.

Starkey, P., Spelke, E.S., & Gelman, R. (1990). Numerical abstraction by human infants. *Cognition, 36,* 97–127.

Steel, J.G., Gorman, R., & Flexman, J.E. (1984). Neuropsychiatric testing in an autistic mathematical idiot-savant: Evidence for nonverbal abstract capacity. *Journal of the American Academy of Child Psychiatry, 23,* 704–707.

Steffenberg, S., Gillberg, C., Hellgren, L., Andersson, L., Gillberg, I., Jakonsson, G., & Bohman, M. (1989). A twin study of autism in Denmark, Finland, Iceland, Norway and Sweden. *Journal of Child Psychology and Psychiatry, 30,* 405–416.

Stephenson, S. (1905). *British Journal of Childhood Diseases, 2,* 550.

Stevenson, J. (1992). Evidence for a genetic etiology in hyperactivity in children. *Behaviour Genetics, 22,* 337–344.

Stiles, J., & Nass, R. (1991). Spatial grouping ability in young children with congenital right or left hemisphere injury. *Brain and Cognition, 15,* 201–202.

Stiles, J., & Thal, D. (1993). Linguistic and spatial cognitive development following early focal brain injury: Patterns of deficit and recovery. In M.H. Johnson (Ed.) *Brain development and cognition: A reader.* Oxford, UK: Blackwells.

Stiles-Davis, J. (1988). Spatial dysfunctions in young children with right cerebral hemisphere injury. In J. Stiles-Davis, M. Kritchevsky, & U. Bellugi (Eds.), *Spatial cognition: Brain bases and development.* (pp 251–272). Hillsdale, NJ: Lawrence Erlbaum Associates Inc.

Stiles-Davis, J., Janowsky, J., Engel, N., & Nass, R. (1988). Drawing ability in four young children with congenital unilateral brain lesions. *Neuropsychologia, 26,* 359–371.

Stiles-Davis, J., Sugarman, S., & Nass, R. (1985). The development of spatial class relations in four young children with right-cerebral-hemisphere damage: Evidence for an early spatial constructive deficit. *Brain and Cognition, 4,* 388–412.

Stoetter, B., Braun, A.R., Randolph, C., Gernert, J., Carson, R.E., Herscovitch, P., & Chase, T.N. (1992). Functional neuroanatomy of Tourette Syndrome: Limbic-motor interactions studied with FDG PET. *Advances in Neurology, 58,* 213–226.

Strauss, H. (1963). Paroxysmal blindness. *Electroencephalography and Clinical Neurophysiology, 15,* 921.

Stroop, J.R. (1935). Studies of interference in serial verbal reactions. *Journal of Experimental Psychology, 18,* 643–662.

Stuart, M., & Coltheart, M. (1988). Does reading develop in a sequence of stages? *Cognition, 30,* 139–181.

Stuart, M. and Howard, D. (1995). KJ: A developmental deep dyslexia. *Cognitive neuropsychology, 12,* 793–824.

Stuss, D.T. (1987). Contribution of frontal lobe injury to cognitive impairment after closed head injury: Methods of assessment and recent findings. In H.S. Levin, J. Grafman, & H.M. Eisenberg (Eds.), *Neurobehavioural recovery from head injury.* (pp. 166–177). New York: Oxford University Press.

Stuss, D.T. (1991a). Disturbance of self-awareness after frontal system damage. In G. Prigatano, & D. Schacter (Eds.) *Awareness of deficit after brain injury.* (pp. 63–83). New York: Oxford University Press.

Stuss, D.T. (1991b). Self, awareness and the frontal lobes: A neuropsychological perspective. In J. Strauss & G.R. Goethals (Eds.), *The self: Interdisciplinary approaches.* (pp. 255–278). New York: Springer-Verlag.

Stuss, D.T. (1992). Biological and psychological development of executive functions. *Brain and Cognition, 20,* 8–23.

Stuss, D.T., & Benson, D.F. (1986). *The frontal lobes.* New York: Raven Press.

Sutherland, R.J., Kolb, B., Schoel, W.M., Whishaw, I.Q., & Davies, D. (1982). Neuropsychological assessment of children and adults with Tourette syndrome: A comparison with learning disabilities and schizophrenia. In A.J. Friedhoff & T.N. Chase (Eds.), *Gilles de la Tourette syndrome.* (pp. 31–322). New York: Raven Press.

Szatmari, P., Offord, D.R., & Boyle, M. (1989). Correlates, associated impairments and patterns of service utilisation of children with attention deficit disorders: findings from the Ontario Child Health Study. *Journal of Child Psychology and Psychiatry, 30,* 205–217.

Tager-Flusberg, H. (1981). On the nature of linguistic functioning in early infantile autism. *Journal of Autism and Developmental Disorders, 11,* 45–56.

Tager-Flusberg, H. (1985). Psycholinguistic approaches to language and communication in autism. In E. Shopler & G. Mesibov (Eds.), *Communication problems in autism.* (pp. 69–87). New York: Plenum Press.

Tager-Flusberg, H. (1989). A psycholinguistic perspective on language development in the autistic child. In G. Dawson (Ed.), *Autism: New directions in diagnosis, nature and treatment*. New York: Guildford.

Tager-Flusberg, H., & Anderson, M. (1991). The development of contingent discourse ability in autistic children. *Journal of Child Psychology and Psychiatry, 32*, 1123–1134.

Tager-Flusberg, H., Calkins, S., Nolin, T., Baumberger, T., Anderson, M., & Chadwick-Dias, A. (1990). A longitudinal study of language acquisition in autistic and Down syndrome. *Journal of Autism and Developmental Disorders, 20*, 1–21.

Tallal, P., Miller, S.L., Bedi, G., Byma, G., Wang, X., Nagarajan, S., Schreiner, C., Jenkins, W., & Merzenich, M. (1996). Language comprehension in language-learning impaired children improved with acoustically modified speech. *Science, 271*, 81–84.

Tallal, P., & Piercy, M. (1973). Developmental dysphasia: Impaired rate of non-verbal processing as a function of sensory modality. *Neuropsychologia, 11*, 389–398.

Tallal, P. and Stark, R. (1981). Speech acoustic cue discrimination abilities of normal developing and language impaired children. *Journal of the Acoustical Society of America, 69*, 568–574.

Tallal, P., Stark, R., Kallman, C., & Mellits, D. (1980). Developmental dysphasia: The relationship between acoustic processing and verbal processing. *Neuropsychologia, 18*, 273–284.

Tant, J.L., & Douglas, V.I. (1982). Problem-solving in hyperactive, normal and reading-disabled boys. *Journal of Abnormal Child Psychology, 10*, 285–306.

Tantam, D. (1991). Asperger's syndrome in adulthood. In U. Frith (Ed.), *Autism and Asperger's syndrome.* (pp. 147–183). Cambridge, UK: Cambridge University Press.

Tantam, D., Monaghan, L. Nicholson, H., & Stirling, J. (1989). Autistic children's ability to interpret faces: A research note. *Journal of Child Psychology and Psychiatry, 30*, 623–630.

Taylor, L. (1989). Personal communication. Cited by Spreen and Strauss, 1991)

Teele, D.W., Klein, J.O., Rosner, B.A., & the Greater Boston Otitis Media Study Group (1984). Otitis media with effusion during the first three years of life and development of speech and language. *Paediatrics, 74*, 282–287.

Temple, C.M. (1984a). Developmental analogues to acquired phonological dyslexia. In R.N. Malatesha & H.A. Whitaker (Eds.), *Dyslexia: A global issue.* (pp. 143–158). The Hague, The Netherlands: Nijhoff.

Temple, C.M. (1984b). New approaches to the developmental dyslexias. In C. Rose (Ed.), *Progress in aphasiology.* (pp. 223–232). London: Plenum Press.

Temple, C.M. (1984c). Surface dyslexia in a child with epilepsy. *Neuropsychologia, 22*, 569–576.

Temple, C.M. (1985a). Developmental surface dysgraphia: A case report. *Applied Psycholinguistics, 6*, 391–406.

Temple, C.M. (1985b). Reading with partial phonology. *Journal of Psycholinguistic Research, 14*, 523–541.

Temple, C.M. (1985c). Surface dyslexia: Variation within a syndrome. In K. Patterson, J.C. Marshall, & M. Coltheart (Eds.), *Surface dyslexia.* (pp. 269–288). Hillsdale, NJ: Lawrence Erlbaum Associates Inc.

Temple, C.M. (1986a). Anomia for animals in a child. *Brain, 109*, 1225–1242.

Temple, C.M. (1986b). Developmental dysgraphias. *Quarterly Journal of Experimental Psychology, 38A*, 77–110.

Temple, C.M. (1987). The nature of normality, the deviance of dyslexia and the recognition of rhyme. *Cognition, 27*, 103–108.

Temple, C.M. (1988a). Developmental dyslexia and dysgraphia: Persistence in adulthood. *Journal of Communication Disorders, 21*, 189–207.

Temple, C.M. (1988b). Red is read but eye is blue: A further comparison of developmental and acquired dyslexia. *Brain and Language, 34*, 13–37.

Temple, C.M. (1989). Digit dyslexia: A category-specific disorder in developmental dyscalculia. *Cognitive Neuropsychology, 6*, 93–116.

Temple, C.M. (1990a). Auditory and reading comprehension in hyperlexia: Semantic and syntactic skills. *Reading and Writing: An Interdisciplinary Journal, 2*, 297–306.

Temple, C.M. (1990b). Developments and applications of cognitive neuropsychology. In M.W. Eysenck (Ed.) *Cognitive psychology: An international review*. London: Wiley & Sons.

Temple, C.M. (1990c). Foop is still floop: A six year follow-up of phonological dyslexia and dysgraphia. *Reading and Writing : An Interdisciplinary Journal, 2*, 209–221.

Temple, C.M. (1991). Procedural dyscalculia and number fact dyscalculia: Double dissociation in developmental dyscalculia. *Cognitive Neuropsychology, 8*, 155–176.

Temple, C.M. (1992a). Developmental dyscalculia. In S.J. Segalowitz & I. Rapin (Eds.), *Handbook of neuropsychology*. Amsterdam/London: Elsevier.

Temple, C.M. (1992b). Developmental memory impairment: Faces and patterns. In R. Campbell (Ed.), *Mental lives: Case studies in cognition.* (pp. 199–215). Oxford, UK. Blackwell.

Temple, C.M. (1993). *The brain: An introduction to the psychology of the human brain and behaviour*. London: Penguin Books.

Temple, C.M. (1994). The cognitive neuropsychology of the developmental dyscalculias. *Cahiers de Psychologie Cognitive/Current Psychology of Cognition, 133*, 351–370.

Temple, C.M. (1995). The kangaroo's a fox. In R. Campbell (Ed.), *Broken memories.* (pp. 383–396). Oxford, UK: Blackwell.

Temple, C.M. (1977). Cognitive neuropsychology and its application to children. *Journal of Child Psychology and Psychiatry, 38*, 27–52.

Temple, C.M., & Carney, R.A. (1993). Intellectual functioning in Turner's syndrome: A comparison of behavioural phenotypes. *Developmental Medicine and Child Neurology, 35*, 691–698.

Temple, C.M., & Carney, R.A. (1995). Patterns of spatial functioning in Turner's syndrome. *Cortex, 31*, 109–118.

Temple, C.M., & Carney, R.A. (1996). Reading skills in children with Turner's syndrome: An analysis of hyperlexia. *Cortex, 32*, 335–345.

Temple, C.M., Carney, R.A., & Mullarkey, S. (1996). Frontal lobe function and executive skill in children with Turner's syndrome. *Developmental Neuropsychology, 12*, 343–363.

Temple, C.M., & Cornish, K. (submitted). *Spatial cognition in school children: Individual differences in relation to sex and handedness*.

Temple, C.M., & Ilsley, J. (1994). Sounds and shapes: Language and spatial cognition in callosal agenesis. In M. Lassonde & M. Jeeves (Eds.), *Callosal agenesis: The natural split brain*. New York: Plenum Press.

Temple, C.M., Jeeves, M.A., & Villaroya, O. (1989). Ten, pen, men: Rhyming skills in two children with callosal agenesis. *Brain and Language*, *37*, 548–564.

Temple, C.M., Jeeves, M.A, & Villaroya, O. (1990). Reading in callosal agenesis. *Brain and Language*, *39*, 235–253.

Temple, C.M. and Marshall, J.C. (1983). A case study of developmental phonological dyslexia. *British Journal of Psychology*, *74*, 517–533.

Teuber, H.L., Milner, B., & Vaughan, H.G. (1968). Persistent anterograde amnesia after stab wound of the basal brain. *Neuropsychologia*, *6*, 267–282.

Thal, D., Bates, E., & Bellugi, U. (1989). Language and cognition in two children with Williams syndrome. *Journal of Speech and Hearing Research*, *23*, 489–500.

Thal, D., Marchman, V.A., Stiles, J., Aram, D., Tranner, D., Nass, R. & Bates, E. (1991). Early lexical development in children with focal brain injury. *Brain and Language*, *40*, 491–527.

Thomas P. (1905). *Opthalmic Review*. (Cited by Hinshelwood, 1917).

Thompson, N.M., Ewing-Cobbs, L., Fletcher, J.M., Miner, M.E., & Levin, H. (1991). Left unilateral neglect in a preschool child. *Developmental Medicine and Child Neurology*, *33*, 636–644.

Thompson, P.J., & Trimble, M.R. (1982). Anticonvulsant drugs and cognitive functions. *Epilepsia*, *23*, 531–544.

Thurstone, L. (1938). *Primary mental abilities*. Chicago: University of Chicago Press.

Tomblin, B. (1989). Familial concentration of developmental language impairment. *Journal of Speech and Hearing Disorders*, *54*, 287–285.

Treiman, R. (1992). The role of intrasyllabic units in learning to read and spell. In P.B. Gough, L.C. Ehri, & R. Trieman (Eds.), *Reading acquisition*. Hillsdale, NJ: Lawrence Erlbaum Associates Inc.

Treiman, R. (1993). *Beginning to spell*. Oxford, UK: Oxford University Press.

Trimble, M.R., & Reynolds, E.H. (1976). Anticonvulsant drugs and mental symptoms. *Psychological Medicine*, *6*, 169–178.

Turner, H.H. (1938). A syndrome of infantilism, congenital webbed neck and cubitus valgus. *Endocrinology*, *23*, 566–578.

Tychsen, L., & Lisberger, S.G. (1986). Maldevelopment of visual motion processing in humans who had strabismus with early onset in infancy. *Journal of Neuroscience*, *6*, 2495–2508.

Tychsen, L., Lisberger, S.G., & Burkhalter, A. (1995). Neuroanatomical abnormalities of primary visual cortex in macaque monkeys with infantile esotropia: Preliminary results. *Journal of Pediatric Opthalmology and Strabismus*, *32*, 323–328.

Tychsen, L., Rastelli, A., Steinman, S., & Steinman, B. (1996). Biases of motion perception revealed by reversing gratings in humans who had infantile-onset strabismus. *Developmental Medicine and Child Neurology*, *38*, 408–422.

Udwin, O. (1990). A survey of adults with Williams syndrome and idiopathic infantile hypercalcaemia. *Developmental Medicine and Child Neurology*, *32*, 129–141.

Udwin, O., & Yule, W. (1990). Expressive language of children with Williams syndrome. *American Journal of Medical Genetics Supplement*, *6*, 108–114.

Udwin, O., & Yule, W. (1991). A cognitive and behavioural phenotype in Williams syndrome. *Journal of Clinical and Experimental Psychology*, *13*, 232–244.

Udwin, O., Yule, W., & Martin, N. (1986). Age at diagnosis and abilities in idiopathic hypercalcaemia. *Archives of Diseases of Childhood, 61*, 1164–1167.

Udwin, O., Yule, W., & Martin, N. (1987). Cognitive abilities and behavioural characteristics of children with idiopathic infantile hypercalcaemia. *Journal of Child Psychology and Psychiatry, 28*, 297–309.

Valdois, S., Gerard, C., Vanault, P., & Dugas, M. (1995). Peripheral developmental dyslexia: A visual attentional account? *Cognitive Neuropsychology, 12*, 31–67.

Vandenburg, S.G., & Kuse, A.R. (1978). Mental rotation, a group test of three dimensional spatial visualisation. *Perceptual and Motor Skills, 47*, 599–604.

Van der Lely, H. (1990). *Sentence comprehension processes in specifically language impaired children*. Unpublished PhD thesis, University of London, London.

Van der Lely, H. (1994). Canonical linking rules: Forward versus reverse linking in normally developing and specifically language impaired children. *Cognition, 51*, 29–72.

Van der Linde, E., Morrongiello, B.A., & Rovee-Collier, C. (1985). Determinants of retention in 8-week-old infants. *Developmental Psychology, 21*, 601–613.

Van Essen, D.C., Anderson, C.H., & Felleman, D.J. (1992). Information processing in the primate visual system: An integrated systems perspective. *Science, 255*, 419–123.

Van Hout, A. (1993). Acquired aphasia in childhood and developmental dysphasias: Are the errors similar? Analysis of errors made in confrontation naming tasks. *Aphasiology, 7*, 525–531.

Van Orden, G., Pennington, B., & Stone, G. (1990). Word identification and the promise of subsymbolic psycholinguistics. *Psychological Review, 97*, 488–522.

Vargha-Khadem, F., Isaacs, E., & Mishkin, M. (in press). Agnosia, alexia and a remarkable form of amnesia in an adolescent boy. *Brain, 117*.

Vargha-Khadem, F., O'Gorman, A.M., & Watters, G.V. (1985). Aphasia and handedness in relation to hemispheric side, age at injury and severity of cerebral lesion during childhood. *Brain, 108*, 677–696.

Vogler, G.P., DeFries, J., & Decker, S. (1985). Family history as an indicator of risk for reading disability. *Journal of Learning Disabilities, 18*, 419–421.

Waber, D.P. (1979). Neuropsychological aspects of Turner's syndrome. *Developmental Medicine and child Neurology, 21*, 58–70.

Waber, D.P., Isquith, P.K., & Kahn, C.N. (1994). Metacognitive factors in the visuo-spatial skills of long term survivors of acute lymphoblastic leukemia: An experimental approach to the Rey-Osterrieth complex figure test. *Developmental Neuropsychology, 10*, 349–367.

Wagner, R.K., & Torgeson, J.L. (1987). The nature of phonological processing and its causal role in the acquisition of reading skills. *Psychological Bulletin, 101*, 192–212.

Wall, M. (1980). A comparison of syntax in young stutterers and non-stutterers. *Journal of Fluency Disorders, 5*, 321–326.

Wang, A., & Norcia, A. (1992). Reversing grating as a simple clinical method to test the symmetry of motion perception and potential binocularity. *Investigative Ophthalmology and Visual Sciences, 33(Suppl)*, 1340.

Warren, D.H. (1974). Early vs. late vision: The role of early vision in spatial reference systems. *New Outlook for the Blind, 68*, 157–162.

Warren, D.H. (1978). Perception by the blind. In E. Cartarette & M. Friedman (Eds.), *Handbook of perception* (Vol. 10). New York: Academic Press.

Warrington, E.K. (1982). The fractionation of arithmetical skills: A single case study. *Quarterly Journal of Experimental Psychology, 34(A)*, 31–51.

Warrington, E.K. (1984). *Recognition memory battery*. Windsor, UK: NFER Nelson.

Warrington, E.K., James, M., & Kinsbourne, M. (1966). Drawing disability in relation to laterality of cerebral lesion. *Brain, 89*, 53–82.

Warrington, E.K., & Shallice, T. (1984). Category specific semantic impairments. *Brain, 107*, 829–854.

Warrington, E.K., & Taylor, A.M. (1973). The contribution of the right parietal lobe to object recognition. *Cortex, 9*, 152–164.

Wechsler, D. (1974). *The Wechsler intelligence scale for children — revised*. New York: The Psychological Corporation.

Weinberger, D.R., Behrman, K.F., Gold, J., & Goldberg, T. (1994). Neural mechanisms of future-oriented processes: In vivo physiological studies of humans. In M.M. Haith, J.B. Benson, R.J. Roberts, & N.F. Pennington (Eds.), *The development of future-oriented processes*. Chicago: University of Chicago Press.

Weintraub, S., & Mesulam, M.M. (1983). Developmental disabilities of the right hemisphere. *Archives of Neurology, 40*, 463–468.

Weiskrantz, L. (1987). *Blindsight: A case study and implications*. Oxford, UK: Oxford University Press.

Weiskrantz, L., & Warrington, E.K. (1979). Conditioning in amnesic patients. *Neuropsychologia, 17*, 187–194.

Welsh, M., Pennington, B.F., & Groissier, D.B. (1991). A normative-developmental study of executive function: A window on prefrontal function in children. *Developmental Neuropsychology, 7*, 131–149.

Welsh, M.C., & Pennington, B.F. (1988). Assessing frontal lobe functioning in children: Views from developmental psychology. *Developmental Neuropsychology, 4*, 199–230.

Welsh, M.C., Pennington, B.F., Ozonoff, S., Rouse, B., & McCabe, E.R.B. (1990). Neuropsychology of early-treated phenylketonuria: Specific executive function deficits. *Child Development, 61*, 1697–1713.

Welsh, M.C., Pennington, B.F., & Rogers, S. (1987). Word recognition and comprehension skills in hyperlexic children. *Brain and Language, 32*, 76–96.

Wetherby, A., & Prutting, C. (1984). Profiles of communicative and cognitive-social abilities in autistic children. *Journal of Speech and Hearing Research, 27*, 364–377.

Weyandt, L.L., & Willis, W.G. (1994). Executive function in school aged children: Potential efficacy of tasks in discriminating clinical groups. *Developmental Neuropsychology, 10*, 27–38.

White, C.P., & Jan, J.E. (1992). Visual hallucinations after acute visual loss in a young child. *Developmental Medicine and Child Neurology, 34*, 252–265.

Wilding, J. (1989). Developmental dyslexics do not fit in boxes: Evidence from the case studies. *European Journal of Cognitive Psychology, 1*, 105–127.

Wilding, J. (1990). Developmental dyslexics do not fit in boxes: Evidence from six new case studies. *European Journal of Cognitive Psychology, 2*, 97–131.

Wilkins, A.J., & Robson, J.G. (1986). *The Cambridge low contrast gratings*. Cambridge, UK: Clement Clark International.

Willerman, L. (1973). Activity level and hyperactivity in twins. *Child Development, 44*, 288–293.

Williams, D., & Mateer, C.A. (1992). Developmental impact of frontal lobe injury in middle childhood. *Brain and Cognition, 20,* 196–204.

Williams, J., Barratt-Boyes, B., & Lowe, J. (1961). Supravalvular aortic stenosis. *Circulation, 24,* 1311–1318.

Williamson, M.L., Koch, R., Azen, C., & Chang, C. (1981). Correlates of intelligence test results in treated phenylketonuric children. *Pediatrics, 68,* 161–167.

Wimmer, H. (in press). Characteristics of developmental dyslexia in a regular writing system. *Applied Psycholinguistics.*

Wimmer, H. and Goswami, U. (1994). The influence of orthographic consistency on reading development: Word recognition in English and German children. *Cognition, 51,* 91–103.

Wimmer, H., & Hummer, P. (1990). How German-speaking first graders read and spell: Doubts on the importance of the logographic stage. *Applied Psycholinguistics, 11,* 349–368.

Wimmer, H., & Perner, J. (1983). Beliefs about beliefs: Representation and constraining function of wrong beliefs in young children's understanding of deception. *Cognition, 13,* 103–128.

Wing, L. (1976). *Early childhood autism.* Oxford, UK: Pergamon Press.

Wing, L. (1981). Asperger's syndrome: A clinical account. *Psychological Medicine, 11,* 115–129.

Wolf, M. (1991 April). *Word-wraiths: The unique contribution of the naming system to reading prediction and intervention in developmental dyslexia.* Paper presented at the Society for Research in Child Development, Seattle, WA

Wolf, M., & Obregon, M. (1992). Early naming deficits, developmental dyslexia, and a specific deficit hypothesis. *Brain and Language, 42,* 219–247.

Wolters, G., Beishuizen, M., Broers, G., & Knoppert, W. (1990). Mental arithmetic: Effects of calculation procedure and problem difficulty on solution latency. *Journal of Experimental Child Psychology, 49,* 20–30.

Wood, F.B., Brown, I.S., & Felton, R.H. (1989). Long term follow-up of a childhood amnesic syndrome. *Brain and Cognition, 10,* 76–86.

Wyler, A.R., Walker, G., Richey, E.T, & Hermann, B.P. (1988). Chronic subdural strip electrode recording for difficult epileptic problems. *Journal of Epilepsy, 1,* 71–78.

Young, A.W. (1992). Face recognition impairments. In V. Bruce, A. Cowey, A.W. Ellis, & D.I. Perrett, (Eds.), *Processing the facial image.* Oxford, UK: Clarendon Press.

Young, A.W., & Ellis, H.D. (1989). Childhood Prosopagnosia. *Brain and Cognition, 9,* 16–47.

Young, A.W., & Ellis, H.D. (1992). Visual perception. In S.J. Segalowitz & I. Rapin (Eds.), *Handbook of neuropsychology: Vol. 7. Child neuropsychology.* Amsterdam/London: Elsevier.

Young, R.M., & O'Shea, T. (1981). Errors in children's subtraction. *Cognitive Science, 5,* 153–177.

Yule, W., Lansdowne, R., & Urbanowicz, M.A. (1982). Early naming deficits, developmental dyslexia, and a specific deficit hypothesis. *Brain and Language, 42,* 219–247.

Zaidel, D., & Rausch, R. (1981). Effects of semantic organisation on the recognition of pictures following temporal lobectomy. *Neuropsychologia, 19,* 813–817.

Zardini, G., Molteni, B., Nardocci, N., Sarti, D., Avanzini, G., & Granata, T. (1995). Linguistic development in a patient with Landau–Kleffner syndrome: A nine-year follow-up. *Neuropaediatrics, 26*, 19–25.

Ziegler, D.K. (1952). Word deafness and Wernicke's aphasia. *Archives of Neurology and Psychiatry, 67*, 323–331.

Zeki, S. (1991). Cerebral akinetopsia (visual motion blindness): A review. *Brain, 114*, 811–824.

Zihl, J., Von Cramon, D., & Mai, N. (1983). Selective disturbance of movement vision after bilateral brain damage. *Brain*, 313–340.

Zilbovicius, M., Garreau, B., Samson, Y., Remy, P., Barthelemy, C., Syrota, A.,and LeLord, G. (1995). Delayed maturation of the frontal cortex in childhood autism. *American Journal of Psychiatry, 152*, 248–252.

Zola-Morgan, S., Squire, L.R., & Amaral, D.G. (1986). Human amnesia and the medial temporal region: Enduring memory impairment following a bilateral lesion limited to field CA1 of the hippocampus. *Journal of Neuroscience, 6*, 2950–2967.

Zung, A., & Margolith, D. (1993). Ictal cortical blindness: A case report and review of the literature. *Developmental Medicine and Child Neurology, 35*, 917–926.

Author Index

Gopnik, M. 59; 60; 61; 63; 64; 78; 79; 81; 320; 325
Gordon, B. 58; 119; 159; 319; 325
Gordon, N. 128
Gordon, P., 68
Gorenstein, E.E., 312
Gorman, R., 306
Goswami, U. 177; 183; 212; 213; 214; 326
Gottesman, I., 71; 329
Goulandris, N. 22; 107; 197; 198
Goy, R.W., 144
Grafman, J. 258; 260
Graham, F., 64
Graham, P., 171
Granata, T. 37
Grant, D.A., 288; 289; 297
Grant, J., 149
Grattan, L.M., 296; 316
Greco, C., 83; 84
Green, K., 313
Greenberg, F. 148
Greenberger, V., 120
Greeno, J.G., 263
Griesler, P., 83
Griffin, F.D., 304
Griffiths, P. 120; 199
Grimm, H., 59
Grodzinsky, G.M., 312
Groenveld, M., 120
Groissier, D.B. 290; 291; 302; 303; 312; 314; 315
Gross, C.G. 127
Gross-Glenn, K., 174
Gross-Tsur, V., 254
Gupta, P.D., 20
Guthrie, R. 303
Guttler, F., 303
Guz, G., 258

Hagram, J.O., 174
Halberg, F., 315
Hall, J., 106; 174
Hall, M., 309
Hall, S.M., 65
Haller, M. 185
Hallgren, B. 171
Halligan, P.W., 127
Halminski, M., 303
Haltiner, A., 91
Hamburger, S., 174; 306; 311

Hamlett, K.W., 312
Hamsher, K. des, 138; 140
Hanahan, A.P., 174
Hanley, J.R., 197; 239; 240
Hanley, W.B., 304
Hansen, D. 62; 63; 79
Harkness, W., 117; 118
Harlow, J.M. 287
Harper, J. 35
Harris, D.B. 147
Harris, E.L., 312
Harris, J.C. 303
Harris, P., 258
Harris, S.M., 311
Harris, W. 116
Hart, J., 58
Harter, M.R. 312
Hartmann, J., 292
Harward, H., 292
Hastie, K., 197; 239; 240
Hatcher, P.J., 212
Hatfield, F.M., 239
Haxby, J., 145; 313
Hayden, M. 145; 313
Hayne, H., 83; 84
Haynes, C., 77
Healy, J.M. 219
Heaton, R.K. 145; 288; 289; 297; 304; 313; 314
Heavens, J., 309
Hecaen, H., 260
Hechtman, L., 312
Heilman, K.M. 228; 229; 247
Held, R., 117; 127
Heller, J.I. 263
Heller, W., 124
Hellgren, L., 71
Hendrick, B., 90
Hendrick, E., 14
Henriksen, L., 311
Hermann, B., 91
Heron, W., 118
Herscovitch, P., 309
Herskowitz, J., 88
Hess, R.F., 127
Hewitt, J.K., 311
Hickmans, E.M. 303
Hicks, J. 65
Hien, T 174
Hinshelwood, J. 164; 165; 166; 167; 168; 169; 170; 171; 175; 221; 225; 249; 256; 257; 260; 272

Hinton, G.E., 184
Hitch, G., 95; 101; 171; 174; 221; 254; 260
Hobson, R., 143; 308
Hoddinott, S., 68
Hodges, J.R., 11; 116; 181; 194
Hoffer, P.B. 309
Hoffman, H., 90
Hoffman, W. 306
Holcomb, P.J., 64
Holligan, C., 106
Holmes, G.L., 36
Holmes, J. 187
Holtzman, N.A., 304
Honeyman, J.C., 174
Hong-Yin, N., 212
Hood, B., 117; 118
Hopkins, J., 312
Horowitz, S.J., 219
Horwitz, B., 145; 313
Houillier, S. 260
Howard, D. 215; 218; 251; 326
Howe, M.L., 85; 86
Howell, P. 107
Howie, P. , 68
Hudson, J., 85
Hughes, C., 308; 315
Hulme, A., 106; 107
Hulme, C. 22; 106; 200; 209; 212; 248
Hummer, P. 177; 217; 226; 227
Humphreys, G.W., 52; 58
Humphreys, M., 106
Hunkin, N.M., 87
Hunt, S. 120
Hurst, J.A., 64
Hyde, T.M., 309; 311
Hynd, G. 174; 290; 292; 311

Ilsley, J. 125; 159
Inhelder, B. 20; 85
Innes, W.C., 120
Isaac, W., 290; 292
Isaacs, E., 88
Isquith, P.K., 315

Jackson, G., 117; 118
Jacobs, P.A., 144
Jacobs, R.A., 23
Jadrisec, D. 309

Subject Index